QUALITY

This textbook is a comprehensive introduction to the theory and practice of quality. The study of the quality movement is set in the context of management thinking throughout the twentieth century. The wide-ranging approach encompasses both traditional approaches to quality, and contemporary approaches based on systems thinking. Features and benefits of the book include:

- a complete introduction to the development, theory and practice of quality
- pedagogical features such as key learning points, boxed features, glossary, classroom discussion and assignment questions
- supplements including OHP bases and a tutor guide
- in-depth review of the contributions of the 'Quality Gurus'
- detailed handbook of methods, tools and techniques
- numerous international public and private sector case studies
- emphasis on both service and manufacturing industry

The comprehensive coverage and user-friendly style make this a valuable resource for all those studying quality.

John Beckford teaches extensively at undergraduate and postgraduate level and works as an independent consultant in organisational effectiveness. He has a Ph.D. in Organisational Cybernetics from the University of Hull.

QUALITY

A critical introduction

John Beckford

LONDON & NEW YORK

First published 1998
by Routledge
11 New Fetter Lane, London EC4P 4EE

Simultaneously published in the USA and Canada
by Routledge
29 West 35th Street, New York, NY 10001

Typeset in Plantin and Rockwell by Keystroke,
Jacaranda Lodge, Wolverhampton
Printed and bound in Great Britain by TJ International,
Padstow, Cornwall

British Library Cataloguing in Publication Data
A catalogue record for this book is available from the British Library

Library of Congress Cataloguing in Publication Data
Beckford, John. 1958–
    Quality : a critical introduction / John Beckford.
        p.   cm.
    Includes bibliographical references and index.
    1. Total quality management–Case studies.   2. Service industries–
    Management–Case studies.   3. Manufacturing industries–Management–
    Case studies.   I. Title.
    HD62.15.B433   1998
    658.5′62—dc21   97–51904
                            CIP

ISBN 0–415–18163–1 (hbk)
ISBN 0–415–18164–X (pbk)

Quality:

n . the essential attribute of anything
(Collins, *New English Dictionary*, 1968)

Contents

Figures

Vignettes

Preface

INTRODUCTION

The pursuit of organisational effectiveness and success – however that may be defined – through higher quality in products and services is a dominant theme for organisations throughout the world. However, many quality initiatives fail to achieve their objectives or only partially succeed, contributing to improvement but not leading to the higher levels of organisational performance expected. This failure perhaps results from the narrow focus of many quality programmes and a consequent lack of breadth in the understanding of the true role and meaning of quality in organisational effectiveness. Contributing to this lack of success is the apparent desire of many organisations and managers to adopt a relatively simple pre-packaged programme based upon a single approach to achievement of quality.

Drawing on case studies from around the world in organisations such as McDonald's, Cathay Pacific, the Hong Kong Police, Fletcher Challenge Steel, China and many other private and public sector organisations this book enables the reader to develop a unique and broad understanding of quality – one which will work for him or herself in a particular organisation. The book shows the full breadth of approaches and tools available to support a quality initiative and considers the importance of the socio-cultural context in selecting and using these approaches.

THE AIM OF THIS BOOK

There is a substantial body of literature already published in the field of quality – so why yet another book? The principal established texts in the field are those produced by the 'Quality Gurus' themselves. Each of these takes only the particular author's view of the subject while books by other writers reflect a bias towards one aspect of the subject or one narrow view of it. None of these provide either the breadth of information or the critical stance adopted in this book. The 'discipline' of quality is now mature – the time is right to develop a non-partisan, complete approach to the subject.

WHO SHOULD USE THIS BOOK?

This book provides a complete and coherent knowledge platform for all those (whether students or managers) wishing to fully understand the theory and practice of quality. It does *not* offer the latest quality focused 'miracle' cure for all organisational ills. Instead the book brings together in a single text the plethora of ideas, approaches and methods espoused in the pursuit of quality in recent years. It draws on the published writings of many quality experts and incorporates the practical experience of the author and his associates in using these ideas throughout the world.

It features:

- a complete introduction to quality in the context of management thinking;
- in-depth reviews of the contributions of the 'Quality Gurus' and contemporary; management authors to quality theory and practice;
- international case-studies drawing on the public and private sectors;
- particular emphasis on the neglected service sector as well as manufacturing industry.

STRUCTURE

The book is divided into four parts. Part one provides a foundation for the book by considering the arguments surrounding the pursuit of quality, the role of quality in the organisation, barriers to its implementation and the developments in management thinking which appear to underpin the quality movement.

Part two provides a critical review of the works of those writers who have made a distinct and valuable contribution to the achievement of quality. These are Philip Crosby, W. Edwards Deming, Armand Feigenbaum, Kaoru Ishikawa, Joseph Juran, John Oakland, Shigeo Shingo and Genichi Taguchi.

Part three moves beyond these traditionally based approaches to consider the value to be derived from contemporary management thinking. This part relates to the quality theme ideas ranging from the emergence of contingency theory to the more radical notions of critical systems thinking, re-engineering and organisational learning.

Part four shifts the focus away from quality theory to quality practice by introducing the methods, tools and techniques used for achieving quality. This section works from basic and common techniques such as process analysis through to current strategies for engaging all of the organisation's stakeholders in the quality process and concludes with guidance on implementing quality programmes.

HOW TO USE THIS BOOK

This book, as with all textbooks, provides a simplified perspective of its topic and of the daily realities of pursuing quality in organisations. The information is presented in what seems to the author a logical, systematic order, teasing apart topics which are necessarily closely inter-related.

The clue to successful reading is to recognise the connections which exist between the various parts and topics (these connections are regularly made within the text). The chapters then, while presented in one particular order, need not be read in that way. If, for example, when reading the chapter on W. Edwards Deming (chapter 6), the reader wishes to understand more about Statistical Process Control, it is easy to jump to the chapter on Statistical Methods (chapter 22) and pursue that theme. Equally, the chapters can be read in a fully sequential manner although each is intended to be able to stand alone offering a perspective on a particular topic. Hence, some chapters are short, some long.

Each part of the book commences with a user guide to the content and makes suggestions about how to maximise learning from it. These introductions each summarise the major points made in the contained chapters.

Practical illustrations and short vignettes will be found in each chapter. These are intended to help consolidate learning as well as being informative and entertaining. Many readers will find that remembering the story helps them to remember the key points of the associated chapter. These illustrations arise from the author's own knowledge and practice, or have been contributed by friends and colleagues drawing on their working experience in positions of responsibility for quality.

Each chapter concludes with a question. This may be used either as a formal assignment, or as a discussion topic for classroom or study group work. Attempting to answer these questions will help to reinforce and consolidate learning. If you cannot adequately answer the question you should revisit the chapter to enhance your knowledge. Working through the book like this will help you to develop your knowledge in a systematic and critical way.

THE AUTHOR

John Beckford is a freelance consultant in organisational effectiveness. He holds a Ph.D. in Organisational Cybernetics from the University of Hull, is a Corporate Member of the Institute of Management Services and a Founder and Council Member of the Institute of Business Process Re-engineering. He has published numerous refereed journal and conference papers and is regularly invited to deliver talks and seminars to organisations in both the private and public sectors.

Commencing his career in branch banking with the Royal Bank of Scotland, John worked as an internal consultant before leaving the bank to complete his doctorate. Since then he has worked with senior managers in the UK, Middle and Far East, Australia and New Zealand in a wide variety of sectors including finance, steel, public and private healthcare, public education, property, food and the motor trade.

John is a Director of SIGMA BETA Research and Consulting and lectures extensively on the University of Hull Doctoral and Masters programmes for which he has researched and developed a series of courses on Total Quality Management. John also works with King Alfred's University College, Winchester, where he is a Visiting Research Fellow and has delivered his ideas at numerous other institutions both in the UK and overseas.

Acknowledgements

I am extremely grateful to all those who have helped in the development and production of this book. First to the many students and managers who have debated quality ideas with me over several years and contributed ideas to the book – especially Bing Zeat Mah, John Cox, Tony Fletcher, Sonal Kumar and Mike Smith – their theoretical and practical contributions have altered and shaped my views. Second are the review panel who have read and robustly criticised every aspect of the text during production – Robin Asby, University College, Winchester; Derek Hill, Salford University; Joyce Liddle, Sunderland Business School. I, of course, remain responsible for any errors, oversights or omissions. Third are the many organisations who have allowed the sharing of their quality experiences – specifically Cathay Pacific; Chesswood Produce Limited; Derwentside District Council; Fletcher Challenge Steel, China; the Hong Kong Police Force (formerly Royal Hong Kong Police Force); Kennet School, Thatcham, Berkshire; McDonald's, Hong Kong, and West Berkshire Music Centre. Fourth are Stuart Hay and the editorial team at Routledge for accepting the idea of the book and supporting its production. Finally I thank Sara, Paul and Matthew for their enormous and continuing tolerance, support and friendship.

part one

INTRODUCING QUALITY

USER GUIDE

This part of the book provides an introduction to the whole quality debate. Chapter 1 examines the arguments for and against the pursuit of quality, examining economic, social and environmental imperatives. Chapter 2 considers the role of quality in the organisation with particular reference to the ongoing debate as to whether it should be considered as a strategic or operational issue. Chapter 3 focuses on barriers to the pursuit of quality, highlighting how the established cultures, systems and processes of organisations inhibit quality initiatives. In chapter 4 the 'classical' and 'human relations' schools of management thinking are introduced and their apparent influence on the thinking of the Quality Gurus elaborated.

This part of the book provides the necessary foundation for a study of quality by examining the four key dimensions:

- the need for quality;
- the role of quality;
- the barriers to its achievement;
- the thinking which underpins dominant approaches.

chapter
one

THE QUALITY
IMPERATIVE

There is a surplus of everything

Tom Peters, 1992

INTRODUCTION

Quality has emerged and remained as a dominant theme in management thinking since the 1940s. While the initial approaches emerged from American theorists and practitioners, early commercial applications were predominantly amongst Japanese companies. The need for enhanced quality was largely ignored or rejected in the West. More recently organisations throughout the world have begun to embrace the theories and practices. This chapter is concerned with 'why' quality has achieved this pre-eminence amongst the concerns of so many managers. It presents three arguments for the pursuit of quality: the economic, the social and the environmental. Each of these is pursued through the author's own perspective on management and achievement of quality.

1.1   THE ECONOMIC IMPERATIVE

During the post-World War Two years consumer demand grew to such an extent that the manufacturing focus in the Western world was on productivity. Effectively, growing markets were starved of products and with increasing economic prosperity, everything that could be produced could be sold. Simply, with unfulfilled demand, organisations were under no pressure to focus on the quality of product and perhaps perceived that they had already achieved the ultimate standards. Coupled to this, consumer expectations of product longevity and reliability were relatively low compared with today as was the technology of both the products and the manufacturing processes.

As markets matured and growth consequently stabilised, organisations, faced with increasing costs of production – particularly the cost of labour and in the 1970s the cost of power – began to challenge their established ways of working. Some organisations further increased the pressure on workers for more productivity gains while pursuing cost reductions in raw materials and through research and development, others relied on the emerging technologies of automation, robotics and electronic data processing; most adopted a mix of these approaches. Where technologically and financially feasible other organisations followed the more conventional approach of exporting jobs to lower cost manufacturing centres especially in South East Asia. Rather than reducing costs through improving their processes, they relocated manufacturing plants to take advantage of lower cost labour.

This phenomenon of chasing cheap labour can be traced from the late nineteenth century when manufacturing emerged in America with its ready supply of cheap land and labour. At that time European organisations began to establish overseas operations. From the mid-1960s Western organisations have developed operations in the so-called 'Tiger Economies' of Asia. The first of these to emerge, Singapore, Hong Kong and Taiwan are now maturing economies (GDP per capita is at or approaching Western levels) and are beginning to lose jobs to their newly emergent and lower cost neighbours such as Cambodia, Indonesia, Korea and Vietnam.

Following changes in the UK economy over recent years, it can be observed that there is a trend by certain Asian companies to relocate manufacturing operations to it as labour is relatively cheaper than before and the workforce has the skills required for high quality manufacturing operations. Notable organisations following this trend include Sony, Nissan, Toyota and Honda from Japan and Lucky Goldstar from Korea. Cathay Pacific Airlines has relocated much of its paper processing and accounting work to Australia from Hong Kong and a UK airline operates its customer call centre from the Middle East.

It seems relatively clear that where technology and total costs enables such a move jobs are attracted to sources of cheap labour. The economic consequences for the originating economies are currently uncertain. However, it is easy to observe relative growth in the wealth of emerging economies and decline in those which are mature. While there may be profits for the 'home' economy to repatriate (after tax!), the jobs and much of the wealth remain in the host manufacturing economy – as this is where the workers spend their wages.

It would seem to be the case that work continues to follow low total production costs. If the observed cycle continues it should be apparent that the long-term decline of the mature economies is guaranteed as emergent economies develop the skills and abilities necessary to absorb a greater proportion of both manufacturing and service sector jobs.

In parallel with this phenomenon and notwithstanding the substantial apparent progress in products, services and information technology in recent years it also appears to be the case that for many products demand, with the exception of certain emerging products and services such as computer games and leisure facilities, is in effect, satisfied.

MANUFACTURING ACTIVITY DRIVES THE SERVICE SECTOR

It can be argued that it is largely the wages of manufacturing workers which drive prosperity in the service sector of an economy. Observation of any community which has lost its manufacturing base will tend to confirm this view. For example, South Wales in the UK, which has largely lost its mining, steel and shipping industries, continues to suffer high unemployment. It has a depressed retail sector, low house prices compared to other areas and relatively lower costs/incomes for professional services such as legal and accountancy. Signs of recovery are now apparent with the planned establishment of high technology manufacturing plants in the area. It is anticipated that, like the North East of England, these will provide the impetus for overall economic recovery in the area extending to the service sector.

Consumers are operating in a replacement cycle for a large proportion of established products: for example cars, domestic appliances, home entertainment equipment, even perhaps personal computers, albeit additional features ensure a degree of obsolescence in some products. In this replacement phase of the product lifecycle consumers are demanding greater reliability and longevity from their purchases and these characteristics are significant in their decision making. It also appears that for many products, diversity and choice are expanding, with competitive products from emergent economies challenging those of the established players. The number of emergent, relatively low cost economies has also increased substantially in recent years, not just with the Far East countries but also those of Eastern Europe. Each of these new producers and economies adds to the level of competition in the established markets. A good example of this is in the motor industry where not only are the products from European, Japanese and US manufacturers available but also those such as Proton, Kia, Hyundai and Daewoo – all with Asian origins. All these are relatively new competitors in the UK and are attempting to establish themselves throughout Europe at the lower end of the market.

So much for private industry, but what of the public sector, does the same economic imperative apply? The pursuit of quality is equally important to this sector of every economy. From their behaviour and actions throughout the world, governments can be observed to be dissatisfied with the cost and effectiveness of many public services. There has been for some years a trend towards privatisation or commercialisation of many public sector bodies, imposing on them many of the same commercial constraints faced by private sector, profit oriented institutions. It seems to be the case that the share of GDP absorbed by governments is unacceptable to many voters and potentially damaging to economies, for example, the tendency for organisations to relocate from high employment cost economies to lower cost ones. Examples of this can be seen in the acquisition by BMW of Rover (the UK is a lower employment cost economy than Germany), Mercedes is believed to be exploring a similar move and has already established assembly plants outside Europe while Siemens, another German company, have made further substantial investment in the UK. The current mantra for many is that low taxation equals greater wealth creation – this in turn implies job creation and a satisfied society.

At the same time in those relatively wealthy established economies such as the UK, there is a drift of public service consumers away from the public offerings towards private services where the public service is perceived to be failing to meet the needs of its consumers: for example the apparent trend in the UK towards private healthcare, the emerging preference for 'grant-maintained' schools. If these public services do not address the problems which their users observe then they must eventually fall into disrepair, either collapsing altogether through lack of public support or offering a second-rate service to less well off members of the society which supports them and increasing the unit cost of such provision. The pursuit of quality in their products and services offers these institutions the opportunity to provide comparable services to those available in the private sector. This author argues that there is nothing inherently *better* about a privately owned and offered service than a public one. It is merely that the economic imperative for survival has traditionally been greater in the private sector.

The economic imperative for quality is then essentially quite simple. The imperative is survival for the individual organisation and ultimately the total economy. The 'gurus' promise that achieving quality will reduce costs and improve productivity and certainly many of the tools will lead towards these things. As consumers become more selective in their choices, quality has ceased to be an optional extra and become essential for any organisation in a saturated market-place. From the perspective of the total economy of a nation, it is more cost effective to cure quality problems than it is to export jobs or lose them to alternative or overseas suppliers.

1.2   THE SOCIAL IMPERATIVE

In common with the developments in technology in the post-war era has been massive development in our understanding of human-kind. Through the works of management writers and practitioners such as Barnard (executive functions), Mayo, Herzberg and McGregor (human psychology), Beer (organisational cybernetics), Ackoff and Checkland (soft systems) management theorists and scientists have become aware of many alternative ways of designing and managing jobs and organisations.

However, with the homespun philosophical and short term arrogance of 'If it ain't broke, don't fix it' managers and academics have collectively failed to embrace the many possibilities that these developments in thinking make available to us. Academics at universities and colleges continue to teach classical methods because either it is all they know or because they reject the 'new' ideas. Practically for managers it is often easier in the short term to keep things as they are – particularly when the financial focus is forced onto the short term by external demands – change always involves the expenditure of energy, usually in the form of money. Consequently, the ways in which we run organisations and manage people are often extremely wasteful of human capabilities and talent.

What is perhaps worse is that many of the people affected by inefficient, ineffective systems know both that the system is ineffective and, importantly, know how to fix it. Such systems are not only wasteful but are demoralising and destructive to the talents of their members and users. It is staggering how often those responsible for a job can identify a 'short cut' which enables the job to be completed on time and in specification, whereas the organisation of the system itself would drive towards at least one and often both of these important parameters being missed.

If, as can be shown, individuals have the capacity to perform more complex tasks to higher standards or greater volume than the system permits then managers are wasting resources. This is in itself sufficient evidence of the need for change quite apart from the potential benefit to human spirit. From the perspective of social cohesion, it must be the responsibility of every manager to maximise the opportunity for development for each of his or her subordinates. This will surely lead to a satisfied workforce, a commitment to the organisation and a society more at ease with itself.

The negative aspect of minimising apparent waste of human resources is that if quality is achieved, and markets do not grow to absorb increased higher volume outputs, there may be a substantial increase in levels of unemployment. This will arise because organisations will find it unnecessary (and costly – since there are indirect additional costs involved in employing extra staff) to retain current numbers of employees. This led in the 1980s to the fashion for 'down-sizing' in organisations, reducing staff numbers to the minimum level.

As has been seen in many conurbations in developed countries since the 1970s, high levels of unemployment tend to create conditions of social isolation, a sense of hopelessness and unease, often leading to unrest and what we call anti-social behaviour such as drug and alcohol abuse or increasing crime rates. Examples of this were riots in Liverpool, Birmingham and other UK cities, the increase in drug abuse reported in crime statistics, increased levels of shoplifting, and the rise in illegitimate births particularly amongst teenagers. It cannot be regarded as acceptable that by achieving quality we also achieve social destruction. Neither can it be regarded as sustainable to produce poor quality outputs in order to maintain employment in the short term – above all else, consumer markets will not allow this. A substantial debate is required to address this issue, after all it may be argued that by succeeding in the pursuit of quality any particular country will act as an attractor of industries leading to economic success for that country. Inevitably this would have international consequences which are beyond the capacity of any individual or normal organisation to address. In the meanwhile the markets will not wait and action must be taken to preserve, maintain and develop all industries.

The second imperative for quality then stems from the responsibility of all managers to minimise waste of costly human resources and maximise satisfaction through work for their subordinates in order to support social cohesion within their own sphere of influence.

1.3　THE ENVIRONMENTAL IMPERATIVE

The final imperative for quality is environmental. Driven by the experiments and perspectives of writers such as Lovelock (1979, 1988, 1991) and the emergence of the environmental movement, it is now widely recognised that the world has finite natural resources, particularly fossil fuels, and that the use of these appears damaging to the total ecology of the planet. Renewable energy sources, such as solar power, wind energy or wave energy, are not yet readily available, nor as cheap as may be possible in the future.

Operating our organisations without a sharp focus on quality is to be wasteful of these limited resources. It is argued that quality products, processes and systems minimise the use of all the factors of production (human, material, land and money) and thereby minimise damage to the environment. For example, a process which achieves Crosby's 'Zero Defects' or Shingo's 'Poka-Yoke' standard involves no rework or rectification. A process such as this then makes minimum use of money, materials and labour in obtaining its output and consequently reduces damage to the environment compared with a process producing any number of defective outputs.

Clearly, with the exception of fictional characters such as Superman, it is too much to expect any one individual or organisation to 'save the world'. Each individual or organisation can however be expected to make a contribution to this at the appropriate level – that is, their own level and the ones above and below. The levels could be thought of as the individual, the organisation, the stakeholders, the local community, the national community and the international community.

The individual has a responsibility to him or herself and the employers to minimise use and waste of resources in the completion of his or her duties. This must be supported by the organisation creating the conditions which enable the individual's work to be carried out with minimum waste, this might for example mean ensuring that tools are properly functional (sharp, accurate) and that sufficient time is permitted for the task to be carried out with appropriate care.

The management of the organisation have the additional responsibility to consider the total effectiveness of the organisation in terms of its use of all resources and the environmental implications of their actions. This may mean undertaking additional investments to reduce environmental damage. This approach must of course be supported by the other stakeholders in the enterprise, in particular the shareholders, who must accept responsibility for the actions of the organisation and be prepared to accept the returns generated by an organisation which fully accepts its responsibilities – even if these are less in the short term than competing investments.

The community in which the organisation exists must hold and impose expectations on the behaviour of the organisation as regards environmental matters whilst at the same time accepting its own responsibilities. For example, the community must impose expectations as regards the dumping of waste, but must also provide an appropriate mechanism for such dumping to take place. Economically, certain resources can only be provided at the community level, for example incinerators and recycling plants – the responsibility of the community is to ensure that these are available.

At a national level, the same considerations apply. The nation has a responsibility to itself, its constituents and the international community. This responsibility includes setting, maintaining and enforcing environmental standards and expectations and creating conditions (perhaps through the use of taxes and duties) which reinforce those expectations.

At the international level, the responsibilities are much the same. Creation and enforcement of environmental standards must be undertaken by the international community. While other aspects of organisational life may be very different, for example wage rates, organisational culture and so on, the international community must demand common environmental standards from all those wishing to be part of that community.

At every level there is a need and a responsibility to educate and inform on environmental matters and to understand the needs from a total rather than partial perspective. Thus the third imperative for quality is to address the rising desire for reductions in environmental damage, helping to ensure the survival of all species. A responsibility which pertains at every level of the world community.

SUMMARY

This chapter has identified and elaborated three imperatives for the contemporary pursuit of quality – economic, social and environmental. From these different perspectives, brief arguments have been developed which not only justify, but collectively demand, that the idea of quality be pursued in every aspect of every organisation.

key learning points

Three arguments for pursuing quality:

economic, social, environmental

Economic
mature markets, saturation coverage; work follows (relatively) cheap labour; manufacturing drives services income – economies must be balanced; the public sector must deliver better services at the same or lower cost to meet public expectations; ultimate demand is economic survival.

Social
non-quality goods and services are wasteful of human capabilities and talent; working in a non-quality environment is ultimately demoralising for the individual; the imperative is to minimise waste of talent and maximise satisfaction.

Ethical
the world has finite material resources; we have a responsibility to minimise waste and environmental damage.

QUESTION

To what extent do the three imperatives for quality apply in your own country?

chapter two

QUALITY: A STRATEGIC DECISION?

focus on quality, not quantity.
Jiang Zemin, President, Peoples Republic of China, 1996

INTRODUCTION

The successful pursuit of a quality programme requires the dedication of substantial organisational resources and it is vital to understand whether and how this generates value for the organisation. It is evident from the citation above that China, the world's largest emerging economy consisting of 1.2 billion potential consumers, is treating quality not just as an organisational issue but as a national one. Such a position reinforces the message that all organisations which want to survive and succeed must take quality seriously.

In this chapter the role and implications of quality in the organisation will be explored through consideration of the conventionally recognised different levels of management decision making (operations, administration and strategy). The idea of 'normative' decision making (Beer, 1979) will be introduced to enhance understanding. The implications for an organisation of pursuing quality will be assessed starting with operational management.

2.1   OPERATIONS

Operational management is concerned with the day to day activities which ensure that the organisation fulfils its present purposes and objectives.

These may include short run profitability, achievement of particular levels of output, yield or productivity. Operational decisions are generally more or less immediate in their impact on the organisation, affecting what happens during a particular day, shift, or even part shift, for example where there are product changes during the course of a shift.

The chapters in part four of this book will show how the traditional tools of quality are predominantly aimed at this operational level. They are intended to assist the manager and staff in the production of quality goods and services on a daily basis, focusing on prevention of error and minimisation of rework or rectification, aiming to minimise inspection and to achieve continuous improvement. These things are achieved through the use of measurement system outputs at the 'shopfloor' level to inform devices such as quality circles and work improvement teams. These engage workers in reflection on the difficulties and problems experienced with a product or service and through their joint efforts seek to reduce them.

In terms of the needs of the organisation an analogy can be suggested with Herzberg's (1959) ideas (figure 2.1) on motivation theory. Herzberg suggested that working conditions affecting motivation fall into two broad bands, hygiene factors and motivating factors. Hygiene factors are those characteristics of the working environment which, if absent, will lead to dissatisfaction. Their presence will not motivate workers but will create conditions in which motivation becomes possible. Motivating factors are those characteristics of the work which will inspire those involved to greater efforts.

For the purposes of this analogy we can equate the hygiene factors to the need for operational quality. The absence of an operational quality focus will mean higher levels of error and failure. Its presence will not guarantee greater quality since so many aspects are driven by other parts of the organisation, e.g. planning, design and marketing.

The role of operational management is to achieve the quality expectations of the organisation – but this can only be done within the constraints

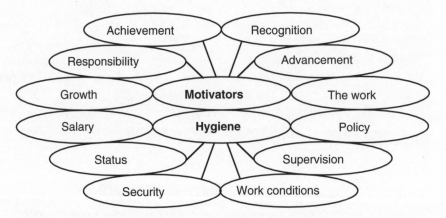

Figure 2.1 **Herzberg's two factor theory of motivation**

imposed by higher order decision making. Clearly, if quality is not an inherent part of the thinking at higher levels in the organisation it will be difficult, if not impossible, to achieve at the operational level.

2.2 ADMINISTRATION

Administrative management is concerned with the allocation, use and control of the current operational resources of an organisation to achieve its present purposes and objectives. It is the control function for operational management. Administrative managers acting within the constraints imposed on them from higher management seek to maximise the use of resources in the pursuit of organisational goals.

At this level the first serious constraint upon the achievement of quality comes into focus. The administrative manager, for example a factory or production manager, may find her or himself in a position of conflict between meeting the customer expectations in terms of volume of product delivered and meeting those customers' expectations on quality of product or service. At this point, the priorities imposed upon this manager from above will determine the outcome of any conflict. The question is simply – 'Which does the organisation regard as more important to deliver, volume or quality?' In addition to observation of the behaviour of the manager, clues to the answer can be discerned in an examination of the performance measurement system of the organisation. If this emphasises volume then delivery of volume will prevail at the expense of quality and vice versa.

The quality management system (whether or not to ISO 9000 or more recently ISO 14000 standards) will, or should, form a significant part of the performance management system employed by the administrative manager. However, if quality is not perceived as a priority within the overall management system then it will probably not be perceived as a priority at this level.

It is also important to realise at this stage that the pursuit of quality does not apply solely to the operational aspects of the organisation but also to all of the support and administrative processes which enable it to function. For example, a personnel recruiting system should be thought of as a productive process delivering to the operational system (its customer) staff who meet the skill and personality criteria necessary to perform the tasks required. If it fails to do this then it is unreasonable to expect the operational processes to function to appropriate quality standards. The same thinking applies to training, to reward systems, to equipment and materials procurement and so on.

The administrative manager then has a dual responsibility for the delivery of quality, neither of which is more important than the other – they are equally necessary. One is to create the operational conditions which make it possible for the product or service to meet customer expectations. The other is to ensure that his or her own systems and processes deliver outputs to the operational 'customers' which meet their needs and expectations.

2.3 STRATEGY

Strategic management is concerned with the scope of the organisation's activities, its markets, products or services and market stance. It deals with the questions of how the organisation should develop and adapt itself for the future. The strategic process necessarily leads to outcomes with a degree of uncertainty. Strategic decisions are then best thought of in terms of probable results rather than the short term absolutes which may be associated with operational or administrative decisions. Despite or rather perhaps because of this, and as with administrative management, quality must be inherent in the strategic process itself to maximise the probability of success and reduce the chances of failed strategic decisions. The classic and often quoted example of such a failure is that of IBM which determined for itself that the future of computing rested in mainframe systems – a decision which led to the organisation falling behind competitors in the development of personal computers with associated failure, at least initially, to gain market share. The strategic process itself then must be subjected to the same rigorous approach to quality as the operational processes. However, we must consider whether the decision to pursue a quality programme or become a quality organisation is itself strategic.

Michael Porter in a *Harvard Business Review* article (1996), in common with this author's thoughts in section 2.1, suggests that 'operational effectiveness and strategy are both essential to superior performance' but also makes the point that 'many companies have been frustrated by their inability to translate those gains [achieved from improved organisational effectiveness] into sustainable profitability'. He suggests that practices such as benchmarking and technology transfers between organisations create conditions where performance gains achieved by one organisation are rapidly replicated in others, potentially leading to a sustained stalemate – no long term winners and no long term losers – with an increasing homogeneity of product and service characteristics. If strategic management is about creating and sustaining competitive advantage for an organisation then this suggests that the pursuit of quality, particularly in a collaborative environment, may be the very opposite of strategic. If it acts to reduce competitive advantage rather than increase it, and to increase similarities between organisations there is potential for all to pursue the same quality goal – which may not represent the true potential of the product or service.

However, that is not to say that the pursuit of quality has no strategic implications. Porter's work implies that every organisation in a particular market will seek to emulate the behaviour of the one perceived as 'best.' This is inevitably not the case. Some organisations will not willingly collaborate. They may regard process knowledge (one key to organisational effectiveness) in the same proprietary manner as they regard a particular brand or item of intellectual property, for example in the petro-chemical industry where the aphorism 'the product is the process' is used. Equally, because of contextual differences, a working practice which delivers benefits for one organisation in a particular cultural setting will not necessarily deliver the same benefits for another in a different cultural setting. Hofstede (1980) has examined this aspect in some depth. Thus the apparent loss of competitive advantage will not spread uniformly and universally across any industry.

Meanwhile, the leading organisations, that is the ones against which others benchmark, will seek continually to further improve their products and processes to sustain their perceived advantage – always providing that they do not become complacent. It is possible to discern then that for any industry there will be leaders and followers with an inevitable time lag between the introduction of an improvement by the leader and its dissemination to others within the industry – either through benchmarking or creative imitation. This time lag will serve to sustain competition within the industry and hence support either price or cost advantage for the leading organisations. It is improbable that any innovation will bring benefits to an entire industry at the same instant except where it is externally driven, such as by governmental or regulatory authority involvement, or where the structure of the industry demands it. Innovation in the banking system, such as a new method of clearing payments between banks, would necessarily have to be adopted by a number of organisations at the same time to actually function. An improvement in operational effectiveness will then, in most circumstances, generate a gain for the innovating organisation until that improvement is emulated by others. A focus on constant innovation and improvement fits quite neatly into Porter's (1980) strategy of 'differentiation', the creation of a market perception of value advantage.

However, the strategic implications go much further than this. The comments on strategic management have, so far, been essentially inward looking – to the organisation and the industry. If we now look outward at the environment the effect of improved quality on customer behaviour can be examined. For perishable or consumption goods, there is perceived to be little impact. Improvement in the quality of a loaf of bread or a mushroom may affect customer choice but, if anything, is likely to lead to advantage for one player against others and a slight overall increase in volume, assuming a relatively mature market. It is when we examine consumer durables that the full impact becomes clear.

Any established consumer durable, that is one in the mature phase of its lifecycle will be subject to constraints of growth in volume. There is only a finite market for items like cars, washing machines, microwaves or dishwashers. Buying activity in these circumstances is determined by the need to replace, or possibly upgrade, existing equipment. The products have entered the buyer's replacement cycle. The quality of these items, in the consumer's mind, is perhaps determined by a number of factors. Inevitably these will include reliability and longevity as well as other factors, such as price, appearance, noise level in operation and brand. If, as a manufacturer of consumer durables, we focus on improving reliability and longevity, then the effect is to stretch the replacement cycle (the period of time between purchases) which has a direct impact on apparent market size. Thus improved quality will act to reduce the overall level of sales of a particular item and, if the market is mature, then the growth opportunity for any one supplier is determined by the number of consumers who can be taken from the competitors. In addition to this, the implications loop back into the organisation to affect the volume of output necessary for the manufacturer to meet demand. This directly affects every strategic decision made by the organisation because those strategic decisions imply the commitment of substantial resources towards a desired outcome. Thinking which follows the pattern:

improving quality =
increased sales =
increased manufacturing volume =
requirement for additional capacity

may be fundamentally flawed. First, because quality improvement should lead to greater volume output from existing facilities. Second, because improvements in quality may substantially extend the replacement cycle, leading to a loss of total market volume. The motor industry exemplifies this potential.

THE MOTOR INDUSTRY

During the 1950s, 1960s and 1970s the products of the motor industry with a few honourable exceptions, whether American, British or European, were in general regarded as unreliable and expensive. These factors coupled to the then enormous labour cost difference across the East–West divide, enabled the very rapid growth of the Japanese motor industry and its substantial penetration to the established markets. Cars were generally considered to have a relatively short life of five or six years and after three years (or around 40,000 miles) to have become so unreliable and prone to breakdown that they needed to be replaced. The ancillary components, for example clutches, steering systems, brake systems and electrical generators, were likely to need replacement at around this mileage.

Faced with the threat of extinction by the rapidly improving quality of imported vehicles, the industry eventually, and with much financial and personal pain, addressed its product quality. It is now accepted as a normal expectation that a car will generally be reliable for perhaps five or six years and that components, such as those specified above, have much longer lifespans than before. Mileage has also become a much less important factor in determining the reliability of a vehicle. Service history (that is, a good maintenance record) has become more important. The collaboration of manufacturers and their suppliers has so dramatically improved the quality of the outputs that, almost without exception, manufacturers are struggling to utilise the capacity of their assembly plants. Although the market for new cars is substantially larger than in the 1950s and 1960s it has not grown to meet the potential numbers of vehicles now available. Consumers are able to rely on second user vehicles, and with improvements in the longevity of body work as well as other components, these maintain a greater proportion of their value. The cost of new vehicles, particularly in the fleet purchaser dominated UK market, has reached levels where the private consumer is unwilling or unable to pay the manufacturer's price. What constitutes value for money for those consumers can adequately be met through the used car market.

These changes in buyer behaviour, driven by the quality improvements made by manufacturers have in effect impacted adversely on the strategic decisions to build new factories, launch new products, expand capacity and so on.

It can be concluded then that the pursuit of quality must be considered as strategic. First, the process for formulating strategy must exhibit quality characteristics – that is, the process itself must be correctly designed and implemented. Second, the impact of the choice to pursue quality fits with the generic strategy of differentiation. Third, the pursuit of quality has an impact on strategic decisions because it may generate changes in consumer behaviour. This in turn may obviate the need to establish additional facilities or new distribution channels.

2.4 NORMATIVE DECISIONS

The conventionally recognised levels of decision making in organisations have been considered. However, the changing nature of the world of organisations and the increasing concern with ethical issues such as morality, environmentalism and so on demands that we go further. Normative management decisions are concerned with these aspects, helping to define the nature of the organisation itself, that is, the values, expectations and beliefs espoused by its members. The norms so derived should ensure that the organisation makes a good ethical fit with all of its stakeholders and with society in general.

An organisation which does not generate this 'fit' with its stakeholders will either lose customers – because it does not reflect their expectations, or fall into disregard, as have branches of the civil service in many countries. While customer loyalty to organisations and particularly brands does exist to the extent that some brands become synonymous with the product – the Hoover, Sellotape, Post-it notes – and is encouraged through various loyalty schemes (e.g. air miles, supermarket bonus cards and so on) – these will not retain customers who are genuinely unhappy with products or services. Political parties are particularly prone to failure of fit when they do not listen to an electorate that holds them in power. When the norms of a particular political grouping no longer reflect the wishes of their society they will be deposed, either through democratic process or by revolution. Similar observations can be made of commercial organisations. When the characteristics of the products or services do not meet the expectations of consumers, or the behaviour of the organisation is considered unacceptable, the customers will 'vote with their feet' and buy elsewhere. One example of this is those organisations which traded with South Africa during the apartheid era. When sales and profit targets are not met, the shareholders in the organisation, increasingly the large financial institutions, will depose the Chief Executive and appoint a new one in an attempt to correct the situation. Thus it is imperative for organisational survival (and for the self-preservation of those in power) that they listen to the demands of customers and formulate organisational norms which will meet them.

The pursuit of quality by so many organisations in recent years is precisely this kind of response. Consumers in mature markets are seeking the reassurance of reliable, high quality (as defined by themselves) goods and services with the number and variety of choices available to them, organisations which do not respond will fail.

The gurus of quality, as will be seen in part two, all stress the need for senior management commitment to the idea of quality in order to ensure its achievement. Normative management is where this commitment arises. The feedback of consumer expectations to senior management closes the loop for the organisation in determining behaviour. This loop explains why senior management must hold and believe in this commitment.

Normative decisions determine what questions and decisions are acceptable to the organisation at the strategic level. They therefore pre-control (Espejo and Schwaninger, 1993) strategic decision making. Strategic decisions create potential new value for the organisation – how profits will be made tomorrow – this, in turn, pre-controls the potential decisions at the administrative and operational levels – today's profits. At this point, and notwithstanding the potential for marketing activity to influence consumer behaviour, the organisation largely loses control to the market. If the normative decisions are incorrect, the consumers will not buy.

In many organisations the normative decisions are expressed through devices such as mission statements or publicised 'visions' which attempt to express the values which the organisation stands for. It is often considered that once this statement has been made the job is complete. However, if the values so expressed are not enacted in the behaviour of the senior management and in the performance measurement and reward systems of the organisation, then the junior management and operational staff will not respond to them. They will, rather, respond to the actual behaviour and expectations of the Senior Management, measured by what they do and how they act, not by what they say. It is vital, as Professor Charles Handy so eloquently puts it, that the Senior Management 'walk the talk'.

SUMMARY

This chapter has reviewed the role and positioning of quality in the context of the four levels of management decision making – operational, administrative, strategic and normative. It has made clear that quality must be inherent throughout the organisation in order for it to survive. While the principal traditional tools of quality focus on the operational and administrative aspects this chapter has shown that it must extend well beyond this. If the Senior Management are not absolutely committed to quality in everything that they say and do, then the organisation will not 'care' about quality. If this caring is absent then it is impossible to build a quality organisation.

---

key learning points

Four levels of management decision:

operational; administrative; strategic; normative

Operational
immediate impacts, day to day activity;

Administrative
allocation of resources to achieve objectives;

Strategic
activity scope, development directions;

Normative
the nature of the organisation, values, beliefs and expectations;
quality must be inherent at every level.

QUESTION

What are the 'norms' of your own organisation (either a business or a university/college)? How do you know?

chapter three

BARRIERS TO QUALITY

Passive resistance is the most potent weapon ever wielded by man.

Benjamin Tucker

INTRODUCTION

This chapter aims to introduce readers to some of the many barriers which prevent the achievement of quality. It will identify what those barriers are, how they arise and how they can be identified or recognised. The barriers have been grouped under four main headings:

- systems and procedures;
- culture;
- organisation design;
- management perspectives.

These headings encompass a variety of other factors which are considered as symptoms rather than fundamental issues. The final part of the chapter will look at identifying the costs of quality (or the costs of a non-quality process or product).

3.1 SYSTEMS AND PROCEDURES

Many organisations, in particular those which are medium to large in size and long established, operate through a more or less bureaucratic process. That is to say that they are organised through a hierarchical system of offices or 'bureaux' (Weber, 1924) and maintain that organisation through formal reports, documents and record keeping. This is not in itself a bad thing, indeed it is essential to the delivery of a standard product – particularly in service organisations or those operating through a distributed delivery network such as retail chains or banks. Without a standardised approach the customer may easily be confused and the organisation itself become out of control.

However, problems can arise with such a system. First, the systems and procedures can become fixed, that is, they become 'frozen' into the organisation such that pressure for change and adaptation encounters high resistance. In this instance when change is necessary to meet a new level of customer expectations it can be difficult to achieve. This is a barrier to the achievement of quality. It can be recognised when staff use expressions such as 'We've always done it like that.' This approach of using precedent as the basis of current decisions is common in many aspects of life, in particular in the practise of law which relies heavily on past cases and in civil administration. Readers may recall Lynn and Jay's *Yes Minister* (1982), when Sir Humphrey and the Minister James Hacker were discussing the Honours system:

> 'I told him not to be silly. This infuriated him even more. "There is *no reason*," he said, stabbing the air with his finger, "to change a system which has worked well in the past."
> "But it hasn't", I said.'

In the contemporary organisational climate, the reliance on precedent must be open to question if emergent threats are to be neutralised and advantage taken of opportunities even if such precedents were at one time reliable.

The second problem, perception, is probably a greater barrier to quality, particularly in the context of a Crosby-style (1979) quality programme. Such a programme relies heavily on an exhortative, evangelical approach. In most cases managers and staff focus on achieving those aspects of performance which are explicitly measured. The systems and procedures of the organisation, especially those involving performance measurement, tend to determine which characteristics of the organisation receive most attention. For example Beckford (1993) reports a case of a cake factory where the performance of the production department was monitored against two simple measures – volume throughput and labour utilisation. The production managers sought to maximise these two characteristics in their daily work with considerable success. Complaints about quality, arising from either the internal quality control function or from the customers, were acknowledged but ignored in pursuit of productivity. While outside the direct scope of Beckford's work, it was necessary for the subject organisation to redesign its measurement system before any sustainable improvement could be achieved.

The barrier to quality revealed here is that of workforce perception – including all managers. Staff in an organisation will seek to achieve the targets which are established through reported measurement – those things which the organisation instructs them through its measurement system to regard as important. Discovering such a barrier in an organisation is easy. It is simply necessary to look at the way in which performance is measured, this tells you what the organisation regards as important. Even where quality performance is formally measured, and it often is not, its importance can be judged against the priority it is given when compared to productivity or other measures.

Overcoming these barriers will be dealt with in later chapters of this book. For now, it is sufficient to say that systems and procedures must be (re)designed to support the achievement of quality with particular attention paid to the selection of performance criteria. If quality is a desired characteristic of the outputs of the organisation, it will somehow and to some degree, have to be measured and must take account of the expectations of customers – whether internal or external.

3.2   CULTURE

The development of a quality culture is a critical area of the achievement of quality, but what is culture? Clutterbuck and Crainer (1990: 195) describe it as:

> a set of behavioural and attitudinal norms, to which most or all members of an organisation subscribe, either consciously or unconsciously, and which exert a strong influence on the way people resolve problems, make decisions and carry out their everyday tasks.

Schein, cited by Clutterbuck and Crainer (1990: 196), suggests that culture describes the '*artefacts, values and underlying assumptions*' that govern behaviour within the organisation. For the purposes of this book it is 'values' and 'beliefs' that are the key cultural drivers although these may be expressed in a variety of ways. They often emerge from the measurement systems and procedures which are seen to communicate to staff and workers what senior management consider important about performance. Eventually, such aspects become culturally embedded, that is, they become a part of the value system of the organisation.

Beliefs and values are also often expressed through the rituals, stories and myths of the organisation. These are exchanged through both formal and informal processes and may be seen as guiding new entrants towards particular forms of behaviour and attitudes. Those who do not conform may be seen as radicals and remain outside the 'cultural web' (Johnson and Scholes, 1993: 60) of the organisation.

Entrenched norms of behaviour are some of the most difficult aspects of an organisation to change. Where achievement of quality has previously not been considered important in comparison to achievement of some other target, it requires considerable determination and effort to change the established values. Again, a case history can perhaps explain the point. Many companies are currently abandoning the formal dress codes which grew up in the post-World War Two period. Perhaps the most famous example of this is IBM which adopted a 'uniform' style of dress – grey suit, white shirt, boring tie. Adoption of this dress standard was seen as acceptance by the individual of his subordination to the organisation – of his becoming a 'company' man. IBM, along with many other organisations have recently formally abolished the requirement to wear standard office clothes – but how long will it be before the staff themselves accept the change? Fletcher Challenge Steel, one of New Zealand's largest companies, formally abandoned its dress code in the 1980s yet the majority of staff still adhere to it. The current Chief Executive of Fletcher Challenge Steel (an Englishman), who has been in the post for over six years, adopts a very informal style – short sleeves, sometimes an open necked shirt – this is remarked upon by others within the organisation, but has not succeeded in changing their approach. Relative to changing attitudes to achieving quality, changing the dress code can be considered as comparatively easy. Contrarily, in some, but by no means every Japanese company, all employees – up to and including the Chief Executive – wear common corporate workwear. They argue that this approach helps to reduce or even eradicate differences between grades, enhances communication and that the sense of uniformity increases the common bond between employees.

It has been shown that culture is often a very strong determinant of behaviour. In the next few pages some specific aspects of organisational culture will be considered.

Politics in the organisational context does not usually refer to overt competition between groups with differing ideologies, although this is possible. Normally, it refers to covert competition between various sub-groups in the organisation for power, that is, for positions of influence and authority from which they can manage the organisation to reflect their own preferences. These groupings may have their roots in a particular technical or functional ability, for example marketing, finance or production, or in common backgrounds, such as groups who joined the organisation at the same time and whose careers developed together, or who share the same school or university background, the same religion, or the same home town. Working as a sub-cultural group within the organisation's total culture, such groups often exercise immense, but tacit influence. If such groupings are strong in an organisation, then their interests may be placed before those of the organisation itself. This presents another barrier to quality. From the perspective of such sub-groups, achievement of quality must come to be seen as a meta-cultural requirement. The interests of the particular group must become aligned with, or subordinated to, the interest of the organisation in pursuing quality.

Linking with some of the points already made about measurement systems and about politics, do the employees of the organisation care about the work and in particular about the quality of the product or service? If they do not, for whatever reason, then quality will probably not be achieved. Such attitudes are often driven by management through the priorities that they set and the results with which they manage the organisation. For example, if those who are rewarded well by the organisation are those who produce most, regardless of quality, then productivity (output) will be the focus of everyone's attention. If, on the other hand, quality is rewarded in preference to volume, then quality will be dominant.

Achievement of quality, particularly in the *kaizen* (continuous improvement) sense, depends upon an adequate level of innovation. Creativity (the origination and implementation of new ideas or innovations) is often suppressed in organisations in pursuit of the status quo. This is revealed through the use of such expressions as 'Don't rock the boat', or 'Yes, you're right, but in the interests of your career/overtime/colleagues . . . ' A lack of creativity in the organisation is not a sign that the people are not creative since creativity is inherent in all of us. More often it is a sign that their creativity is stifled within the organisation and thus has become expressed outside the workplace.

Large or successful organisations often emit a *hum* of satisfaction. They have an air of complacency and contentment with the way things are which can be almost tangible in the atmosphere. Such a situation imposes an immense barrier to quality since there is no apparent compulsion or impetus for change. Frequently such satisfaction is present in organisations which have a short term focus – perhaps a lack of foresight. They assume that if everything is alright in this period, then everything will surely be alright in the next. Disasters and near disasters frequently overtake such organisations.

COMPAQ COMPUTERS

It has been widely reported that in 1990 Compaq, then one of the world's top 400 companies, achieved sales of US$3.6 billion and profits of US$455 million. In the second quarter of the following year profits fell by 80 per cent, the third quarter produced a loss! The business had been built on an unrivalled reputation for quality, price was seventh on their list of procurement criteria. Thus, while their products enjoyed high quality, prices to consumers were higher than for their rivals. When market conditions changed so that price became a priority issue for customers the drone of satisfaction from the company drowned out the warning signals from the market-place. Compaq subsequently went through a major re-appraisal of its strategy in its efforts to return to profit.

This may appear a somewhat perverse story in a book about quality, but it usefully emphasises the point that quality is not only about quality!

Perhaps the best illustration of lack of foresight is given by Handy (1990a: 7–8):

I like the story of the Peruvian Indians who, seeing the sails of their Spanish invaders on the horizon put it down to a freak of the weather and went on about their business, having no concept of sailing ships in their limited experience. Assuming continuity, they screened out what did not fit and let disaster in. I like less the story that a frog if put in cold water will not bestir itself if that water is heated up slowly and gradually and will in the end let itself be boiled alive, too comfortable with continuity to realize that continuous change at some point becomes discontinuous and demands a change in behaviour.

In the turbulent contemporary business environment the assumption of continuity is highly dangerous. While pursuing quality with its implications of continuous improvement, standardisation and regularity, it is equally vital to be alert to the potential for discontinuous change, especially since strategic advantage may rest in such discontinuities.

The last barrier to quality which will be briefly explored under the general heading of culture is that of accountability. Achievement of quality requires that errors be acknowledged, that sources of error be tracked down and rectified and that both curative and preventative action be taken by those involved.

In many organisations this process is inhibited by a sub-culture which adopts a penal attitude. The realisation of error is followed by a process of detection, prosecution – sometimes persecution – and punishment. This book is not the place for a debate on the societal value of such an approach but it can be suggested that it is likely to be essentially negative in its effects. This may in turn lead to a situation where, as Deming (1982: 107) suggests 'fear grips everyone'. In such a situation, errors may be suppressed or hidden. Where this is not possible, for example in manufacturing organisations, there will be a tendency to avoid punishment by blaming others and by a refusal to accept responsibility.

This barrier can be overcome by recognising that errors are often opportunities for learning and are the basis for modifying a process or system to inhibit or prevent future occurrences. Naturally there must be a limiting case, when the error is consciously or deliberately provoked, when those responsible must be found and an appropriate response generated. However, in most organisations, and in many circumstances, the cause of error can be traced to some failure in the design or execution of a process, in the training of the employee or in the equipment provided for the completion of the task. These aspects should be the first focus of attention and, in a quality organisation, will inhibit the use of disciplinary action. In many cases though, they are the last. Managers often prefer to find someone to blame, perhaps because it is easier to do that than to accept responsibility for their own failure – from this approach arises the blame culture. For example, one organisation employed a group of administrative staff to operate a post office and administration system, servicing the needs of an off-site sales force. The sales people rarely visited the office and relied heavily on the administrators to maintain diaries and timetable customer visits. An activity based reward system meant that the sales force were absolutely reliant on the administrative system to ensure that they were paid the correct amount for the work done. Time lags in the system caused regular delays in payment. Work done was not paid for and adventurous sales staff submitted claims for work which was incomplete, relying on the time lags to beat the system. Inevitably, problems arose in this operation. Members of the sales force began to fall behind with commitments, others received no pay at the end of certain months. After some delay, an administrator and two of the sales force left the organisation, their temporary contracts were not renewed due to poor performance. Today, no member of the workforce will take any action without at least one management signature. This ensures that they have to take no responsibility. The system, the driver of the problems, is unchanged.

3.3   ORGANISATION DESIGN

When discussing organisation design, it is not simply the organisation structure – the classic pyramidal hierarchy, or more recently the very flat organisation chart – which is to be considered. It must also incorporate the interactions between units, the information and management systems and their total inter-relatedness. As Beer (1985: i) suggests, the organisation chart may be seen as 'frozen out of history,' revealing who to blame when things go wrong but not showing how the organisation actually works. A number of barriers to achievement of quality can be found in this area.

The first, and most frequent, error is what can be called institutionalised conflict. This means that an organisation has been designed in such a way that conflict between quality and some other characteristic, such as productivity, is inherent. This is commonly found where the Quality Control or Assurance Manager reports to the Production Manager. In such a case, the need to meet customer orders will often override the need to achieve quality standards. The Quality Manager is, in effect, redundant, since no value is added to the operation of the organisation by his or her presence. Flood (1993: 210–221), reports how when production fell short of customer orders at 'Tarty Bakeries' the Production Manager would pass as acceptable output which had already been rejected by the Quality Inspectors.

This situation, replicated in many organisations, presents a major barrier to quality. A structure must be created in which the quality function is independent of the production function, and as shall be seen, where quality is inherent in the product, the process and, importantly, the culture. This leads to a situation where rather than rejects and errors being *inspected out*, quality can be *baked in* to the product.

The second barrier to quality in this context is the design of the organisation's information systems. This does not simply mean the computerised management or executive information system, but the whole of the information generating and processing activity of the organisation, both formal and informal. These activities must generate the right information, in the right format, at the right time and deliver it to the right decision maker(s) if it is to be of any benefit. Most frequently, users of information spend much time analysing and discussing yesterday's or last week's errors whilst paying no attention to today or to the future. While they may be criticised for this it is as much a function of the design of the information system as a matter of managerial desire. Hindsight is always twenty-twenty and a common requirement in organisations is for managers to explain what went wrong, to justify mistakes and failures. Such organisations are attempting to manage their past and not their future, perhaps because they find this easier to do – a little like driving a car by looking in the rear view mirror to see where you have been!

The informal system refers to communication through devices such as unions and other staff bodies and the grapevine. Beer (1985: 58–59) encourages this informal communication between functions, which may be concerned with immediate operational matters such as the timing of the next batch of a product, or with longer term issues such as competition for capital. However, he specifically sees this communication as supplementary to and not in the place of the formal systems. Beckford (1993: 300–323) shows how the union and the grapevine were perceived by both management and staff as the most reliable information sources in an organisation. It is worth making the point at this stage that managers cannot stop communication within an organisation. Data will find a means of transmission whatever barriers are placed in the way, but the organisation will only be effective if the communication channels are properly designed.

Another aspect of this information system is performance measurement. Briefly recapping on section 3.1, performance measurement tends to determine which aspects of the organisation will be perceived as important. Those characteristics or outputs which are measured will be the focus of work, that which is not measured may well be ignored. Thus the design of the measurement system, its prime content and the way its outputs are responded to by managers, may be expected to drive the performance of the organisation.

Similarly, many organisations operate with no formal measurement system at all, everything is done by 'gut feel' and rule of thumb. In these circumstances, quality simply cannot be known to have been achieved since, even if it has been defined, it is not being measured. As the conversation goes in *Alice in Wonderland* (Carroll, 1866):

> 'Would you tell me, please, which way I ought to walk from here?' [Said Alice]
> 'That depends a good deal on where you want to get to.' [Said the Cheshire Cat]
> 'I don't much care where.' [Said Alice]
> 'Then it doesn't matter which way you walk.' [Said the Cheshire Cat]
> 'So long as I get *somewhere*.' [Said Alice]

An appropriate form and degree of measurement is vital. That is enough to know what is happening but not so much that the 'measured' feel burdened or oppressed by the system since in such a case they may seek to pervert the results. Perhaps, as Beer (1985: 102) proposes in the context of autonomy, we should have as much measurement 'as guarantees cohesion'.

The next barrier to quality is one of role understanding and articulation within the organisation, particularly amongst the staff involved in the control and development functions – general management, marketing, human resource management, accounting, strategic planning and so on. There is a tendency amongst many such staff to delve down into the operations of the organisation, perhaps taking direct control when errors occur or the unexpected happens. While doing so they may be neglecting their own roles within the organisation. This 'firefighting' or 'crisis' style of management is seen in many organisations as heroic, with plaudits and awards handed to those who perform in this way. However, as the apocryphal saying goes: 'when you are up to your armpits in alligators, it's easy to forget that the original objective was to drain the swamp'.

Solving today's crisis is extremely important but as suggested by Senge (1990: 15) that is to deal with 'symptoms not underlying causes'. A low level intervention by senior management will rarely address the root, or fundamental cause of the problem, and *that* is their proper role, not to deal with operational matters. The operational managers must be allowed the freedom and given the support to solve their own problems. If senior management continually intervene in a junior manager's daily problem solving activity two things will occur. First, the junior manager will never learn to solve his or her own problems thus reducing organisational effectiveness and increasing costs. Second, the senior manager's work will never get done and consequently the organisation will hurtle out of control into the nearest obstacle because nobody is watching where it is going.

The final barrier which we will explore in this section is that of irrelevant, or inappropriate, activities. This section is titled 'Organisation design', frequently the truth is that an organisation has not been designed, it has grown and metamorphosed almost of its own accord. Many features of an established organisation, whether they be structural, such as departments or units; organisational, that is, activities and procedures; or cultural and attitudinal, have been not intentionally and deliberately created. Often they just grow. They develop, perhaps to support some long forgotten or superseded purpose of the organisation and are simply never stopped. Cases are common where procedures have become institutionalised and carried on for years. In one example a manager once requested a particular report which had to be produced by hand. That the manager had long since moved on (and retired) and no further request had ever been received for the report was not seen as a reason for stopping, 'after all, you never know'! Equally, that a computerised version of the same report was available had not been noticed and 'anyway, the technology is unreliable'.

A similar process occurs with what, in Business Process Re-engineering (BPR) are known as cowpaths: these are the routes through an organisation which develop naturally without the purposeful intervention of the staff. A procedure in use may never have been the subject of deliberate design, it may have simply developed and its users become accustomed to it, complete with all its unique peculiarities and foibles. Such processes are often inefficient, sometimes ineffective, everybody complains about them, but they are seen as nobody's responsibility.

These cowpaths and inappropriate processes may well present barriers to the achievement of quality, since they are an 'unconscious' part of the organisation and their quality achievement inhibiting properties may not be recognised.

3.4   MANAGEMENT PERSPECTIVES

Management perspectives does not simply refer to the attitude to quality, but to the whole management ethos of the organisation as it impacts on quality – a subject which was touched upon in the previous chapter. The issue of corporate politics has already been raised in section 3.1 so will not be covered again here.

In order for an appropriate attitude to be developed to quality it must be recognised as a cause for concern. That is, the lack of quality in a product or service must be recognised. Frequently, companies adopt an ostrich-like attitude to quality finding it easier to blame poor performance on a host of other reasons. For example, when a previously successful sales performance declines, a common reaction is to focus on market changes, the sales team or activity by competitors, rather than on the product or service itself. Issues such as pricing and margins are often raised, perhaps leading to a focus on manufacturing performance in terms of productivity. Rarely is quality of product or service considered as a potentially primary issue at the outset.

It is essential that quality be treated as a potential part of the problem and be considered as a possible cause of decline. Even where a company is performing well, a positive attitude to quality needs to be developed and maintained. A product which is considered 'good enough' probably isn't so in today's competitive markets. There is no room for such complacency.

A further barrier to achievement of quality is a focus on short term results only, that is, the result in a particular shift, day, week, quarter or even year. Often salary or wage packages and performance bonuses are related directly to current period performance. Therefore currently acceptable performance parameters are used as a reason (or excuse) for not addressing the issue of quality. While not necessarily so, it is often the case that a focus on quality, or any other major change programme, will lead to a short term decline in performance (particularly of productivity) whilst staff and management adjust to changes – this is known as the 'hockey stick' effect. This may be related to a complete change of emphasis, where achieving quality of output needs to override, perhaps for the first time, achieving quantity of output. The change required in management attitudes is fundamental, away from pure productivity to productivity with quality. After all, output which is rejected, either internally or by the customer, cannot really be considered as output at all – it represents waste.

Thus a major barrier to quality may be built in to the reward system of the organisation. This can only be overcome by changing that system – it cannot be overcome through exhortations, evangelism, penal action or statistical measurement. Effective change may mean negotiating fresh terms with a variety of stakeholders in the enterprise, from the workforce and their bonus system, to the shareholders or providers of equity and loan capital whose short term interests may be affected and will need to be addressed.

Management often focuses on 'output today at all costs'. No concern with or interest in quality is evident. In order to boost performance a focus is maintained exclusively on current output. In the event of an apparent or expected shortfall in output the rate of production is increased in an attempt to compensate. Such increases are usually doomed to failure unless the system of production itself is addressed.

A food factory case study highlights the problem. The production lines had an established level of throughput for each of their various product lines, an optimal rate at which the equipment and operators could cope and a 'satisfactory compromise' was reached between productivity and quality. The established or recorded reject rate, with which the management were quite content, was 10 per cent.

In the event that production was likely to fall short of customer orders, the throughput rate across the product range would be increased from an average of 12 units per minute to an average of 16 units per minute. It was assumed by the factory management that this would give a net increase of around 33 per cent in output over the running time compared to optimal rate running. In practice, an increase of only about 10 per cent was achieved, the balance of additional throughput being rejected for failing to achieve the required quality standard. Naturally, the management's reaction was to speed up the process even further seeking to gain the elusive extra output. Figure 3.1 shows the effect of *slipping clutch syndrome* diagramatically.

While portrayed for the sake of simplicity as a step change, in practice, the quality gap widened on a progressive basis with every small increase in output. The greater the throughput the greater the reject rate, every increase in running speed generating an ever-reducing increase in acceptable output. One other major factor in this case was that the necessary work rate of the individual members of staff had to increase in line with the speed of the production belt – something which would not generally be sustainable regardless of the quality issue. The major solution applied in this particular case was to reduce throughput and thereby reduce the quality gap, ensuring that operators had sufficient time with each unit to reach the appropriate quality standard. A series of other measures were also taken – simply changing production rates was not the entire solution to the subject company's quality problems.

Each of the barriers highlighted in this section reflects a common mindset on the part of management. That mindset is called reductionism, the belief that anything can be understood by continually breaking it down into parts, breaking the parts down into further parts – and so on – this is often called

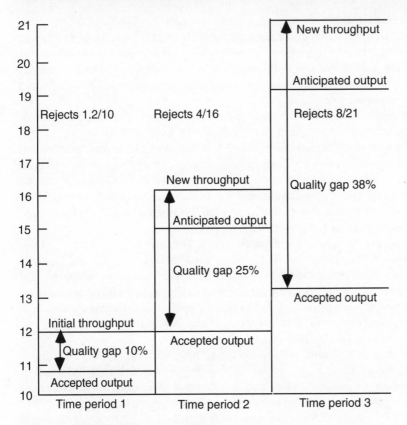

Figure 3.1 **Slipping clutch syndrome**

an analytical approach. The reductionist mindset seeks singular causes for singular effects and reflects the mechanistic thinking which has dominated science in the twentieth century.

Contemporary thinking suggests that a holistic approach to problem solving is more effective. That is one which deals with systems as wholes, which recognises the inter-relationships and interdependencies between parts of a system and which acknowledges that fixing one part of a system will not necessarily improve the whole. Such an approach broadens the attack on a problem by widening the scope of enquiry to study also those factors which influence it – its inputs – as well as considering the consequences of any changes – the effect on outputs. For example, simply replacing the tyres on a motor car, whilst potentially improving grip, will do little or nothing to improve the overall performance of the car.

3.5 COSTS OF QUALITY

The last issue to be briefly explored in this chapter is the costs of quality. This means the direct and invisible costs unnecessarily incurred by any organisation which does not have an effective quality system in place.

Direct costs in this context means those costs arising as a result of the non-achievement of quality and visibly attributable to that fact. Invisible costs in this context means those costs arising in the organisation as a result of not achieving quality but not visibly attributable to that fact – those where the relationship between non-quality and the cost may not have been discerned by the organisation.

Any production system for a product or service which is not designed to achieve the quality standard 'first time, every time' will incur rework and rectification costs. These are the costs of putting right errors, performing again a particular task or disassembling and reassembling (or scrapping) a product. Traditionally such costs have been treated by organisations as part of the overall cost of production and a percentage is included in the price of every item sold for the ones that go wrong. Thus acceptance of error is both institutionalised and carefully hidden!

In the era of quality, with lean production systems and just-in-time delivery, these costs need to be uncovered, and attention paid to their reduction and eradication. They must be challenged, not accepted. All processes receive inputs in the form of either materials or information from prior steps in the chain. That is to say, that each process is the customer of either an internal or external supplier. If the inputs received are defective, then costs may be incurred in a number of ways.

The first way, and potentially the most damaging, is that entire consignments have to be returned, holding up or stopping production and leading to unfilled orders and lost revenue. A commonly used answer to this is to increase holding stocks (ensuring that there is sufficient to cover a break in supply). Such an approach simply increases stocking costs, reducing the supply of working capital available to the organisation and inhibiting its overall performance – it does nothing to solve the quality problem.

The second way is that costs are incurred in validating the quality of goods or information received before it is processed, inspecting out failures from suppliers and, in effect, absorbing part of the suppliers' operating cost. Costs can also be incurred by not inspecting goods received, leading to the use of defective parts or information at the next stage of production. This ensures that the final product will also fail, leading back to rework and rectification.

A third way is that goods received are inspected and defective parts rectified before use. This again generates cost which should have been incurred by the supplier. Strategies to address some of these issues are incorporated in chapter 24 – Supplier development.

Inspection, as an auditing activity, can never be completely eradicated. Reports generated by inspection provide higher level management with information necessary for them to control and develop the operation. However, inspection is most commonly used as the quality mechanism, the one procedure which attempts to ensure that products and services are being provided at the agreed level. For such an approach to quality to work it requires at least a statistically valid sampling approach, and 100 per cent confidence requires 100 per cent inspection – an impossible task in some industries, for example, the manufacture of sweets or biscuits or other very high volume, low margin products. Although frequently attempted, this is rarely successful and always inordinately expensive. It is often impractical. Beckford (1993: 308) refers to an inspection system with a notional target of 100 per cent – in practice 5 per cent was supposedly achieved. The target figure was not practical given throughput, and was in any case irrelevant, since the product to be inspected was sealed into a plastic bag, inside a cardboard box – the only inspection was of the box, provided by an independent external supplier, not the product!

The level of inspection can be significantly reduced where quality is inherent in both the product and the process. Effective auditing can be substituted. This has a direct impact on both the cost of the activity and its utility.

Invisible costs are much harder to identify and specify, but are nonetheless incurred when quality has not been addressed properly. They may include:

- dissatisfied customers who fulfil future needs with an alternative supplier;
- in-process rework costs (costs incurred by reworking unfinished products within a process). Beckford (1993: 300–323) reports a case where the reported reject figure of 10 per cent ignored in-process rectification which amounted to a further 25 per cent of throughput;
- high staff turnover leading to increased recruitment and training costs as a result of dissatisfied staff leaving;
- capital costs for equipment and warehousing to provide for rectification of defective parts and storage of additional materials;
- reduced availability of internal working capital leading to unnecessary reliance on loan/overdraft capital (i.e. increased gearing).

Such costs are rarely attributed directly to the quality issue. However, they are in an interdependent relationship with all the other factors of the business and so to a large extent they are related to and driven by quality.

SUMMARY

This chapter has reviewed a number of the barriers to quality, looking particularly at the issues of systems and procedures, culture, organisation design and management approach. The chapter concluded with a brief look at some of the costs of quality.

key learning points

Four principal barriers to quality:
Systems and procedures, culture, organisation design, management perspectives

Systems and procedures
supporting or inhibiting the pursuit of quality?

Culture
attitudes, values and beliefs. Is the culture supportive of quality?

Organisation design
does the organisation design support or inhibit quality achievement?

Management perspectives
is quality recognised as a problem? Is the focus right for achieving quality? Is the mindset holistic or reductionist?

Two categories of quality cost:
direct, invisible

Direct costs
rework, rectification, defective inputs, inspection

Invisible costs
These include:
Lost customers, in-process errors, high staff turnover, unnecessary capital costs, reduced availability of working capital

QUESTION

Identify the barriers to quality in your own organisation (or one which is well known to you). Justify your choices and outline ways in which they might be overcome.

chapter _four_

THE EMERGENCE
OF MANAGEMENT

These all look like 'Whats'. Its the 'Hows' that I have trouble with.
Winnie the Pooh: (Allen, 1995)

INTRODUCTION

The purpose of this chapter is to introduce the principal models that still appear to govern much management behaviour. The formal study of management has only emerged as a discipline in its own right over the last hundred or so years – indeed it is still considered by many (particularly practising managers) as being at least as much 'black art' as science.

Theoretical and practical development of the discipline have more or less paralleled the emergence of the major corporations. Prior to the industrial revolution, the only permanent large scale organisations (other than states which were then extremely volatile) were the various religious churches and the standing armies and navies of the wealthier nations. The majority of the workforce were either agricultural labourers living at not much better than a subsistence standard of living, land-owning farmers, craftsmen or professionals such as doctors and lawyers.

Following the industrial revolution, the agricultural workers moved from the country to the towns and cities to improve their standard of living often becoming factory workers. The increasing size of such organisations (and the increasing wealth and desire to pursue other interests of the factory owners) created the opportunity for the emergence of the professional manager –

those whose job it was to oversee and supervise the activities of the workers on behalf of owners. The need to manage these large scale organisations and the drive for additional profitability can be interpreted as having given impetus to the study of management. The development of early management theories is the topic of the next sections.

The principal early models in organisation (or management) theory are the 'Classical', also known as the Traditional or Rational, and the 'Human Relations'. These two approaches have their own particular strengths and weaknesses which will be explored. These theories are considered to some extent as the causes of many quality problems and as being reflected in the dominant quality models which will be considered in the next part of the book.

4.1   CLASSICAL THEORY

The classical or 'machine' (Morgan, 1986: 20) model of organisation reflects the scientific management approach developed by Frederick Taylor, the classical theory of Henri Fayol and Max Weber's Bureaucracy Theory. These collectively still dominate mainstream management thinking. Each of these approaches regards the design of organisations as a technical exercise and depends upon fragmenting or dissecting an organisation into its component parts for analysis and efficient operation.

FREDERICK TAYLOR

'develop a science for each element of a man's work, which replaces the old rule of thumb method'.

'scientifically select and then train, teach and develop the workman, whereas in the past he chose his own work and trained himself as best he could'.

'heartily co-operate with the men so as to insure all of the work being done in accordance with the principles of the science which has been developed'.

ensure that 'There is an almost equal division of the work and the responsibility between the management and the workmen. The management take over all the work for which they are better fitted than the workmen, while in the past almost all of the work and the greater part of the responsibility were thrown upon the men.'

Figure 4.1 **Principles of scientific management: Frederick Taylor**

The 'machine' approaches to organisation arose as suggested in the late nineteenth and early twentieth centuries and may be considered as logical extensions of the advances then being made in machine technology. Machines are, in general, designed to perform specified tasks at known input/output rates and within specified tolerances; these management approaches assume that organisations can be similarly designed.

Frederick Taylor's scientific management (Taylor, 1911) is based on four key principles (see figure 4.1) of scientific task design, scientific selection, management-worker co-operation and equal division of work. Huczynski and Buchanan (1991: 282–283) see Taylor's objectives as being: first, to improve efficiency by increasing output and reducing 'underworking', what Taylor described as 'natural soldiering' and 'systematic soldiering'; second, to achieve 'standardisation of job performance, by dividing tasks up into small and closely specified sub tasks'; finally, to instil discipline, 'by establishing hierarchical authority and introducing a system whereby all management's policy decisions could be implemented'.

Whilst Taylor recognised that the worker in a given situation had a 'mass of rule of thumb or traditional knowledge', which constituted his 'principal asset or possession', he had a poor view of the capabilities and intelligence of the worker. For example, he believed that:

> the science of handling pig iron is so great and amounts to so much that it is impossible for the man who is best suited to this type of work to understand the principles of this science, or even to work in accordance with these principles without the aid of a man better educated than he is.

Taylor, saw the organisation as a machine, capable of being specified, designed and controlled by management to achieve a given purpose. The workmen were viewed as standardised machine parts, interchangeable with every other of like design and to be used at the discretion of management. His approach was later followed by Gilbreth and Gantt who both attempted to humanise Scientific Management, recognising the need for rest (Gilbreth) and human needs and dignity (Gantt). Taylor's key assumption that the worker was principally motivated by money was maintained.

Henri Fayol (1916) used the 'machine' metaphor in writing that:

> The body corporate of a concern is often compared with a machine or plant or animal. The expressions, 'administrative machine,' 'administrative gearing,' suggest an organism obeying the drive of its head and having all of its effectively interrelated parts move in unison towards the same end, and that is excellent.

This perception of the excellence of the 'machine' view is evident in his proposals for organising and managing. He proposed that 'to organise a business is to provide it with everything useful to its functioning: raw materials, tools, capital, personnel' and saw six sets of activities as producing the organisation: Technical, Commercial, Financial, Security, Accounting and Managerial. Fayol's proposed duties of managers reinforce this view, these

HENRI FAYOL

To ensure that the plan is judiciously prepared and strictly carried out:

See that the human and material organisation is consistent with the objectives, resources and requirements of the concern.

Set up a single, competent, energetic guiding authority.

Harmonise activities and co-ordinate efforts.

Formulate clear, distinct, precise decisions.

Arrange for efficient selection - each department must be headed by a competent, energetic man, each employee must be in that place where he can render greatest service.

Define duties clearly.

Encourage a liking for initiative and responsibility.

Have fair and suitable recompense for services rendered.

Make use of sanctions against faults and errors.

See to the maintenance of discipline.

Ensure that individual interests are subordinated to the general interest.

Pay special attention to unity of command.

Supervise both human and material order.

Have everything under control.

Fight against excess of regulation, red tape and paper control.

Figure 4.2 **Duties of managers: Henri Fayol**

are given in figure 4.2. The managerial duties reflect Fayol's fourteen principles of management shown in figure 4.3.

Some of these managerial duties and principles of management appear to conflict with the machine view and with each other. For example, 'Define duties clearly' and 'Encourage a liking for initiative and responsibility', or 'specialisation' and 'initiative', the first of which in each case would appear to preclude or at least make difficult the second.

The admonition to managers to 'fight against excess of regulation, red tape and paper control' stands in sharp contrast to his view that the work should be 'clearly divided', 'judiciously planned and strictly carried out', aspects which carry with them an implication of machine-like precision and heavy reliance on record keeping.

The overall impression remains that Fayol, like Taylor, viewed the organisation as a machine. The management were responsible for forecasting,

---

HENRI FAYOL

Division of work (specialisation)

Authority

Discipline

Unity of command

Unity of direction

Subordination (the interest of the organisation is more important than that of the individual)

Remuneration

Centralisation (a question of continuously varying proportion)

Scalar chain

Order

Equity

Stability of tenure

Initiative

Esprit de corps

Figure 4.3 **Principles of management: Henri Fayol**

planning, organising, commanding, co-ordinating and controlling whilst the 'workers', distinguished by 'technical ability characteristic of the business', were component parts to be fitted into the machine at the most appropriate place with 'a place for everyone and everyone in his place'.

Max Weber's 'Bureaucracy Theory' is developed from his views of three types of legitimate authority in organisations: rational, traditional and charismatic. Traditional authority rests on established acceptance of a natural order of society – the rulers and the ruled, perhaps reflecting the idea of monarchy. Charismatic authority rests on the personal devotion of individuals to a particular leader. Both of these styles of management exist in organisations today. For example, traditional authority is found in many of the patriarchal family owned businesses of Asia while charismatic authority may be considered as the style of organisations such as Body Shop or Virgin Atlantic. However, rational authority is the principal interest in this text as it has come to dominate many large organisations.

Rational authority was seen by Weber (cited in Pugh, 1990: 3–13) as representing legal authority, with 'obedience owed to the legally established impersonal order'. He considered that the 'purest type of exercise of legal authority is that which employs a bureaucratic administrative staff', and that bureaucracy was not simply desirable but indispensable to cope with the, then, complexities of organisations. He considered that the increasing

---

MAX WEBER

Specialisation: Each office (or 'bureau') has a defined area of expertise;

Hierarchy: Supervision and control or lower offices by higher ones;

Rules: Exhaustive, stable rules, learned by all;

Impersonality: Equality of treatment for all according to the rules;

Appointment: Selection according to competence not election;

Full-time: Occupation of office as the primary task of the individual;

Career: Promotion, tenure and seniority within the system;

Segregation: The official activity is distinct from the private individual.

Figure 4.4 **Principles of bureaucracy: Max Weber**

general technical knowledge had as a consequence, a need for an increase in the particular technical knowledge of individuals, in order for them to effectively administer an organisation.

A bureaucracy (see figure 4.4) was seen by Weber as being composed of a hierarchical organisation of 'offices', each acting according to the rules and norms of the organisation within a specified area of competence. Individuals within this structure were appointed on rational grounds to perform a specified function, without gaining rights to that appointment or having ownership of the organisation. All decisions, rules and acts were to be recorded in writing, in order, together with the 'continuous organisation of official functions', to 'constitute the office'. Weber saw a clear choice in organisations between 'bureaucracy and dilettantism' and proposed that bureaucracy was an inevitable requirement to support large organisations.

The machine view is evident again in this case, Weber proposing that every function, and every act of every office is capable of being specified to an exact degree. People were clearly viewed as functionaries within the bureaucracy, bringing no human element to the conduct of the affairs of the organisation.

4.2   CRITICAL REVIEW

Several assumptions about the world and organisational life seem to underlie these three rational views of organisation. These need to be stated before considering their strengths and weaknesses.

The first assumption is that an organisation can be regarded as isolated from the influence of its environment. While this may have been an acceptable view in a fast growing producer-led economy, it clearly cannot be considered appropriate in consumer led, low-growth and highly competitive markets. Despite the observations of Galbraith (1974) concerning producer dominance, organisations must respond to the needs and demands of external stakeholders if they are to survive.

The second assumption is that an improvement in the performance of a part of the organisation will necessarily improve the performance of the whole. There appears to be some merit in this idea at the purely mechanical level – the repair or replacement of a defective part will possibly generate some improvement. However, the approach ignores interdependence within the organisation. This means that the whole will only perform at the level of the weakest or slowest part. Similarly, the idea of 'emergent properties' is ignored – the conception that the whole may be more than the sum of the parts. The ideas of systemic thinking will be pursued explicitly in part three of this book, meantime it is sufficient to suggest that organisations often have characteristics or properties which belong only to their entirety and not to any of their individual parts, these characteristics cannot be addressed except by considering the capacity for interaction.

The third assumption is that the organisation must be studied only from the perspective of the goals of management. Later studies have shown that organisational effectiveness depends on the co-operation of many parties to the organisation. Commonly called 'stakeholders' these parties include owners, employees, customers, suppliers, and those outside the organisation who are affected by its activities and behaviour. The contemporary concept of 'good corporate citizenship' recognises the need for organisations to take account of the wishes of the community in which they exist.

The final assumption is that an organisation can be designed and understood in 'machine' terms. It can be created to perform a given task and once designed need not be adapted. Operating in a global economy which is best characterised as turbulent and dynamic and subject to rapid changes in technology and customer expectations, any organisation which cannot adapt reasonably readily cannot expect to survive.

Apart from the foregoing comments, each of these assumptions has been challenged through developments in thinking about organisations and in ideas about human well-being during the twentieth century. Practical experience of using the model in organisations has also shown that the assumptions are flawed.

4.3   REITERATION

Flood and Jackson (1991: 8–9) provide a useful summary of the 'machine' view which forms the basis of this section. They consider that it is useful in practice when the organisation operates in a stable environment, performing a straightforward task, such as repetitive production of a single product and when the 'human parts' are prepared to follow 'machine-like' commands. They consider that its usefulness is limited since it reduces the adaptability of organisations and the 'mindless contribution' is difficult to maintain with 'mindful parts', leading to dehumanisation or conflict.

The strengths of the model are:

- systematic, methodical analysis of specific tasks;
- assistance in establishing order in organisations;
- a useful guide to creating organisations where demands on individuals need to be precise or exact, for example, in the nuclear industry or multiple-outlet operations such as banks.

Its weaknesses are thought of as:

- its failure to recognise environmental interaction;
- the lack of acknowledgement of the interdependence of parts;
- no inherent capacity for adaptation;
- the model is static, not dynamic;
- people are 'dehumanised';
- goals are inherent in the design;
- the focus on control may encourage inefficiency;
- it cannot help with informal organisations such as network arrangements which are increasingly common;
- it is diagnostic but not prescriptive.

It can be seen then that whilst the machine view offers some assistance, its weaknesses are such that it must be considered an inadequate approach for managers today. The impact of this thinking on quality will be considered in section 4.7.

4.4   HUMAN RELATIONS THEORY

Whilst benefits could and can still be obtained from the rational approaches, their lack of humanity is demonstrated by the difficulties which emerge during their application with the people involved. The human relations model of organisation emerged as a means of addressing these difficulties and was the first significant challenge to the 'machine' view.

The 'organic' or 'organism' (Morgan, 1986: 39–76) analogy stems from the origins of modern systems thinking in the biological sciences and attempts to deal with attainment of survival of the system or organisation rather than achievement of particular goals. While survival may be seen as a legitimate goal it may not sufficiently represent the purpose of the organisation. This organic view first found expression in organisations through what has become known as the Human Relations Model. This considers that attention must be paid to the human aspects of organisation and gives primacy to the roles, needs and expectations of the human participants. Particular emphasis is given to issues of motivation, management style, and participation as critical success factors.

The 'Hawthorne' studies of Roethlisberger and Dickson with Elton Mayo (Mayo, 1949) may be interpreted as an early systems approach to management (Flood and Carson, 1988). Although they were originally focused on the application of scientific management principles the findings led away from this perspective. They later recognised the need to capture and understand the relatedness of all the parts involved. Further work in this field by Maslow, Herzberg etc., did not adopt the systemic perspective. These later developments still adopt a reductionist and 'closed system' view of the organisation, concentrating on improving the performance of parts, not wholes, and emphasising internal rather than external influences on the organisation.

Mayo (1949) argued that:

In modern large-scale industry the three persistent problems of management are:-
- The application of science and technical skill to some material good or product.
- The systematic ordering of operations.
- The organisation of teamwork – that is, of sustained co-operation.

Following Chester Barnard, Mayo saw that the first two of these would operate to make an industry effective, the third to make it efficient. He considered that the application of science and technical skill and the systematic ordering of operations were attended to, the first by continuous experiment, the second being already well developed in practice. He saw the third element as neglected but necessary if the organisation as a whole was to be successful.

Mayo became involved in the 'Hawthorne' studies after they had examined the effects on workers of changes in the physical environment. Experiments had shown that social and psychological factors were present and the studies became focused on these human issues. Records were kept of every aspect of changes made and their impact to establish a 'systemic' view. Further experiments were conducted and followed by formal interviews which revealed that many of the particular organisations' difficulties related to emotional rather than rational conditions. Further experiment showed that informal group pressures had more influence on output and performance than the economic pressures of the formal organisation.

The 'Hawthorne' studies are credited with having discovered the importance of groups in organisations, the influence of the observer on the observed, and the need to ensure that the goals and objectives of staff are not in conflict with those of the organisation. Notwithstanding subsequent criticisms of the research methodology and interpretation of the findings, the studies are generally seen as the foundations of the human relations approach.

Maslow (1970), whilst seeing that the 'individual is an integrated, organised whole', proposed a hierarchy of human needs. These needs were: physiological (food and health), safety (security), belongingness and love (the need to belong to a group), esteem (the need to be valued by oneself and others), and self-actualisation (the need to be all that one can be). He suggested that the needs were all contained within each other such that 'if one need is satisfied then another emerges' although the satisfied need remains present. That means that each need is ever present even when not 'prepotent'. Maslow's 'hierarchy of needs' is usually presented as in figure 4.5.

Frederick Herzberg (1959), in his studies of motivation in the industrial and commercial context, built upon the foundation laid by Maslow. Through a series of observations and interviews with samples of people at work, he found that two sets of factors influenced the level of motivation. These were the 'hygiene' and 'motivating' factors discussed in chapter 2. Briefly, 'hygiene' factors concerned the maintenance of conditions that were conducive to satisfaction. If satisfactory conditions did not pertain then the worker would be dissatisfied with his job position; conversely, achievement of a satisfactory standard would not positively motivate. Positive motivation would be derived from 'motivators', factors which were seen as actively encouraging an increased contribution. These factors were summarised in figure 2.1.

Herzberg concluded that in order for organisations to achieve improved levels of performance they must address both types of factor. He considered that 'good hygiene will prevent many of the negative results of low morale', but this on its own was not enough, suggesting: 'our emphasis should be on the strengthening of motivators'. This he saw as being achieved by: restructuring jobs; providing workers with some degree of control over their achievement; meaningful job rotation; selection of staff to match the needs of the task; effective supervision through planning, organising and support (a link with Taylor's work); and, appropriate participation.

Finally, Herzberg recognised that 'there are large segments of our society to which these prescriptions cannot possibly apply'. He considered that these people could obtain a good life from 'fruitful hobbies and improved lives outside the job', and that 'the greatest fulfilment of man is to be found in activities related to his own needs as well as those of society'.

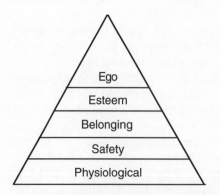

Figure 4.5 **Maslow's hierarchy of needs**

4.5   CRITICAL REVIEW

Again, several assumptions about the world and people seem to underpin the human relations approaches to organisation some of which represent a major shift in thinking from the machine view. From the organisation design perspective, the influence of the environment is still largely neglected and there is still a focus on improving the performance of parts rather than the whole.

The first major shift, and perhaps the most significant, is the assumption that people may be motivated by rewards from work other than money. This assumption is of great significance in mature economies where ever rising salaries and wages are not a realistic prospect. If motivation is to be maintained in such circumstances it is vital that managers recognise this assumption and discover what characteristics of the work and its environment are likely to stimulate staff.

The second assumption is concerned with the abilities of people. Whereas the machine view largely assumes limited ability and finite competence, the human relations view assumes much greater, albeit variable, competence and encourages a greater degree of autonomy and flexibility. It stresses delegation of decision making and enrichment of jobs in direct contrast to the simplification associated with classical theory.

4.6   REITERATION

The human relations model gives primacy to the role of the people in the organisation and suggests ways of increasing their satisfaction. However, it does nothing for the achievement of the objectives of the organisation and says little about how the complex tasks of the organisation could be structured.

Flood and Jackson (1991: 10) consider that the 'organic' view is of practical value when there is an open relationship with the environment, when survival or adaptation needs are predominant and when the environment is complex. They believe that the Human Relations view fails. First, because it does not recognise that organisations are socially constructed phenomena which, it can be argued, need to be understood from the perspective of the participants. Second, because the emphasis is on harmonious relations, whereas conflict and coercion are often present. Third because change is often environmentally driven, rather than driven by the organisation itself.

The principal strength of the 'organic' model is the emphasis that it places on the human element of organisations, recognising that people are not 'machine' parts but individuals who have needs and desires.

There are, though, a number of weaknesses in this approach that make it inadequate for the needs of contemporary managers. First, notwithstanding the warning from Herzberg, that human needs could be, and for some people, need to be met, outside the workplace, the assumption underlying many applications of the Human Relations approach is that these needs must be met at work. Second, the human relations model does not allow for the supremacy of organisational goals and objectives, its needs driven by technology, or the operating environment, over human goals and needs. Such supremacy may be necessary to ensure the survival of the organisation. Finally, the model does not assist with the specifics of designing and structuring organisations to cope with the complex tasks faced by contemporary managers nor with the interface of the organisation with its environment.

This 'organic' view, whilst offering some significant advantages over the 'machine' view still appears inadequate.

4.7   RELEVANCE TO QUALITY

The Classical and Human Relations theories of management have relevance to quality for a number of reasons. First is simply that they remain the dominant approaches to management in many cultures and contexts. They retain this dominance because they do have considerable value and appear to offer simple, fast solutions to management problems while serving to support the currently powerful groups in organisations. The second reason is that a lot of management schools and training organisations do not teach many of the more contemporary and arguably radical ideas, rejecting them in favour of the traditional approaches. It must be acknowledged that in a newly developing country where the workforce are unfamiliar with even the concept of having a job the highly disciplined and autocratic styles which fit with the traditional view or organisation may offer advantages in the short term. In more sophisticated contexts this is less likely to be the case.

A further point which needs to be recognised is the loss of skill and status associated with the introduction of modern highly productive and factory based methods of working. For example, when agricultural or craft workers left the land or traditional occupations to work in factories, their accumulated store of knowledge became redundant. The progressive deskilling of the workforce particularly associated with increased specialisation and mechanisation in factories has served to reinforce this situation. Previously a worker would have exercised a large share of his or her skill, knowledge and abilities in the completion of a task. However, the factory-style operation required none of this and for this reason much of the pride of the worker in the job was lost. This may reasonably be considered to be a primary driver of quality problems in organisations. Trist and Bamforth (1951 in Pugh, 1990: 393–416) make this point in relation to the sociological idea of 'responsible autonomy' in a three man coal getting team.

While the 'human relations' approach, which emerged in response to the problems associated with the classical school, may appear to offer the solution this is not the case. The 'HR' view gives priority to the needs of the individuals over the organisation. In this case the potential exists for the needs of the customers to be completely ignored in the pursuit of employee satisfaction. Thus it may be considered more important to go home on time, or take a tea break, than to meet a customer's expectations. Similarly, the organisation may develop products and services which exercise the skills knowledge and aspirations of its workers rather than fulfilling a customer's needs.

Clearly, both of these schools of thought offer advantages to the organisation. All too often these advantages are pursued internally (because they are internally focused) and the needs of the customer are neglected.

Part two of the book considers the work of those we call the 'Quality Gurus'. The influence of the 'classical' and 'human relations' schools of management thinking on these writers will be apparent. While all stress the importance of the customer, perhaps in response to the internally focused approaches just outlined, they place emphasis on tools and techniques which seem to sit most comfortably with the traditional approaches, and suffer from many of the same problems in the contemporary context.

SUMMARY

This chapter has, through a critical review, shown the inadequacy of the dominant classical and human relations theories used by managers to deal with the complexity of contemporary organisations. In the final section, a comment was offered on the relevance of these theories to quality.

---

key learning points

Study of managing has emerged in parallel with emergence of large organisations.

Principal dominant models of organisation
- *classical*: 'machine' model;
- *human relations*: 'organic' model.

Classical management theorists
- *Frederick Taylor*: scientific management;
- *Henri Fayol*: administrative management;
- *Max Weber*: bureaucracy theory.

Human Relations theorists
- *Elton Mayo*: the Hawthorne studies;
- *Abraham Maslow*: the hierarchy of human needs;
- *Frederick Herzberg*: two factor theory of motivation.

Each model is considered responsible for some aspects of contemporary quality problems.

QUESTION

Compare and contrast the machine view of organisations with the organic view. Suggest other metaphors which might be appropriate for these styles of management.

part
two

THE QUALITY
GURUS

Kaoru Ishikawa, Joseph M. Juran, John Oakland, Shigeo Shingo and Genichi Taguchi. Seven have been selected as having made the most significant and enduring early contributions to quality management, Oakland is incorporated as the dominant European contemporary practitioner of quality management. The work of each is explored through a five point critical framework:

- philosophy;
- assumptions;
- methods;
- successes and failures;
- critical review.

Through this approach the reader should develop a platform for understanding the strengths, weaknesses and different perspective of each writer. While each of those featured has much in common with the others, there are significant differences in their views of the quality problem. None of these views are 'right' or 'wrong' they are simply different, formed from the differing backgrounds, knowledge and experiences of the various writers. Each is based on the particular guru's view of the world and is valid from his theoretical and practical perspective. While being critical of these perspectives in our own contemporary contexts it is important to respect the contexts in which the approaches were developed.

chapter five

PHILIP B. CROSBY

Quality is free!
       Philip Crosby, 1979

INTRODUCTION

Philip Crosby is a graduate of Western Reserve University and has a professional background in quality. Following military service he went into quality control in manufacturing where he worked his way through from Line Inspector to Quality Director and Corporate Vice-President of ITT. Based on many years of practical experience, his first book became a best seller and led him to establish the consulting organisation 'Philip Crosby Associates Incorporated' and the 'Quality College' based in Florida. He is described by Bendell (1989) as 'particularly well marketed and charismatic', by the *Financial Times* (26 November 1986) as having 'the look of a sunbelt Senator rather than a man from the quality department' and by Bank (1992) as exhorting his message with 'almost religious fervour'. Clearly he is a man who acts as he speaks or 'walks the talk'. His approach has been well received, over 60,000 managers have been trained at the 'Quality College' and his quality books, particularly *Quality is Free* and *Quality without Tears* continue to sell well.

5.1 PHILOSOPHY

Crosby's philosophy is seen by many, for example Gilbert (1992), to be encapsulated in his five 'Absolutes of Quality Management' (figure 5.1). Each of these absolutes will be examined in turn to consider its meaning.

PHILIP B. CROSBY

- Quality is defined as conformance to requirements, not as 'goodness' nor 'elegance'.

- There is no such thing as a quality problem.

- It is always cheaper to do it right first time.

- The only performance measurement is the cost of quality.

- The only performance standard is zero defects.

Figure 5.1 **Five absolutes of quality management: Philip B. Crosby**

First is Crosby's definition of quality. It suggests that when he talks about a quality product or service he is referring to one which meets the requirements of the customer or user. This means in turn that those requirements must be defined, in advance, and that 'measures must be taken continually to determine conformance' (Flood, 1993: 22). The requirements may, of course, include both quantitative and qualitative aspects although, as shall be shown, Crosby's target emphasis is towards the quantitative, that is 'Zero Defects'. The first fundamental beliefs then are that quality is an essentially measurable aspect of a product or service and that quality is achieved when expectations or requirements are met.

Crosby's second absolute is that 'There is no such thing as a quality problem.' It can be suggested that his meaning here is that poor management creates the quality problems, they do not create themselves or exist as separate entities from the management process. In other words, the product, and its quality, do not exist in a vacuum, they are a result of the management process and if that is a quality process then a quality product will emerge. The second belief then is that management must lead the workers towards a quality outcome.

Third, 'It is always cheaper to do it right first time.' Logothetis (1992), suggests that, 'A company which relies on mass inspection of the final output to improve quality is doomed to stagnation.' It is possible to go further than this and suggest that a company focused on inspection will be achieving more than it deserves if it stagnates. It is more likely, in the long run, to fail altogether. Here, Crosby is making clear his belief that inspection is a cost and that quality needs to be *designed into* a product, not that flaws should be inspected out. This we take as a belief in the potential to achieve quality, that is, conformance to requirements, by developing a quality process and product from the outset with no expectation of failure. Prevention of error is considered better than rectification.

Fourth, 'the only performance measurement is the cost of quality'. Crosby clearly believes that the cost of quality is always a measurable item, for example rework, warranty costs, rejects, and that this is the only basis on which to measure performance. It is as suggested by Logothetis (1992: 85) the 'price of non conformance'. As a practical measurement of quality this might generally be considered to be useful although it cannot be seen as the only measure of business performance, rather the only measure of quality. Nonetheless, Crosby's belief in a quantitative approach is evident.

Finally, 'The only performance standard is zero defects.' The idea here is that perfection is the standard to aim for through continuous improvement, and underpinning that, zero defects is an achievable and measurable objective. Here again Crosby's fundamental belief in the quantitative approach to quality is made clear with perfection, that is, 'Zero Defects', suggested as the target.

Summarising Crosby's perspective on quality, there appear to be three essential strands:

- a belief in quantification;
- management leadership;
- prevention rather than cure.

Quality is then considered by Crosby to be an inherent characteristic of the product not an added extra. He believes, for example, that 20 per cent of manufacturing cost relates to failure, whilst for service companies this is around 35 per cent. He considers that the workers must not be blamed for error, but rather, that management should take the lead and that the workers will then follow. Crosby suggests that 85 per cent of quality problems are within the control of management.

5.2   ASSUMPTIONS

The assumptions about the world that seem to underpin Crosby's approach will now be considered.

First, it can be clearly seen that Crosby focuses attention on the management process as the key driver of quality. That is to say, that if the management process is not functioning to achieve quality then a quality product or service will not arise. If a causal chain view of the development of a product or service is adopted then it is easy to see value in this assumption. For example, with quality defined as 'conformance to requirements' then it is absolutely essential that requirements are defined and communicated amongst all stakeholders. If this first step is not taken, for example the company manufactures what it can rather than what the consumers demand, then there will be an eternal quality problem since the customer's requirements will never be conformed to. This constraint, to define conformance requirements, must be met for every aspect of the product, design, function, colour, delivery, price and so on.

The second assumption is that 'Zero Defects' is an achievable objective. The implication here is that any product can reliably be made, in relevant volumes, entirely free of defects. This raises the question of exactly what constitutes a defect. We must work in this respect from Crosby's quality definition – conformance to requirements – and say that any product which conforms to requirements is defect free. This again highlights the importance of the product specification in determining what constitutes quality.

The third assumption is that it is possible to establish a company that 'does not start out expecting mistakes', where errors are not expected or inevitable. While this is an admirable ideal, it must be considered exceedingly difficult to achieve in practice. Differing cultures, staff turnover, levels of training and skill, aptitude for the particular task are all aspects that change and develop over time. In any large manufacturing facility, for example, labour turnover at the shopfloor level is likely to run at a rate of around 8–10 per cent simply from natural causes such as ill-health and retirement. To achieve and maintain a consistency of expectation of zero defects in these circumstances may be seen as unreasonable – unless the management is sufficiently firm in its resolve to achieve quality. Operationally, and particularly where some qualitative or subjective judgement element applies to a product, managers are often faced with a choice of meeting either the customer's product volume requirement or their quality requirement.

This problem was frequently met by management at 'Tarty Bakeries' (Flood, 1993: 209–221) making hand-decorated cakes, where the Production Manager could fulfil one or the other requirement exactly. More often he would make a subjective decision that cakes rejected at inspection actually conformed to requirements! This again leads back to the basic issue of 'requirements', – what are they, how are they defined, who decides them?

Crosby is not particularly illuminating on this issue which, as can be seen, has critical impact. In the context of a physically hard and readily definable product, specifying requirements is essentially straightforward. In the context of natural products such as foods, whether processed or not, and services, certain characteristics of the product are less tangible, or even intangible, except at the point of consumption. Consequently it is very difficult to specify requirements and even more difficult to know whether these have been met. The Chesswood Produce Ltd story illustrates this point. Since you cannot have your cake and eat it, it is difficult to know if it matched the requirements unless these requirements are so loosely specified as to be almost meaningless.

CHESSWOOD PRODUCE LIMITED

Chesswood Produce Limited, a subsidiary of Rank Hovis McDougall is a long established and successful mushroom growing business. Operating from two sites in the UK it supplies mushrooms to the major supermarket chains and the wholesale market. Mushroom growing is a 24 hour per day, all year round business.

As with other production businesses the keys to success in a highly competitive market are productivity, yield and quality. To ensure that quality standards are maintained the staff at Chesswood adhere to rigorous controls in the entire process of growing, cropping and packing the mushrooms – over 400,000 lb of them per week – around 200 tons!

The eight week growing process starts with the preparation of compost which is mixed and matured to a standard 'recipe' consisting of straw, different kinds of manure, water and various trace ingredients. Once pasteurised the compost is run with spawn, placed in trays and cased with a protective layer of peat. The mushroom spawns are sourced from a single supplier and, once again, adhere to rigorous quality and performance standards. The cased trays are then moved to climate controlled growing sheds where they are monitored during the growth period. The monitoring system controls the air temperature, moisture content of the trays and air movement with the aim of maximising yield and minimising damage to the very delicate crop. To meet the demands of the supermarket customers, careful planning is required to enable sufficient quantities of mushrooms to be available on the correct day of each week – mushrooms have a very short shelf life.

Despite these efforts and the considerable skill and expertise of the mushroom growers, the crop matures at slightly different rates so that the mushrooms do not all appear at the same time or the same size, each one doubling in size every 24 hours in the final stage of growth. Some are early, being ready to pick ahead of the others, some late.

This presents a problem. The mushrooms will not grow to accurately meet the exacting specifications laid down by the supermarkets. Each quality specification fills a binder covering around eight product categories from buttons, through closed cups and open cups to flats (open field type mushrooms). The specification covers the size, shape and colour of the mushrooms as well as the packaging and labelling standards. While these latter standards can be specified and met exactly, when it comes to the mushrooms themselves Chesswood and their customers are relying on the judgement of individuals. This natural product just cannot be 'made' to a standard specification.

Chesswood is continually under pressure from its customers to improve quality – whatever that may mean in the circumstances. Eight lorry loads a day leave their site in Sussex – very few mushrooms are returned as out of specification!

5.3 METHODS

Crosby's principal method is his fourteen step programme (see figure 5.2) for quality improvement. It is essentially very straightforward and relies on a combination of both quantitative and qualitative aspects. The first two steps may be seen as addressing cultural aspects of the organisation. The first is about management commitment, this literally means the management accepting responsibility for, or an obligation to, achieving quality. Such a commitment then constrains management to consistently behave in a quality achievement oriented manner. This may proscribe or inhibit many

PHILIP B. CROSBY

Step 1 *Establish management commitment* - it is seen as vital that the whole management team participates in the programme, a half hearted effort will fail.

Step 2 *Form quality improvement teams* – the emphasis here is on multi-disciplinary team effort. An initiative from the quality department will not be successful. It is considered essential to build team working across arbitrary, and often artificial, organisational boundaries.

Step 3 *Establish quality measurements* – these must apply to every activity throughout the company. A way must be found to capture every aspect, design, manufacturing, delivery and so on. These measurements provide a platform for the next step.

Step 4 *Evaluate the cost of quality* – this evaluation must highlight, using the measures established in the previous step, where quality improvement will be profitable.

Step 5 *Raise quality awareness* – this is normally undertaken through the training of managers and supervisors, through communications such as videos and books, and by displays of posters etc.

Step 6 *Take action to correct problems* – this involves encouraging staff to identify and rectify defects, or pass them on to higher supervisory levels where they can be addressed.

Step 7 *Zero defects planning* – establish a committee, or working group to develop ways to initiate and implement a Zero Defects programme.

Step 8 *Train supervisors and managers* – this step is focused on achieving understanding by all managers and supervisors of the steps in the quality improvement programme in order that they can explain it in turn.

Step 9 *Hold a 'Zero Defects' day* to establish the attitude and expectation within the company. Crosby sees this as being achieved in a celebratory atmosphere accompanied by badges, buttons and balloons.

Step 10 *Encourage the setting of goals* for improvement. Goals are of course of no value unless they are related to appropriate timescales for their achievement.

Step 11 *Obstacle reporting* – this is encouragement to employees to advise management of the factors which prevent them achieving error free work. This might cover defective or inadequate equipment, poor quality components, etc.

Step 12 *Recognition for contributors* – Crosby considers that those who contribute to the programme should be rewarded through a formal, although non-monetary, reward scheme. Readers may be aware of the 'Gold Banana' award given by Foxboro for scientific achievement (Peters and Waterman, 1982).

Step 13 *Establish Quality Councils* – these are essentially forums composed of quality professionals and team leaders allowing them to communicate and determine action plans for further quality improvement.

Step 14 *Do it all over again* – the message here is very simple – achievement of quality is an ongoing process. However far you have got, there is always further to go!

Figure 5.2 **Fourteen step quality programme: Philip B. Crosby**

of the traditional ways in which they have managed – however effective or ineffective.

When linked to the second step – the formation of quality improvement teams – a further traditional boundary is broken. Organisations are still structured predominantly on functional lines. Crosby specifically requires multi-disciplinary teams. This means that managers and other staff must break out of their 'comfort zones' and, inevitably, relinquish some of the 'expert' and 'position' power (Handy, 1985: 124–126) that goes with the functional organisation. A whole hearted embrace by management of these two steps alone may be considered a major achievement!

The third and fourth steps are quantitative and directly linked again – the fourth is simply not possible without the third. Measurement is a necessary precursor to evaluation.

These steps in turn provide a platform for the fifth step – raising quality awareness, a more qualitative issue. To make the quality training relevant for supervisors and managers it needs to be set firmly in the context of the quality status of the firm as evidenced by the measurements. This step also may be seen to act as re-affirmation of the first two steps – gaining commitment and the multi-functional approach. Through measurement and evaluation the interrelatedness of quality issues across internal boundaries can be highlighted.

Step 6 is to take action, unless they result in corrective action the other steps are worthless. This step is where the management and staff really must 'walk the talk'. It has both qualitative and quantitative aspects. If the numbers generated through the measurement system are simply used as clubs to beat over the heads of the staff they are unlikely to prove very helpful. The numbers must be used to provide guidance and support to the action taken and the actions taken must be in harmony with the words spoken!

Once step 6 has commenced, the organisation can be seen to have established a sound platform for quality improvement – staff and management are committed and action is being taken. It could be argued at this stage that provided the momentum of improvement is maintained quality will continuously improve. Crosby's process however sees this as insufficient; with the process firmly established he proposes an increased effort and impetus towards 'Zero Defects'. This is the thrust of step 7 – Zero Defects Planning – which strives to establish a ZD programme, an essentially quantitative target but achieved through both soft and hard approaches. Step 8 involves training of supervisors and managers so that they can pass on the programme to their subordinates.

Step 9, Zero Defects day, may be seen as both a celebration of achievements to date and a new beginning to the quality improvement programme. This now takes Zero Defects as a very precise and quantifiable objective. Step 10 is a natural consequence of step 9 and requires commitment to achieving goals for improvement tied to defined and relatively short term timescales. Again it is quantitative in nature, the results being directly measurable.

Step 11 – obstacle reporting – is a communication device which recognises that failure to achieve quality in one area may be related to failure in another, or to local factors which inhibit quality achievement. This process enables those facing problems to report them, and importantly, it places obligations on management to address those issues. Time frames for response and action are built into this step which requires both a change in culture – the acceptance by management of criticism from the workers – and a change in the nature of managers' roles. Particularly for problems which cross functional boundaries, it will no longer be enough for managers to concentrate on their own direct areas of responsibility, they will have to work with managers of other areas to achieve the objectives set.

Step 12 requires acknowledgement of the contribution of staff to the process – a direct reward for the efforts made. Crosby is very specific that these rewards should be formal but non-monetary. This step is largely cultural in its impact. Recognising and rewarding the contributors to the programme is a device for reinforcing amongst the whole staff a particular kind of behaviour, further embedding the quality culture.

The establishment of Quality Councils at step 13 is seen as 'institutionalising' the quality programme – making it a part of the embedded culture. It becomes at this stage an integral part of the way in which the company is managed and controlled. Mainly qualitative in nature, it will affect many aspects of the way in which the staff of the company behave in the future.

The final step – 'Do it all over again' – should be seen as a reminder that quality improvement never stops. Any programme such as this will, over time, lose impetus and thrust simply because the original, perhaps revolutionary, leaders will achieve the objectives which they set themselves. They may find it difficult to maintain the initial enthusiasm and drive. In order to maintain and develop the programme it will be necessary to pump new energy into it by the appointment of fresh people and the establishment of new objectives.

Crosby's 'Quality Vaccine' (Logothetis, 1992: 82–83) is an essential part of his process. It is based on three principal ingredients:

- integrity;
- dedication to communication and customer satisfaction;
- company wide policies and operations which support the quality thrust.

Logothetis (1992) proposes a triangle (figure 5.3) of interaction between these three ingredients which must be supported by Crosby's belief in how the vaccine is administered. This again has three strands:

- *determination* – awareness that management must lead;
- *education* – for management and staff;
- *implementation* – creating an organisational environment where achievement of quality is regarded as the norm, not the exception.

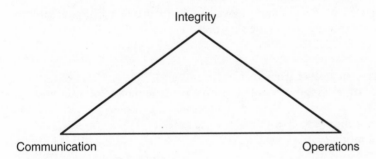

Integrity

Communication   Operations

Figure 5.3 **Triangle of interactions**

This chapter is not intended to provide an exhaustive account of methods, tools and techniques, that is for part four. Aspects of Crosby's approach will be returned to in more detail, dealing with 'How' rather than 'What' in the appropriate chapters. This section has however provided an introduction to the principal strands of Crosby's method which can be seen as based largely in quantitative outcomes and to rely heavily on an evangelical attitude, amongst both the management and the staff.

5.4   SUCCESSES AND FAILURES

Quality Gurus, like doctors, are prone to advertising their successes and burying their failures. Companies act similarly: a successful quality programme will be advertised in order to attract customers – a failure will be swept under the carpet, with executives pretending that it never happened. It thus becomes impossible to find reported empirical evidence of failure.

Success on the other hand is shared. The guru proclaims the success of his method, while the company proclaim the success of their strategy and acknowledge the contribution made by their interpretation of the particular guru's approach. Chrysler's Lee Iacocca for example, cited by Bank (1992: 75), says:

> we established our own Chrysler Quality Institute in Michigan, modelled after his [Crosby's] operation – our company's put about twenty thousand of our people through it . . . and I admit they do return with QUALITY stamped on their foreheads.

It can be explicitly seen here that Crosby's contribution has been acknowledged but that Chrysler have used this work as a model. What we cannot see is how closely the model follows the original!

With his consulting company, Quality College and overseas operations firmly established Crosby must be acknowledged as having been successful. It is also the case that sufficient client organisations must have found the approach useful to have sustained the development and growth of that organisation over a lengthy period of time. It must be concluded that there is some real value to be found in his approach.

Flood (1993: 27–28) acknowledges this in identifying five strengths to Crosby's work. Summarising, he sees these as:

- clarity;
- recognition of worker participation;
- rejection of a tangible quality problem, acceptance of the idea of solutions;
- Crosby's metaphors – 'vaccine' and 'maturity';
- Crosby's motivational style.

Flood also criticises perceived weaknesses. He sees:

- danger of misdirected effort from 'blaming' workers;
- emphasis on marketing more than recognition of barriers;
- the management and goal orientation of the fourteen step programme as failing to 'free workers from externally generated goals'.
- potential for 'Zero Defects' to be interpreted as zero risk;
- Ineffectiveness in coercive power structures.

Looking at the strengths, it could be argued that clarity and simplicity of approach are not necessarily beneficial in dealing with increasingly complex problems. It is perhaps rather that the potential richness of any problem solving tool must be adequate for the situation being addressed. The issue of appropriateness must be considered when selecting an approach.

The value of worker participation cannot be denied. First, since the workers may be the only people who can recognise the roots of a particular problem. Second, because their involvement implies easier acceptance of ownership of the programme and the solutions.

The conception that all quality issues can be resolved is very useful in provoking ideal goal seeking behaviour amongst the participants in the situation. Bank (1992: 23) compares this to the ice-skaters Torville and Dean aiming for perfect scores even though they may not be attainable. He cites Thomas J. Watson, founder of IBM, as saying 'It's better to aim at perfection and miss than it is to aim at imperfection and hit it.' Acceptance that certain problems cannot be solved could be seen as reinforcing behaviour and attitudes which ensure that they never will be.

Creativity and leadership must be seen as essential strands in quality improvement. However, while some writers see great strength in Crosby's approach to this there is also, perhaps, inherent danger. The 'charismatic' or 'evangelical' style adopted by Crosby has also been criticised by Juran. Crosby, cited by Bank (1992: 76) says 'Dr. Juran seems to think I am a charlatan and hasn't missed many opportunities to say that over the years.' The founding charge here seems really to be one of a lack of substantial underpinning to Crosby's approach, perhaps reflecting other comments about promotion 'through slogans and too often full of platitudes'.

There can be no doubt that many of the most sustained management theories and approaches through the years have been well marketed, yet when examined by others have been demonstrated to have either theoretical or methodological weaknesses. This is almost inevitably true. Theories validated within one paradigm can probably always be disputed from within another. Similarly, it is often said that there is no such thing as bad publicity, and to quote Oscar Wilde in *The Picture of Dorian Gray*, 'There is only one thing in the world worse than being talked about, and that is not being talked about.'

That Crosby is an effective self-publicist cannot be denied, however, this does not necessarily detract from the value of what is being said. Perhaps the comments of another great self-publicist, Winston Churchill, Britain's World War Two Prime Minister, should be noted. Churchill is known to have annotated his speeches with what might be seen as 'stage directions'. One of his most well known is the reported admonition in the margin of a speech, 'Weak point – SHOUT!'

Regarding the weaknesses, it is arguable whether the interpretation of Crosby as blaming the workers is reasonable. Bendell (1989) for example, states that Crosby 'does not believe that workers should take prime responsibility for poor quality; the reality, he says, is that you have to get management straight first'. Bendell further suggests that in the Crosby approach, 'management sets the tone on quality and workers follow . . . the initiative comes from the top'. Thus it could be argued that rather than creating a 'blame the workers' culture, the Crosby approach is a form of empowerment, led by the management.

The issue of platitudes and lack of substance has already been largely addressed and goal orientation comes into focus. It is clear that Crosby only considers one goal for the organisation and that is 'Zero Defects'. Flood's criticism here is much better founded. The external setting of goals by the management is far from empowering or emancipatory and neglects to address workers' perception of their own values and needs. It must be recognised however that the requirement for quality is being driven from the environment of the organisation. If survival of the firm is to be achieved then quality products are an essential feature.

Misinterpretation of 'Zero Defects' as meaning the avoidance of risk is another reasonable point. There will always be an element of risk involved in a change of behaviour or process. To overcome the danger of risk aversion, management must develop a cultural environment where risks can be calculated and minimised and where learning from mistakes is encouraged, perhaps incorporating ideas of the Learning Organisation (Senge, 1990: see chapter 19 of this book).

Flood's strongest criticism is of the assumption that people will work in an open and conciliatory manner. He makes it clear that in a political or coercive context this will not apply. Many management writers agree that an element of politics and coercion is present in most organisations, whether or not this is explicit. There will always be a dominant group or sub-group and it is suggested that the fully open and conciliatory atmosphere is an ideal rather than an easily achievable objective.

5.5   CRITICAL REVIEW

Overall, the foundation of Crosby's approach can be seen in two elements. First, his extensive professional background in quality will have provided the quantitative bias to his method and, second, his reportedly charismatic personality will have provided the qualitative aspects.

The general value of measurement in establishing standards and objectives for quality is readily recognisable while the principles are transferable between organisations and people. The value of the qualitative issues are much harder to evaluate and transfer. The majority of managers would not perhaps consider themselves to be 'charismatic' leaders, an epithet more readily used in respect of others than it is ourselves. A wholehearted commitment to quality achievement throughout the organisation is undoubtedly required; what is questionable is whether the exhortative, inspirational slogans and platitudes will work in all circumstances and for all managers.

It has to be concluded for Crosby that the process, and quantitative aspects of his programme – a word which in itself implies a discrete activity rather than an ongoing management approach – may be readily transferable. However, the management style adopted will have to reflect the needs, values and personalities of those involved in the programme.

Similar comments can be applied to other aspects of the approach. For example, while encouraging reward Crosby suggests that these should not be monetary. It is perhaps the case that the reward, to be truly meaningful to the recipient, should reflect his or her needs and aspirations. For an individual whose focus is professional achievement then public recognition of his or her contribution may be all the reward that is required. For an individual on low wages, perhaps seeking to reduce personal indebtedness or, in an extreme case to pay for life preserving medical treatment, a monetary reward may be precisely right.

Reflection is also necessary on the suitability of the approach for different industries. With his manufacturing background Crosby has developed an approach which reflects that – it is essentially possible, in the manufacturing environment to know when a defect free product is achieved. This is far more difficult in the service sector where definitions of the product are harder to generate and delivery is almost impossible to control.

Certain aspects of service are relatively straightforward to quantify, for example how many times the telephone rings before it is answered, or precisely what words of greeting are used. Other aspects are less susceptible to measurement and control, for example tone of voice. The nature of many of these transactions is that the service is provided and consumed instantly. While they can, to some extent, be designed and planned, their production is uncontrollable. They also depend on factors which are perhaps outside the ability of the organisation to effectively influence. These factors include the expectations of the customer, his or her mood, the sort of day they have already experienced and the level of service they have received before. These factors cannot be known until after service has commenced.

Therefore Crosby's approach has to be marked with some cautions about its general applicability across a range of industries and cultures. What works very well for Philip Crosby at ITT, or for Lee Iacocca at Chrysler, may not work in a bank in Hong Kong, or on a North Sea Oil production platform.

SUMMARY

This chapter has presented the work of Philip Crosby through a five point critical framework. It has described his philosophy and its underpinning assumptions, outlined his principal methods, examined the successes and failures of the approach and summarised this in a brief critical review. Readers may refer to Crosby's own works, particularly *Quality is Free* (1979), to enhance and develop their own knowledge and understanding.

---

key learning points

PHILIP B. CROSBY

Definition of quality
conformance to requirements

Five absolutes of quality management
- quality as conformance;
- no such thing as a quality problem;

- always cheaper first time;
- only measurement of performance is the cost of quality;
- zero defects

Three key beliefs
quantification; management leadership; prevention

Principal methods
Fourteen step quality programme; the 'Quality Vaccine'

QUESTION

Discuss Crosby's assertion that 'There is no such thing as a quality problem.'

chapter
six

W. EDWARDS
DEMING

A prophet is not without honour, save in his own country.
Matthew, 13: 57

INTRODUCTION

W. Edwards Deming, who died in 1994, is considered by many to be the
founding father of the quality movement. He is perhaps the most widely
known of the gurus both within, and outside, the quality field. Deming held
a doctorate in Physics from Yale and was a keen statistician, working in the
US Government for many years in the Department of Agriculture and
the Bureau of Census. According to Bendell (1989: 4) Deming rose to
prominence in Japan where he was closely involved in the post-war
development of quality for which Bendell suggests 'he is considered largely
responsible'. Heller (1989) sees Deming as having a 'passionate belief in
man's ability to improve on the poor and the mediocre, and even on the
good', a belief which shall be seen is evident in both his theory and his
practice. Logothetis (1992: xii) sees Deming as advocating 'widespread use
of statistical ideas, with management taking a strong initiative in building
quality in'. Bank (1992: 62), cites Hutchins' belief that a major contribution
made by Deming to the Japanese quality movement was in helping them to:
'cut through the academic theory, to present the ideas in a simple way which
could be meaningful right down to production worker levels'.

Summarising, Deming's approach can be seen as founded in scientific method (his physics and statistics background) whilst he was also a very capable communicator. Although, as Bendell (1989: 5) suggests, it is 'difficult to delimit his [Deming's] concepts' due to the constant refinement and improvement of his ideas, his successful and widely read book *Out of the Crisis* (1986) presents his approach to both management and quality in its most succinct, coherent form.

6.1 PHILOSOPHY

Deming's initial approach, largely rejected by American industry at the outset, was based on his background in statistical methods. His quantitative method provided a 'systematic, rigorous approach to quality' (Bendell, 1989: 4). Drawing on the work of the statistician Walter Shewhart – his tutor – Deming urged a management focus on causes of variability in manufacturing processes.

Deming's first belief can be seen here, that there are 'common' and 'special' causes of quality problems. 'Special' causes are seen as those relating to particular operators or machines and requiring attention to the individual cause. 'Common' causes are those which arise from the operation of the system itself and are a management responsibility.

Deming believed in the use of Statistical Process Control (SPC) charts as the key method for identifying special and common causes and assisting diagnosis of quality problems. His aim was to remove 'outliers', that is, quality problems relating to the special causes of failure. This was achieved through training, improved machinery and equipment and so on. SPC enabled the production process to be brought 'under control'. Remaining quality problems were considered to be related to common causes, that is, they were inherent in the design of the production process. Eradication of special causes enabled a shift in focus to common causes to further improve quality.

Deming's second belief is apparent here, that of a quantitative approach to identifying problems. It is suggested by Bendell (1989: 4) that this statistically based approach brought its own problems. He reports lack of technical standards and limitations of data, and perhaps more importantly 'human difficulties in the form of employee resistance and management lack of understanding as to their roles in quality improvement', particularly in the American applications. Bendell considers that perhaps 'too much emphasis was being given towards the statistical aspects'. It can be suggested that Deming's approach reflects to a significant degree the 'machine' view of organisations outlined in chapter 4.

Notwithstanding these problems Deming became a national hero in Japan and his methods were widely taken up. In 1951 the 'Deming Prize' for contributions to quality and dependability was launched, and in 1960 he was awarded the 'Second Order of the Sacred Treasure', Japan's premier Imperial honour.

A third strand to Deming's work was the formulation of his systematic approach to problem solving. This has become known as the Deming, Shewhart or PDCA cycle – Plan, Do, Check, Action, illustrated in figure 6.1. This cycle is iterative, once it has been systematically completed it recommences without ceasing. This is in agreement with Crosby's admonition, already considered, to 'Do it all over again.' The approach is seen as re-emphasising the responsibility of management to be actively involved in the organisation's quality programme, while Logothetis (1992: 55) considers that it provides the basis for a 'self-sustaining quality programme'.

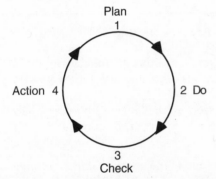

Figure 6.1 **The Plan-Do-Check-Action cycle**

Two further beliefs can be derived here. The first, is in a systematic, methodical approach contrasting sharply with the ad hoc and random behaviour of many quality initiatives. The second is in the need for continuous quality improvement action. This contrasts sharply with the overtones in Crosby's approach which suggest a discrete set of activities.

Deming's later work focused on Western, and particularly American management. Here Deming (1986: 97–148) elaborated seven fundamental beliefs (the 'Seven Deadly Sins' – figure 6.2) about bad management practices which he considered must be eliminated before western styles of management could be transformed to support the implementation of a successful quality initiative.

Sin 1, 'lack of constancy' is seen by Logothetis (1992: 46) as urging 'an absolute and constant commitment on the part of senior management to quality, productivity and innovation'. Inherent in this is a continuing drive towards better quality and reliability of product in order to drive down costs, protect investment and employment, create and enlarge markets and hence generate more jobs. It is seen as providing a positive and achieve-ment oriented focus for the organisation. Deming (1986: 98) criticises management, particularly in American industry, for being 'run on the quarterly dividend'. It is certainly true that even today many organisations throughout the world are managed according to the '*flavour of the month*'

W. EDWARDS DEMING

Sin 1   Lack of constancy;

Sin 2   Short term profit focus;

Sin 3   Performance appraisals;

Sin 4   Job-hopping;

Sin 5   Use of visible figures only;

Sin 6   Excessive medical costs;

Sin 7   Excessive costs of liability.

Figure 6.2 **The Seven Deadly Sins: W. Edwards Deming**

with senior managers flitting from miracle solution to miracle solution, while more junior managers keep their heads down and wait for the passion to pass.

Sin 2, 'short term profit focus', is seen as challenging and potentially defeating the 'constancy of purpose' previously urged. Deming (1986: 99) suggests that:

> Anyone can boost the dividend at the end of the quarter. Ship everything on hand, regardless of quality: mark it shipped, and show it all as accounts receivable. Defer till next quarter, so far as possible, orders for material and equipment. Cut down on research, education, training.

Here, Deming is making clear his belief in a management approach with a long term orientation. Deming gives explicit recognition to the need to satisfy shareholder expectations, but points out that these expectations often go beyond immediate return on capital to consider the future.

Much criticism has been levied in recent years at what is now known as 'short-termism' in the City of London, on Wall Street, in Exchange Square or Raffles Place. The underlying reasons and causes are not the subject of this book but readers may wish to consider issues such as the increasing ownership of shares by financial institutions and the difficulties of making money by making products in a harsh business environment. Pension and investment companies are frequently the largest stockholders in public companies; it is worth thinking about their requirements and the reward packages of their employees which are often tied to short term performance measures.

Sin 3, performance appraisal, is considered by Deming (1986: 102) to 'nourish short-term performance' . . . and . . . 'leave people bitter, crushed, bruised, battered, desolate, despondent, dejected, feeling inferior', a somewhat damning indictment. Logothetis (1992: 47) sees appraisal as encouraging 'rivalry and isolation' and demolishing teamwork, again leading back to a focus on individual and short term results, noting that 'people who attempt to change the system (for the better) have no chance of recognition'.

While acknowledging Deming's belief in the potential damage that a poor appraisal system can cause, this is rather more a function of a badly designed system than a necessary outcome of performance review. As with the quality of a manufactured product, the quality and impact of an appraisal system will depend upon the quality of its design. Most of us need and enjoy recognition of our achievements and can benefit from the guidance delivered through a constructive and effective appraisal system. This perhaps partly reflects the esteem element in Maslow's hierarchy of needs.

Job-hopping, regular movement of management between jobs either within or between organisations, is the fourth sin. Originally seen as a particular attribute of Western management, this is increasingly common in Far East locations such as Singapore and Hong Kong. Job-hopping is considered to lead to instability and further reinforce the short term orientation of the organisation. Logothetis (1992: 39) suggests that it again destroys teamwork and commitment and ensures that many decisions are taken in whole or partial ignorance of the circumstances surrounding them. The belief this time is in the need for commitment of management to the long term future of the organisation.

Sin 5 is 'the use of visible figures only'. Here Deming criticises failure to recognise and evaluate the intangible aspects of the organisation, for example, the additional sales generated through satisfied customers, the benefits to productivity and quality derived from people feeling part of a success story and the negative impact of performance appraisal or barriers to achieving quality. Deming (1986: 123) considers that managers who believe that everything can be measured are deluding themselves and suggests that they should know before they start that they will be able to quantify only 'a trivial part of the gain'. This should be seen as a belief in intangible, invisible benefits arising from good management practice. It does however conflict with his espousal of statistical methods since the reliable measurement of intangibles is notoriously difficult. Lessons could perhaps be drawn here from organisational psychology which can help to measure some of the aspects that Deming considered intangible.

The sixth and seventh sins while revealed by Deming, are given little attention by other writers on his work. His points are simply made. The sixth sin, medical costs, both in direct lost labour costs and indirect in the sense of medical insurance premiums, are met largely by the employer. Thus they are an additional cost to be recovered in the price of the product. Deming (1986: 98) refers to William Hoglund of the Pontiac Motor Division informing him that the direct cost of medical care to the company exceeded the amount spent on steel for every vehicle produced!

The cost of insurance is driven by claims experience and actuarial expectation and it is arguable whether Deming is making a fair point. Medical costs are currently covered in every developed nation. If they are not supported by private insurance schemes such as prevail in the USA,

France, Singapore and many other nations, they may be met by a national scheme such as the NHS in the UK. Either way, the company may be considered to bear the cost, through direct contribution, or by increased basic wages which enable the employees to meet the cost themselves. For example, in the UK, employees receiving an appropriate level of income pay between 7 per cent and 9 per cent of their wages into a National Insurance scheme intended to cover costs of primary health care and provision of a state pension. In addition, employers pay a contribution of around 10 per cent of total salary costs into the same scheme on behalf of the employees. It is doubtful whether there is any real difference in the cost related to this between employers in the USA or the UK.

The seventh and final sin is one that is now considered to be gaining further ground, that is 'liability costs'. There is evidence throughout the developed world of an increasingly litigious public perhaps encouraged by lawyers working on a 'no win, no fee' basis. While many potential liability issues are insurable many others are not. The costs of these must be borne by the organisation. Whether management and manufacturers can reasonably be blamed for this issue is certainly arguable and it is questionable whether it is within their power to effectively control. It is suspected that it relates to broader societary changes such as an increasing trend towards individual rather than collective values and the hunt, whenever things go wrong, for the often elusive 'someone to blame'.

Summarising Deming's philosophy we can identify a number of clear strands. There are evident beliefs in:

- quantitative, statistically valid, control systems;
- clear definition of those aspects under the direct control of staff, i.e. the 'special causes' and those which are the responsibility of management, 'the common causes'. Deming suggests that these are as high as 94 per cent!;
- a systematic, methodical approach;
- continuous improvement;
- constancy and determination, which taken together cover the first five of his 'Deadly Sins' the other two being highly arguable.

Along with Crosby, Deming (1986: ix) considers that quality should be designed in to both the product and the process. He believes that 'transformation of the style of American [*sic*] management' is necessary requiring a 'whole new structure, from foundation upward'.

6.2   ASSUMPTIONS

The assumptions about the world that Deming seems to make in order to underpin his approach will now be explored.

First, it can be seen that while initially focusing attention on existing processes to derive immediate improvement – the eradication of 'special causes' of failure – it is rapidly refocused to the management process and attitudes. Deming seems to believe that these must be, in his own words, 'transformed', in order for sustained improvement to be achieved. The management are seen to be responsible and, significantly, to be capable of undertaking the proposed transformation. He does not suggest, in organisation design terms, how this should be achieved.

Second, is the assumption that statistical methods, properly used, will provide quantitative evidence to support changes. At the same time he recognises that some aspects cannot be easily measured and suggests that managements frequently fail to take seriously those aspects which they consider unmeasurable.

The third key assumption is that continuous improvement is both possible and desirable. Taking his definition of quality as 'meeting the needs of the customer, both present and future' (1986: 5), this has to be questioned. If the needs of the customer are met where is the benefit in further improvement?

A further aspect to this is perhaps more significant in the 1990s. The assumption is that continuous improvement supported by a long term orientation will enable the organisation to meet customers' 'future needs'. If, however, the contemporary world is characterised as Handy (1990a) suggests by 'discontinuous change' then a long term view and continuous improvement may no longer be enough. Perhaps organisations must be built which can anticipate and prepare for sudden, maybe catastrophic, change. The Compaq example in chapter 3 illustrates the point – continuous improvement and incremental change may not be sound recipes in a discontinuous world.

Deming's final assumption, as with Crosby, is about the service sector. Simply, he sees that the prime role of the service sector, in the context of a national economy, rests in enabling manufacturing to do its job. He suggests (1986: 188), for example, that:

> A better plan for freight carriers would be to improve service and thus to decrease costs. These cost savings, passed on to manufacturers and to other service industries, would help American industry to improve the market for American products, and would in time bring new business to carriers of freight.

While offering specific advice in the same text about quality improvement in the service sector, Deming, unlike Crosby, does explicitly recognise the difficulty of measuring certain aspects of it. He seems also to assume an initially altruistic effort which contrasts sharply with his accusations of short termism. To some extent he is possibly correct, cost savings should be passed back down the chain and in a systemically developed solution this could occur. Such a move though is probably a function of a competitive and open market rather than an altruistic gesture.

The implications of his assumption about the role of services should also be considered. As suggested in chapter 1 (manufacturing activity drives the service sector) it can be observed that few local communities thrive when their manufacturing base is lost, for example, the shipbuilding and coal-mining communities in the UK suffer major economic difficulties, social fragmentation and mass unemployment. Notably, many service sector jobs and organisations can now be clearly seen to have depended upon local manufacturers through the direct purchase of services by the major organisations and the expenditure of wages by the employees. The wealth generated by the employer was in large part expended in the same community. As the manufacturing sector has declined, so too has the service sector.

Those sectors where services have continued to thrive are in areas of specialist technical expertise such as banking, insurance, finance and other knowledge based industries. These industries have a less dependent relationship on the manufacturing sector than say, retailing and real estate. Notwithstanding these particular aspects, there is perhaps a warning at a national and multi-national level. If individual communities cannot be adequately sustained when manufacturing is lost to them, then is there any future for nations if the manufacturing base as a whole is lost?

6.3   METHODS

Deming has four principal methods:

- the PDCA cycle;
- statistical process control;
- the 14 principles for transformation;
- the 7 point action plan.

The first of these has been introduced and will not be dealt with further here. The second, Statistical Process Control, will be introduced but is fully elaborated in chapter 22. The fourteen principles for transformation and seven point action plan will provide the major content of this section.

Statistical Process Control is a quantitative approach based on measurement of process performance. Essentially, a process is considered to be under control, that is, stable, when its random variations fall within determined upper and lower limits. That is seen by Deming as the process having achieved a position where the special causes of failure have been eradicated.

A control chart, a sample of which is provided at figure 6.2, is used to record the value of a measurement associated with an event in a process. Statistical analysis of the values recorded will reveal the mean value. Normal variation from this mean value for the particular process in its established state is conventionally taken as any value within $\pm$ 3 standard deviations of the mean. Events which fall outside that normal variation are considered as 'special' and should prove tractable to individual diagnosis and treatment. Events falling within the norms are considered to have 'common' causes, that is, they are a product of the organisation of the system and require treatment at the system level. Here we can refer directly to Deming (1986: 315) and re-emphasise the role of management in the development of quality:

I should estimate that in my experience most troubles and most possibilities for improvement add up to proportions something like this:

> 94% belong to the system (responsibility of management)
> 6% special.

A sample control chart is provided in figure 6.3.

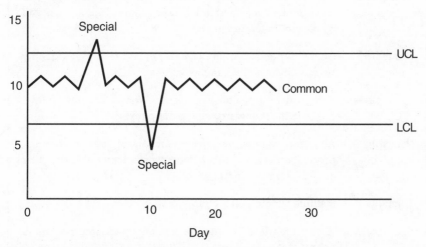

Figure 6.3 **Sample control chart**

It has to be acknowledged here that Deming's split of special and common causes, and consequently his allocation of responsibility for error relates directly to the product of SPC. At ± 3 standard deviations in a stable system it is inevitable that 95 per cent of errors will belong to the system – 95 per cent is only 2 standard deviations in a normal distribution. Three standard deviations (99.7 per cent approximately of results) are recognised through SPC as representing stability – the system is under control. The standard (± 3 sigma) was originally devised by Shewhart to minimise net economic loss from rectifying mistakes, the objective of Taguchi's 'quadratic loss function' to be elaborated in chapter 12.

We can now turn to the first main focus of this section, Deming's fourteen principles for transformation (see figure 6.4). These, like Crosby's fourteen steps are essentially straightforward and rely on a combination of statistical and human, or cultural, aspects. The principles will be reviewed in turn.

The first three principles, creating constancy of purpose, adoption of a new philosophy and ceasing dependence on mass inspection may all be seen as focused on the cultural aspects of the organisation. The first principle is aimed at creating a 'team' type of environment where all are working together towards a common goal. It requires the management to commit themselves to achieving ever improving quality as a primary objective of the organisation. The story of the regeneration of Kennet School illustrates this point.

W. EDWARDS DEMING

Principle 1 Create constancy of purpose to improve product and service.

Principle 2 Adopt a new philosophy for the new economic age with management learning what their responsibilities are and by assuming leadership for change.

Principle 3 Cease dependence on mass inspection to achieve quality by building quality into the product.

Principle 4 End awarding business on price. Award business on total cost and move towards single suppliers.

Principle 5 Aim for continuous improvement of the system of production and service to improve productivity and quality and to decrease costs.

Principle 6 Institute training on the job.

Principle 7 Institute leadership with the aim of supervising people to help them to do a better job.

Principle 8 Drive out fear so that everyone can work effectively together for the organisation.

Principle 9 Break down barriers between departments. Encourage research, design, sales and production to work together to foresee difficulties in production and use.

Principle 10 Eliminate slogans, exhortations and numerical targets for the workforce since they are divisory and anyway difficulties belong to the whole system.

Principle 11 Eliminate quotas or work standards and management by objectives or numerical goals: leadership should be substituted instead.

Principle 12 Remove barriers that rob people of their right to pride in their work.

Principle 13 Institute a vigorous education and self-improvement programme.

Principle 14 Put everyone in the company to work to accomplish the transformation.

Figure 6.4 **Fourteen principles for transformation: W. Edwards Deming**

KENNET SCHOOL: A TALE OF CONSTANCY AND DETERMINATION

Until January 1989, Kennet School presented a disappointing picture. The lack of coherence and consistency in support to the teachers constrained them from exploiting their talents and abilities. While some pupils performed exceptionally well, certain parents perceived the school as a 'glorified youth club' – somewhere to send the children to keep them occupied while they were out at work. Limited leadership was in evidence – there was little communication between members of staff, parental complaints were ignored and the buildings were neglected. The school was suffering a falling pupil roll threatening the sixth form of only 90 pupils with closure. In measured performance terms only 28 per cent of pupils obtained 5 or more passes at grades A–C in the General Certificate of Secondary Education (GCSE) examinations – a dismal record.

In 1997, despite the provision of extra buildings, the school is nearing capacity in pupil numbers – 43 per cent growth in five years – and the sixth form is thriving. The 1997 examination results show 60 per cent of pupils obtaining 5 or more GCSE passes at grades A–C (against a 1996 national average rate of 44 per cent) and a pass rate of 93 per cent at A level (against a national average rate of 87 per cent) with 50 per cent achieving grades A–C. The standards attained by the school led to it being listed in early 1997 as outstanding in examination results and inspection. Kennet School is one of only 63 secondary schools in England and Wales recognised in this way, and the only school in the Royal County of Berkshire.

The achievement of this turnaround has been through 'constancy and determination' rather than the use of a 'miracle cure', or the adoption of any particular gurus' methodology. The new headmaster appointed in 1989 adopted a 'classical' approach to management in the early days. He imposed discipline both on the children and the staff, letting 'nothing go by that [he] didn't like'. Development and imposition of rules and standards for staff and children was immediate. These covered issues such as movement, behaviour, uniform and homework and were supported by action on his part – the smooth functioning of the school now rests on these rules which received high visibility at the outset. A staff handbook is in use which sets out the aims of the school and is supported by clarity of responsibility with everyone now knowing 'who is responsible for what'.

The priority of the school is academic excellence. Sporting success (a regular achievement) and pastoral issues are regarded as important in supporting the academic objectives, the means to achieve educational ends, rather than ends in themselves. The creation of an 'inner cabinet', chaired by the headmaster emphasises this priority. The cabinet consists of the heads of the eleven academic faculties within the school together with one head of house. This unbalanced representation confirms in action the words of the headmaster – 'walking the talk'!

The headmaster recognised that some 'early wins' were required to ensure that his different way of running the school would be perceived as correct. Ten members of staff left in the first three years, some voluntarily, some less so. Two children were expelled. There was necessarily some conflict during those early days and while there was much discussion with the people affected, the head held, and still holds an absolute veto on all matters – although he exercises extreme caution in using it. He recognises the need to achieve a balance between making things happen and doing everything himself – a possible outcome of an autocratic approach.

With a system of rules in place and acceptance by the staff of the new way of working much of the decision making power has been passed to the heads of departments (notwithstanding the headmaster's veto). Their decisions (as well as those referred to the headmaster) rest on one simple question – 'What is the benefit in the classroom?' If there is no benefit then the proposal will fail. The criterion for the introduction of new ideas or approaches is simply educational benefit.

Creation of a three year rolling development plan for the school is undertaken by the heads of departments and their staff and subjected to a 'round robin' process of modification and refinement. Every member of staff receives a copy of the completed plan. The final column of the plan shows who is responsible for which aspects – making accountability open and public. The senior staff undertake a review and re-focusing of the plan at termly intervals.

The school, now managed in a much more decentralised manner with trust given to staff and pupils wherever possible, still adheres to three global targets:

- continuous improvement in academic standards;
- staff development;
- improved behavioural standards and sustained improvement in the environment of the school.

In the words of the headmaster: 'There is so much more to do.'

The second principle, that of embracing management learning and a leadership based style of management, concerns acceptance by the management that the responsibility for developing and achieving the changes is theirs. It requires explicit recognition by management that the workers are not necessarily to blame for quality deficiencies. This may well require a dramatic change in both words and actions on the part of management, particularly if they have been accustomed, as so many are, to pushing the blame down through the hierarchy!

The third principle, ceasing dependence on mass inspection by building quality into the product, requires a further dramatic change in management approach and has major implications for issues such as organisation structure and information management. A simple abandonment of mass inspection not supported by changes in other aspects will potentially be disastrous. A successful example of such a change is the introduction in recent years of multi-disciplinary product development teams in organisations such as John Deere Tractors. These teams include both design and production engineers so that products are now designed with production requirements in mind rather than having to be re-engineered for production. This speeds up the development of new products, reduces manufacturing complexity and leads to improved quality. Other major manufacturing companies are following the same route.

The fourth principle, the ending of awarding business on price rather than total cost, is a recognition that the invoiced unit price of a sub-assembly or part is only a fraction of its total potential cost (or value) to the organisation. For example, a part which has the lowest unit cost may carry with it a high level of rejects. This leads to either high inspection costs to identify poor quality parts or to a poor quality of finished product leading in turn to high inspection and rework costs and potential for product failure in the hands of the customer.

A number of aspects need to be considered in the identification of the total cost of a purchased item. These may include unit cost, quality (failure and reject rate), inspection costs, inventory costs (for example the potential for implementing a 'just-in-time' or *kanban* system) and ease of use in the manufacturing environment – that is, the impact of the supplied item on labour and other costs. The other aspect which must be considered is the purchase of items which support the manufacturing process such as machine tools, conveyor systems and control systems. Particularly with these latter items the ongoing running costs are often a far greater part of the total lifetime cost than the initial purchase price. Significant benefits can be obtained by bearing a higher initial cost in order to generate longer term savings. A prime example of this is with Mercedes motor cars. While the initial capital cost is significantly greater than for the competitors' equivalent models, the Mercedes is reputed to depreciate at a far lower rate (under 40 per cent over the first three years of life compared to more than 60 per cent) than those competitors and, with greater component reliability and longevity, also has lower running costs.

Deming also recommends a move towards single suppliers. As with so many things, this approach has both advantages and drawbacks. The principal advantages are that it provides the purchaser with significant leverage in negotiating improvements in product quality and price, it enables long term relationships based on trust and mutual support to be established and it provides a more secure financial platform for the provider. Conversely, reliance on a single source of parts supply makes the purchaser vulnerable to any failure by the supplier, either financially, or in quality. Such exposure may give cause for concern to bankers and other financiers. A worthwhile approach here would be to consider the use of a single supplier based on Porter's (1980) model for competitive rivalry. Where supplier power is weak (there are many suppliers and the product is un-differentiated or non-critical), a single supplier strategy may bring significant benefits to the company, enabling it to take effective control of its supplier. Where supplier power is strong (there are few suppliers, the product is differentiated or critical), the organisation may maximise its position by supporting more than one supplier.

The fifth principle, aim for continuous improvement, if considered appropriate to the customer's needs and industry circumstances, gives greater substance and focus to the first two by focusing attention on productivity, quality and decreasing costs. Objectives at this stage can be made more quantifiable, moving from the ideals of the first principles to a more practical, achievement orientation.

The sixth principle, 'on the job training', emphasises the need to improve competencies and skills in the practical context. While not excluding classroom based training, this principle suggests that the objective of continuous improvement applies at least as much to people as it does to processes.

The seventh principle, 'leadership' is again qualitative and cultural and is closely associated with the eighth, 'drive out fear'. These principles are connected with the management style of the organisation. The objective here can usefully be seen as a requirement to move away from an adversarial style of management towards a collaborative style. Effective management in this way, supported by the SPC techniques, will focus attention on how to improve the individual (special causes) or the system (common causes) rather than on who to blame. The approach will again target curing the diseases rather than convicting the victims.

The ninth principle, 'breaking down barriers', can be seen as linked to the fourth. The suggestion here is, in effect, for the creation of multi-disciplinary teams for product and service development aiming to enhance the development, production and delivery of new products or services. Deming does not discuss how this can be achieved or specifically recognise the difficulties that can be associated with it. There are a number of cultural and professional issues which often emerge in the creation of multi-disciplinary teams and any reorganisation into either a matrix form of management, or project teams, needs to be associated with commensurate changes in salary and bonus packages to enable congruence of individual and organisational goals.

The tenth principle, 'eliminate slogans, exhortations and numerical quotas', is again more a cultural than a quantitative statement. Here Deming is suggesting that these features act more to vex the staff than encourage them. His argument is simple. If through the use of SPC the 'special causes' of failure related to individual machines and workers have been removed, then all other causes of failure relate to the system itself. These are seen as the responsibility of management so no amount of slogans, exhortations and quotas will have any positive effect. Instead, Deming (1986: 67) suggests they will 'generate frustration and resentment'. This principle clearly links to the second which required management to accept their responsibilities.

The eleventh principle, 'eliminate quotas, work standards and management by objectives or numerical goals and substitute leadership' seems to be something of a contradiction. Improvement targets must be an inherent part of measuring and monitoring achievement, and statistical process control provides one form of measurement of achievement.

Deming's point here is, that if the system is stable, as will be revealed by the control charts, then its performance cannot be improved by the setting of targets, only by changes to the system. As with slogans and exhortations,

Deming sees the setting of targets and quotas as potentially both meaning-less and divisive unless accompanied by a specific action plan to improve the process. This may well mean re-appraising what the system is designed to achieve.

Removal of barriers that rob people of their right to pride in their work is the twelfth principle. Deming distinguishes management and workers from each other here. He sees that annual appraisal or merit review focuses the attention of management on the matters that will be covered in the appraisal or merit system. He implies that they will strive to achieve those things regardless of the impact on quality or productivity, that is they will do the right thing by the appraisal system, not by the customer!

The workers he sees as being constrained by uncertainty of employment, by the lack of definition as to what constitutes acceptable workmanship, by poor quality materials, tools and machines and by ineffective supervision and management. He suggests that if these aspects are corrected, then quality products will follow. Deming (1986: 85) suggests 'Give the work force a chance to work with pride, and the 3 per cent that apparently don't care will erode itself by peer pressure.' He seems to ignore the idea that the whole organisation of many factories, based on the principles of classical management theory, is established to remove pride in achievement from the workers by fragmenting tasks.

Principle 13 is to institute a vigorous education and self-improvement programme. This is Deming's recognition that if the organisation is to continuously improve, then the people must continuously improve. He suggests that future competitive advantage will be achieved through knowledge, a conclusion that there can be little argument with.

The fourteenth and final principle is to put everyone to work to achieve the transformation. This suggests that the whole programme can only be successful if a 'total' approach is taken. This will require a strong, unified and cohesive culture within the organisation with commitment from top to bottom. Such a culture can only be achieved when the behaviour of management is consistent with their words, i.e. when they 'walk the talk'.

Taken together, these principles can be summarised as proposing wholesale attitudinal change throughout the organisation (a qualitative approach), supported where appropriate by reliance on validated statistical analysis (quantitative).

To enable the principles to be implemented, Deming proposed a seven point action plan (see figure 6.5). This action plan is perhaps best inter-preted as a series of statements about 'what' to do, rather than the more important 'how' to do it.

The first three points clearly focus attention on the top management group and are based on attitudes and communication. They suggest that this group must understand what they are trying to achieve, commit themselves to a successful outcome and then explain to the subordinates throughout the organisation why it is necessary. This has distinct over-tones of Crosby's more directly evangelical approach and reflects what can be thought of as the ethical aspect of the programme, that is, the need for

---

W. EDWARDS DEMING

Point 1   Management must agree on the meaning of the quality programme, its implications and the direction to take.

Point 2   Top management must accept and adopt the new philosophy.

Point 3   Top management must communicate the plan and the necessity for it to the people in the organisation.

Point 4   Every activity must be recognised as a step in a process and the customers of that process identified. The customers are responsible for the next stage of the process.

Point 5   Each stage must adopt the 'Deming' or 'Shewhart' Cycle – Plan, Do, Check, Action – as the basis of quality improvement.

Point 6   Team working must be engendered and encouraged to improve inputs and outputs. Everyone must be enabled to contribute to this process.

Point 7   Construct an organisation for quality with the support of knowledgeable statisticians.

Figure 6.5 **The seven point action plan**

quality to be embraced in the values and beliefs of *all* members of the organisation. It can surely be agreed that if the management are not wholly committed to the programme and are unable, or unwilling, to communicate it effectively to the workforce, who must similarly accept it, then it will not work.

The fourth point recognises the process based workflow of most organisations and calls for the processes to be divided into stages. Each stage becomes a clear task with the recipients of its outputs being treated as its customers. Thus at every stage there are customers whose needs must be identified and satisfied. This can be seen as an attempt to overcome the problem of workers in many processes, for example in the manufacture of sub-assemblies. These staff are often unaware of customers and do not recognise the sub-assembly as a product in its own right, but rather as a part of a larger product which perhaps they never see. It is suggested that this shift of emphasis enables workers to take a pride in their work that is otherwise absent.

The fifth point is simply to implement continuous improvement at every stage through the PDCA cycle. Achievement of implementation in this way implies acceptance, by both management and workers within each process, of responsibility for the process. This in turn implies that higher management must allow them authority to develop and implement the changes.

The next point, participation in teamwork to improve all inputs and outputs, can be seen to operate at several levels. First, a team culture must be developed within each process to improve it internally. Second, since changes in one area may have implications in another, a team culture must be engendered between process owners (the management) to enable effective communication between them. Third, to be truly effective a means of sharing and developing improvements across processes must be developed – this links the whole programme back to top management.

The seventh point, construction of an organisation for quality, is perhaps a further development of the third part of stage six, improvement across processes. The requirement is to build an organisation which reflects and nurtures the achievement of quality. Deming suggests the use of knowledgeable statisticians to support this aspect, perhaps reflecting his own background. It is useful to go well beyond this and propose the support of a multidisciplined team of management scientists and experts such as cyberneticians, psychologists, statisticians and accountants to work with the management team in the pursuit of the programme. This emphasises the collaborative nature of achieving quality. It is not suggested that the management scientists develop and impose a programme of change, this will be almost certainly doomed to failure. It is suggested, rather, that the management and workers should be responsible for the whole programme, having both control and ownership. The role of the management scientists is to use their expertise in a supportive, guiding manner, as experts within the team.

The introduction to Deming's approach is now complete. Statistical Process Control and methodologies for implementing quality will be addressed in the appropriate chapters. Let this section conclude by reaffirming the view that while initially Deming's approach was rooted in quantitative methods it later came to be supported by more qualitative techniques.

6.4 SUCCESSES AND FAILURES

While overall Deming can be said to have been very successful in his achievements there have been both successes and failures. His movement into Japan, for example, was to some extent a result of the early rejection of his ideas by American managements. This perhaps reflects the maxim that 'a prophet is not without honour, save in his own country'. It was only after his substantial successes with Japanese industry that Deming was able to turn his attention again to the problems of industrial America.

Here, what Flood (1993: 14) calls Deming's fundamentally 'mechanistic' approach ran 'into strong workforce resistance, from both the managers and the workers'. Deming, taking account of these issues together with matters of reliance on technology, standards of practice and the cultural issues, substantially revised his methods. This is reflected in the shift in emphasis from quantitative to qualitative approaches and in the codification of the 'Seven Deadly Diseases'.

Adapting from Flood (1993) the principal strengths of Deming's approach are considered as:

- the systemic logic, particularly the idea of internal customer–supplier relationships;
- management before technology;
- emphasis on management leadership;
- the sound statistical approach;
- awareness of different socio-cultural contexts.

There are also significant weaknesses recognised:

- lack of a well defined methodology;
- the work is not adequately grounded in human relations theory;
- as with Crosby, the approach will not help in an organisation with a biased power structure.

Reviewing the strengths, the value of the systemic and logical approach cannot be denied, put simply, it is an organised and systematic rather than chaotic approach. The 'Plan, Do, Check, Action' cycle as a mechanism for organisational learning is recognised in other areas of management as a 'learning cycle'. Handy (1985) for example refers to a process of:

- *questioning and conceptualisation*: – fundamental parts of effective planning;
- *experimentation*: trying out ideas, the testing and evaluation of hypotheses;
- *consolidation*: the alteration of habits, the basis for future action.

Handy sees this as the basis of human learning, that is, continuous personal improvement. It is unsurprising that a similar process works for organisations which, after all, have people as their fundamental organisational units.

Deming's prioritisation of management before technology represents a reversal of the attitudes of many managers. The British adage that 'a bad workman always blames his tools' recognises that the tendency for most managers is to look at external rather than internal factors as responsible for failure. If, as Deming suggests, 94 per cent of problems belong to the management then acceptance by them of responsibility is a primary step in enabling change. Equally even the worst tools can be made to perform better in the hands of a good workman, but a bad workman will not achieve good performance however good the tools.

The recognition of the importance of leadership and motivation can be seen to reflect the development of human relations theory as a major strand of management thinking, although Deming does not draw heavily on the body of knowledge that became established in that area during his productive years.

Regarding the strong quantitative base, perhaps Flood does not go far enough and it could be suggested that some form of measurement system, whether relying on hard, physical measures, or on softer aspects using techniques from organisational psychology is fundamental to achievement of quality. A simple attempt to 'do better', will always be followed by questions such as 'how much' or 'when'. Vagueness on these issues would be expected to have a dispiriting effect on the participants while a form of achievement target orientation would be motivational. Success is said to breed success, but first of all it must be known that success is being achieved!

The recognition by Deming of different cultural contexts is a vital strength. His failure to draw heavily on the literature of human relations theory for this aspect suggests that his embrace of it was driven by pragmatism rather than desire, perhaps a reluctant recognition that it was necessary to allow the other ideas to work. Nonetheless, the recognition of different cultures, and adaptation to them are essential in achieving success. Hofstede (1980) produced the principal work in this area. In the context of quality the recognition needs to go well beyond the country differences highlighted by Hofstede to recognise the particular culture of organisations themselves, and even sections, functions and departments within organisations. These frequently have unique, perhaps very strong, cultural contexts.

Flood's criticism of a lack of a clear 'Deming method' can be seen as reasonably well justified. Like many gurus and experts, Deming suggests what to do without indicating very precisely how to do it. While perhaps constraining on the one hand, this lack of precision can be seen as potentially disemprisoning and empowering. It encourages experimentation and debate within each individual context to find an approach which will work there rather than using an approach which was developed in another time and context. Perhaps the most important issue is reliance on Deming's principles.

The second weakness having been covered within the strengths, we can examine the third. Deming is criticised for saying nothing about intervention in political and coercive situations. Perhaps, following the previous point, nothing needs to be said. The second principle and the first three points of the action plan all call on management to accept their responsibility for quality and productivity and to embrace a new philosophy. These remarks are targeted directly at the most senior members of the management team, that is, those who hold power in a political or coercive context. If they do not accept responsibility at the outset, they are ignoring the principles, and by default, not following the Deming method. If they seek to impose a quality approach on others, failure will certainly follow. Deming's whole approach rests on the attitude of management!

6.5 CRITICAL REVIEW

The foundation of Deming's approach can be seen in his statistical background and his training in the science of physics. These essentially 'hard' sciences based in scientific method will have informed the development of his early approaches. It must be acknowledged that they make a major contribution to work in the field of quality.

The principles and practice of Statistical Process Control have been demonstrated over time to have considerable value to organisations in both the service and manufacturing sectors. They also have value for the workers who use them, providing rapid and personal performance feedback information, enabling them to recognise their own successes and failures and to take corrective action where appropriate.

Deming's work in relation to the softer issues is considered to be narrow and underdeveloped, failing to take account of much of the thinking in that area over the period of his career. It must though be acknowledged that Deming did not claim to be an expert in this field! Nevertheless, the value of his approach could have been further enhanced by a clearer focus on that aspect.

The Plan, Do, Check, Action, cycle, is a clear directive to both management and workers that achieving continuous improvement is the purpose of the quality activity. This contrasts directly with the overtones of a discrete programme suggested in Crosby's work.

Deming makes quite clear reference to the service sector in his work, but again places much emphasis on quantitative aspects of this area. For example he refers to aspects such as how long a telephone is out of action before it is repaired. While this is of great importance, of equal importance is the tone of voice which a person uses in answering the telephone when it rings. This may be a stronger determinant of how the customer perceives the level of service quality than the number of times that it rings, or even the words that are said. Interestingly, it was reported in the business press in May 1997 that one organisation, having focused on answering the telephone at the first ring was improving its service by allowing eight seconds to elapse before answering. Apparently the prompt responses had been putting customers off!

It is often the case that managers take measurements of the things which are easy to measure, rather than the things which, while difficult to measure, are of greater importance. In a world which relies ever more heavily on telecommunications devices these aspects, which are more difficult to quantify, will have increasing importance. The reliability and clarity of modern digital telecommunications systems are such that these are no longer significant issues and many businesses are run entirely through them, for example, telephone based banking and insurance services. Of increasing importance then is tone of voice since technical issues are less problematic and digital technology makes tone of voice transparent to the listener. The more recent development of videophone technology will have as yet unknown impacts on this area of service.

It is accepted that Deming has probably made the most substantial contribution to quality management. However, enthusiasm must be tempered with the knowledge that a clearer method, a more explicit and developed recognition of the human aspects and a precise focus on what constitutes quality of service in the contemporary world would enhance the value of his work.

SUMMARY

This chapter has presented the main strands of the work of W. Edwards Deming through the five point critical framework. Readers wishing to develop their knowledge further should read the relevant chapters in part four of this book and refer to Deming's own work, in particular *Out of the Crisis*.

---

key learning points

W. EDWARDS DEMING

Definition of quality
a function of continuous improvement based on reduction in variation around the desired output

Seven deadly sins and diseases
- lack of constancy;
- short term profit focus;
- performance appraisal;
- job-hopping;
- use of visible figures only;
- excessive medical costs;
- excessive liability costs.

Five key beliefs
quantification, recognition of failure causes, systematic approach, continuous improvement, constancy

Principal methods
Fourteen principles for transformation, the 7 point plan

QUESTION

Deming suggests that 94 per cent of quality problems are the responsibility of management. Review this statement.

chapter seven

ARMAND V. FEIGENBAUM

quality is simply a way of managing a business organisation.
Logothetis, *Managing for Total Quality*, 1992

INTRODUCTION

Armand Feigenbaum originated the approach to quality known as 'Total Quality Control' (TQC) which has a clear industrial focus. After completing a doctorate at MIT (Massachusetts Institute of Technology), Feigenbaum joined the General Electric Company where he was manager of worldwide manufacturing operations and quality control before becoming President of General Systems Company. His book, *Total Quality Control*, completed whilst he was still a doctoral student, and his other works, were discovered by the Japanese in the early 1950s. He was also involved with them through his business contacts with Hitachi and Toshiba.

Bendell (1989: 15) states that Feigenbaum presented a case for a 'systematic, or Total approach to quality', and it is argued by Bank (1992: xv) that he was the first to do so. Logothetis (1992: 94) suggests that to Feigenbaum 'quality is simply a way of managing a business organisation', while Gilbert (1992: 22) concurs with that and adds that Feigenbaum sees 'quality improvement as the single most important force leading to organisational success and growth'.

Feigenbaum's contribution has been widely recognised. He was founding chairman of the International Academy for Quality and is a past president of the American Society for Quality Control which awarded him the Edwards Medal and Lancaster Award for his international contribution to quality and productivity (Bendell, 1989: 15).

7.1 PHILOSOPHY

Feigenbaum's philosophy is clearly founded in his early idea of the 'total' approach, reflecting a systemic attitude of mind. He saw it as fundamental to quality improvement that all functions in an organisation should be involved in the quality process and that quality should be built in to the product rather than failure be inspected out.

He defines quality as 'best for the customer use and selling price' and quality control as:

> an effective method for co-ordinating the quality maintenance and quality improvement efforts of the various groups in an organisation so as to enable production at the most economical levels which allow for full customer satisfaction.

Reflecting on Feigenbaum's approach there is no difficulty in accepting the systemic nature of his philosophy. While the work of both Deming and Juran can be interpreted in a systemic manner, Feigenbaum is explicit from the outset that this is vital. In the contemporary, complex world of organisations there is every need to manage from a systemic perspective – recognising and dealing with interactions across arbitrary organisational boundaries and at all levels within them as well as with the suppliers, customers and other stakeholders in the enterprise.

The issue of building quality in can also be addressed here. This recognises that organisations do not simply manufacture products, they also design and develop them. Feigenbaum appears to be suggesting that many quality problems can be eradicated from both the products and the manufacturing process by paying attention to the quality issue from the conception of the idea, right through to delivery of the first and subsequent items. Techniques here might include, colour coding wires so that electronic products cannot be incorrectly wired or varying bolt positions in otherwise apparently symmetrical pieces of metal so that they cannot be mounted incorrectly.

Looking at Feigenbaum's definition of quality two constraints are discovered which have not previously been seen, 'customer use' and 'selling price'. The first of these is perhaps no different from Deming's, 'needs of the consumer', or Crosby's 'conformance to requirements' but it suggests a constraint, rather than an ideal to aim for. It seems to imply that there are, perhaps, limits to useful quality. The issue of selling price has not previously been met and clearly indicates that for any given price Feigenbaum perceives limitations to the expectations of quality. This can perhaps be interpreted as saying that a quality differential, of perhaps performance or reliability between, say, a car costing US$10,000 and one costing US$100,000 is to be expected and is acceptable.

His definition of quality control emphasises the integral nature of the quality process, stressing 'co-ordination' of maintenance and improvement efforts across 'groups'. It is notable that he does not say 'functions' or 'departments'. This is a clear recognition of the human relations aspects of organisations.

Summarising Feigenbaum's philosophy, a commitment to a systemic, 'total' approach and an emphasis on designing for quality and involving all departments is evident. Supporting this is recognition of, and reliance on, the human aspects of the organisation with statistical methods being used as necessary. This contrasts quite sharply with the greater statistical emphasis in the work of Deming.

7.2   ASSUMPTIONS

Turning now to Feigenbaum's apparent assumptions about the world a different understanding is perceived to those gurus already reviewed.

First, is his explicit assumption of a world composed of systems. He works with the interrelationships that he perceives to exist between all aspects within the organisation, and importantly, in its environment. He recognises the contribution made by suppliers and the constraints, particularly on performance expectations and price, imposed by customers.

The systemic view is clear again in his second assumption, that human relationships are a basic issue in quality achievement. This concurs with the developments in management thinking – the human relations school – that were occurring at the time of his early work.

In these assumptions he clearly focuses attention on the whole enterprise, from suppliers to users, through every function and to all the groups who are involved in it. The development in more recent times of global businesses serving global markets, of ever more complex and inter-dependent relationships between organisational, social and individual well-being and the continuing emergence of newly industrialising nations, leads to the conclusion that this systemic view must be sustained.

An organisation can perhaps be seen to exist within an ecological economic system in which it will ultimately either thrive or become extinct. Although not explicitly referring to adaptation of the organisation, Feigenbaum's commitment to 'full customer satisfaction', implies constant awareness of customer needs and expectations within the organisation and the need for change to satisfy them.

MCDONALDS, HONG KONG: FULL CUSTOMER SATISFACTION

McDonalds, Hong Kong, which has built its business on three characteristics – food quality, convenience and price has clearly developed a unique approach to the idea of full customer satisfaction. The two letters reprinted below show that McDonalds has recognised that customer satisfaction in their case goes well beyond simply serving the right food, at the right time and price. The first letter demonstrates their commitment to the total McDonald's experience. The customer doesn't mention food but is impressed by the quality of overall service and the hygiene standards of the washrooms.

January 19, 1996

The Managing Director
McDonald's Restaurant (HK) Ltd
Upper G/F, Park Vale
1060 King's Road
Quarry Bay, H.K.

Dear Sir:

I would like to draw your attention to the outstanding performance and good job done by your staff of the Sai Kung Court outlet.

I live in Sai Kung, occasionally I pay visits to your Sai Kung Court outlet for afternoon coffee. In each of these visits, I am so impressed by the cleanliness and tidiness of the shop. Your staff work hard to do the cleaning work in turns, while the staff at the counters handling customers efficiently. In addition, the lady's room is not big though, it is always filled with paper rolls and smells pleasant. The excellent quality of hygiene standard and customer service should be considered as a model among the McDonald's shops.

Congratulations for hiring such a team of good staff, in providing comfortable environment. I'll certainly keep visiting this shop with my family.

Best regards,

Christine Chan

Christine Chan
A Fan of the McDonald's

cc: Shop manager, Sai Kung Court

The second letter shows how far McDonalds has gone in becoming a part of the community in which it thrives as a business. Again, food is not the issue, it is service which counts.

March 19, 1996

Miss Doctor Law
First Assistant
McDonald's Restaurants (H.K.) Ltd.
Upper G/Fl., Park Vale
1060 King's Road
Quarry Bay
Hong Kong

Dear Miss Law,

I wanted to write to you to express my deep thanks for looking after my daughter Erin yesterday. The first aid assistance and the very helpful and concerned attitude you showed greatly helped her. It took me 2 hours to drive from my office to your restaurant due to heavy traffic and your understanding was much appreciated.

McDonald's is an amazing part of the community. When Erin was looking for somewhere safe and friendly to shelter she headed straight for the familiar "Golden Arches".

She has had her leg stitched and is resting comfortably now. Thank you again for your help and I hope you enjoy the chocolates.

Kind regards,

Mark I. McCallum

cc : Mr Don Dempsey (McDonald H.K.)

Feigenbaum further assumes that continuous improvement is both desirable and achievable. Referring again to his definition of quality we can see the potential for conflict and contradiction. For example, if customer expectations on performance and price are met then quality, by his definition, has been achieved. However, unless the process of TQC ends, then further improvement will arise. This in turn implies a need for the organisation to interact with its customers, aiming to alter their expectations of quality, perhaps as suggested by Galbraith (1974). There is a danger, therefore, that as with Crosby, Feigenbaum's approach can be interpreted as a finite, ends-oriented and discrete programme, whereas his intent appears to have been for continuous improvement.

7.3 METHODS

While Flood (1993: 35) reduces Feigenbaum's philosophy through a four step approach, these steps (figure 7.1) should be viewed as a simplification of his overall method. These steps may certainly be seen as capturing the fundamental essence of Feigenbaum's approach which is intended to lead to a 'Total Quality System'. This is defined by Bendell (1989: 16) as:

> The agreed companywide and plantwide operating work structure, documented in effective, integrated technical and managerial procedures, for guiding the co-ordinated actions of the people, the machines and the information of the company and plant in the best and most practical ways to assure customer quality satisfaction and economical costs of quality.

The Weberian, bureaucratic overtones and dangers inherent in this definition are quite clear. A heavy reliance on documentation and integration of procedures and on co-ordinating the people, machines and information certainly present an opportunity to those 'keener on talking about work than doing any' (Beckford, 1993).

ARMAND V. FEIGENBAUM

Step 1   Set quality standards.
Step 2   Appraise conformance to standards.
Step 3   Act when standards are not met.
Step 4   Plan to make improvements.

Figure 7.1 **Four steps to quality: Armand V. Feigenbaum**

To counter the dangers of this, Feigenbaum uses in the first sentence the word 'agreed'. This stresses that everyone must be committed to the design of the organisation through effective communication. However, while proposing that gradual development of the programme is preferred, little is said about how agreement is achieved which permits scope for either autocratic or democratic processes to be employed. While Feigenbaum proposes participation as a means of harnessing the contribution of people and encouraging a sense of belonging it remains the case that the approach need not be used in this participative manner.

A further tool is the measurement of what Feigenbaum calls 'operating quality costs'. These are divided into four self-explanatory categories and have been met before in chapter 3:

- *prevention costs*, including quality planning;
- *appraisal costs*, including inspection costs;
- *internal failure costs*, including scrap and rework;
- *external failure costs*, including warranty costs and complaints.

It can be seen again how Feigenbaum's concept of total quality extends from product development right through to product use, that is, product quality in the hands of the consumer. Bendell (1989: 16) states that:

> reductions in operating quality costs result from setting up a total quality system for two reasons:
>
> 1. Lack of existing effective customer-orientated customer standards may mean current quality of products is not optimal given use.
> 2. Expenditure on prevention costs can lead to a several fold reduction in internal and external failure costs.

The proposal overall is that by measuring quality at every critical stage the total costs of running the organisation will be reduced. A similar concept is met in the food manufacturing industry which uses a system called 'HACCP' – Hazard Analysis Critical Control Points to evaluate and ensure food product quality and safety at points of risk. This would include aspects such as temperature change. If, for example, a product must be boiled then the HACCP system would test it to ensure that boiling point is actually reached. The emphasis on design again stresses the importance to Feigenbaum of designing quality in to the product.

Overall, Feigenbaum's approach is best seen as part of the *kaizen* management practices which are management responsibility oriented and involve effective teamworking across the organisation. These tools will be examined in more depth in the appropriate chapters.

7.4   SUCCESSES AND FAILURES

Feigenbaum's approach has undoubtedly been successful and has been adopted in whole, or in part, by a number of organisations. There is little doubt that his recognition of quality as a way of running an organisation, rather than as a subset activity, is a major breakthrough to thinking in this area, yet even today many organisations consider quality as an added extra rather than a fundamental of organisational effectiveness. Similarly, his systemic concept of 'total', that is, quality running throughout the organisation, from its inputs to its outputs, has immense value.

Flood (1993: 36) again provides a summary of the principal strengths and weaknesses of Feigenbaum's approach from which the following is adapted. He sees the main strengths as:

- a total or whole approach to quality control;
- emphasis on the importance of management;
- socio-technical systems thinking is taken into account;
- participation is promoted.

Principal weaknesses identified are:

- the work is systemic but not complementarist;
- the breadth of management theory is recognised but not unified;
- the political or coercive context is not addressed.

It can be added to this critique that the industrial orientation of the approach provides little of real value for service based organisations. Similarly, it could be said that as with Deming, there is a lack of clarity of method: ample instruction in what to do is not supported by guidance on how to do it.

The necessity and contribution of the systemic view proposed has already been acknowledged. Similarly the focus on the importance of management to the process is supported, although as Bendell (1989: 16) suggests: 'modern quality control is seen by Feigenbaum as stimulating and building up *operator responsibility* and interest in quality'.

While this is achieved through management commitment to the programme, the need for management to *sell* the ideas is stressed, suggesting a certain resistance by employees to accept the concepts of quality. While fully accepting the value of a participative approach, the question has again to be raised – how is such participation to be achieved. Even Flood's choice of the word 'harnessing' in respect of individual contributions is suggestive of a less than wholehearted commitment, having overtones of compulsion.

Looking at the weaknesses, Feigenbaum's work says nothing about the identification and selection of tools, whether management theories or systems approaches, which are most appropriate for a particular organisational or national context. For contemporary managers this issue is of great importance. Many organisations are globally based, and to achieve agreement, which Feigenbaum requires amongst the top management, account must be taken of the varying cultures and expectations of the participants. An approach which works well in Hong Kong, may fail completely in Tokyo, Los Angeles or London.

Finally, Flood's comment that nothing is said about political or coercive contexts is valid. Feigenbaum's assumption that people can and will work together for the improvement of the organisation and its outputs is clear in his work. However, his recognition of the need to *sell* the total quality concept perhaps suggests that a degree of political or coercive pressure may, for him legitimately, be brought to bear to achieve the end result. That being said, it is perhaps a little unfair to criticise someone for not offering a solution to a problem he did not set out to address!

7.5 CRITICAL REVIEW

There appear to be three founding ideas to Feigenbaum's work. First, is his acceptance of the systems paradigm, second, is a belief in appropriate measurement, third, is the recognition of participation as a means of developing and encouraging support for change and enabling creativity.

Feigenbaum's strong academic background in issues of quality control, supported by his extensive practical managerial experience, undoubtedly provided a substantial platform for the further development and successful application of his ideas with considerable success.

The apparent lack of a well developed, clear methodology telling managers how to proceed with his approach is a major drawback. It is suspected that personal and management styles are much greater factors in the success or failure of a Total Quality Control initiative than is normally recognised. The adoption by top management of a collaborative, team-based working pattern is not easily achieved or maintained.

Functionally structured companies, for example, normally have power bases within each function. If these power bases are strong then they may resist the perceived loss of individual or function power that arises from any other orientation. Companies are often heard of which are 'production led', 'marketing led' or 'accounting led'. These are companies which are dominated by a particular power group within a professional specialisation. They appear to perceive the world from a particular professional stand-point, and in so doing, perhaps undervalue the contribution of other professions. Adoption of a team-based approach where each profession is valued for its contribution to the whole, perhaps in the form of a project or matrix management system is unlikely. Similar comments can be made about issues such as sexual orientation, gender and race; for example the 'WASPs' (White Anglo Saxon Protestants) in the USA, Oxbridge graduates in the UK, *bumiputras* (indigenous Malaysians) in Malaysia. Professional and other biases must be overcome in the creation of organisations based on expertise, Feigenbaum says nothing of how to achieve this.

The quantitative aspects of Feigenbaum's approach are welcome. Reliance on statistics 'where appropriate' is a useful guide encouraging managers to use discretion in their choice of measurements. This contrasts quite sharply with the strong emphasis on measurement proposed by Deming. Feigenbaum is quite selective about what it is useful to measure and when. Like Deming he proposes, through the four way division of operating quality costs, a form of customer chain analysis which can be seen to be helpful not simply in identifying the costs of quality but very importantly, where they arise.

It is accepted that Feigenbaum has made a substantial contribution to work in the field of quality, but enthusiasm for his approach is tempered by recognising some weaknesses in respect of methodology and cultural context and the important understanding that his work does not go beyond the industrial sector.

SUMMARY

This chapter has introduced the principal strands of the work of Armand Feigenbaum, presenting and reviewing his philosophy, assumptions, methods and successes and failures. Readers may wish to refer to Feigenbaum's own work *Total Quality Control* (1986) to enhance and further develop their understanding.

key learning points

ARMAND V. FEIGENBAUM

Definition of quality
quality is a way of running a business organisation

Key beliefs
systems thinking, relevant measurement, participation

Principal methods
the four steps to quality, operating quality costs

QUESTION

The chapter suggests difficulties might arise from Feigenbaum's definition of a 'Total Quality System' with its 'Weberian, bureaucratic overtones'. Defend Feigenbaum's work against this suggestion.

chapter
eight

KAORU ISHIKAWA

'At last,' he said, 'el pueblo.'
Salvador Allende, President of Chile: (Beer, 1981: 258)

INTRODUCTION

Kaoru Ishikawa, who died in 1989, was a Chemist, held a doctorate in Engineering and was Emeritus Professor at Tokyo University. Bank (1992: 74) cites him as the 'Father of Quality Circles' and as a founder of the Japanese quality movement. He became involved in quality issues in 1949 through the Union of Japanese Scientists and Engineers (JUSE) and subsequently became a world-wide lecturer and consultant on quality. Gilbert (1992: 23) suggests that Ishikawa was the first guru to 'recognise that quality improvement is too important to be left in the hands of specialists'. Ishikawa's writings explaining his approach include the *Guide to Quality Control* (1986) and *What is Total Quality Control? The Japanese Way* (1985) which have both been translated into English. Ishikawa was widely honoured for his work, receiving the Deming, Nihon Keizai Press and Industrial Standardisation prizes and the Grant Award from the American Society for Quality Control.

8.1 PHILOSOPHY

Gilbert (1992: 23) and Logothetis (1992: 95) see the philosophical roots of Ishikawa's work in the concept of Company-Wide Quality. Ishikawa himself, cited by Bendell (1989: 18) said:

The results of these company-wide Quality Control activities are remarkable, not only in ensuring the quality of industrial products but also in their great contribution to the company's overall business.

Bendell (1989) considers that Ishikawa defines quality as meaning 'not only the quality of the product, but also of after sales service, quality of management, the company itself and the human being'.

Flood (1993: 33) interprets Ishikawa's approach as involving 'vertical and horizontal co-operation'. Thus the approach takes account of communication and co-operation between different levels of managers, supervisors and workers and from suppliers to customers. Ishikawa's first belief then is that everyone involved in or affected by the company and its operations should be involved in the quality programme. This is similar to the 'total' approach advocated by Feigenbaum which has already been reviewed.

The level of involvement proposed is also significant, Ishikawa asks that the programme not just be company wide (and beyond) but that it involve active participation. His approach to participation emphasises greater worker involvement and motivation which Bendell (1989: 19) sees as being created through:

- an atmosphere where employees are continuously looking to resolve problems;
- greater commercial awareness;
- a change of shopfloor attitude in aiming for ever increasing goals.

These strands stress three words, all of them qualitative rather than quantitative; atmosphere, awareness and attitude. They are cultural requirements which have direct implications for the behaviour of management.

An 'atmosphere where employees are continuously looking to resolve problems' implies acceptance by management that:

- workers have the ability to recognise both problems and solutions;
- management will either, accept the need for change and implement proposals or, explain why a proposed change is not possible or desirable in a way which maintains the employees' enthusiasm.

A 'greater commercial awareness' imposes two responsibilities on management. First, is to provide or enable training and education for the workforce in this area. Second, is to provide to the workforce accurate, meaningful and timely data in respect of the company's performance as well as that of its competitors. Although commercial awareness is stressed in this regard, these matters should be considered equally important in a public sector or not-for-profit organisation which, rather than focusing on profit should be focused on delivering the maximum level of service within a constrained resource; that is value for money.

The third strand, 'a change of shop floor attitude' towards a focus on ever increasing goals – the culture of continuous improvement – again implies management responsibility. It is considered that management must adopt this attitude in their behaviour as well as their words to make its achievement possible. Deming's concern about 'exhortations' is important here as well as Crosby's promotion through slogans and platitudes.

Clearly Ishikawa believed that effective participation, like effective communication, is a two-way street and as suggested by Hagima Karatsu, Managing Director of Matsushita Communication (cited by Bendell, 1989: 19) 'creative co-operation' between people is an absolute requirement for a quality organisation.

A third element to Ishikawa's work is the emphasis on direct, simple communication. Bendell (1989: 17) states that Ishikawa saw 'open group communication' as critical, particularly in the use of his tools for problem solving. A fundamental part of communication for Ishikawa seems to have been an emphasis on simplicity in his methods. For example the book *Guide to Quality Control* was deliberately written as a 'non-sophisticated' (ibid.) text and Bank (1992: 75) suggests that Ishikawa worked in a 'straightforward manner'. Logothetis (1992: 95) stresses that Ishikawa concentrated on 'simple statistical techniques for data collection and presentation'. The requirement for simplicity covers both the qualitative and quantitative issues.

The emphasis on simplicity and using what might be called the language of the shopfloor is considered to have an empowering effect. The workers, having been trained in the appropriate methods, are not obliged to use obscure or arcane terminology. Management are unable to hide behind complex approaches and sophisticated language. Since training is given to all levels of employee a common quality language is spoken by all which in turn aids and enhances communication.

Three principal elements can be identified in Ishikawa's philosophy. First, is the systemic or holistic approach advocated by 'Company-Wide Quality', an all-embracing view. Second, is participation, active and creative co-operation between those affected. The third element is the emphasis on communication through two strands of thinking, simplicity of analysis and method and commonality of language.

8.2   ASSUMPTIONS

Ishikawa's apparent assumptions about the world will now be explored.

It can be seen that Ishikawa's first assumption is concerned with interrelatedness, a 'total' or systems view. He explicitly recognises that every aspect of the organisation and the relevant parts of the environment must be considered. As with Feigenbaum it is difficult to argue with that approach, although whether Ishikawa's techniques and methods may be thought of as systemic will be considered in the next section, since some of these seem to rely heavily on a reductionist perspective.

Ishikawa's second assumption is that a fully participative approach can be adopted. This implies a belief that every individual within the organisation can, and will, commit themselves to addressing the quality issue.

This suggests that a quality 'religion' or creed must become established and the achievement of higher quality become a superordinate goal, overriding all others as a requirement for organisational success. The primacy of this goal, while perhaps accommodating the requirements of the management or even the owners or shareholders, seems to assume that the primary goals of the workforce will be congruent with those of the organisation. However, little is said about how such a state can be achieved and, for example, Bendell (1989: 19) says that '[quality] circle members receive no direct financial reward for their improvements'. Commitment to quality then, very like religious belief, is considered to be its own reward!

A further assumption implied is that the quality activity takes place in an organisational environment which is free from politics and power relations between participants. While this may be an admirable ideal, it must be perceived as being unrealistic. Both Eastern and Western organisations are subject to internal issues of power and potentially coercion. These may be dominant or subordinate issues in the management of the organisation but they nonetheless exist. Ishikawa is silent on this aspect and how it may be addressed, perhaps reflecting the strength of his own position, or a lack of awareness of the problems faced by others, less educated, or in less privileged positions. Alternatively, it may simply reflect the strongly collective nature of the Japanese value system.

The third assumption, effective communication, is to some extent associated with the second. Participation relies on effective communication for its success. While the development of a common 'language' for discussing quality issues throughout the company is considered to be a substantial benefit in this regard it is still possible that communication will be inhibited by cultural or political issues which prevent viewpoints from being expressed. For example, respect for age or status or fear of loss of face, may prevent an open exchange of views, without which no real communication takes place and the 'loser' in the transaction, who may have a valid viewpoint, is not heard.

Finally, we can turn to the assumption that 'simplicity' in technique and method is useful. While acknowledging that the sophistication of tools must match that of the people who work with them, Ishikawa's work to some extent may be seen as undervaluing the people in the organisation in assuming that they can only cope with simple concepts and methods.

If the complexity of life for an individual is considered, in either the West or the East, it must be recognised that the majority of people deal extremely well with a highly complex existence. For example, coping with accommodation requirements, raising children and managing families (surely the ultimate management challenge), organising pensions and health matters, dealing with state bureaucracies, even driving a car, require complex problem solving and organisational skills. These skills are rarely articulated and acknowledged but none the less they exist and are used for the most part very well. To assume, as Ishikawa appears to, that everything must be simplified is perhaps arrogant. To forget that starting from simple skills that we all acquire as children we can develop, through education and experience, the ability to handle greater complexity is to underestimate the potential of the workforce and perhaps sow the seeds of future discontent.

A second assumption apparently being made is that problems of quality will be tractable when examined using simple methods and approaches. Products and services are considered by many to be becoming more complex, as are the environments in which organisations exist and the organisations themselves. There are increasing numbers of interrelationships between factors; at the same time there are perhaps more factors to be considered. The complexity of any situation may be suggested to be increasing through these two prime driving forces. Experience suggests that simple problem solving approaches are unlikely to be adequate in these circumstances. Other, more sophisticated but not necessarily less accessible, tools must be used. Despite their increasing availability and prominence during Ishikawa's time he does not appear to have taken account of them. Some, as will be seen in part four of this book reflect values in relation to the workforce which accord well with those of Ishikawa and would have, perhaps, enhanced his approach.

8.3   METHODS

Ishikawa's overarching method is 'company-wide quality control.' This he sees as being supported by the 'Quality Circles' technique, and the 'seven tools of quality control.' These will be dealt with in turn.

Company-wide quality control has already largely been addressed as the founding philosophy of Ishikawa's approach and deals with organisational aspects. It is seen as embracing all departments and functions and uses the tools which will be described in the following pages. Bendell (1989) suggests that 15 effects arise from this approach (figure 8.1).

While acknowledging that these are benefits which may arise from the approach, it cannot be agreed that they are necessarily consequent upon the company-wide quality control approach being adopted. Perhaps, as Logothetis (1992: 96) suggests, '*kaizen* consciousness [implied within Ishikawa's work] can only be established when management changes the corporate culture,' an area which is not discussed.

Quality circles are Ishikawa's principal method for achieving participation, composed of between 4 and 12 workers from the same area of activity and led by a workman or supervisor. Their function is to 'identify local problems and recommend solutions' (Gilbert: 92). Bendell (1989: 18) identifies three aims:

- to contribute to the improvement and development of the enterprise;
- to respect human relations and build a happy workshop offering job satisfaction;
- to deploy human capabilities fully and draw out infinite potential.

Gilbert (1992: 92) suggests that there are a number of 'cornerstones' to successful quality circles (figure 8.2). The first four of these factors apply

KAORU ISHIKAWA

Effect 1   Product quality is improved and becomes uniform. Defects are reduced.

Effect 2   Reliability of goods is improved.

Effect 3   Cost is reduced.

Effect 4   Quantity of production is increased, and it becomes possible to make rational production schedules.

Effect 5   Wasteful work and rework are reduced.

Effect 6   Technique is established and improved.

Effect 7   Expenses for inspection and testing are reduced.

Effect 8   Contracts between vendor and vendee are rationalised.

Effect 9   The sales market is enlarged.

Effect 10   Better relationships are established between departments.

Effect 11   False data and reports are reduced.

Effect 12   Discussions are carried out more freely and democratically.

Effect 13   Meetings are operated more smoothly.

Effect 14   Repairs and installations of equipment and facilities are done more rationally.

Effect 15   Human relations are improved.

Figure 8.1 **Fifteen effects of company-wide quality control: Kaoru Ishikawa**
Source: **Gilbert: 1992**

to every successful quality programme – management at all levels must be committed and workers must be trained and willing participants. The 'shared work background' has some limitations as it may fail to address cross-functional or inter-departmental needs. Solution orientation is a means of ensuring that quality circles do not simply descend into complaint sessions where the focus is on what the management, or adjacent processes, could do or not do.

Recognition of efforts is a difficult area, if there is only effort and no achievement then should this be recognised? To maintain efforts and encourage further attempts it is probably valuable to recognise the work done. However, the difference between effort and substantial achievement should also be acknowledged.

J. GILBERT

- Top management support;

- Operational management support and involvement;

- Voluntary participation of the members;

- Effective training of the leader and members;

- Shared work background;

- Solution oriented approach;

- Recognition of the quality circle's efforts;

- Have an agenda, minutes and rotating chairmanship;

- Keep to the time allowed for the meeting;

- Members should inform bosses of meeting times;

- Make sure that quality circles are not hierarchical. If seniority plays any sort of part you'll find the MD's [CEO] secretary thinks she's too good to attend the regular secretaries' Quality Forum.

Figure 8.2 **Cornerstones to successful quality circles: J. Gilbert**
Source: **Gilbert: 1992**

Minutes and an agenda provide, in essence, control devices for the circle. They enable the circle to consider what has or has not been achieved since the last meeting, to keep track of implementation of solutions and to maintain a focus within the circle on innovation rather than reiterating old points. The agenda provides the opportunity both to control the discussion once a meeting has started and, if issued in advance, to give thinking time to the participants before the meeting to consider the issues to be raised. Keeping to time is a matter of good discipline which will be supported by the previous two items.

Informing bosses of meeting times is both courteous and good communication practice. He or she may wish to attend or to provide some input to the meeting, either in the form of ideas or implementation progress, or to support the effort in other ways.

Ensuring a non-hierarchical approach will very much depend on the culture and political issues within the organisation. If an ethos of equality in problem solving has genuinely been achieved there will be little difficulty with this aspect. However, experience of working within quality circles and other team-type environments suggests that hierarchy, of some sort, will very often emerge.

QUALITY CIRCLES INACTION

In the late 1970s a retail distributor with several hundred outlets decided to launch a service quality initiative to improve its performance in an increasingly competitive and over-supplied market. The organisation, apparently committed to this initiative at its head office, selected 'quality circles' as the driving mechanism to be used at the outlet level.

The senior management of the organisation at head office attended training sessions to learn the rules for quality circles and this training was then extended to the outlet managers themselves. After some time had elapsed, all of the training events had been completed and the programme was ready to be launched. Staff were informed by a letter to each outlet from the head office that the organisation was to adopt quality circles as a device for improving service quality. The letter further informed them that the local manager would be arranging these events. Other than the outlet managers, no one at the local level was provided with any training whatsoever.

The local managers then called the staff together – at the end of the working day – and informed them that the first meeting of the quality circle would take place at 5 p.m. the following Wednesday. Overtime would not be paid and all staff were expected to volunteer to join the circle. At the first meeting the rules would be explained and roles allocated within the circle.

The first meetings took place, at which the managers naturally took the role of chairperson and explained the purpose of the circles. The meetings were then thrown open to suggestions from the staff to improve service quality. Discussion in one outlet focused on the number of ashtrays in the customer facing areas – were there enough, not enough, too many? Another focused, perhaps quite usefully on the issue of opening hours, until the manager ruled the discussion 'out of order' since opening hours fell beyond the scope of the outlet to change – a constraint applied in many outlets and to many suggested discussion topics. In most cases, the manager's secretary recorded the discussion and produced minutes. The managers edited these and despatched the edited version to head office as evidence of the meetings having taken place.

While the organisation persisted with these events for around 12 months no significant or useful ideas emerged and were implemented across the organisation. No major changes took place in the organisation's systems and procedures which would improve service quality to either internal or external customers. The whole exercise was a waste – although it could be argued that awareness of quality of customer service was raised amongst the staff, perhaps bringing some intangible benefit.

There were perhaps four major mistakes made by the organisation in pursuing this quality circles initiative. First, the absolute lack of training for the staff involved. Second, the structure of the circles with managers appointed (or appointing themselves) as QC leaders thus maintaining the apparent hierarchy. Third, the attempt to achieve participation was by unilateral diktat or coercion, quite apart from the staff not being persuaded that there was a problem to solve. Fourth, was the failure by the senior management to understand the structure of the enterprise which they managed, a structure which, in effect, determined where problems could be solved. Any large retail organisation adopts standardised systems and procedures to ensure continuity and accuracy of service delivery across its outlets. Even in the 1970s these were increasingly tied to the capabilities of centralised computer networks. The operation of these networks controlled large parts of the customer facing activity, dictating what it was, or was not, possible to deliver. Changes proposed to these systems were ruled 'out of order' by managers, thereby closing off any possible communication to those running the organisation of the customer needs as perceived by the staff who actually dealt with those customers. What it was possible to change locally was the way in which individual staff members dealt with customers – a change which could not be created through the chosen mechanism.

This was a classic case of the senior management of the organisation appearing to 'blame' the staff for poor customer service, whilst blinding (or perhaps deafening) themselves to the potential for improvement which lay only within their own power.

Ishikawa suggests that quality circles should be an integral part of the quality effort, not an isolated approach. They have met with success and failure both in the West and in Japan. Bendell (1989: 19) comments that 'Even in Japan, many quality circles have collapsed, usually because of management's lack of interest or excessive intervention.' Both Crosby and Juran are stated to have questioned their effectiveness in the West and the experience outlined in 'Quality Circles Inaction' demonstrates some of the scope for failure. Crosby is reported to consider that quality circles are abused as a cure for poor employee motivation, productivity and quality, while Juran suggests that if an organisation's management are not trained in quality then quality circles will have limited effectiveness.

The quantitative techniques of Ishikawa's approach are referred to by Bendell as the 'seven tools of quality control' (Figure 8.3). Taken together they are a set of pictures of quality, representing in diagrammatic, or chart form, the quality status of the operation or process being reviewed. Ishikawa considered that all staff should be trained in these techniques. They will be fully discussed in chapter 22 as they have a useful role to play in managing quality.

This chapter will examine only the Ishikawa or fishbone diagram since this is the only technique that originated with Ishikawa. He developed the approach while at the University of Tokyo to explain relationships between factors. It subsequently became part of his quality tools portfolio and has been widely adopted throughout industry.

The Ishikawa diagram, figure 8.4, is essentially an end or goal oriented picture of a problem situation. The goal or objective is placed at the head of the fish and contributing factors categorised. Gilbert (1992: 111) suggests that major categories such as 'Men, Machines, Materials and Methods' may provide a useful first set of categories, each of these categories is then subdivided again, the 'fishbones' gaining further ribs and subribs as the whole issue of concern is explored. Other forms of categorisation such as

KAORU ISHIKAWA

Tool 1 *Pareto charts:*   used to identify the principal
                                      causes of problems.

Tool 2 *Ishikawa/fishbone diagrams:* charts of cause and effect in
                                      processes.

Tool 3 *Stratification:*   layer charts which place each set
                                      of data successively on top of the
                                      previous one.

Tool 4 *Check sheets:*   to provide a record of quality.

Tool 5 *Histograms:*   graphs used to display frequency
                                      of various ranges of values of a
                                      quantity.

Tool 6 *Scattergraphs:*   used to help determine whether
                                      there is a correlation between two
                                      factors.

Tool 7 *Control charts:*   Used as a device in Statistical
                                      Process Control.

Figure 8.3 **Seven tools of quality control: Kaoru Ishikawa**

processes, technology, knowledge or information systems may also be appropriate. The approach is also useful in enabling and encouraging participants to express their views.

The approach does not carry with it any automatic means of prioritisation of issues and ideas emerging are not constrained by any limitations. The pragmatic world of management however does impose constraints of issues such as time, technology and capital and these may affect the value of the approach. Issues emerging, which are not responded to adequately by those responsible will cause discontent, and perhaps, fragmentation of the quality effort. The diagram can easily be used as a device for apportioning blame instead of one for enabling improvement.

Summarising Ishikawa's approach it can be seen to contain both quantitative and qualitative aspects which taken together focus on achieving 'company-wide quality'.

8.4   SUCCESSES AND FAILURES

Ishikawa's world-wide status and the widespread acceptance of his ideas suggest that his approach has met with considerable success. That he is best known for the fishbone diagram should not inhibit appreciation of the value of his other works. Similarly, that quality circles have been successful cannot be doubted, notwithstanding the level of failure that has been seen in some organisations. An organisational idea such as quality circles,

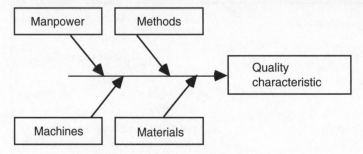

Figure 8.4 **The Ishikawa or 'fishbone' diagram**

which has been adopted to the extent that Bendell (1989: 19) reports – 'more than 10 million circle members' in Japan alone – has undoubtedly been a successful, useful idea.

Summarising from Flood (1993: 34–35) the strengths of Ishikawa's approach are:

- emphasis on participation;
- variety of quantitative and qualitative methods;
- a whole system view;
- QCC's are relevant to all sectors of the economy.

The main weaknesses can be viewed as:

- fishbone diagrams are systematic but not systemic;
- QCC's depend upon management support;
- there is a failure to address coercive contexts.

Looking first of all at the strengths, participation and the development of tools usable by the stakeholders are of undeniable value. They enable people at all levels in the organisation to make a meaningful contribution, in their own terms, to the process of achieving quality. Promoting creativity and increasing motivation have value both for the organisation and the individual.

The choice of a mixture of methods and tools which are both qualitative and quantitative is seen as encouraging a broader understanding of the organisation than would be achieved with a simple focus on either a single tool, or a purely qualitative or quantitative approach. The 'holistic' perspective proposed is again supported by the current view that a systemic approach is vital in the contemporary organisational context.

While agreeing that Quality Control Circles are relevant to all economic sectors, there remain considerable reservations as to their practical value. It is rare in the West to discover an organisation where more than 'lip-service' is paid to the QCC movement. It is very often used as a device for allowing workers to feel that they are involved but with little real commitment from managers. That is to say that the theory in practice is rarely as successful as the theory in theory!

Turning to the weaknesses, it is easy to concur with Flood's view that the 'causal chain' or linear view of problems proposed by the fishbone diagram is limited in its use. It would perhaps be better to recognise that problems are often interacting and far more complex than the fishbone approach will reveal.

The second weakness identified by Flood is the failure faced when management is not prepared to listen to the ideas emerging from quality circles, an aspect which has already been covered. In this case, the organisation is probably facing the third weakness, that the approach would struggle in a political or coercive context. The view has already been espoused that any human system is to some extent political and/or coercive and a particular tendency currently prevalent in the West is that of seeking 'someone to blame.' In a culture such as this, genuine commitment and participation in the quality issue is unlikely to emerge since it implies acceptance of responsibility for both successes and failures. In a 'blame' culture, wholehearted participation will not easily occur since failure is met with some form of disciplinary action or punishment rather than being treated as an opportunity to learn.

8.5 CRITICAL REVIEW

There seem to be three founding elements to Ishikawa's work; an attempt at a holistic view, participation and communication through a common language and simplicity of approach.

The first of these should be valued highly, as with the work of the other gurus, however, its use is limited by two failures. First, it does not take full account of interrelationships (the linear view of the fishbone diagram). Second, it fails to break down and work across organisational boundaries in any systemic sense, for example quality control circles are focused on a single area, or workshop, rather than being formed along interacting processes. These represent severe limitations of the approach in the contemporary context.

Participation is again highly valued and the idea of training everybody in the same tools, language and techniques is a sound method to encourage this. However, it again relies rather too heavily on a willingness to participate which is often not easily found. The third strand, simplicity, is criticised for ignoring the complexity and interrelationships of organisations.

The roots of Ishikawa's approach can be found in his early training and development as a chemist. That is a science which has traditionally been associated with a reductionist, 'scientific method', heavily reliant on analysis and fragmentation of problems. This is clearly carried across into the quality sphere with the use of simple analytical tools and the 'breaking down' of processes into manageable parts.

Similarly, and as with Feigenbaum, there does not emerge from Ishikawa's work an overarching methodology which binds together and integrates all of the different strands of his thinking. Thus, while many of the tools and techniques are useful in isolation there is no clear means of implementing an 'Ishikawa' programme.

This element may itself explain, to some degree, the failure of quality circles in so many organisations. They appear to stand alone as a device for quality improvement rather than being seen as one part of a complete process of management leading towards quality improvement. Taken in isolation they are almost certainly doomed to failure since the changes in management attitudes and the development of a common language and a common set of problem solving tools have not been developed to go with them.

Ishikawa appears to have taken account of developments in management thinking relating to people, what has been called the 'Human Relations' school, emerging in the West from the works of those such as Mayo, Maslow and Herzberg. However, he does not seem to have given recognition to other developments, such as the emergence of the systems approaches, for example organisational cybernetics, soft systems thinking and the variety of other tools. It is considered that recognition of these approaches would have enhanced and further enriched his already substantial contribution.

Finally, recognition must again be given to the multi-dimensional approach espoused by Ishikawa. Unlike Deming his methods are not predominantly quantitative (although he uses these methods widely) but incorporate a substantial qualitative element. Aspects such as attitudinal change, participation and communication are seen as vital elements in the management process.

Ishikawa's substantial contribution to the quality movement must be recognised although the lack of a clear methodology is an obvious weakness.

SUMMARY

This chapter has outlined the principal work of Kaoru Ishikawa through the five point critical review. Interested readers should refer to Ishikawa's own works to further develop their knowledge and understanding.

---

key learning points

KAORU ISHIKAWA

Definition of quality
quality of product, service, management, the company itself and the human being

Key beliefs
systemic approach, participation, communication

Principal methods
Seven tools of quality control, fishbone diagram, quality circles

QUESTION

Quality circles are Ishikawa's principal method for achieving participation. Critically evaluate quality circles in your own cultural context.

chapter nine

JOSEPH M. JURAN

the vital few, the useful many

Joseph M. Juran, 1988

INTRODUCTION

Joseph Juran is a naturalised American. He commenced his initial career as an engineer in 1924, subsequently working as an executive, civil servant, professor, arbitrator, director and management consultant. This strong professional background supported his first work in the quality field, the *Quality Control Handbook*, which is seen by some, for example Bendell (1989: 8), as having led to his international pre-eminence in the field of quality. Along with Deming, Juran worked extensively with the Japanese in the 1950s where the focus of his work was with middle and high ranking executives since he considers that 'quality control should be conducted as an integral part of management control' (ibid.).

He has received numerous awards for his work including, again like Deming, the 'Second Order of the Sacred Treasure' by the Emperor of Japan in recognition of his contribution to Japanese Quality Control and friendship with America.

Juran is described by Bendell (1989) as charismatic, by Bank (1992: 70) as 'perhaps the top Quality Guru', and by Logothetis (1992: 62) as having made 'the greatest contribution to the management literature of any quality professional'. Juran has published 12 books which have been translated into 13 languages. Perhaps the most relevant of these is the work entitled *Juran on Planning for Quality* (1988). This is seen as the definitive guide to his thinking on company wide quality planning.

9.1 PHILOSOPHY

Juran's philosophy is perhaps best summed up in the saying, cited by Logothetis (1992: 62) 'quality does not happen by accident, it has to be planned'. This is reflected in his structured approach to company wide quality planning, an aspect already met in the work of other gurus, for example Ishikawa and Feigenbaum. He is considered by Logothetis (1992) and Bendell (1989: 8) to emphasise management's responsibility for quality with Bendell (1989: 10) quoting him as saying that 'management controllable defects account for over 80% of the total quality problems'. The emphasis of his work is on 'planning, organisational issues, management's responsibility for quality and the need to set goals and targets for improvement' (Bendell: 1989: 8).

Juran's first two beliefs can be derived from this. First, that management are largely responsible for quality. Second, that quality cannot be consistently improved unless the improvement is planned.

Logothetis (1992: 64) considers another aspect to Juran's work – the avoidance of slogans and exhortations. He cites Juran's view that 'the recipe for action should consist of 90% substance and 10% exhortation, not the reverse!' Here can be seen Juran's third belief, that planned improvement must be specific and measurable. Logothetis sees in this aspect a 'formula for results' which consists of four elements:

- establish specific goals to be reached – identify what needs to be done, the specific projects that need to be tackled;
- establish plans for reaching the goals – provide a structured process for going from here to there;
- assign clear responsibility for meeting the goals;
- base the rewards on results achieved – feed back the information and utilise the lessons learned and the experience gained.

This approach indicates a clear reliance on quantitative methods, rather than any vague or 'woolly-minded' aspirations to higher quality, what Flood (1993: 19) refers to as Juran's concern that 'Quality has become too gimmicky, full of platitudes and supposed good intentions, but short on real substance.'

Juran's definition of quality constitutes another strand of his philosophy. He defines quality as 'fitness for use or purpose' (Bank, 1992: 71). Bank suggests that this is a more useful definition than 'conformance to specification' since a dangerous product could conform to all specifications but still be unfit for use. This may be compared with Crosby's definition of 'conformance to requirements'. It would probably be reasonable to assume that safety in use would be a requirement for Crosby – although he does not say so! The final important strand to Juran's thinking is in his trilogy of: quality planning, quality control and quality improvement (figure 9.1).

This essentially simple approach encapsulates the demand for substantial action inherent in all of Juran's work. Juran's emphasis in this respect is in

---

JOSEPH JURAN

- *Quality planning*:   determine quality goals; implementation planning; resource planning; express goals in quality terms: create the quality plan.

- *Quality control*:   monitor performance; compare objectives with achievements; act to reduce the gap.

- *Quality improvement*:   reduce waste; enhance logistics; improve employee morale; improve profitability; satisfy customers.

Figure 9.1 **The quality trilogy: Joseph M. Juran**

three areas: changing management behaviour through quality awareness, training and then spilling down new attitudes to supporting management levels. This top-down approach reflects Juran's belief that management is largely responsible for quality problems.

FLETCHER CHALLENGE STEEL, CHINA

Planning and Politics

In 1995, Fletcher Challenge Steel formed a joint venture with Datong City Government in China – Fletcher Challenge Steel, China – to upgrade the Datong iron making plant and build a new melt shop to melt and cast steel billets. The team from Fletcher Challenge had created a plan for the venture involving increases in both volume and quality of output and reductions in manning levels. Making a significant investment in new equipment, the overall aim was to achieve levels of performance comparable to Western mills. Fletcher Challenge had previously undertaken best practice studies and were successfully implementing performance improvements in their domestic steel operations in New Zealand.

Following the formation of the joint-venture company a management team was appointed composed of some of the established local Chinese managers, the project team from New Zealand and selected new appointees with Chinese origins but Western technical education and knowledge. It was recognised right from the outset that cultural barriers to success would exist and that effective communication would be vital. In part, this communication was seen to rest on common language and shared cultural background.

In 1997, well behind the planned timescale, the plant began to approach the levels of output performance necessary to be self-supporting in the long run and to justify the substantial investment made in it by Fletcher Challenge. The initial financial investment consisted of US$25 million, but this was supported by a substantial investment of personal credibility by Fletcher Steel Chief Executive, Mike Smith. Smith, an Englishman, had persuaded the group board of Fletcher Challenge to make the investment and despite his success in the New Zealand plants could not afford to have this venture fail.

The delays in achieving the planned performance improvements did not result from poor technical planning but from an inadequate appreciation of the political difficulties and resistance that would be met from the Chinese partners. The local managers were suddenly faced with both technical and managerial challenges to the ways in which they had been accustomed to run their business. Such challenges alone are often sufficient to inhibit any change programme. When those challenges are reinforced by cultural and language differences between the parties then significant problems are almost inevitable. Equally, the plans were externally derived. The local established management were not involved in the planning process, rather the results of that process were presented to them, a factor which would further inhibit acceptance – particularly when the standards of performance proposed were considered unachievable as they were outside the scope of local experience. These factors combined to generate significant internal resistance to the implementation of the plans and, without the commitment of the local senior management, workforce acceptance was also inhibited.

Despite the technical successes, the 'political' battles continue. The final outcome is awaited with interest.

Summarising Juran's philosophy five key beliefs can be identified:

- management is largely responsible for quality;
- quality can only be improved through planning;
- plans and objectives must be specific and measurable;
- training is essential and starts at the top;
- three step process of planning, control and action.

9.2   ASSUMPTIONS

The assumptions about the world which seem to underpin Juran's approach are discussed below.

The first point to be examined is Juran's assumption, along with Deming, that there is a quality crisis. It is certainly the case that consumers' expectations of products and services have increased and there is a lower tolerance of faults than was once the case. We all expect our watches to keep time, our cars to start every day and that services will be reliably and consistently provided.

There are at least three potential views of the quality problem. First, it could be argued that the Quality Gurus 'created' the quality crisis by raising awareness of the quality issue, focusing attention on the negative aspects and driving up consumer expectations which in turn has forced producers and providers to improve. A second argument is that awareness of the costs of poor quality amongst providers and producers increased, leading managements to focus their attention on improving quality which then became a virtue for their product (and bottom line!). A third view is that consumers have driven the quality movement through increasing expectations and an unwillingness to tolerate defective or shoddy goods and services.

The truth probably lies in a combination of all of these arguments with interrelationships between the factors being the driving force. This moves the quality argument away from the linear view of the world, seen in Crosby and Ishikawa, towards a more holistic approach.

Looking at wider issues it can certainly be argued that in the world of relatively mature consumer markets which was evident in Europe and North America in the 1980s, and increasing industrialisation of the Asia-Pacific region, the substantial growth in availability of goods and services was sure to lead to a focus on performance. Thus poor quality represented a major threat to organisational survival. Achievement of quality became not an ideal to aim for but, like profit, a fundamental requirement for staying in business.

To argue that there was a 'quality crisis' implies a decline in quality, it is considered more likely that there was an increase in expectations. As has often been said 'if we can put a man on the moon, why can't we make a toaster that works?'

A second assumption is that both management of the organisation and quality are processes. This idea has considerable appeal. Management is often thought of as a set of discrete, separate activities, but this view is rather narrow and simplistic. To recognise that management is a process, with all actions and decisions interacting with all others is a much broader and perhaps more realistic view. There can be little argument with Juran in this respect especially as much current thinking in management revolves around the ideas of organising ventures on process lines and on 're-engineering' those processes.

A third assumption is of the potential for continuous improvement, this has already been addressed in the sections on Deming and Ishikawa. Briefly reiterating, continuous improvement is a reasonable view in a continuous world; however, when change becomes discontinuous such an approach loses its value.

The fourth and final assumption to be examined is that relating to quantification. Juran's work focuses very clearly on measurement and specific objectives. Again, as with other gurus, the validity of this approach must be questioned. Many aspects of quality, particularly in the service sector, are difficult to accurately and reliably quantify. Significantly, some aspects are outside the control of the organisation providing the service. This leads us to two problems. The first is the tendency to measure those aspects which are easily accessible, rather than those which are most important. The second is how to measure individual customer expectations, expectations which may vary each time the service is purchased. The normal route here is to provide a standard service and educate the customer to understand what they can expect. A different, and rather more difficult route, is to adapt the service to meet individual expectations.

There is a clear bias in the use of quantitative methods which can be considered to arise for Juran in the industrial/manufacturing base to the greater part of his work. This perhaps provides a certain limitation on the application of his ideas in the service sector.

9.3 METHODS

While Juran's 'quality trilogy' of Planning, Control, Improvement, offers the guideline to his approach, his overarching methodology for achieving quality is the 'quality planning road map' (Bendell 1989: 9). Recognising both external and internal customers, the 'road map' (figure 9.2) offers a nine step guide. These steps will be briefly reviewed in turn.

The first two steps refer not just to external customers but also to the customers of processes within the organisation. This is normally seen as identifying the single next step in the process, although it might be thought that a more useful view is to identify the whole chain and all of the inter-relationships. It could be the case that a particular feature of a product is of no significance to the immediate customer but has enormous impact for one at a later stage of the process. It is therefore important to recognise and take account of the requirements of all possible customers in the chain.

The third step is really about effective communication. A package of requirements that is expressed in a language unknown or unfamiliar to the

---

JOSEPH M. JURAN

Step 1 Identify who are the customers.

Step 2 Determine the needs of those customers.

Step 3 Translate those needs into our language [the language of the organisation].

Step 4 Develop a product that can respond to those needs.

Step 5 Optimise the product features so as to meet our [the company's] needs as well as customers needs.

Step 6 Develop a process which is able to produce the product.

Step 7 Optimise the process.

Step 8 Prove that the process can produce the product under operating conditions.

Step 9 Transfer the process to operations.

Figure 9.2 **The quality planning road map: Joseph M. Juran**

people in the organisation will be of no help. Obvious examples of this are converting words in general or common usage, the customer's language, into the specific technical 'jargon' of the organisation. Less obvious are internal requirements. Here it is important that the requirements are expressed in terms meaningful to the working group involved, for example, a condition expressed in the language of accounting to meet a particular budget in terms of profit and loss may be meaningless to a group of engineers. It is essential that their 'budget' be expressed in relevant terms such as required throughput, machine utilisation, or levels of waste.

Developing a product that responds to customer needs takes the quality issue back to its most fundamental aspect – building quality in rather than inspecting defects out. This is one aspect where other gurus agree. It is better and cheaper to establish quality from the outset than to engage in rectification. Optimising the product to meet the organisation's or department's needs as well as those of the customer should ideally be seen as a constraint on the development process of the previous step rather than as a separate issue. It is, or should be, a design constraint that the product meets these requirements simultaneously.

The development, optimisation and testing of a production process, making it operational, is an area that historically has received little attention. Consulting experience has shown that often products have been developed by the research and development staff then simply handed over to the production staff with the instruction to make it. More recently many companies are taking account of manufacturing requirements in the development process. Ease of manufacture is becoming accepted as a design constraint.

The final point is to transfer the process to operations. Again, historically this has been done very badly and there is no argument with Juran's proposal. A useful device to assist with this aspect, and something which is being adopted by many companies, is to create teams for product development which include operational staff and managers. If the idea of designing for manufacture is adopted, then this step becomes very straightforward.

Supporting this fundamental approach to designing quality in to the systems and processes is what Bank (1992: 70) refers to as Juran's 'ten steps' to continuous quality improvement (see figure 9.3). Here it can be seen how Juran's philosophy is carried across into practice. The first step begins to establish a quality oriented culture in the organisation through the process of raising awareness of the need and scope – a qualitative approach. The second is quantitative, establishing objectives – goals – for improvement. The third step is an attempt to institutionalise quality, to embed the quality process in the management process so that it becomes an ingrained part of the organisation.

The fourth step takes the organisation forward to train the entire staff. This is seen as helping to make quality an integral part of everyone's thinking.

The fifth and sixth steps 'carry out projects,' and 'report progress', recognise that while continuous improvement is the objective, it must be

JOSEPH M. JURAN

Step 1   Create awareness of the need and opportunity for quality improvement.

Step 2   Set goals for continuous improvement.

Step 3   Build an organisation to achieve goals by establishing a quality council, identifying problems, selecting a project, appointing teams and choosing facilitators.

Step 4   Give everyone training.

Step 5   Carry out projects to solve problems.

Step 6   Report progress.

Step 7   Show recognition.

Step 8   Communicate results.

Step 9   Keep a record of successes.

Step 10   Incorporate annual improvements into the company's regular systems and processes and thereby maintain momentum.

Figure 9.3 **Ten steps to continuous quality improvement: Joseph M. Juran**

achieved within visible and measurable elements. The reporting process is seen as enabling experience and learning to be shared and to allow those involved to share their sense of achievement. This also allows the seventh step, 'show recognition', to be actioned. The sixth and eighth steps are linked, 'communicate results' being a call to share the successes (and failures) throughout the organisation.

The ninth step, keeping a record, is again an aid to organisational learning. A record may be thought of as an organisational 'memory' to which reference can be made in the future. While Juran suggests that this record should be of successes, it is arguably just as important to memorise strategies and schemes that do not work as those that do. This may enable the organisation to avoid those forms of behaviour in the future.

The tenth step is a corporate level and public commitment to the achievement of higher quality. This should be seen as reaffirming the quality process in the minds of both employees and customers.

Juran shows awareness of the phenomenon of resistance to change which is so common in organisations. Logothetis (1992: 75) reports Juran's belief that 'resistance to a technological change is due to social and cultural factors'. Juran proposes two principal methods for dealing with this. First, he considers that all those affected by the change should be 'allowed to participate' (1988), second that 'adequate time should be allowed for the change to be accepted'. These approaches are seen as providing an opportunity for evaluation and experimentation, promoting ownership of the changes and helping to overcome resistance.

Underpinning the two processes outlined above – 'the road map' and the 'ten steps' – Juran uses a variety of statistical methods. Like Deming, Juran studied under Shewhart and so shares many of the same approaches, for example control charts. Perhaps one of the best known of his approaches is using Pareto analysis to help separate the 'vital few' problems from the 'useful many'. Pareto analysis is included in chapter 22.

9.4   SUCCESSES AND FAILURES

Like the other gurus, it must be accepted that Juran has been hugely successful in developing and promoting his ideas. That his books have been translated into thirteen languages and his ideas accepted and exploited by so many organisations and in so many different countries is a measure of the perceived value of his contribution. However, the work has not been universally applied and can be seen to be less effective in the service sector than in manufacturing.

Adapting from Flood (1993: 21–22) the strengths of Juran's approach are:

* concentration on genuine issues of management practice;
* a new understanding of the customer, referring to both internal and external customers;
* management involvement and commitment;

The main weaknesses are perceived as:

* the literature on motivation and leadership is not addressed;
* workers' contributions are underrated;
* methods are traditional, failing to address culture and politics.

It can be added to these criticisms that the body of systems knowledge, and in particular management and organisational cybernetics, which could have enhanced and enriched Juran's approach, has, like human relations theory, been largely ignored.

The first strength identified is one with which most people would agree, although a programme which fails to motivate and develop the majority of the workforce, is one which may well be seen as consisting of 'hype'.

The second strength, that of recognising other parts of the organisation as customers, is again welcome. Readers will recall that this can also be found in the work of Deming.

The third strength is management commitment and involvement. This is not simply because by Juran's measure, 80 per cent of the total quality problem resides there, but also because the power, control and leadership reside there. A management which is seen by the workforce to be committed to quality will 'breed' a quality ethos for the organisation. Workers wishing to progress and be content within a quality oriented environment will probably emulate the behaviour and attitudes of their managers. If this occurs then the quality ethos will tend to spill down through the organisation over time.

Turning to the weaknesses, Flood's understanding that Juran fails to adequately incorporate theories of motivation and leadership is accepted. However, Juran is a practitioner, he deals best with the practice of quality, rather than the theory. It might be suggested that the second statement of weakness, that Juran undervalues the contribution of the worker, is countered to some extent by the explicit incorporation of participation. This was shown in the previous section.

Flood further suggests that Juran emphasises a somewhat 'mechanistic' view of the organisation although he does take account of the organisation's environment, that is, of the customers. The view is largely evident in the unstated assumption that what is good for the organisation – higher quality – is also good for the individual. This perhaps reflects the thinking of the early management theorists such as Taylor, Weber and Fayol. In the contemporary world of 'knowledge workers', high-technology equipment and increasing emphasis on human rights, quite often what is good for the organisation may appear to be bad for the workers. This applies to both the short and long term views. A company operating in the face of maturing or mature markets and not positioned to exploit emerging markets, with fresh, lower cost base competitors from newly industrialising countries may be unable to absorb spare capacity through growth. This leads to the need, to use the politically correct terminology, to 'retrench' workers.

The interests of the organisation and the individual worker may come into direct conflict. The organisation wishes to improve quality to preserve and protect its customer base, to reduce its costs and ensure its survival. The workers may recognise that these same attributes can have different consequences for them, for example, job losses, pay freezes, reductions in overtime, loss of other benefits. Often it can lead to 'deskilling' of jobs and the loss of craft skills in which individuals take great, and justifiable, pride. There is then little incentive for the workforce to contribute to the quality programme if a successful outcome for the company threatens their own – short term – sense of security. They may well seek to preserve their position in the short term while accepting the inevitable longer term threat. Events in France and Germany during 1997 perhaps give this point extra emphasis. Compared with the UK, organisations in those nations had undertaken little by way of radical change and restructuring. Despite the emergent threat to jobs in those economies arising from high costs, questionable productivity and overseas competition, the workers, as represented by the unions, were strongly resisting change. The appeal for participation must deal with issues of this type if it is to have any hope of success. Juran offers little in this regard.

9.5   CRITICAL REVIEW

The founding idea of Juran's work might almost be called 'Design and Build'. His approach stresses planning as the fundamental requirement for quality, followed by action. This orientation towards the setting and achievement of objectives perhaps reflects Juran's engineering and statistical background.

The 'Quality Trilogy', 'Quality Road Map,' and 'Ten Steps to Quality' may all be considered as systematic, somewhat mechanistic, approaches. While Juran established a new understanding of customers (the internal and external), he does not explicitly recognise the importance of the inter-dependence of processes and the interactions between people within the organisation. This prevents his systematic approach from becoming systemic. Juran seems to be making the assumption that improvement in the individual parts will necessarily improve the whole organisation, a view which is challenged by the systems thinking community.

With regard to management, two issues should be stressed. First, that Juran views management as a process. Second, that he sees management as responsible for quality, having control of 80 per cent of the problems. Dealing with the first of these, Juran's view is to be welcomed. An organ-isation which recognises that every action and decision is inextricably linked with every other in a continuous process of management must be considered to be on the verge of a breakthrough in its behaviour. Even today management in many organisations is fragmented into pseudo-independent functions: marketing is separate from finance which is in turn separate from production and so on. Each of these units attempts to fulfil its own functions independently from the others. Similarly, even within departments, tasks are often seen as independent, rather than inter-dependent. For example, recruitment is often seen as a separate function within the personnel or human resource function, having no relationship with training and development and, crucially, no relationship with the units where those recruited will work. In this sort of organisation it is not surprising that there are conflicts, disputes and difficulties in matching people to tasks. A more holistic integrated and interdependent 'process' view is essential. It may be considered that while Juran moves towards this approach, he does not go far enough.

Turning now to the second issue, management responsibility, perhaps the question that should be asked is: why 80 per cent? Deming, for example, has provided statistics suggesting that the figure is 94 per cent, while Crosby's work may be interpreted as suggesting that the bulk of the responsibility lies with the workers. An argument can be proposed whereby management take complete responsibility for quality. If, as Fayol (1916) suggests, it is the responsibility of management to 'Plan, Organise, Command, Control and Co-ordinate', then responsibility should lie with them. The argument is this: management are expected to have control of every aspect of the organisation:

- what is done;
- how it is done;
- when it is done;
- where it is done;
- who does it;
- why it is done.

This suggests that there ought to be nothing internal to the organisation which it is beyond the scope of management to address. Random errors in production for example might be eradicable through changes in design or process such that it becomes impossible to incorrectly assemble a part. Human error might be eradicable through training, adjustment of work rates, increases (or reductions!) in relaxation time or a range of other variables which could be altered to enable improved performance.

It is suggested that the ultimate responsibility for quality should rest with all those who are involved in the production of a good or a service, that is, every employee within every part and function of the organisation. However, the power to achieve higher quality rests in the hands of those who have authority (power) to change things. If that power is in the hands of the management alone, then they have full responsibility. If on the other hand the power is shared throughout the organisation, perhaps through empowerment schemes, quality circles and other participative approaches, then everyone who shares in that power is responsible.

The strong emphasis by Juran on management responsibility fails to adequately address the needs and aspirations of workers. He does not properly take into account the contribution that they can make to the achievement of quality, nor does he provide mechanisms through which this can be done.

Finally, the issue must again be raised of the applicability of Juran's work. It seems to be most suitable for the industrial and manufacturing sectors. It is suggested that it has limited application in service organisations since it does not adequately deal with human issues.

SUMMARY

This chapter has reviewed the major contribution made to the quality movement by Juran. Students should refer to Juran's (1988) own work to further inform and develop their views.

key learning points

JOSEPH M. JURAN

Definition of quality
fitness for use or purpose

Key beliefs
management responsibility, planning, measurability, training, process

Principal methods
company-wide quality control, the quality road map, the ten steps to quality improvement

QUESTION

Juran defines quality as 'fitness for use or purpose'. Critically evaluate this definition.

chapter

ten

JOHN S. OAKLAND

TQM starts at the top.
                    John S. Oakland, 1993

INTRODUCTION

John Oakland was until recently Professor of Total Quality Management and Head of the European Centre for TQM at the University of Bradford Management Centre. Oakland is considered by many as the British guru of quality. His current practice, Oakland Consulting plc, is internationally based and he has provided substantial support to the development of quality in the UK, particularly to the quality initiatives of the government.

Oakland's early industrial career focused on research and development and production management. He holds a Ph.D., is a Chartered Chemist, Member of the Royal Society of Chemistry, Fellow of the Royal Statistical Society, Fellow of the Association of Quality Management Consultants, Fellow of the Institute of Quality Assurance and Member of the American Society of Quality Control.

The approaches used by Oakland and his colleagues in Oakland Consulting plc are essentially pragmatic and are understood to have been used in thousands of organisations.

10.1 PHILOSOPHY

The philosophy underpinning Oakland's view of quality is perhaps best shown in the emphasis he places on its importance, saying:

We cannot avoid seeing how quality has developed into the most important competitive weapon, and many organisations have realised that TQM is *the* [sic] way of managing for the future.

(Oakland, 1993: Preface)

Through this statement Oakland gives absolute primacy to the pursuit of quality as the cornerstone of organisational success. While it can be agreed that organisations which do not achieve quality in the contemporary environment will probably fail in the long term, it is more difficult to accept the concept of its absolute primacy. Although quality has strategic implications (as discussed in chapter 2) and is a strategic issue, it cannot be accepted that it is the *only* strategic issue.

The concept of TQM as the way of managing for the future on the other hand does have considerable value. If TQM is thought of as a way of managing (as seen with Feigenbaum's work) rather than an added extra, then other management philosophies, methods and tools must be subsumed within it. This idea reinforces Oakland's view that 'quality starts at the top', with quality parameters inherent in every organisational decision. He emphasises seven key characteristics of pursuing TQM (see figure 10.1).

JOHN S. OAKLAND

1 Quality is meeting the customers' requirements.

2 Most quality problems are inter-departmental.

3 Quality control is monitoring, finding and eliminating causes of quality problems.

4 Quality assurance rests on prevention, management systems, effective audit and review.

5 Quality must be managed, it does not just happen.

6 Focus on prevention not cure.

7 Reliability is an extension of quality and enables us to 'delight the customer'.

Figure 10.1 **Seven key characteristics of TQM: John S. Oakland**

First, is Oakland's definition of quality. This definition is simple and very hard to disagree with as it emphasises that quality is a characteristic or attribute defined by the customer, not the supplier. Oakland also stresses the importance of the quality chain. He emphasises the internal supplier–customer relationships, stressing in the second characteristic that most problems are inter-departmental – that is, they occur at the interface between steps in a process.

The third and fourth characteristics emphasise the purposes of quality control (QC) and quality assurance (QA). These definitions move the focus away from criticism and blame often associated with these mechanisms and towards the reason they need to be carried out, which is quite simply to improve quality performance. All too often the QC and QA functions in organisations become self-serving activities, focusing on apportioning blame and identifying guilty parties rather than on improving the performance of the organisation. Because of this they frequently fall into disrepute and become disregarded by the operational personnel – who focus in turn on not getting caught rather than on not failing.

The fifth and sixth characteristics focus on the pro-active nature of the quality drive. The statement that 'quality must be managed, it does not just happen' and reflecting Juran's suggestion that 'quality must be planned', sharpens the recognition that quality is not accidental, or achieved through reactive measures. Quality for Oakland, that is, meeting customer requirements, must be a parameter of every decision made within the organisation, whether operational, administrative or strategic. Quality must then be inherent in management thinking, which in turn means that it must be part of the norms of the organisation. This view is supported by the sixth characteristic of prevention not cure. Oakland suggests that one-third of all organisational efforts are wasted in error based activity, for example rework, rectification, inspection and so on, with an even higher proportion in service based organisations. Working from experience, these proportions are difficult to argue with and in some cases represent an underestimate. If quality can be achieved at the outset, rather than through detection and rectification the total costs of the organisation will always be reduced. The limitation to achieving this arises very often from the functionally based budgeting common in organisations where each budget responsible manager seeks to reduce his or her own short term, that is current period, costs with no regard to the effect in other parts of the organisation.

The final characteristic deals with quality as more than a momentary attribute. Reliability has two dimensions which are related to the nature of the product itself. The first is reliability in use and relates to durable products such as cars, domestic appliances, watches and so on. In this case, what 'delights the customer' is enjoying the uninterrupted use of the product, other than for routine, service based maintenance. A motor car which breaks down will not delight the customer, regardless of how it met the quality criteria upon delivery. The customer requirement is to be able to turn the key and make a journey without fear of non-completion. Services require a different form of reliability, that is consistency. This means that each time the service is delivered it must meet the customer requirements. In this context, reliability means consistency and to achieve consistency of service means there must be consistency and reliability of the delivery process.

Quality is considered by Oakland then to be an organisation wide and fundamental requirement, driven by top management commitment and created through reliable, consistent organisational processes.

10.2   ASSUMPTIONS

The assumptions about the world that seem to underpin Oakland's approach will now be considered.

The first assumption which Oakland makes is that quality is the only issue for organisational survival. While this may be true of some organisations in fully developed, highly competitive and mature economies (those in which Oakland predominantly operates) it is certainly not true of all. Some organisations will succeed (at least in the short to medium term) because they have established such market dominance (and perhaps customer reliance) that the issue of quality simply does not arise. Customers buy the products or services through lack of an alternative rather than through choice. For example, the majority of personal computer users purchase Microsoft operating system compatible software, not necessarily because it does exactly what they require, but because it is what is readily available – and works with their Microsoft based operating systems. With banking and other financial services providers, until very recently, the issue of customer choice did not arise – the products, services and costs were all substantially undifferentiated. When one supplier is as good or as bad as every other the product or service becomes a commodity and choice ceases to be a meaningful word. In other contexts, the sophistication of consumers and state of development of the market still means that providers of goods or services can predominantly focus on their own requirements, not those of the customers. Other suppliers enjoy state sponsored or supported supply positions and as such, quality is not a concern for them – the consumer again has no choice. Oakland's first assumption can be challenged then on the grounds that while perhaps correct as a matter of value, the constraint does not apply across global markets.

The second assumption, that quality must be driven from the top carries complete support. Unless this commitment is achieved at the outset of a quality programme and maintained at a high level of enthusiasm, the initiative will fail.

The third assumption is that errors can always be prevented, through planning, design and effective processes. This is probably true, but requires a substantial shift in the traditional mindset of those in the organisation, and a full appreciation of the soft issues particularly in service based organisations. As has been mentioned before, while the process operation can be designed to operate in an error free way, the actual minute by minute delivery of service depends very largely on the personal interaction between customer and supplier. However robust the technical process may be, there is always scope for error to arise in this context. No standard form of words can cater for the vagaries of mood, sense and interpretation which influence the outcome of such transactions and determine whether customer requirements are met – Oakland's measure of quality.

The fourth assumption is that quality is an organisation-wide issue. This is in common with Flood's call for quality 'across all functions and all levels' and again cannot be argued with. Quality must pervade the whole organisational atmosphere. This suggests that Oakland's approach is systemic. While he makes no direct reference in his work to the systemic approaches to management, there is a systemic as well as systematic attitude reflected in his approach.

Finally, Oakland assumes the involvement of all people through communication, teamwork and participation, in other words through redeveloping the culture of the organisation. This view is again supported and reflects the systemic nature of his approach.

10.3   METHODS

While Oakland quite rightly capitalises on the many well established methods, tools and techniques for achieving quality he does offer his own overarching approach for TQM and some new insight. The overarching method is his 'ten points for senior management' (figure 10.2). Oakland represents the major features of this in his 'Total Quality Management model', figure 10.3.

Unlike some of the other gurus, Oakland focuses on the total process of achieving a TQM organisation without relying inordinately on either qualitative or quantitative aspects. He recognises that both are necessary and, if anything, is slightly biased towards softer aspects as the initial drivers of quality.

JOHN S. OAKLAND

Point 1   Long term commitment;

Point 2   Change the culture to 'right first time';

Point 3   Train the people to understand the 'customer–supplier relationship;

Point 4   Buy products and services on *total cost* (*sic*);

Point 5   Recognise that systems improvement must be managed;

Point 6   Adopt modern methods of supervision and training and eliminate fear;

Point 7   Eliminate barriers, manage processes, improve communications and teamwork;

Point 8   Eliminate, arbitrary goals, standards based only on numbers, barriers to pride of workmanship, fiction (use the correct tools to establish facts);

Point 9   Constantly educate and retrain the in house experts;

Point 10 Utilise a systematic approach to TQM implementation.

Figure 10.2 **Ten points for senior management: John S. Oakland**

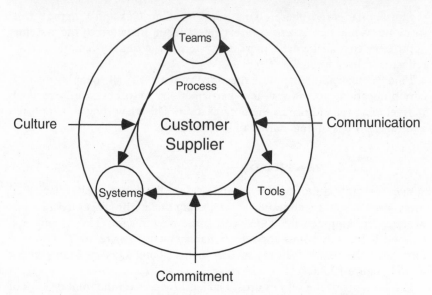

Figure 10.3 **Total Quality Management model: John S. Oakland**
Source: **Adapted from Oakland, 1993**

The ten point process begins with the absolute commitment of senior and middle management to constant improvement. Oakland suggests that the quality process must start in the boardroom. Adoption of quality at that level is fundamental to its achievement since it is then a normative decision – a decision about the sort of behaviour that is desired. Unfortunately, this is rather more difficult to achieve in practice than is recognised. The senior management may say that they are committed to quality, but unless they change their behaviour (that is, the decisions they make, the things they say and do, the ways in which they measure and reward performance) then the commitment is not genuine. This will soon be detected at other levels within the organisation.

THE HONG KONG POLICE FORCE

(Formerly The Royal Hong Kong Police Force)

In March 1995 the Commissioner of the Royal Hong Kong Police Force (an organisation consisting of some 40,000 personnel) publicly announced his strategy for the introduction of a service quality approach to meet the need for change in the culture and work attitudes within the force. At that time there was no clear driver for change, but the force recognised the need for this initiative to meet the challenges ahead, and before it was forced upon it. The programme gives equal focus to internal customers and external customer relationships.

The envisaged change is being implemented in a 'step-by-step' approach and it is anticipated that the development and implementation of the strategy will take at least five years, probably longer. This process has been nominally structured into five phases:

- awareness;
- understanding;
- favour;
- involvement;
- commitment.

Early work focused on generating an understanding of the kinds of changes that were planned. Activities included a road-show for middle to senior level management, a video presentation for viewing by all personnel, publication of the strategy in various internal communications media, development of performance pledges (for the public) and internal service level agreements (for internal customer interactions), the encouragement of voluntary work improvement teams in the work environment and the commissioning of the first of a series of regular public opinion surveys.

However, although the project team assigned to undertake all these activities was reasonably clear as to its objectives, there was a perceived lack of expertise in knowing exactly how to achieve them. The team was also driving these changes from too far down the organisational 'food chain' and the lack of commitment from senior management was seen as a threat to success. It was at this stage, in November 1995, that assistance was sought from a management consultancy.

After an initial scoping study, the consultants recommended refocusing the project team's efforts away from the customer interface towards a more holistic approach. This entailed a more detailed examination of the overall purpose of the organisation and how it was going to set about achieving this, and that this process needed to commence at the very top of the organisation.

Until the advent of the consultancy, the project team's activities and proposals for change lacked credibility. Overnight, senior management were confronted with arguments that they could not refute and, quickly, decisions were made and commitments pledged to a broad front of force-wide changes. The key thrust for these changes was to develop a corporate vision and mission which was to be entitled the Force Vision and Statement of Common Purpose and Values.

From the outset it was recognised that the force would be undertaking a process of change requiring a strong sense of direction provided by solid organisation vision, mission and values. To this end the Commissioner and his senior management team attended a series of workshops, facilitated by the consultants, to identify the themes and elements of the Force Vision and Statement of Common Purpose and Values.

The outcome of this workshop has been further refined by a team of middle level managers broadly representative of the myriad of functional areas within the force. The result was a draft document ready for a consultation process designed to underscore force management commitment to the change process in an unprecedented and structured communications approach. This was to be undertaken by way of discussion groups, rather than using the more traditional paper exercise.

Each member of the force from Chief Superintendent down attended a discussion group run by one of their managers, assisted by a consultation pack and a discussion guide. This was seen as a new approach, designed to involve and commit commanders at all levels to visibly seek genuine feedback from their staff. Over 1,400 such discussion groups were held.

The results of this consultation were made available to force management, and the Commissioner and his management team attended further workshops to consider the feedback and agree on the final version of the statement.

At these workshops the first steps towards developing formal strategic directions for the force were also outlined. The finalised statement was launched at the Force Open Day on 7 December 1996, and widespread publicity of the document followed. The process from inception to launch took just over one year. This signals not the end of the exercise, but completion of the first stage. The next phase is probably the more important: that is, the introduction of a strategy to give life to the vision, common purpose and shared values that all have agreed to. This is now being undertaken through a programme called Living-the-Values with the intention of preparing senior managers for the change in culture and attitudes that will need to follow on from the launch of the statement, and then cascading this message down through the organisation to the constable on the beat.

Following on from the strategic workshops held in connection with the Vision and Statement of Common Purpose and Values, the consultants have facilitated similar workshops for each of the force departments with a view to drawing up Departmental Strategic Direction Plans. Once all departments have been through this process, the various departmental plans will be incorporated into the Force Strategic Directions Document.

Finally, it is worth clearly stating that it is not intended that the force lift a TQM package from a shelf – there is no cookbook which tells us how to do it. There are plenty of success stories and there are plenty of examples of what not to do – the force will consider adopting only those things which should support, as the Commissioner has said, 'Our pursuit of excellence in providing a service of quality'.

The second point, spilling out of the first is to change the culture of the organisation at all levels to focus on 'right first time'. Oakland sees this as based on awareness of customer needs and teamwork, enabled by participation and use of the 'EPDCA helix'. This is a more dynamic representation of the Deming cycle already seen with explicit recognition of the need for evaluation before planning. There is much else required in a cultural change as is implied in the ideas of teamwork, participation and customer needs.

The third point represents the orientation of the organisation, through training, towards customer–supplier relationships – both externally and internally. Oakland suggests this must be achieved for everyone. This is a particularly difficult area which will meet with much resistance in many organisations. This is especially so where the staff of a particular process or function are traditionally poorly regarded, where there is functional organisation design or a major difference of perceived relative expertise with the customer regarded by the supplier as being of a 'lower order'. This is a particular concern in organisations which employ highly qualified professional staff for certain processes and these interact with 'customers' whose perceived level of professionalism is much lower, for example, medical doctors and nursing assistants or porters; chefs and kitchen assistants or waiters/waitresses.

Point four moves away from the culturally oriented changes to examine cost. Here Oakland recognises, like Deming, that purchase price is not the sole determinant of the cost of any input. He calls for continuous improvement in everything to reduce the total cost of doing business, that is, the higher initial cost of a purchase may be more than outweighed by its reduced lifetime cost to the organisation – its cost including running costs and depreciation over time. For example a stainless steel machine may be initially more expensive than its mild steel equivalent, but if the maintenance and running cost is significantly lower, the total cost may be less over time.

Point five examines the systems used to manage the organisation and calls for them to be actively managed to achieve improvement. While this may seem like common sense, it is an often neglected area.

Point six calls for modern methods of supervision and training. This recognises that many traditional supervision and training approaches no longer have great value in organisations. These were very often sterile, having no relationship to the particular job undertaken and not being reflected in individual performance expectations. Similarly the 'kick butt and take names', militaristic approach to performance management is not applicable in a more enlightened environment and is particularly foolish in an economic context of full or near full employment.

Point seven calls for organisations to be managed along processes rather than up and down functional silos. While many process based organisations have already achieved this, it is still the case that significant numbers adopt functional specialisms as the basis of organisation. In these cases, there remain many hand-offs (breaks within processes) which extend the range of customer–supplier relationships and create opportunities for the buck to be passed. In the process the consumer (the ultimate customer) is often forgotten. If the organisation is process based this tends not to happen and communication and teamwork can be encouraged around the process flow since all parties can visualise and share the team objective(s).

Point eight could be called the elimination round. Here Oakland again reflects the ideas of others. He wishes to see arbitrary goals eliminated – it is useless to call for improvement without supplying the facilities necessary for those goals to be achieved and without a formal basis for evaluation. He wants an end to standards based only on numbers, that is on volumes. Purely volume based output measures will always lead to quality problems. As a minimum it is essential to measure quality performance as well – and to recognise that this may mean a lesser initial output – but that the output received should all be perfect! His third requirement is to eradicate barriers to pride of workmanship. Apart from purely measuring output volume (which is one barrier) this means the design and redesign of jobs as suggested in other parts of the literature to enable the particular worker to have pride in the completion of a meaningful task. Lastly, he calls for reliance on facts not fiction, proposing costs of quality and level of firefighting as measures of internal health. The important characteristic here is to recognise measurements that are both meaningful and factual – that is, numbers which cannot be manipulated to present a particular picture. While doctors bury their mistakes, managers frequently recategorise theirs, even to the extent in one factory of 'making for reject to maintain production efficiency'. The particular factory supplied excess or sub-standard output in alternative packaging to a secondary market and repackaged and labelled perfect goods to meet the needs of this secondary market. This was despite their inability to recover more than raw material costs from the purchaser. That secondary purchaser consequently made greater unit profit than the major and highly respected principal customer – while the factory itself lost money.

Stating quite rightly that 'the experts . . . are the people who do the job every day' Oakland calls at point nine for their constant education and retraining. The dynamics of contemporary business and the rapid changes in the business environment render this absolutely essential. For maximum benefit such training must be related back to job performance and expectations, that is, it must link to further improvement.

Finally at point ten, Oakland calls for a planned, systematic approach to the operational implementation of TQM to realise the vision. Again, this cannot be disagreed with as a platform for improvement. However, such systematisation and planning must not preclude capitalising on spontaneous and unexpected successes. The potential opportunist gain must not be lost through rigid adherence to a particular plan.

To support the implementation process, Oakland predominantly relies on what can be thought of as standard tools for achieving quality, such as statistical approaches, quality circles, process analysis and review and so on. He does however enrich his approach by capitalising on particular developments in the pursuit of quality.

First of these is 'quality function deployment'. This is a systematic approach to the design of a product or service around the expressed requirements of the customers. It involves members from across the organisation in converting customer requirements to a technical product or service specification. The QFD process is based around seven activities (figure 10.4) and is intended to ensure that the product or service meets the customer requirements first time and every time. Oakland stresses the importance of recognising the design input of those whose jobs do not include an evident design element. Second, Oakland stresses the importance of teamwork in his approach and draws extensively on the established literature in this area to explain and elaborate his approach.

This chapter is intended only to provide an introduction to Oakland's approach. Methods, tools and techniques will be elaborated in part four of

---

JOHN S. OAKLAND

- Market research;
- Basic research;
- Invention;
- Concept design;
- Prototype testing;
- Final product or service testing;
- After-sales service and trouble-shooting.

Figure 10.4 **Quality function deployment activities: John S. Oakland**

this book. This section has introduced Oakland's primary method which relies heavily on absolute management commitment and leadership of the quality process supported by a wide selection of tools and techniques.

10.4   SUCCESSES AND FAILURES

The use of Oakland's approach to TQM by thousands of companies speaks volumes for its utility. Quite simply, no programme could achieve such sustained success without substantial benefits being delivered to many customers.

The establishment of the European Centre for TQM and of Oakland Consulting plc further confirms that Oakland's approach adds value to quality practice.

A number of strengths and weaknesses can be identified in Oakland's approach. The strengths are:

- systematic, methodical approach;
- process based view of organisations;
- capitalises on developments in quality practice;
- participative approach which utilises the literature on teamwork;
- stresses the importance of management commitment and leadership.

The weaknesses are:

- ignores many developments in organisation theory, especially the systems literature;
- fails to offer assistance in coercive contexts;
- justifies quality in terms of developed economies (the focus on competition);
- ignores other aspects of strategy formulation;
- does not explain how to obtain the commitment from senior management on which the whole process relies.

Turning first to the strengths, the systematic and methodical approach provides a straightforward, coherent platform for the quality initiative. Unfortunately it assumes that there is established agreement about the need for quality. Second, the process based view adheres to current developments in the understanding of how organisations actually function and how effectiveness is improved. Third, the capitalisation on current developments in quality practice ensures that 'best practice' is achieved – a fundamental characteristic of quality.

Oakland's emphasis on teamworking, and in particular his utilisation of the literature on effective teamworking, is to be admired. This shows that he has moved outside the relatively narrow discipline of pure quality to embrace other ideas which support his activities.

The final strength, emphasising the importance of management commitment, is again fundamental to effective pursuit of quality. It is unfortunate that (as suggested by the weaknesses) he says little about how such commitment can be achieved. While the point has been made before it is so important that it must be made again. If senior management are not passionately committed to the achievement of quality throughout every aspect of the organisation then it will not happen. Unfortunately, Oakland does not advise on how to achieve this passionate commitment, nor how to overcome the many functional and professional barriers which may obstruct it.

Turning to the other weaknesses, the failure to explicitly incorporate other aspects of organisation theory and especially to have ignored the value to be derived from a systems based understanding of organisation (together with the associated methodologies) detracts substantially from Oakland's work.

The failure to deal with coercive contexts is common to all quality approaches and is perhaps a little unfair as a criticism. Nonetheless, there are many organisations in the world which are characterised by potentially abusive power relations and one responsibility of the management guru or scientist must include attempting to ameliorate such conditions.

Perhaps because Oakland's practice is centred on Europe, the focus of his justification for pursuing quality is, if not entirely euro-centric, at least based on a perception of the problems and opportunities facing Western organisations in developed economies. These economies are dominated by industrial oligarchies (a small number of major players in each industrial sector). It can be argued that effective competition on strategic issues has almost disappeared and been replaced by a high degree of collaboration and to some extent a tacit acceptance of established market shares. For example, in the motor industry there are many interrelationships between manufacturers who promote distinct brands. Thus Volvo make use of Renault engines, Volkswagen and Ford collaborate in the production of the Galaxy and Sharan – essentially the same vehicle but differently badged. Globally the inter-relationships become even stronger.

Developing economies on the other hand often experience much lower levels of consumer sophistication, which means that the customers are perhaps not as discriminating in their purchasing choices, placing a lesser credence on Western perceptions of quality. These countries often have much more diverse industrial bases with a greater proportion of small to medium sized businesses and less dominance by major players. These two factors taken together generate scope for strategic advantage to be obtained through routes other than quality.

10.5 CRITICAL REVIEW

Overall the foundation to Oakland's work can be seen in his professional background and practical experience of quality. The approach is broadly enough based for it to be regarded as reflecting a systemic as well as systematic view, but it fails to capitalise on developments in systemic thinking.

Oakland is clearly concerned about management commitment with his calls for passionate leadership, but the approach falls down in not making a mechanism available by which such passion can be engendered. It may be thought that the fear of competitive failure is enough to stimulate this response but that is to rely on people running away from something, a negative reaction – rather than running to something, a positive reaction. In the first case as soon as the stimulus is relaxed, that is, the current danger subsides to a comfortable level, the negative response will cease and with it the passion for quality. There is clearly a need to develop an ethos where management want quality as a means to a positive end rather than as an alternative to failure, but no tools are made available to support this.

One very positive feature is that the generality of Oakland's overarching methodology renders it potentially useful in service as well as manufacturing industry. While he says little of the public sector it is quite clear that the method will also work there, although again the senior management motivation stemming from fear of competition is absent.

Summarising, support has to be given to Oakland's approach while recognising that it relies very heavily on well established techniques with all the drawbacks those entail. On the other hand he has capitalised on recent developments and drawn on at least part of the relevant management literature to support and enhance his work. The practical success speaks for itself.

SUMMARY

This chapter has presented the quality approach of John Oakland through a five point critical framework. Readers may wish to refer to Oakland's own work *Total Quality Management*, 1993, 2nd edition, to further develop their understanding and knowledge.

key learning points

JOHN S. OAKLAND

Definition of quality
quality is meeting the customers requirements

Key beliefs
quality is the only issue, quality from the top, errors can be prevented, quality is an organisation-wide issue, quality involves everybody

Principal methods
ten points for senior management, EPDCA cycle, TQM model, quality function deployment

QUESTION

Oakland proposes that 'Quality is the only issue for organisational survival.' Discuss this proposal in the light of the challenges facing contemporary organisations.

chapter eleven

SHIGEO SHINGO

Admit your own mistakes openly, maybe even joyfully.
Robert Townsend, *Further up the Organisation*, 1985

INTRODUCTION

Shigeo Shingo, who died in 1990, is perhaps the least well known in the West of the Japanese Quality Gurus. Educated as a mechanical engineer he became a consultant in 1945, subsequently working with a wide variety of companies in many industries. These companies included Toyota, Mitsubishi, Matsushita and Sony. During his later career he became involved with a large number of Western organisations. Norman Bodek, President of Productivity Incorporated, in the Foreword to *The Sayings of Shigeo Shingo*, (1987) cited by Bendell (1989: 11), says:

> If I could give a Nobel Prize for exceptional contributions to world economy, prosperity and productivity, I wouldn't have much difficulty selecting a winner – Shigeo Shingo's life work has contributed to the well-being of everyone in the world.

He is regarded by Gilbert (1992: 24) as 'one of the 20th century's greatest engineers' and he made a number of significant contributions in this area. He wrote 14 major books with several translated into English and other European languages.

11.1   PHILOSOPHY

Shingo's early philosophy embraced the 'scientific management' ideas originated by Frederick Taylor in the early part of this century. Taylor's (1911) approach was based on what is now called the 'economic man' theory of motivation. Taylor's approach was briefly reviewed in chapter 4. This approach was adopted extensively by Shingo until in his 40s he became aware of the methods of 'Statistical Quality Control.' He adopted these methods until in the 1970s he was 'finally released from the spell of statistical quality control methods' (Bendell, 1989: 12). The breakthrough in his thinking arose when he came to believe in defect prevention. This led to his major contribution to the quality debate.

Essentially, Shingo believed that 'statistical methods detect errors too late in the manufacturing process' (Flood, 1993: 28). He suggested that instead of detecting errors it was better to engage in preventative measures aimed at eliminating error sources. Gilbert (1992: 166) suggests that Shingo meant that we need to change our 'attitude of mind' and 'to organise and then behave in a way' which allows mistake proofing to happen.

Thus, over time, Shingo effectively rejected the scientific management, 'economic man', theory with all its attendant difficulties, rejected control after the event and focused on prevention. He became concerned with the total manufacturing process and Gilbert (1992: 24) cites him as saying that:

> he would prefer to be remembered for his promotion of the understanding necessary behind the concepts of looking at the total manufacturing process and the elimination of transportation, storage, lot delays and inspection.

Shingo continued to believe in mechanising the monitoring of error, considering that human assessment was 'inconsistent and prone to error'. He used people to identify underlying causes and produce preventative solutions.

There is a clear belief, like Crosby, in a 'zero defects' approach. However, unlike Crosby who's ideas emphasise worker responsibility, exhortations and slogans, Shingo's approach emphasises zero defects through good engineering and process investigation and rectification. Bendell (1989: 12) reports that Shingo shared the concern of Deming and Juran that 'posting defect statistics is misguided, and that instead the defective elements in operations that generate a lot of defectives should be hunted down.'

11.2   ASSUMPTIONS

The assumptions about the world that seem to underpin Shingo's approach will now be reviewed.

Perhaps unsurprisingly, given his mechanical engineering background and training, Shingo can be seen to have adhered to a mechanistic approach to organisation throughout his career. From engineering jobs and people in the scientific management approach of his early work, he moved to the quantitative methods of statistical quality control and, finally to error prevention through good engineering.

The mechanistic view of organisation has been challenged by many management theorists and practitioners. It has been criticised for failing to take account of human needs and desires, for failing to recognise interactions within the organisation and between the organisation and its environment. Further criticisms have been aimed at the reductionist nature of the approach which tends to fragment organisations rather than deal with them as wholes. An approach which does not take account of these factors in an increasingly complex and dynamic world must be considered flawed.

The adoption, then abandonment, of statistical methods rests on the assumption that it is possible to develop processes which are error free. While it can be seen that in an engineering context it may be possible to achieve the zero defects objective, it is considered unlikely that the same can be done in other sectors. Food production, as was seen with Chesswood Produce Ltd relies on natural processes which cannot yet be engineered to a significant extent. While it is possible to improve materials and yields, the processes are still subject to forces which are outside the influence or control of the organisation and its people, for example temperature, humidity, wind, soil condition, crop diseases. Similarly in the service sector, as has previously been discussed, there are many variables which cannot be controlled to the extent that Shingo's approach requires.

It has been consistently argued in this book that an appropriate balance of both qualitative and quantitative approaches is most useful. Here Shingo's assumptions must be challenged by suggesting that ignoring the human relations aspects of organisation and abandoning statistical methods largely limits the potential applications to the manufacturing sector.

11.3 METHODS

It could be considered that Shingo was the first management thinker and practitioner to engage in what has come to be called 're-engineering' (Hammer and Champy, 1993). His achievement in reducing hull assembly time from 4 months to 2 months at Mitsubishi, and the development of the SMED System at Toyota (Single Minute Exchange of Die) as part of the 'just-in-time' concept were both substantial contributions in their own right.

However, his principal contribution to the quality field is the mistake proofing concept, Poka-Yoke, 'Defect = 0'. This approach stops the production process whenever a defect occurs, defines the cause and generates action designed to prevent recurrence. Alternatively, 'on-line' adjustment to the product or process may be made, enabling continuous processes to be managed. For example, in the chemical and steel industries it may be both impractical and expensive to stop a production process.

Poka-Yoke relies on a process of continuously monitoring potential sources of error. Machines used in the process are equipped with feedback instrumentation to carry out this task as Shingo considered that human personnel are 'fallible' (Bendell, 1989: 12). People are used to trace and resolve the error causes. Installation of the system is expected to lead over time to a position where all likely recurring errors have been eradicated.

CYBERNETIC SYSTEMS

The idea of Poka-Yoke is similar to the concepts employed in cybernetic systems, that is, systems which in the process of going out of control put themselves back in control again. The simplest and commonest form of cybernetic system is a domestic heating system which on receipt of 'feedback' information about the air temperature from the thermostat turns the heating system on and off in the attempt to maintain a set temperature. A similar example is the cooling system on an engine where the thermostat opens and closes to allow or inhibit the flow of cold water to circulate, keeping the engine at an optimum operating temperature.

The 'goal' of these systems is a particular temperature. In the case of 'Poka-Yoke' the goal of the system is zero defects. In each case the goal is determined outside the system, for example, by the house owner in the case of the heating system, or the factory management in the case of a production process.

The concept is now widely employed in industrial control systems for production processes. For example, the baking industry uses a system of this type to control the chamber temperatures in travelling ovens aiming to ensure that the product is appropriately heated at each stage of the cooking process.

The employment of these techniques can reduce or eliminate the need for human monitoring of processes and, as Shingo suggests, enhance reliability.

The concept has been adopted to some extent in the food processing industry through the system known as 'HACCP', (Hazard Analysis Critical Control Points) which has already been outlined. Clearly, it would be unacceptable for even one defective food item to move through a system where that generated risk to health. However, as is regularly seen, even such rigorous systems cannot entirely remove the risks, for example the 'e.coli' food poisoning outbreak in Scotland during 1996 which led to several deaths.

11.4   SUCCESSES AND FAILURES

There is no doubt that Shingo's ideas have made a substantial contribution in a variety of areas. The adoption of all or some of his methods by companies throughout the world and his extensive consulting in many countries stand as testament to his success. There are, though, apparent limitations.

While Gilbert (1992: 166) suggests that the Poka-Yoke concept can be applied equally to administrative procedures and production processes, this is arguable. A production process may well be fully, or extensively, automated, minimising the opportunity for human or machine error.

Administrative and book-keeping procedures, which rely for the most part on the communication and transcription of information, cannot be automated to the same extent – there is then scope for error. Human interaction and intervention in the system is inevitable, and as Shingo himself said, humans are fallible. A second strand to this is the potential for misinterpretation of data. Language relies on two levels of understanding, the syntactic (signs) and semantic (meaning). While syntactic under-standing can be relatively reliably conveyed, even automated, semantic understanding cannot be guaranteed. It is not therefore possible to build an administrative system which can guarantee that the message, including its meaning, transmitted by one party is received and understood in the same way by the other party.

Flood (1993: 29) provides the basis for the main strengths of Shingo's approach:

- on-line, real-time control;
- Poka-Yoke emphasises effective control systems.

The main weaknesses are:

- source inspection only works effectively in manufacturing processes;
- Shingo says little about people other than that they are fallible.

Examining the first of these points, there is little doubt that in a fast moving and rapidly changing world, on-line real time information is not just desirable but arguably essential. However, the feasibility of halting many production processes is questioned.

The use of automated feedback and control mechanisms is a sound starting point for the control of a process in operation and is to be welcomed. However, little is said about the management attitudes towards accountability and responsibility that must go with it. It could be argued that a management unsupportive of this approach would not implement it. However, a technical system of this sort provides information which an autocratic management could use in a way which might be considered inappropriate, that is, it could be used as a stick with which to beat people rather than a tool for improvement. Nonetheless, as Wiener (1948) stated in the early stages of the development of modern cybernetics there are 'great possibilities for good or evil' and it is up to managers to use the knowledge wisely.

Turning to the weaknesses, the applicability of the ideas to the service sector has already been questioned. Regarding the attitude to people it is clear that Shingo's work assumes a willing co-operative workforce although he says nothing of how this state can be achieved and maintained. The body of literature concerning this topic which has arisen during the middle and later years of the century has not been accounted for.

11.5   CRITICAL REVIEW

There appear to be some consistent themes to Shingo's views, despite the apparent developments in his thinking, from scientific management through statistical quality control to mistake proofing.

He seems to have adhered, in the main, to an 'economic man' view of the people involved in the organisation. The wisdom of this view, and his failure to address the body of theoretical and practical knowledge which challenges it, has to be considered a major weakness of his work. While in some Eastern cultures there remains a strong allegiance to collective societary values, notably in Japan, other nations have moved away from this. Many Western countries have seen a significant move towards the pursuit of individual values and objectives which often translates into the pursuit of individual rather than corporate benefit from work. In a situation where that is the case, the individual may not be willing to contribute in the way that Shingo's work suggests is necessary.

A second clear and consistent theme has been the concentration on good engineering. This is unsurprising given Shingo's background and his contribution must be considered substantial in this area. However it does limit the application of his ideas to organisations and processes where the concepts are most readily applied.

The concept of mistake proofing, by refining and redesigning processes is of great importance. While it will generally be most easily applicable in the manufacturing sector, there is little doubt that the concept if not the practice can be carried across into service organisations. The danger is that it may give rise to additional administrative, auditing and checking procedures, which far from reducing costs and speeding up processes may well serve to increase costs and slow down service. A second danger associated with this is that the procedures may become 'institutionalised', inhibiting or preventing adaptation and learning by the organisation. Nonetheless, the underlying emphasis on prevention of error is to be welcomed.

SUMMARY

This chapter has reviewed the major contribution of Shigeo Shingo to the quality movement. Students should refer to Shingo's (1987) own work to develop and enhance their own understanding.

key learning points

SHIGEO SHINGO

Definition of quality
defects in process

Key beliefs
defect prevention through eradication of defective processes, human fallibility, 'mechanistic' view of organisations, real-time information processing

Principal method
poka-yoke (zero defects)

QUESTION

Shingo's approach to measuring quality through technical, automated systems is criticised for being open to abuse by autocratic managements. Consider how this problem might be overcome while preserving the value of Shingo's ideas.

chapter
twelve

GENICHI TAGUCHI

All things are numbers.
Pythagoras

INTRODUCTION

Genichi Taguchi trained as a textile engineer prior to his service in the
Japanese Navy. He subsequently worked in the Ministry of Public Health
and Welfare and the Institute of Statistical Mathematics. In that post he
learned about experimental design techniques and orthogonal arrays.
He began his consulting career whilst working at Nippon Telephone and
Telegraph.

His early work in the field of quality was mainly concerned with
production processes, the shift to a focus on product and process design
occurring during the 1980s. It was during this period that his ideas began to
be adopted in the USA. Logothetis (1992: 17) describes Taguchi's contribution as an 'inspired evolution' in the quality movement by eliminating the
need for mass inspection through his process of building quality into the
product at the design stage.

Taguchi was awarded the Deming prize and the Deming award for
literature on quality. His best known work is *Systems of Experimental Design*
(1987), and *Management by Total Results* which he co-authored.

12.1 PHILOSOPHY

The two founding ideas of Taguchi's quality work are essentially quantitative. First, is a belief in statistical methods to identify and eradicate quality problems. The second rests on designing products and processes to build quality in, right from the outset. Logothetis (1992: 13) sees Taguchi's view of quality as a negative, the cost of non-quality, that is, 'the loss imparted to society from the time the product is shipped'. Taguchi's prime concern is with customer satisfaction and with the potential for 'loss of reputation and goodwill' associated with failure to meet customer expectations. Such a failure he considered would lead the customer to buy elsewhere in the future, damaging the prospects of the company, its employees and society. He saw that loss not only occurred when a product was outside its specification but also when it varied from its target value.

Flood (1993: 30) suggests that Taguchi's view 'steps back one further stage on the technical side,' pulling back quality management into design. This is achieved through a three stage prototyping method (figure 12.1).

GENICHI TAGUCHI

- System design;

- Parameter design;

- Tolerance design.

Figure 12.1 **Three stage prototyping method: Genichi Taguchi**

The first stage is concerned with system design reasoning involving both product and process. This is an attempt to develop a basic analytical, materials, process and production framework. This framework is carried forward into the second stage, parameter design. The search at this stage is for the optimal mix of product variation levels and process operating levels, aiming to reduce the sensitivity of the production system to external or internal disturbances. Tolerance design, the third stage, enables the recognition of factors that may significantly affect the variability of the product. Additional investment, alternative equipment and materials are then considered as ways to further reduce variability.

Here a clear belief can be seen in identifying and, as far as possible, eradicating potential causes of 'non-quality' at the outset. This ties in with Flood's (1993: 32) view that Taguchi's work perceives quality to be a 'societal rather than organisational issue'. He further recognises that Taguchi's method relies on a number of organisational principles (figure 12.2).

Clearly, Taguchi recognises organisations as 'open systems', interacting with their environment. The emphasis on communication and control, the

---

GENICHI TAGUCHI

Principle 1   Communication;

Principle 2   Control;

Principle 3   Efficiency;

Principle 4   Effectiveness;

Principle 5   Efficacy;

Principle 6   Emphasis on location and elimination of causes of error;

Principle 7   Emphasis on design control;

Principle 8   Emphasis on environmental analysis.

Figure 12.2 **Organisational principles: Genichi Taguchi**

systems view, recognises interdependence between processes, something which he has been criticised for ignoring. Logothetis (1992: 340) considers this unreasonable and says that:

> Taguchi, contrary to common opinion does recognise interactions – saying:
>
> > 'If one assumes a linear model thinking it correct, then one is a man removed from natural science or reality, and commits the mistake of standing just upon mathematics which is nothing but idealism.'

Summarising, there appear to be several beliefs. The first is in quantitative methods, providing measurements for control. The second is in the eradication, as far as possible, of causes of failure at the outset. The third is in the societary cost of non-quality. The fourth perhaps reflects the third, and is the systems view of inter-dependence and interrelationship both within the organisation and with its environment.

12.2   ASSUMPTIONS

Assumptions which are considered to underpin Taguchi's approach will now be addressed.

The first and quite critical feature is that he seems to assume that quality can always be controlled through improvement in design. While this may be the case for many aspects of manufacturing, its validity in the service sector must be questioned. Similarly, where products exhibit either natural characteristics – as in the case of food, or contain aspects of 'craft' skill – cabinet making, pottery or precious metal work, this may be inappropriate.

A second assumption relates to his attitude to people. While it will be clearly seen in the next section that he values their creative input to the design and development process, it is perceived that they are not considered a significant factor in the production of quality goods. Little or nothing is said about them or the management process.

It has already been mentioned that the work has a clear focus on the manufacturing sector. Nothing is said about how to manage the quality process in service industries.

The next assumption is again quite critical. Taguchi seems to assume that the organisation can wait for results – that delays between product conception and production will be acceptable. While these delays are to some extent inevitable, the contemporary market demands are such that they need to be minimised. It is essential therefore if Taguchi's ideas are to be fully implemented that they are integral to the product development process, not additional. In this way maximum benefit can be gained and delays minimised. Adopting the Taguchi method after initial product design must be seen as unacceptable. It could even be suggested that quality parameters should be seen as being as much a part of a basic design brief as target markets and prices.

It is easy to see that much of Taguchi's work has been informed by his background in engineering and quantitative methods. What is less obvious is how his 'systems' perspective, with which there is no disagreement, arose. The adoption of a systemic view, while not apparently extending to the management process of the organisation, is certainly a step forward from the work of many of his fellow gurus.

12.3 METHODS

The principal tools and techniques espoused by Taguchi centre around the concept of *kaizen* thinking, that is, continuous improvement. His backward step into the design process helps to ensure a high basic quality standard. Other than the 'quadratic loss function' the other statistical methods are common to many thinkers and will be reviewed in the appropriate chapter. In this section concentration will be on the following:

- suggested steps for experimental studies;
- prototyping;
- quadratic loss function.

The suggested steps (figure 12.3) fall into the 'parameter design' (Logothetis, 1992: 306) stage of product development. It is within this process that Taguchi utilises people. This scientific method is very reminiscent of Demings' 'Plan, Do, Check, Action' cycle. This should perhaps not be surprising given their common background in statistics.

The first stage is concerned with developing a clear statement of precisely what problem is to be solved. Taguchi considers it of great importance that the experiment should be exactly targeted. The second stage links with the first. It is important to determine what output characteristics are to be studied and optimised through the experimental process, and

GENICHI TAGUCHI

Stage 1　　Define the problem.

Stage 2　　Determine the objective.

Stage 3　　Conduct a brainstorming session.

Stage 4　　Design the experiment.

Stage 5　　Conduct the experiment.

Stage 6　　Analyse the data.

Stage 7　　Interpret the results.

Stage 8　　Run a confirmatory experiment.

Figure 12.3 **Eight stages of product development: Genichi Taguchi**

what measurements are to be taken. It may be necessary to run control experiments in order to validate results.

The third stage is brainstorming. At this point, all the managers and operators related to the product or process are required to come together and determine the controllable and uncontrollable factors affecting the situation. Here the aim is to define an experimental range and suitable factor levels. Logothetis (1992: 306) suggests that Taguchi prefers to consider as many factors (not interactions) as is economically feasible. Whether this represents a sufficient involvement by people in the solution development process is debatable. It might be considered that they should be involved at all stages. Nonetheless, their involvement in experiment design, and their contribution of knowledge to the debate, must be considered invaluable. It is normally the case that those who actually perform a task know more about it than anybody else. The opportunity for them to articulate that knowledge in an informal session such as brainstorming is to be welcomed.

The fourth stage is experiment design. At this point the controllable and uncontrollable (noise) factors are separated for statistical monitoring purposes. This is followed by the fifth stage, the experiment itself.

The sixth stage is to analyse the performance measures recorded, using appropriate statistical methods. This is followed by interpretation of the results at the seventh stage. This aims to identify optimal levels for the control factors which seek to minimise variability and bring the process closest to its target value. Prediction is used at this stage to consider the performance of the process under optimal conditions.

The eighth and final stage is to validate the results so far obtained by running further experiments. Failure to confirm results by further experimentation generates a need to revisit stages 3–8.

This whole process may be regarded as similar to the 'black box' technique used in cybernetics. In that case, altering inputs and monitoring the effect on outputs is used as a device for determining the function of a unit. This technique could be used from a 'macro' perspective in a production or manufacturing facility to determine areas of maximum concern for detailed analysis through the Taguchi methods. Interested readers should refer to the work of Beer (1981) for a more detailed discussion of this approach.

Prototyping, is the technique which Taguchi uses to develop what Gilbert (1992: 24) calls the 'up and limping' prototype. This has already been seen in the review of Taguchi's philosophy. The technique consists of three stages. The first, System Design, is aimed at applying scientific and engineering principles to the development of functional design. It has two elements, product design and process design. The second stage is Parameter Design. This looks at establishing process and machine settings that minimise performance variation. A distinction is made at this stage between controllable and uncontrollable factors (parameters and noise). The specification criterion is for optimisation and is usually expressed as monetary loss arising from variation. The third stage is Tolerance Design. This is aimed at minimising the total sum of product manufacturing and lifetime costs.

PROTOTYPING SERVICES

Taguchi's approach to prototyping products can also be applied to the service sector. It is common practice for service organisations to develop new processes or products and test market them in selected areas, modifying them before a full launch through all outlets. This is a very similar approach to that which should be taken by manufacturing industry – although it often is not! It is far less common practice though to prototype other changes, particularly in the way that the organisation is run. These changes, which may have much more substantial and long term impact than a new service, are often developed in secrecy for political reasons and imposed overnight on a surprised workforce.

This is not the only approach to organisational change, and certainly not necessarily the most successful. In 1990, a major retail organisation with many outlets decided that its distribution strategy needed to be revised to meet the changing needs of its customers, to enhance the effectiveness of service delivery and reduce costs relative to income. The organisation saw the priorities in the stated order. The three strands were seen as directly correlated, that is an improvement in either of the first two would increase income, a consequence of achieving the first two would be the third. Steps were also taken to directly reduce costs by eliminating inefficiency and waste within the organisation.

A substantially revised organisation was designed based on 'natural' geographical and business communities. For each such community there was recognised to be a 'lead' outlet offering a full range of services but specialising in more complex, higher value activities requiring greater internal expertise. The 'subordinate' outlets were focused on the precise needs of their particular community taking the normal requirements of 99 per cent (approximately ± 3 standard deviations!) of their customers as the benchmark. The relationships with the 1 per cent of exceptional requirements were to be dealt with by staff from the 'lead' outlet.

The principles and broad approach were agreed by the board of the organisation and a series of 'pilot' communities were created. This commenced with a prolonged period with one community where the principles were put into practice for the first time. This was used as a 'learning' situation. The staff of the community were fully involved in the process. While the principles were strictly adhered to, the implementation process was filled with experimentation, reflection, critical review and modification. Once running satisfactorily the test bed community was visited by representatives from six other communities. These visitors studied what had been achieved, including the mistakes, and with expert facilitation developed solutions appropriate to their own circumstances, providing altogether seven 'up and limping' prototypes.

Once 'tested to destruction' and suitably modified the revised organisation design was rolled out across the organisation.

The quadratic loss function is Taguchi's principal contribution to the statistical aspects of achieving quality. The point of this calculation is to minimise the cost of a product or service. In this, a particular quality characteristic (x) is identified and a target value (T) set for it. Proximity to the target value is expressed as $(x-T)$. The result of exceeding, or failing to achieve T is a financial loss to the organisation, hence the result must always be positive, this is achieved through squaring the answer, $(x-T)^2$. This result is multiplied by a cost co-efficient (c) which puts a price on failing to meet the target (T). A further co-efficient (k), representing the minimum loss to society with a value always greater than 0, is added. The sum represents the total loss (L) to society. Thus:

$$L = c\,(x-T)^2 + k$$

This may be viewed, in some respects, as a measure of efficiency and of effective utilisation of resources. Of critical importance to its use are the correct selection of criteria and the accurate development of the co-efficients c and k. If any of the values selected for the calculation are incorrect then the whole process becomes useless.

12.4   SUCCESSES AND FAILURES

As with each of the other gurus reviewed, Taguchi has to be accepted as having made a substantial contribution to the field. His books, and his consulting, indicate the wide acknowledgement of the utility of his approach.

Adapting from Flood (1993: 32–33) the following strengths to Taguchi's work are suggested:

- quality is a design requirement;
- the approach recognises the systemic impact of quality;
- it is a practical method for engineers;
- it guides effective process control.

The principal weaknesses are:

- usefulness is biased towards manufacturing;
- guidance is not given on management or organisational issues;
- it places quality in the hands of the experts;
- it says nothing about people as social animals.

Looking at the strengths, it can again be argued that Taguchi does not go far enough backwards into the design process. Quality parameters are to some extent already determined once the product has moved beyond the initial concept stage, since certain factors such as market and price range will often be decided at that point.

The recognition of the total cost to society of defective products is useful. However, since, as Flood suggests, little account is taken of the people or management process in the organisation, the definition of 'total cost' has to be open to question.

That the method is developed for practising engineers, rather than theoretical statisticians, perhaps serves to make it useful. However, the validity of the quadratic loss function should be questioned if each application is not properly understood and underpinned by a validated statistical base.

Turning to the weaknesses, Flood's assessment that the model is of no use where measurement produces no meaningful hard data can be supported. This perhaps limits its usefulness outside the manufacturing sector. That nothing is said about managing people and the organisation is also agreed and is considered to be a major drawback to the whole approach.

Taguchi's failure to recognise organisations as social systems contrasts quite sharply with his recognition of quality as a societal issue. There is no explanation in his work for this. He appears to consider the people within the organisation as 'machine parts' who will perform whatever function they are allocated to. No account is taken of human variability in the measurement of processes, perhaps he regards this, unsympathetically, as noise!

12.5 CRITICAL REVIEW

There can be little doubt that Taguchi's work makes a substantial contribution to the quality movement. This contribution has, however, been focused very narrowly.

His engineering and statistical background quite clearly underpins the approaches which he espouses and this, to some extent, has limited the value of his work. He relies absolutely on quantitative measures of quality and this makes his approach quite unsuitable for application to the service sector where quality is often defined by observers at a much more subjective level.

Contrasting with this, his emphasis on quality of design and the process of prototyping are invaluable, even if perhaps not far reaching enough. The impact on total (organisation) cost of developing quality products and processes must not be underestimated. They will enable substantial reductions, if not eradication, of processes of inspection, rework and reject. Each of these items add substantially to the operating costs of many organisations and often increase directly with the inadequacy of the design and development work.

Taguchi's lack of concern with people and managing organisations must be considered the second major flaw in his approach. He says nothing of how to implement his approaches, which from experience, would meet major resistance in many organisations. The necessary re-organisation and alteration of corporate structures, the shifts in power, and perhaps the change in budgets associated with his method, would all be expected to generate substantial resistance within the organisation. Handling this resistance is not addressed.

SUMMARY

The review of the work of Genichi Taguchi is now complete. Readers should refer to his original work, (Taguchi: 1987), in order to develop their own appreciation of his contribution.

---

key learning points

GENICHI TAGUCHI

Definition of quality
the loss imparted to society from the time the product is shipped

Key beliefs
statistical methods, quality as inherent in design, quality is a societal issue

Principal methods
prototyping method, eight steps of parameter design, quadratic loss function

---

QUESTION

Taguchi believes that quality is a societal, rather than an organisational issue. Discuss.

part three

CONTEMPORARY

THINKING

USER GUIDE

Part one of this book, particularly chapter 4, showed how quality has become a major organisational issue and placed it in the broader context of early management thinking. In part two, the work of the 'Quality Gurus' arising from this thinking was considered. The purpose of part three is to bring quality thinking up to date by placing it in the context of contemporary approaches to management.

Management thinking has developed substantially since the 1960s yet the dominant literature about quality does not appear to have embraced the potential benefits emerging from that development. It was shown in part two that the work of the Quality Gurus relies principally on the 'machine' view of organisation, with some writers moving towards 'human relations' theory but failing to take full advantage of the substantial body of work in that area. For example, Ishikawa emphasises participation and provides a potentially useful tool for achieving it, but says nothing of the aspects of human behaviour which enable or inhibit meaningful participation. Similarly, the value of holistic or systemic thinking about organisational issues is achieving increasing prominence in other areas of problem solving (for example Senge's 'Fifth Discipline') but is largely ignored in the quality literature.

Part three of the book explores and explains these holistic approaches to understanding organisation. Holistic thinking moves away from treating quality as a largely technical exercise and embraces the softer issues of culture, stakeholder relations and organisational politics as well as offering assistance on the technical aspects. Whilst quality purists might argue the point, it is believed that from a holistic perspective the pursuit of quality is just one strand of many in the achievement of organisational effectiveness.

Selecting strands of thought to include in this section was very difficult, there are so many books and ideas published each year in the field of management. The works and authors selected have met five criteria. They are (or purport to be):

- systemic;
- contemporary (either recently produced or currently popular);
- practical (they have a well worked out and tested methodology);
- original;
- directly relevant to the pursuit of organisational effectiveness through quality.

These criteria led to the exclusion of specific or extended study of many other significant management thinkers and writers, for example Drucker, Peters, Kanter, Mintzberg. It is not the intention to detract from or deny their substantial contributions to management thinking and readers are encouraged to study their work. Their exclusion simply means that they did not meet the criteria established for this book.

The chapters in this part are organised along two broad lines. First they are (more or less) in 'date order', that is, the earliest ideas are in the earliest chapters. Second, they broadly follow a continuum from 'hard' thinking – how to solve a defined problem, to 'soft' thinking – defining the problem itself. Readers may again work through the chapters in the order presented or 'dip in' to the ideas they find most interesting or relevant to their particular interest. The aim of this section is to help the reader identify and understand the various strands of management thought which are currently emerging and to enable informed selection from amongst those approaches.

chapter thirteen

CONTINGENCY THEORY

Sir Roger told them, with the air of a man who would not give his judgement rashly, that much might be said on both sides.
Joseph Addison, *The Spectator*: 68,
adapted from Martial, xii, 47

INTRODUCTION

Contingency theory initially arose from the body of work concerning leadership and motivation. The principal proponent of this psychology based approach is Fiedler (1967) whose work suggested that the best leadership style depended upon the particular set of circumstances of the organisation. He identified two styles of leadership, 'relationship-motivated' and 'task-motivated' which were equally valid under different conditions. 'Relationship-motivated' leadership is seen as appropriate when the technical task is relatively easy but the relationships are difficult to manage, 'task-motivated' leadership in the opposing circumstances. There is a 'sliding-scale' or continuum of variations between these two extreme positions. Overall, Fiedler's work, unlike that of earlier writers suggests that there is no 'one best way' of leading or managing.

13.1   CONTINGENCY THEORY AND ORGANISATION DESIGN

During the 1970s contingency theory developed from those roots in leadership and motivation theory to became the dominant approach to organisation design and management. Theoretically it reflects some of the development of systems thinking, to be discussed in the next chapter, but it is based on observation and practice and to a large extent pre-dates much of the work in the systems field.

Contingency theory considers the organisation systemically as an interacting network of functional elements bound together in pursuit of a common purpose. Each element is essential to the success (that is the survival, efficiency and effectiveness) of the organisation and the needs of each element must be met within the context of the organisation. In other words, an appropriate balance must be struck between the elements – this balance being dynamic since the environment and the needs of the elements may be continually changing. Like systems thinking, but unlike the classical and HR theories, contingency theory recognises that the organisation is contained within an environment with which it interacts – influencing and being influenced.

Burns and Stalker (1961) proposed that 'organic' organisation structures and systems were most relevant to organisations in a dynamic state where conditions and requirements were continually changing. They identified the key variables influencing the structure as the product market and the manufacturing technology. Joan Woodward (1965) and her colleagues studied the relationship between technology and organisation design through a survey of manufacturing organisations in south-east Essex. Woodward found that there were substantial variations between the organisational characteristics of different firms with notable differences in the number of reportees, the number of levels of management and the formality of communication. Further research showed that a key factor in these differences was not the size of the organisation, as was originally assumed, but the technology employed and the production method. This led to the suggestion (Pugh and Hickson 1989: 16–21) that the 'objectives of a firm . . . determine the kind of technology it uses' and this in turn may be seen as driving the organisational structure – that is the design of the organisation is to some extent 'contingent'. Jackson (1990) considers that there are five 'strategic contingencies' which affect each other and influence the choice of organisation structure. They are:

- goals;
- people;
- technical;
- managerial;
- size.

The goal sub-system is concerned with the survival of the organisation in both the long and the short terms – with normative, strategic and operational objectives. These goals need to meet the aspirations of the stakeholders, to match the dynamism of the environment of the organisation which in turn needs to be reflected in its decision making structure. Contemporary mantras such as 'think global, act local' reflect this demand for appropriate autonomy in goal setting.

Goals should be determined within the organisation, although the normative goals (decisions about the nature of the organisation) must be strongly influenced by the socio-economic context in which the organisation exists. All goals need to be thought of as dynamic and evolutionary to avoid the danger of a sense of complacency emerging. The goals are driven by a number of aspects. The influence of the environment (socio-economic context) has already been mentioned. The expectations of the managers or controllers of the organisation are significant as are the expectations and needs of the workforce and of the community of shareholders and other stakeholders surrounding the organisation.

The people or 'human' sub-system is concerned primarily with the evolving needs of the employees of the organisation. These needs must be met if people are to be content within the organisation, to be attracted to it and to be fulfilled by their work. It is reasonable to suggest that these needs will vary with the context in which the individuals are employed, that is, the demands of London based employees may be very different to those in New York, Melbourne or Hong Kong. Essentially, the design of the organisation must take account of the needs and capabilities of the staff.

While Jackson draws a boundary which emphasises differing perspectives for people within the total system to those outside in the 'environment', it must not be forgotten that the boundary is itself arbitrary, usually reflecting legally established relationships. Reflecting briefly on the work of the 'gurus' and others, the notions of 'supplier development', the 'value chain', the 'internal supplier–customer chain' and 'customer feedback' all imply a much closer relationship between the system and its environment – almost to the point that the boundary ceases to exist, perhaps as Beer (1979: 94–95) suggests, creating a 'diffusion' of information within the larger system. Thus while a distinction may be drawn between suppliers, staff and customers it may be more appropriate to see staff as both *in* and *of* the system, that is, they work within it and are largely loyal to it. Customers and suppliers are *in* but not *of* it. They work *with* or *buy from* the system but not for it – their loyalty lies elsewhere. They do not necessarily share in or benefit from the systems objectives.

The technical sub-system refers to the technology employed by the organisation in carrying out its work. As already stated, it was found by Woodward that organisations employed different forms of organisation according to their size and production technology. She discovered that 'typical' organisational forms had developed within particular industries and that the most successful firms employed these structures. To some extent this may be regarded as a predictable result – the practice now called benchmarking is not new. Although the more formal exchanges which take place today may be more rigorous in their use, there is little doubt that there has always been a fluid movement of ideas between participants in the same industry particularly when there was high mobility of labour and low job security. Equally, if a particular technology is appropriate to production of a particular product group, it should be no surprise that the organisational forms which succeed with the product will share many of the same characteristics.

The role of the managerial sub-system is to co-ordinate and enable the activities of the others. Current thinking recognises that the management of an organisation can enable it to respond, through the implementation of strategic choices, to developments in the environment. Thus, rather than being at the mercy of the environment the organisation can, through its management decisions, be active in dealing with it. Since the scope for the organisation to influence the environment is recognised, the management sub-system as observer can, to some extent, create the environment through its observations and its interference with it.

Jackson (1990) suggests that what he calls the deterministic origins of contingency theory are flawed and that the managerial sub-system is an important determinant of organisational success. This criticism pushes the argument away from the 'mechanistic' view of Woodward – 'technology determines structure' – towards a more organic, interactive view.

The importance of size as a factor in organisational structure was recognised by Pugh and the Aston group in studies (Pugh and Hickson, 1976; Pugh and Hinings, 1976) which considered larger organisations than those studied by Woodward. Their work showed that increasing size reinforces the need for delegation and decentralisation of decision making, while simultaneously increasing the need for structured, formal activities. This perhaps can be linked to Fayol's call for an appropriate balance between centralisation and decentralisation.

While not listed as one of Jackson's key factors, the environment is important to the effectiveness of the organisation. It is considered that differing environmental demands and constraints require different organisational formats to be employed. Overall there appears to be a correlation between the level of environmental complexity and turbulence and the requisite level of adaptability or flexibility of an organisation. To ensure long term success, that is, survival of the organisation, it must be capable of responding at an appropriate rate to changes in its environment, and, perhaps through marketing activity, of influencing the environment in favour of itself.

13.2   REITERATION

Summarising, contingency theory views the organisation as existing at the confluence of interactions between its goals, people, technology, management and size. These factors in conjunction with the environmental influences feed managers' decisions about the shape of the organisation leading to a particular structure which in turn pre-controls organisational performance. These ideas are represented in figure 13.1.

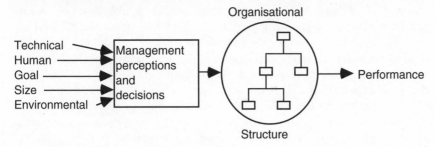

Figure 13.1 **The contingency perspective**
Source: **Adapted from Jackson, 1990**

13.3   IS QUALITY CONTINGENT?

This question has two distinct dimensions. The first is concerned with quality as an output measure of the organisation's performance. The second is concerned with defining quality itself.

Dealing with the first question, the answer must be yes. The quality of any product or service is a function of the interaction of all of the elements of the system itself and its environment. If any of the inputs, procedures or processes of the organisation are flawed, if the demands or influences of the environment are not accounted for, or if the expectations of the customers in the environment are not understood, then the product or service may be considered by those customers not to be 'quality'. Therefore, achievement of quality must be contingent upon the effectiveness of every part of the system. This perception demands a holistic approach to achieving quality.

Dealing with the second question is much harder since this is concerned with the definition of 'quality' itself. The 'gurus' reviewed in part two of this book each offered definitions of quality resting on well-defined, measurable characteristics of a product or service. These are expressed in the form of 'the one best way'. In one form or another they state that *this is quality* (their various definitions) and *this is how it is achieved* (their different method-ologies). It is clear that there are substantial differences between them: for example, Deming's statistically based approach compared with Ishikawa's participative approach, the internal evangelical focus of Crosby's work compared with the societal concerns expressed by Taguchi.

Are they *all* right, or are *none* of them right? *What is quality?* For Crosby it is 'conformance to requirements', for Deming and Shingo it is eradication of error, for Feigenbaum 'best for customer use and selling price', for Ishikawa it is the product, service, management, the company and the people – very near to the contingency view of organisation. Juran sees quality as a function of planning, while Taguchi focuses on the cost imparted to society.

It is suggested here that, in the contemporary dynamic and turbulent organisational environment, quality cannot be adequately defined in these absolute terms as something fixed and necessarily quantifiable. Perhaps as

Hume ('Of Tragedy', *Essays*) suggests, quality is like beauty: 'Beauty [quality] in things exists in the mind which contemplates them.' Perhaps customers experience rather than receive quality of service or product. As each of them has different expectations, they (the customers) continually and individually redefine quality in terms of their past experience and their changing expectations. This means of course that the pursuit of quality, like the hunt for the Loch Ness monster, is doomed to failure because, like the monster, quality is mysterious and ethereal rather than substantial and absolute. Quality then *is* contingent, but upon the customer *not* the organisation, its products or services.

This perspective on quality poses a problem for organisations pursuing quality programmes. If quality is not an absolute, then what are they aiming for and how do they know when they have achieved it? The answer seems to be that the quality target is continually shifting and that organisations must pursue 'rightness' or 'appropriateness' in their products or services. Products and services must fulfil the varying purposes for which they are purchased. They, and the processes and procedures by which they are produced, must be error free – within the limits of expectations already created in the customer's mind. Those processes and procedures must minimise cost (land, labour, capital and entrepreneurship – the four factors of production), and crucially every aspect and activity of the organisation and its management must be focused on doing the right job right.

The key to success in such a scenario rests on communication both within the organisation and between the organisation and its environment. If internal communication is defective then staff may do the right job wrong, or the wrong job right. Communication with the environment rests in understanding the expectations of customers (communication in to the organisation) and creating or modifying the expectations of customers (communication out from the organisation). If this communication is not effective then there will be flawed understanding on either (or both) sides and hence there will not be quality – because however technically good the product or service may be the expectations of one party from the other will not be met.

'THAT'S QUALITY!'

During a doctoral seminar on quality in Hong Kong, a student and I went for lunch together, taking an opportunity to discuss his forthcoming project work. The purpose of the lunch was the discussion, eating was incidental, a necessary activity. We found a run of the mill Italian fast food restaurant. The menu was predictable – pasta, pizzas and pollo. The decor was unassuming. The food served quickly and as ordered was fully acceptable. The service was surprising – just the right blend of courtesy and friendliness to meet our, admittedly not very high, expectations. We thoroughly enjoyed both our meal and our discussion, paid, walked out into the street, turned to each other and said in unison 'That's quality!' We had experienced it but could not adequately describe it – the best that can be achieved is to say that it was *all* right on *all* counts.

If asked to nominate a 'quality' restaurant in advance neither of us would have chosen the chain to which that restaurant belonged. The experience though has changed our expectations. If we went there again, would we be disappointed with exactly the same experience?

SUMMARY

This chapter has briefly introduced the concept of thinking in terms of a contingent view of the world. The emergence and background of contingency theory was explored and its roots in the empirical study of organisations explained. Readers wishing to extend their knowledge should refer directly to the work of the various authors to whom reference has been made.

---

key learning points

CONTINGENCY THEORY

Definition
organisational effectiveness is the product of the adequacy of managerial response to five key effectors on the organisation: technology, human, goal, size and environment

Key belief
there is not one best way of structuring an organisation

Contingency and quality
quality is contingent upon the expectations of the customer, not on the products or services offered

---

QUESTION

Evaluate the contribution of contingency theory to the pursuit of quality.

chapter fourteen

ORGANISATIONS AS SYSTEMS

'Contrariwise,' continued Tweedledee,
'if it was so, it might be; and if it were so,
it would be; but as it isn't, it ain't. That's logic.'
Lewis Carroll, *Through the Looking Glass*

INTRODUCTION

While contingency theory is seen as systemic, its roots lie in an essentially practical rather than theoretical domain and its main tenets are drawn from observation of organisations, that is, empirical data. Thinking about organisations as systems must have strong theoretical foundations if this strand of organisation theory is to be more than simply 'best observed practice'. Theory enables the development of general principles upon which rigorous and coherent practice can be originated rather than copied. This chapter briefly focuses on the theoretical development of systems thinking and provides the platform for the various approaches outlined in subsequent chapters.

14.1   SYSTEMS THINKING

Systems thinking emerged as a further challenge to the traditional and human relations models and falls within a view of organisations as organisms. The systems approach is fundamentally different to the reductionist view on which much of modern science rests. The shift in thinking is 'not a gradual evolution, but a discontinuity' (Singleton, 1974: 10–11). A discontinuity in this context means a total change of paradigm – a complete break from traditional, reductionist approaches. While reductionism implies breaking down and analysing organisations on a piecemeal basis, systemic thinking implies stepping back from the organisation and its individual parts and understanding its behaviour and interactions as a whole.

Systemic thinking attempts to deal with organisations as 'wholes' rather than parts, hence the expression 'holistic'. It considers the organisation (as with contingency theory) as a complex network of elements and relationships, and recognises the interaction with the environment in which the organisation is contained. Thinking about organisations as 'systems' builds upon the early work of Barnard, Selznick and von Bertalanffy and has become a major, if not yet dominant, approach for management thinkers and practitioners. Practically, thinking systemically has profound implications for organisations, but is not easy to grasp for those of us educated in a reductionist approach to the world. An explanation of systemic thinking is attempted below.

If we remove the engines from a jet aircraft neither they nor the aircraft will fly – flight is a product of their interaction and interconnectedness, a synergistic outcome. It is a property which belongs to the complete aircraft but not its parts. Properties such as this are called 'emergent' – they 'emerge' from the interaction of the various system elements. This means that when examining the properties and behaviour of an aircraft we must look at it in its totality, not just at its components, since the whole may have properties not found in the components. Equally, the parts may have properties not found in the whole. For example, the turbine of a jet engine rotates at high speed while the engine as a whole does not. Similarly, where is the voice in a radio, or the picture in a television. These things are observable outputs of the interactions within such systems and with their environment (the reception of radio or television signals) but cannot be found by reductionist examination or analysis of them.

Ackoff (1981: 18) perhaps offers the most lucid explanation of thinking systemically:

> suppose we bring one of each of these . . . [types of automobile] . . . into a large garage and then employ a number of outstanding automotive engineers to determine which one has the best carburettor. When they have done so, we record the result and ask them to do the same for engines. We continue this process until we have covered all the parts required for an automobile. Then we ask the engineers to remove and reassemble these parts. Would we obtain the best possible automobile? Of course not. We would not even obtain an automobile because *the parts would not fit together,* even if they did, *they would not work well together. The performance of a system depends more on how its parts interact than how they act independently of each other* [sic].

14.2   SYSTEMS THINKING AND ORGANISATIONS

Parsons and Smelser (1956) attempted to 'elaborate four functional imperatives to be fulfilled for a system, by its sub-systems, if that system is to continue to exist' (figure 14.1). The imperatives they identified are adaptation, goal attainment, integration and latency (pattern maintenance) and make up the AGIL mnemonic.

PARSONS AND SMELSER

Imperative 1   A = *Adaptation*: the system has to establish relationships between itself and its external environment.

Imperative 2   G = *Goal-attainment*: goals have to be defined and resources mobilised and managed in pursuit of those goals.

Imperative 3   I = *Integration*: the system has to have a means of co-ordinating its efforts.

Imperative 4   L = *Latency (or pattern maintenance)*: the first three requisites for organisational survival have to be solved with the minimum of strain and tension by ensuring that organisational 'actors' are motivated to act in the appropriate manner.

Figure 14.1 **Functional imperatives of a system: Parsons and Smewer**

Jackson (1990) interprets this somewhat differently, seeing four primary sub-systems of an organisation – goal, human, technical and managerial, which reflect his contingency theory perspective, as essential prerequisites (see figure 14.2). He considers that effectiveness and efficiency are attained through the interaction of the sub-systems in pursuit of the purpose of the system in its environment.

The goal sub-system is concerned with the purpose of the system and the means of achieving that purpose; the human sub-system deals with the people and their management and motivation; the technical sub-system handles the operations (that is, input – transformation – output); and the managerial sub-system co-ordinates and manages each of the others, balancing their relationships and attending to the environmental interaction.

The systems model adds value to the practice and theory of management since it demands explicit recognition of the environment and of interactions within the organisation. The generic system model is of great utility in a descriptive mode, enabling the elaboration of the elements and interactions

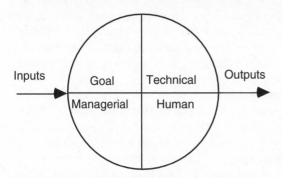

Figure 14.2 **The organisation as a system**

of the system. However, while this description frequently enables diagnosis of faults and failures in the connectivity of the system, it does not offer a prescriptive model based on a projection of an organisational ideal. In terms of weaknesses the systems model perhaps underplays the essential, purposeful role of the individuals within organisations and the extent to which human interactions can affect outputs unless the context of the discussion fully embraces systemic thinking.

The systems model takes account of the environment and focuses on the generality of survival rather than specific organisational objectives. It does not attempt to quantify the success of an organisation, and says little about 'how' organisations adapt. The potential for relative autonomy is not explored and little advice is offered in terms of specific, general remedies for ineffective organisations.

The emphasis in this view is on harmonious internal interaction, whereas conflict and coercion are often present amongst the human actors. Change is perceived as being environmentally driven, rather than instigated by the organisation.

14.3   SYSTEMS THINKING AND QUALITY

The shift from the classical management school of thought to the human relations school represented a change of emphasis within the reductionist paradigm. This shift is from a focus on the needs of organisations to a focus on the needs of the individuals and groups within them. The shift in thinking has not been strongly reflected in the quality literature, although the Quality Gurus do generally recognise in their work the importance of the commitment of all staff to quality initiatives and some acknowledge the importance of dealing with the totality of the organisation. The shift from reductionist to systemic thinking about quality is much more fundamental, involving the acceptance of a new paradigm, a reframing of the entire way in which the individual thinks about the world. The impact on thinking about quality is substantial.

When thinking systemically about quality the performance of individual parts of an organisation becomes less important with emphasis shifting to their total interacting performance. This means examining not just the performance of functional units such as production, sales, finance, personnel (as would be the case in a reductionist approach) but, crucially, how the performance of those parts is enabled or inhibited by other parts, that is, how they interact to produce goods or services.

Conventionally, most quality initiatives focus on the technical performance of production systems, whether for products or services. They examine in detail the characteristics of machines (Shingo), they study the accuracy and reliability of the human and technical inputs to the production system (Deming's special causes of error) and they sometimes look at the internal supplier–customer relationships. Few quality programmes go beyond these technical aspects in any substantial manner.

In a systemic world the examination needs to draw back and consider how each of the parts of the organisation interact with every other. So, for example, financial objectives, recruitment and training policies and inbound logistics all impact on production capability and the ability to meet quality targets. Similarly, the sales function and the commitments given to customers by sales personnel are strong determinants of the level of after-sales service which must be provided to meet customer expectations, and of the cost of providing it. These sales commitments also interact with the production elements of the organisation, creating demands which need to be met. Overlaying all of these aspects are the internal politics of the organisation, that is, the ways in which people interact, the coherence or otherwise of their behaviour, the degree of mutuality in their objectives given that individuals tend to compete for preferment within the organisation – and sometimes at its expense.

A SYSTEMS PROBLEM

The following story, received from a reliable source in the IT industry, is:

1 reported as true;
2 an illustration of the need to think systemically about problems.

Dialogue between a customer and Customer Support Help Desk:

CS: 'Ridge Hall computer assistant, may I help you?'
CUSTOMER: 'Yes, well, I'm having trouble with WordPerfect.'
CS: 'What sort of trouble?'
CUSTOMER: 'Well, I was just typing along, and all of a sudden the words went away.'
CS: 'Went away?'
CUSTOMER: 'They disappeared.'
CS: 'Hmm. So what does your screen look like now?'
CUSTOMER: 'Nothing.'
CS: 'Nothing?'
CUSTOMER: 'It's blank; it won't accept anything when I type.'

CS:	'Are you still in WordPerfect, or did you get out?'
CUSTOMER:	'How do I tell?'
CS:	'Can you see the "C" prompt on the screen?'
CUSTOMER:	'What's a sea-prompt?'
CS:	'Never mind. Can you move the cursor around the screen?'
CUSTOMER:	'There isn't any cursor: I told you, it won't accept anything I type.'
CS:	'Does your monitor have a power indicator?'
CUSTOMER:	'What's a monitor?'
CS:	'It's the thing with a screen on it that looks like a TV. Does it have a little light that tells you when it's on?'
CUSTOMER:	'I don't know.'
CS:	'Well, then look on the back of the monitor and find where the power cord goes into it. Can you see that?'
CUSTOMER:	'. . . Yes, I think so.'
CS:	'Great. Follow the cord to the plug and tell me if it's plugged in to the wall.'
CUSTOMER:	'. . . Yes. It is.'
CS:	'When you were behind the monitor, did you notice that there were two cables plugged into the back of it, not just one?'
CUSTOMER:	'No.'
CS:	'Well, there are. I need you to look back there again and find the other cable.'
CUSTOMER:	'. . . Okay, here it is.'
CS:	'Follow it for me, and tell me if it's plugged securely into the back of your computer.'
CUSTOMER:	'I can't reach.'
CS:	'Uh huh. Well can you see if it is'?
CUSTOMER:	'No.'
CS:	'Even if you maybe put your knee on something and lean way over?'
CUSTOMER:	'Oh, it's not because I don't have the right angle – it's because it's dark.'
CS:	'Dark?'
CUSTOMER:	'Yes, the office light is off and the only light I have is coming in from the window.'
CS:	'Well, turn the office light on then.'
CUSTOMER:	'I can't.'
CS:	'Why not?'
CUSTOMER:	'Because there's a power outage.'
CS:	'A power . . . a power outage? Aha! Okay, we've got it licked now. Do you still have the boxes and manuals and packing stuff your computer came in?'
CUSTOMER:	'Well, yes, I keep them in the closet.'
CS:	'Good! Go get them, unplug your system and pack it up just like it was when you got it. Then take it back to the store you bought it from.'
CUSTOMER:	'Really? Is it that bad?'
CS:	'Yes, I'm afraid it is.'

CUSTOMER: 'Well, all right then, I suppose. What do I tell them?'
CS: 'Tell them you're too stupid to own a computer.'

The point is, not that we are too stupid for the organisations in which we work, but that the conventional reductionist mindset leads us to explore only the issue of immediate concern and to ignore the wider issues which a systemic mindset suggests may have implications for the resolution of our particular problem.

Complicating the situation further is the issue of measurement (and the associated rewards and punishments related to performance). It has already been suggested in chapter 3 that in general 'we get what we measure' and for many organisations, and the individuals within them, the measurements are narrow and simple. Such systems tend to lead to a focus on one aspect of performance at the expense of others. So for example if the measurement system emphasises production efficiency that is what the management will aim for. In a systemic world, production efficiency cannot be measured in isolation but must be related to the demands of the market-place, the availability of inputs to the system (land, labour, raw materials etc.) and to the capacity of the organisation to provide financial support.

Systemically, quality is not something which can be achieved through enhancing only independent functional units – however effective they may become individually. Equally, quality cannot be measured in purely technical terms by some inherent and visible characteristics of the product or service such as size, shape, colour or conformance to requirements. Systemically, quality must be recognised as a more or less measurable property of the total organisation. It must be inherent in each process and each interaction within the system and must persist in the organisation's dealings with its environment. For example, the products or services of a company may be admired for their apparent quality. However, if the process by which they are made is unnecessarily environmentally damaging or the management system abuses the employees within the organisation then it cannot be considered a quality organisation – except by that single output measure of operational performance. In the event that the processes are environmentally damaging or abusive of people, then quality is achieved at some other cost which may not be acceptable at a societal level.

SUMMARY

This chapter has briefly introduced the idea of thinking about organisations as systems and attempted to explain systemic thinking. The implications of systems thinking for quality have been addressed. In subsequent chapters three different strands of the development of systemic thinking will be explored. Organisational cybernetics stems from the relatively hard, solution oriented approaches while soft systems thinking reflects a more means oriented approach. Critical systems thinking embraces both of these strands in a systemic enquiry process.

key learning points

ORGANISATIONS AS SYSTEMS

Key definition
the study of organisations and their interactions as wholes, not as an assembly of individual parts

Key beliefs
the 'system' exhibits behaviour which is not exhibited by any of the parts and has 'emergent' properties which belong to none of those parts individually

Implications for quality
shift of focus from just the individual parts to embrace the interactions between those parts, recognition that the internal customer chain creates the organisation, quality must be recognised as an emergent property of the system rather than just a technical measure of output

QUESTION

What do you think might be the 'emergent' properties of a University? Why?

chapter fifteen

ORGANISATIONAL CYBERNETICS

I'm not complaining, but There It Is.
Eeyore in *Winnie the Pooh*, A. A. Milne

INTRODUCTION

The science of cybernetics emerged during the 1940s as a part of the systems thinking movement. Norbert Weiner was the founding driver of contemporary cybernetics working primarily on machine systems. His work has subsequently been developed extensively by others in the modern field of robotics.

Stafford Beer has for nearly forty years led the development of cybernetics in the study of organisations creating a branch which we now call 'management' or 'organisational' cybernetics. This work extends from the 1950s and is undergoing continued development by Beer and others including this author. Beer defines cybernetics as the 'science of effective organisation' – something from which quality may be considered to result.

This chapter is concerned with the theory of cybernetics and its relationship to the achievement of quality in organisations. Organisations are conceived here as societies, composed of people and existing, as proposed in the previous chapter, as the product of their actions, interactions and of the technical artefacts which link and support them. Early work, from which the cybernetic principles were developed, addressed such diverse fields as automation, computing and radar and built upon previous discoveries such as Watt's steam engine governor, which are used to illustrate what Jackson (1991) has called 'management cybernetics'.

Organisational cybernetics builds upon and draws ideas from that fundamental work, but 'breaks somewhat with the mechanistic and organismic thinking that typifies management cybernetics' (Jackson, 1991: 103). The distinction is drawn by Jackson on the basis of two differences between the work of Stafford Beer and that of others in this field. First, in *The Heart of Enterprise* Beer (1979) builds a model of 'any organisation' from first principles of cybernetics. Second, he pays significant attention to the role of the observer whose presence influences the situation observed. Accepting the intellectual insights of Stafford Beer, it is possible to make use of the principles of cybernetics without relying on analogies between the organisation observed and other natural phenomena – although analogies are useful as ways of helping us to order our thoughts about a situation. It can be recognised that the existence and behaviour of the organisation studied is, to some degree, a function of the perceptions of the observer.

The role of cybernetics is to help the manager (defined as any person legitimately attempting to command and control an organisation) to understand:

- how an organisation works (or doesn't work);
- why it works that way;
- what to do about the organisation to influence the outcome in a way which is beneficial to the purposes perceived as being served.

This is because 'Cybernetics . . . treats, not things but *ways of behaving*' (Ashby, 1956).

15.1 CYBERNETIC SYSTEMS

The truths of cybernetics are not conditional on their being derived from some other branch of science.

(Ashby, 1956: 1)

This section deals with the major characteristics of systems suitable for the cybernetic approach. Notwithstanding the above quote from Ross Ashby, a number of the principles have been derived from 'some other branch of science'. It is in taking account of the role of the observer that they reflect the essentially cybernetic operation of those natural systems which have been studied. The principles of cybernetics can be observed operating in nature (viz.: Gell-Mann, Gleick, Lovelock, Hawking, Penrose) and are concerned with 'general laws that govern control processes, whatever the nature of the system under governance' (Jackson: 1991: 92) and that includes quality systems.

Beer (1959) considers that, in order to be a worthwhile subject for the application of the cybernetic approach, the organisation will be likely to demonstrate three characteristics (figure 15.1)

STAFFORD BEER

Characteristic 1   extreme complexity;

Characteristic 2   a degree of self-regulation;

Characteristic 3   probabilistic behaviour.

Figure 15.1 **Characteristics of cybernetic systems: Stafford Beer**

Beer (1959: 12) designates as 'exceedingly complex' any organisation which is so complicated that it cannot be described in a precise and detailed fashion. To explain this point, the wiring loom of a car is, in Beer's terms, 'complex but describable', its design and connectivity can be, and, in fact, are recorded. An example of an exceedingly complex organisation would perhaps be an interaction between two people in a meeting. This transaction while apparently simple to observe and record, would, in fact, not be describable. The individual interpretation of words, inflections of speech, degree of eye contact and bodily postures adopted, all form a part of the transaction.

Self-regulation describes the ability of an organisation to 'manage' itself towards its purposes or goals despite environmental disturbance, for example, maintenance of body temperature in humans and animals. The temperature control system behaves in an autonomous manner, needing no active direction or management from the brain – although the brain is where the rules of temperature control are generated.

Probabilism exists where there are elements of the organisation whose behaviour is at least partly random. Returning to the example of the car wiring loom, it is not only 'complex but describable', it is also 'deterministic'. Its behaviour can be known in advance as any given input to the system, for example, operating a switch, will generate a precisely predictable outcome. The outcome of the meeting between two people would be 'probabilistic'. This is because, while the agenda for discussion may be known in advance, and a 'most likely' outcome predicted, the variables in the meeting, such as mood, posture and experience of the parties, separately and together, make the outcome uncertain.

15.2   TOOLS OF CYBERNETICS

There are three principal cybernetic tools for dealing with these exceedingly complex, self-regulating, probabilistic organisations (figure 15.2). Complexity is dealt with by the black box technique. Schoderbek *et al.* (1990: 94) consider that complexity is a property of an organisation, which, when examined from a non-quantitative viewpoint, is the product of the interaction of four main aspects – the number of elements, their interactions, their attributes and their degree of organisation.

Tool 1   the *black box* technique – to address extreme complexity;

Tool 2   *feedback* – to manage self regulation;

Tool 3   *variety engineering* – to handle probabilism.

Figure 15.2 **Tools of cybernetics**

It should be apparent that the interaction of those four 'determinants' can generate what would be seen as an exceedingly complex organisation. As such, it does not lend itself to the reductionist analysis of a classical or human relations view as such an approach would break down the organisation and cause the emergent properties to disappear. The organisation then examined would be different from that which was initially identified.

The need to study the organisation, while interfering minimally with its internal operation, leads to the use of the black box technique. This is a way of gaining knowledge about the operations carried out by an organisation without the need to reduce it to its component parts. The black box technique involves manipulating the inputs to an organisation and recording the effect on its outputs in order to establish patterns or regularities in its behaviour. As knowledge or understanding of the organisation's behaviour is acquired, the manipulations can become more structured. The black box technique is shown diagramatically in figure 15.3.

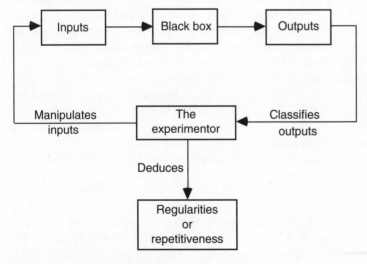

Figure 15.3 **The black box technique**

All of us are familiar with and deal with complex black box organisations in our daily lives without ever needing to know or understand how they work. Indeed, the black box technique will never reveal how the transformation process works or how efficient it is.

EVERYDAY BLACK BOXES

1 Drivers need not know how an engine works in order to drive a vehicle.

2 No understanding of electronics is needed in order to use the computer on which this book is being written.

3 Children need know nothing of the internal workings of a video recorder in order to record and view their favourite programmes.
(Something which so many adults cannot manage.)

4 Facsimile machines and photocopiers.

5 Finally, parents learn to manage their children (and children their parents) long before they have a common spoken language with which to communicate and explain their actions. Nobody would propose a reductionist analysis of a baby to 'find out how it works' in order to control it – it is simply managed as a black box.

Managers in organisations, usually unknowingly, perform many tasks using the black box technique. It is not possible to grasp the full complexity of the organisations which are managed. Management is achieved by manipulating the inputs to the organisation, recording the outputs, and deducing patterns of response. These patterns can then be used to inform future actions.

Feedback is the process which makes self-regulation possible and describes 'circular causal processes' (Clemson, 1984: 22). Self-regulation occurs in both an organisation and its environment and is consequently of major importance. If it is not understood that an exceedingly complex probabilistic organisation to some extent regulates itself and how this occurs then the predictability of the outcomes of managerial actions in relation to that organisation is reduced. Self-regulation generates a degree of stability, but, if an intervention is undertaken, either in an organisation or by an organisation in its environment, this stability may be disturbed. If the 'circular causal chains' have not been adequately understood then the intervention may produce unmanageable instability.

The simplest form of feedback occurs when two parts of an organisation continuously interact with each other such that the output of one determines the next action of the other. There are two types of this 'first order' feedback behaviour. In the first, negative feedback or goal seeking behaviour, the organisation will resist disturbances that take it away from its goal. That is to say, that the reaction of the one element is to inhibit the change in the other and vice versa. A common example of first order feedback behaviour is the thermostatic control of a heating or air conditioning system, the thermostat switching the system on and off in order to maintain a given temperature.

The opposite of negative feedback is positive feedback. In this case, deviation by one element will be amplified rather than reduced by the action of another. These systems whilst potentially highly unstable are also useful. A good example of this is the level of interest acting on a bank account. Positive feedback results in the interest compounding – in effect running away out of control.

A second order feedback system is capable of choosing between a variety of responses to environmental changes in order to achieve its goal. A third order system is still more sophisticated. It is capable of changing the goal state itself in response to feedback processes, determining the goal internally as opposed to externally, as in the first and second order systems. Figure 15.4 shows an example of a closed-loop feedback system.

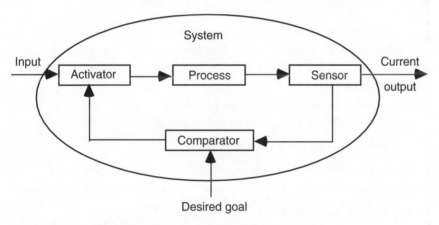

Figure 15.4 **A closed-loop, first-order feedback system**

This description of feedback has so far dealt with simple situations. In organisations the feedback systems may be highly complex, containing large numbers of elements, connected in a number of ways and consisting of both positive and negative loops. It may also be the case that at any time the 'sum' of the loops may operate in a positive or negative manner and in human systems (such as organisations) they need not be physical.

PSYCHOLOGICAL FEEDBACK

Given two teams that are roughly evenly matched, if one team plays very well and begins to pull slightly ahead, the other team is stimulated to greater effort and tends to catch up, i.e. the two function as a negative loop in minimising the score difference between them. However, suppose one team is having a horrible night and gets completely demoralised in the first ten minutes. As the game goes on and they get more and more hopelessly behind they will tend to play less and less well and the better team will relax and everything will go right for them. In this case, the two teams are functioning so that the overall feedback loop is positive in maximising the score difference.

(Clemson, 1984: 23)

Clemson draws from this that: '. . . there is nothing structural or in the "essence" of the system, about whether the loop is positive or negative'.

Ultimately, systems that include feedback loops are capable of demonstrating exceedingly complex behaviour, and large changes in that behaviour may be brought about by small changes in the internal relationships. There are several key criteria for the design of effective feedback mechanisms (figure 15.5) these will be further elaborated in chapter 27 when effective organisation in practice is considered.

Criterion 1	All the elements of the system must be working properly and the communication channels between them must be adequate.
Criterion 2	In an organisation, responsibility for action, (which carries with it accountability), must be clearly allocated.
Criterion 3	Controls must be selective.
Criterion 4	The control must highlight the necessary action.

Figure 15.5 **Design criteria for feedback systems**

Variety is the measure of complexity in an organisation: that is, the number of possible states it can exhibit; probabilistic behaviour exists when the behaviour of some of the elements of the organisation is considered to be at least partly random. A principal argument of cybernetics is that the mechanisms that are used to manage this complexity must answer to Ashby's 'Law of Requisite Variety' which states that 'only variety can destroy variety'. This means that, in order to effectively manage a situation, the management must command as much variety as the operation(s) it seeks to control.

Variety engineering consists of the two prime methods of achieving this control, either reducing the variety of the organisation to be controlled (variety reduction), or, increasing the variety of the management (variety amplification). In fact, variety can neither be absolutely reduced nor absolutely increased, only managed through appropriate techniques (figure 15.6). This process must be undertaken in a manner which is suitable for the particular organisation being managed and should contribute to the achievement of its goals. There are a number of management techniques

---

VARIETY MANAGEMENT

Reduction

Structural:	delegation (autonomy or decentralisation), functionalisation or divisionalisation;
Planning:	establishing objectives and priorities;
Operational:	budgeting, management by exception;
Rules/policies:	instructions and 'norms' of behaviour.

Amplification

Structural:	teamwork and groups;
Augmentation:	recruit/train experts, employ independent experts;
Information management:	management or executive information systems (which may also act as attenuators).

Figure 15.6 **Variety reduction and amplification techniques**

which are in common use and may be seen as the tools of variety engineering if employed appropriately. These techniques need to be used thoughtfully and with full awareness of their possible consequences, rather than randomly, or politically, as often seems to happen in organisations. Actions or processes that work to reduce the variety faced by managers are known as filters or attenuators, whilst those which act to increase the variety of the manager are amplifiers.

Recursion is the final topic for this section. In this context recursion refers to the 'organisational and interactional invariance' (Beer, 1981: 72) between levels of an organisation. In essence, each level of an organisation contains all the levels below it, and is contained in all the levels above it. The organisation then exists within a chain of embedded systems – a sample chain is provided in figure 15.7. In the cybernetic context, the structure of information flows and interaction within the organisation is perceived as identical at every level. This provides for great ease of understanding of the structure at every level and provides for the determination of the relevant autonomy of the system studied. Each level of organisation then manages surplus variety from its contained levels and enjoys a degree of freedom in managing variety at its own level constrained by its membership of the next higher level.

15.3 CYBERNETICS AND QUALITY

While the 'systems' and 'contingency' approaches to management progress well beyond the clear limitations of the 'classical' and 'human relations' schools of thought, they each only offer a way of describing organisations.

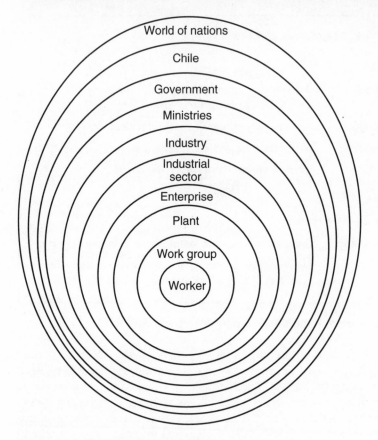

Figure 15.7 **Recursions of a system**

They are descriptive models. However, the ability to describe a situation or problem does little to improve or solve it. The cybernetic model like these other models can be used to provide a description of how the organisation works but through the work of Beer adds to this the capability to diagnose organisational faults and thence to provide a prescription of changes to enhance the situation. The cybernetic approach then, through Beer's Viable System Model, can be used to provide a description, diagnosis and prescription for any organisation. The application of that model will be revealed in full in chapter 27.

The adoption of cybernetic principles generates several challenges to the established ways of thinking about organisations and achieving quality. First, the cybernetic model of organisation relies on appropriate distribution of information. That is to say, that information is held at the lowest level in the organisation where it is relevant. The design of the information system ensures this and provides the opportunity for local decision making – metaphorically the equivalent of reflex reactions in the human body. Information received locally may be reacted to locally provided that reaction is consistent with the needs of the whole organisation. Every feedback loop contains a comparator which implies the capacity for making decisions. The organisation provides as much autonomy as is consistent with organisational cohesion. Therefore, the local operation may not undertake activities or engage in reactions which are different from its agreed role or which challenge or threaten the organisation, but does have the freedom to react to those matters which are only of concern to itself.

This raises the second issue. If information is distributed, then power is distributed. A common basis of operation in organisations is for power (the right to make decisions) to be relatively highly centralised. Beer, using the expression 'dysfunctional overcentrality', contends that in many organisations decisions are taken at higher levels than is necessary or desirable for their effective functioning and raises two points relating to this. First, it is highly inefficient and therefore wasteful of resources. Second, it reduces the adaptability and flexibility of the organisation inhibiting the ability to react to threats and opportunities. In some cases the result of this will be the demise of the organisation since failure to respond appropriately and rapidly to a threat may cause 'organisational death', that is, liquidation, receivership, bankruptcy.

A third issue directly challenges a key assumption which underpins much of early management thinking concerning the abilities of workers. Taylor (1911) provided a prime example of this thinking when he suggested that 'no man suited to the task of handling pig iron is capable of understanding the science that applies to it'. This negative view of the capabilities of workers suggests of course the opposite view of management – omniscient, 'god-like' creatures of a higher order of intelligence than workers. Whether this view had validity in Taylor's time may be considered open to debate. Its relevance to the contemporary world is highly questionable. The generally higher levels of education now in evidence coupled with the technology driven move towards 'knowledge industries' have created a situation where Taylor's view is clearly unacceptable.

This generates a significant difficulty. The adoption of cybernetic principles in the design of organisations demands that those who currently hold power in organisations must release it. Thus the solution to many problems rests in the hands of those least likely to use it. This is a major criticism of cybernetic thinking. In a highly political or coercive situation the solutions which cybernetics proposes would not be applied. The approach is also criticised for being open to abuse by those with autocratic intentions. It is certainly the case that the concepts and principles underpinning cybernetics may be used in this way. Such applications though would be to corrupt the intent of the work of cyberneticians and in the medium to long term would be likely to fail. They would in any event be highly inefficient, demanding a high level of inspection or 'policing' to maintain themselves.

Comparing the cybernetic approach with the various approaches to quality, a number of parallels are revealed. The cybernetic demand for distributed information, coupled with the devolution of decision making in the organisation, reflects the demand in the quality literature for participation and improvement centred on the particular process or workshop. The idea of 'knowledge workers' supports the concept of quality circles – the assumption that the workforce do have the capacity to bring about substantial and constructive improvement in quality performance. Cybernetics demands that power be distributed in the organisation and utilised by those who have the information to make a decision, rather than those whose position on the organisation chart suggests that they have power. This in turn reflects the quality call for management commitment. A management which is serious about the pursuit of quality will facilitate and encourage this distribution of power, recognising that it is both necessary and desirable. If their managerial actions and behaviour do not support their public calls for improvement, then the psychological feedback loops inherent in any organisation will act to inhibit quality performance improvement.

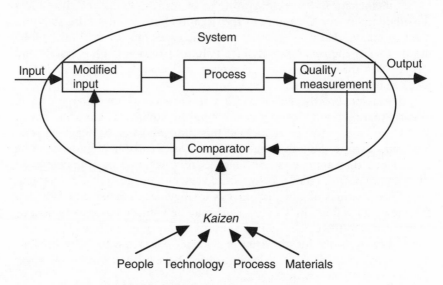

Figure 15.8 **A closed-loop, quality feedback system**

The achievement of quality itself may also be seen as a cybernetic function. Any production process (whether for goods or services) will include a feedback system of the type shown in figure 15.3. This was a model of any feedback system. In figure 15.8 the same model is used but this time modified to be explicitly about quality improvement. In this more specific model it can be seen that the input to a process is modified to reflect some desired quality improvement. The output of the process is measured in some way and the results fed back to a comparator. This compares the actual output with the desired output. The desired output is itself being continually modified by the *kaizen* process. Results are used to further modify the input to bring the actual output closer to that which is desired. The *kaizen* process itself consists of a further and similar set of feedback systems dealing with people, technology, processes, materials and so on. Each time a quality improvement is made in one of those aspects there is a consequent change in the desired output.

The cybernetic view considers organisations as made up of closely interacting feedback systems. The action of each system is continually modified by the actions, changes and outputs of each of the others. This conception of organisation serves to bring the organisation 'alive' – it can be imagined as constantly active – engaged in a continual process of self-maintenance and self-improvement, steering itself towards a better future rather than as the static, management driven and controlled machine of earlier views.

SUMMARY

This chapter has provided a brief overview of the field of organisational cybernetics and its relationship with quality. Many writers (for example, Beckford, 1993, 1995; Beer, 1959, 1979, 1981, 1985; Espejo and Schwaninger, 1993) have worked with and sought to develop cybernetic ideas on effective organisation. In chapter 27 these ideas will be applied in practice.

---

key learning points
ORGANISATIONAL CYBERNETICS

Key definition
the science of effective organisation

Key beliefs
quality is a product of effectiveness, organisations are extremely complex, exhibit self-regulation, are probabilistic

Tools of cybernetics
the black box technique, feedback, variety engineering, recursion

Cybernetics and quality
descriptive, diagnostic and prescriptive model, offers parallels to mainstream quality thinking, knowledge workers supports quality circles approach, distributed power demands management commitment, the cybernetic view supports and enables *kaizen*

QUESTION

Attempt to describe your class or tutorial sessions in terms of cybernetic processes.

chapter sixteen

SOFT SYSTEMS
THINKING

It ain't necessarily so.
Ira Gershwin and Dubose Heyward, *Porgy & Bess*

INTRODUCTION

No matter to what extent an organisation is automated and its products or services are believed guaranteed by the excellence of its technical artefacts, every venture has a fundamental reliance on human input for control and development. If the aim is to create a quality organisation then it is vital that those people, whether they are relatively unskilled workers or highly qualified experts in a consultancy or research organisation, are committed to that aim. This cannot be achieved if they are excluded by the management from the development and decision processes of the quality programme. They may tolerate the programme or accept it at a superficial level, but they will not take ownership of it, regard it as their own and drive it forward. A programme for quality which is not actively supported at every level in the organisation will fail.

16.1   SOFT SYSTEMS EXPLAINED

Organisational cybernetics, is often considered by those not fully familiar with its breadth and depth, as applicable to 'hard' problems. Soft systems thinking, largely represented in the work of Peter Checkland (1981), proposes the study of human activity systems, those 'soft ill-structured problems of the real world'. Checkland suggests that in 'soft' problems, the identification of the objectives themselves is problematic and his work focuses on defining a systemic methodology which helps participants to understand social systems.

The study of 'soft systems' is considered as ends orientated. It is concerned with discovering the purpose of the system. It presumes that the problem of what to do must be solved before the problem of how to do it can be addressed.

Hard systems thinking assumes that the problem to be tackled 'is to select an efficient means of achieving a known and defined end' (Checkland, 1978) – a criticism often levelled at the cybernetic understanding discussed in the previous chapter. Soft systems thinking supposes multiple perceptions of reality. This simply means that reality is not assumed to be the same for every observer. The existence and purpose of the organisation are considered to be functions of the observer rather than objective statements of fact. Contrasting with the hard approach, the desired end needs to be defined because only limited agreement about it is believed to exist.

For example, a rainbow exists as a result of the action of light through water droplets suspended in the air, but it can only be observed from the outside, and from particular angles; when approached, it disappears; it is a mirage. While we cannot grasp or physically handle a rainbow, we can describe it and understand how it is structured even though from a different perspective, the rainbow simply isn't there! Another example is to consider an entity such as the City of Kowloon in Hong Kong. There is only one Kowloon and all parties can agree about its objective existence. However, consideration of Kowloon from vantage points on the eight hills surrounding it would generate different descriptions of that objective existence. Each of the descriptions would be 'right' for the particular observer and viewpoint, but each would describe a different reality.

Similarly each observer's perception is prejudiced by past experiences, personal desires and expectations. Each observer is unique. This means that even if the same organisation is studied from precisely the same physical viewpoint by a variety of people differing aspects of the organisation will be highlighted. Examining Kowloon through a fixed set of binoculars from a hilltop will reveal different sights to different people, an architect may see the buildings, a town planner the roads, an anthropologist the people and an entrepreneur the profit opportunities.

Accepting this very different, 'interpretive' (Burrell and Morgan: 1979) perspective on organisations demands a completely different approach to problem solving and organisational management. The nature and existence of an organisation and its purposes can no longer be taken as facts within an established framework, they must be agreed through the participation of the members. The first step in any problem solving or improvement process then becomes to develop consensus about the organisation and the problems or issues to be addressed.

The adjective 'soft' does not refer to a characteristic of the system itself but is a function of the perspective taken of the system by those who set themselves up as its problem solvers. It reflects their particular interpretation of how organisational problems should be solved. Thus soft systems thinkers propose that the dominant element in a problem solving situation is generating agreement amongst the participants, with this agreement itself leading to improvement in the situation. This is because the generation of agreement will highlight aspects of the organisation which do not meet the terms of that agreement and must therefore be modified to fit.

Two well established methodologies for using soft systems thinking will be explored in chapter 28.

16.2   TOOLS FOR SOFT SYSTEMS

At a fundamental level, the tools of soft systems may be seen to be cybernetic. That is, effective communication may be interpreted as operating through positive and negative feedback loops, comparators of expectations against achievements and adaptation or modification of attitudes in order to work towards defining goals. The processes by which this takes place though make more explicit use of interpersonal action and debate. For example, in Strategic Assumption Surfacing and Testing (Mason and Mitroff, 1981) there are four phases (figure 16.1).

MASON AND MITROFF

Phase 1   Group formation;

Phase 2   Assumption surfacing;

Phase 3   Dialectical debate;

Phase 4   Synthesis.

Figure 16.1 **Four phases of SAST: Mason and Mitroff**

Each of these phases relies heavily on open, effective communication (speaking *and* listening) between the participants. Phase one is concerned with structuring groups on the basis of some common ground. Phase two involves the individual groups developing an agreed perspective on the problem. Phase three is based on advocacy with each group presenting its approach and explaining the assumptions which underpin it. Dialectical debate orientated around the underpinning assumptions of the respective arguments follows between the groups. Dialectical debate is debate based on logical argument. At phase four, the attempt is made to converge the two different views into a consensus view shared by all the participants. Reiteration of the process with additional information is encouraged where consensus cannot be achieved.

It can be seen that this process relies on a number of key characteristics:

- agreement by the participants to open debate;
- a common language – both syntactic and semantic;
- freedom of expression;
- advocacy skills;
- the capacity of the individuals to express themselves, hence freedom from fear;
- sufficient commonality of opinion at the outset for agreement to be a feasible potential outcome.

The tools then are the tools of human communication, perhaps best understood and expressed through the science of human psychology. Whilst admirable in theory, some of the characteristics of debate outlined above can be difficult to achieve in practice.

CATHAY PACIFIC

Service Straight From The Heart

Cathay Pacific Airline, launched the programme called 'Service Straight From The Heart' (SSFTH) as a means of developing cultural change within the airline focused on improving customer service. As airline users will know, service is the principal means of differentiating between airlines and is highly influential in customer choice.

Cathay Pacific recognised in early 1995 that the organisation and management style of the company needed to create the conditions which would make it possible for SSFTH to be delivered to the customers. A leadership training programme was developed with the purposes of enabling managers to:

- focus on developing a culture supportive to SSFTH;
- understand the company's expectations of its managers;
- understand the impact of personal and organisational styles;
- understand how personal leadership affects service quality;
- experience leadership of high performance teams;
- identify and plan for the challenges to be faced in delivering enhanced service.

The programme addresses a number of leadership behaviours:

- sharing the strategy and vision;
- supporting others;
- enabling others;
- encouraging others;
- modelling – leading the way.

Crucial in this process of development is the emphasis on enabling the effective participation of staff in decision making. For example, in the section on 'Enabling others', managers are required to involve others in planning, to develop co-operative relationships, to treat others with dignity and respect. Under 'Encouraging others' the programme suggests celebrating achievements, recognition of contributions and sharing successes. These aspects are all expected to have the effect of encouraging and enabling a sense of community and shared purpose within the organisation.

Cathay Pacific has expressed within this programme its understanding of the importance of the people within the organisation and its recognition of the contribution of those people to its success. By putting people at the heart of its own efforts, they can expect those people to put the customers at the heart of theirs.

The company has enjoyed considerable success with the SSFTH programme and these results are fast becoming measurable where it matters – that is where the airline serves its customers.

16.3   SOFT SYSTEMS AND QUALITY

The traditional approaches to quality predominantly focus on its technical aspects, paying relatively little attention to the human side. They are 'hard' approaches which assume that the pursuit of quality necessarily leads to improvement. This is, however, to examine quality only from the perspective of the owners or managers of the organisation. If quality means less cost and higher profits, then in a profit oriented world, quality is good for managers and owners. The assumption which underpins those approaches is that 'economic man' will fall in line with the corporate expectations.

However, as has been discussed by numerous writers since the 1960s, the theory of man as purely economically motivated does not stand up to practical examination. People work for many different reasons and while for some, money is a strong, extrinsic motivator, others derive the greater part of their value from the intrinsic value of the work itself. From yet another perspective it is argued that people work simply because man is a social animal and needs both company and work for social and psychological reasons.

If the motivation underpinning an organisation's drive for quality is simply economic (as it so often is) then the probable outcomes include reduced numbers in the workforce (assuming a stable output) and changes to working practices and the established social mores of the organisation. If the management does not appreciate the differing perspectives of the other members of the organisations and accommodate them within their mental models of what is to be achieved then they will meet varying degrees of resistance to those changes. This resistance will arise from the different interpretations which the individuals put on the organisation and its actions.

When resistance to the quality programme is met, the programme will almost certainly fail to fulfil all its stated objectives. Blame will be placed on the 'workers' – 'they failed to make it happen'. The soft systems thinker will immediately recognise that the failure belongs to management because they failed to create the conditions which would have made it possible for the programme to succeed. The management have failed to discover and accommodate the different viewpoints within the organisation.

This thinking re-emphasises the points made in earlier chapters about the need for effective communication and is a reminder of the comments made by various gurus that most of the responsibility for quality lies with the management.

SUMMARY

This chapter has introduced the concept of 'soft systems'. In this view organisations are not products of objective reality but products of the interpretations put on them by their members. The different approach to solving organisational problems necessitated by this view was introduced and the implications for the pursuit of quality discussed. Readers wishing to expand their knowledge of soft systems should consider the work of Checkland (1981), Mason and Mitroff (1981), Checkland and Scholes (1991).

---

key learning points

SOFT SYSTEMS

Key definition
the study of problems in human activity systems

Key beliefs
objectives must be agreed through participation before the study of methods becomes meaningful

Tools of soft systems
participation, debate, consensus building

Soft systems and quality
participative approaches can reduce conflict, quality programmes must address hearts as well as minds

---

QUESTION

How do *you* use 'soft' approaches to problem solving in your day-to-day life?

chapter
seventeen

CRITICAL
SYSTEMS
THINKING

to transcend their alterable, historical and essentially ideological limitations.

John C. Oliga, 1988

INTRODUCTION

Critical Systems Thinking which began to emerge in the late 1970s and early 1980s is founded on the pursuit of three goals 'complementarism', 'sociological awareness', and 'emancipation'.

Complementarism recognises that different situations lend themselves to different problem solving approaches. Therefore critical systems thinking proposes that the most appropriate methodology should be applied to a problem but that this *must* be done with understanding of and respect for the theoretical underpinnings of the approach.

Sociological awareness is simply a commitment to the understanding that the nature and culture of societies is different between varying organisations and nations and alters over time. It is suggested that choice of methodology must be guided by the acceptability of a particular approach in a given context. Without such contextual awareness any approach is likely to fail. It is essential that the conditions demanded by a methodology or way of working are met. Thus it might be of limited value to apply a very 'hard' methodology in a very liberal environment for example, a creative organisation. Similarly, it might be inappropriate to apply a very 'soft' approach in a prison camp or a dictatorship since the approach would be doomed to failure by the power relations within the system studied.

Emancipation and human well-being are cornerstones of the critical systems approach and act to support the development of human potential and freedom from externally imposed constraints. Theoretical support for this aspect is drawn from the work of Habermas (cited by Flood and Jackson, 1991) who suggested that the two fundamental conditions underpinning the 'socio-cultural' form of life are 'work' and 'interaction'. Work is goal oriented and enables improvement in material things, generating a 'technical interest' in control. Interaction is a 'practical interest' concerned with the development of understanding between people. A further and major concern is with the way in which power is, and has been, exercised in forming social arrangements. Awareness of the power of individuals or groups in a given organisational context frequently disrupts the free flow of discussion, inhibiting the potential for genuine debate.

It should be clear that taking these three strands of thought together creates the potential for management problem solving through all available and theoretically substantiated routes enabling technical, practical and emancipatory interests to be fully served.

17.1 TOTAL SYSTEMS INTERVENTION

Flood and Jackson (1991) suggest that the world of management problem solving and systems thinking has divided itself along three principal routes – pragmatism, isolationism and imperialism.

The first of these concentrates on practical solutions – what works for the manager or consultant. Concern is expressed that solutions developed without the appropriate theoretical underpinnings are somewhat sterile as we cannot learn from them (since they only apply in the given situation) and that such solutions lead to distortion or abuse such as 'simply serving the powerful'. It is also observed that without the ability to move from the particular to the general, there is no management science which can usefully be passed on to future generations of managers.

Isolationism on the other hand suggests that only one method, based on only one rationality is appropriate in *all* circumstances – in other words it fits the problem to the solution, rather than the solution to the problem.

The dangers of 'imperialism' are also highlighted. Imperialism occurs when alternative methodologies are subsumed into the preferred theoretical position of the user. We must be concerned about this when, as was seen in part two of this book, each different approach is based on a particular set of assumptions about the world. The results postulated by the approach can only be achieved if that set of assumptions is recognised, respected and adhered to by the user.

Hence, in chapter 15, the application of organisational cybernetics required the devolution of power within an organisation to achieve maximum benefit. Such devolution forms part of the philosophy of the approach. It is undeniable that the understanding of organisational interaction derived from the cybernetic approach can be used, at the 'tool' or 'method' level to achieve greater centralisation of power. There is nothing inherently devolutionary about cybernetic interactions. However, to use the tools in this way is a denial of the founding philosophy – quite apart from being less effective in improving the total efficiency and effectiveness of an organisation.

Taking action on this theoretical work and connecting it with the work of Jackson and Keys (1984) on the development of a 'system of systems methodologies', Flood and Jackson have developed a meta-method for problem solving which enables the informed use of each systems methodology in its most appropriate context. This approach is called 'Total Systems Intervention' (TSI).

17.2   PRINCIPLES OF TSI

The practice of Total Systems Intervention (TSI) in the quality context will be considered in chapter 26. In this chapter we are concerned with its principles and philosophy. There are seven underpinning principles to TSI (figure 17.1) which it is reasonable to consider briefly in turn and reflect on their relevance. Taking the first, it is certainly the case that the many extremely large organisations of today are very complicated and that the complexity of their problems is beyond what could have been envisaged by the management writers of the earlier parts of the century.

But what of small organisations – those which make up the bulk of the world's economies. A significant proportion of the world's businesses are classified as 'small to medium' (as defined by the Companies Act, 1985, criteria of turnover below £5.75m, and less than 250 employees). These are generally owner managed, independent organisations with minimal influence on pricing within their industry or sector. In these cases it might be thought that lesser tools would be adequate. However, it seems to be the case that the problems of these organisations are in many ways more complex than their larger brethren. On the economic side, the smaller business is seeking to maintain viability in a market-place dominated by large organisations which have significant advantages in cost and in economic information, increasing the challenge to the small player. In human terms, the intimacy of small organisations may be considered to lead to an increase in the relevance of people management and relationship issues, where people are often personal friends not simply reference numbers on a payroll. In management terms the small business is again at a disadvantage. They are relatively unattractive to many managers because they often cannot, or do not, offer the same level of either monetary or non-monetary

FLOOD AND JACKSON

Principle 1   Organisations are too complicated to understand using one management 'model' and their problems too complex too tackle with the 'quick fix'.

Principle 2   Organisations, their strategies and the difficulties they face should be investigated using a range of systems metaphors.

Principle 3   Systems metaphors, which seem appropriate for highlighting organisational strategies and problems, can be linked to appropriate systems methodologies to guide intervention.

Principle 4   Different systems metaphors and methodologies can be used in a complementary way to address different aspects of organisations and the difficulties they confront.

Principle 5   It is possible to appreciate the strengths and weaknesses of different systems methodologies and to relate each to organisational and business concerns.

Principle 6   TSI sets out a systemic circle of enquiry with iteration back and forth between the three phases.

Principle 7   Facilitators, clients and others are engaged at all stages of the TSI process.

Figure 17.1 **Seven principles of TSI: Flood and Jackson**

reward as the larger organisations. They are not well placed to attract the highest calibre staff and frequently lack the resources to properly educate and train those which they do attract.

Turning to complexity, it must be suggested that this is not necessarily a function of the size of the organisation. Complexity may be seen as a product of dynamism (the frequency of interaction), the number of elements (the number of relevant sub-systems within the organisation studied) and the necessary rate of change of the organisation and its environment – factors which may be considered to be more predominant in small organisations than in larger ones.

BUSINESS BANKING

Size doesn't matter

In the late 1980s a major high street bank reviewed the way in which it managed its relationships with business customers – those whose accounts were not held purely for personal purposes. This review led to the development of a wholly new operating structure based on dividing customers according to their industry rather than the traditional alphabetic division. It was felt that in this way the bankers could develop higher levels of industry focused expertise and understanding generating in turn higher levels of customer service and lower levels of risk.

This new form of division created difficulties of its own. It was no longer considered adequate to simply 'lump' customers together and shuffle their problems up and down the hierarchy as had traditionally been done. If 'relationships' were to be the basis of satisfying customers, it was thought essential that the customer facing member of staff must be able to deal with the majority of the particular customer's problems and needs.

Traditionally the organisation had assumed that size (particularly borrowing requirements), complexity and risk were positively correlated – the bigger the amount borrowed, the greater the complexity and risk associated with the account. It was suggested, by the staff, that this assumption may be flawed and that an alternative division based on complexity of requirements and difficulty of control should be considered.

The staff involved undertook the task of dividing the relationships into industry, at the same time allocating a complexity code (which would determine the seniority of the member of staff who subsequently managed the relationship) according to their knowledge and experience of the customer. It emerged that many of the largest accounts (either by turnover or borrowing requirements) were the simplest to manage – being categorised as 'simple' by the staff. The requirements were simple to understand and relatively unchanging and the sophistication of the customer matched the needs of the organisation. In contrast many much smaller accounts were designated 'very complex'. These smaller accounts often had rapidly changing requirements (because of rapid growth, or the unexpected demands and opportunities facing small businesses) and had less financially sophisticated staff requiring a greater degree of more sophisticated support from the bank.

The second principle, use of systems metaphors, is useful because it enables individuals to generate high level descriptions of their circumstances without the need for great elaboration or reductionist analysis. The 'meaning' conveyed by descriptions such as 'prison', 'brain', 'culture' is normally relatively clear to the listener since there exists a common understanding. Thus the use of metaphor provides a systemic language which can be easily shared. A good source for further exploration of the use of metaphors in this context is Morgan (1986).

The third principle follows from the second. The image generated by a particular metaphor is linked to a group of methodologies. The methodologies so identified are considered applicable to organisations which display the 'metaphorical' characteristics. The assumptions about the world which underpin the methodology match the behaviour of the actors within the organisation. Thus a 'prison' is suggestive of a coercive environment with a relatively low level of interaction between the stakeholders – one group is dominated by the other. The methodology proposed for this situation is 'Critical Systems Heuristics' which will be introduced in chapter 29.

The fourth principle addresses the issue of 'complementarity' which has already been adequately elaborated at the outset of this chapter.

The fifth principle is of particular importance. It acknowledges that any given methodology has both strengths and weaknesses, situations for which it is good and situations for which it is not. This specifically addresses the issues of isolationism and imperialism raised in the previous section. No craftsman uses only a single tool for the completion of all his tasks. He or she selects from the range of tools available one which is appropriate for the task in hand. Management scientists should be no different.

The sixth principle reflects the dynamic nature of contemporary organisations. TSI is proposed as setting out a 'systemic circle of enquiry' with iteration back and forth. This issue is perhaps understated in much of the literature. A key assumption which underpins much of management thinking is that problems can be solved. Beer (1981) prefers to think that, through the application of organisational cybernetics, rather than being solved, problems can be dissolved. While there is truth in both of these positions, the current author tends to the view that rather than problems being solved, situations can be managed. While any particular and discrete management problem may have a definable solution, the overall problem of managing can never be complete. The continual changes both within the system of interest and in its environment ensure that effective management is a non-stop activity.

Thus it may be more helpful to think of TSI as a systemic meta-model for managing, rather than as a meta-methodology for problem solving. Taking this view it is easier to understand that the process may be simultaneously at different stages for different problems, and that more than one metaphor may be employed simultaneously with another to describe a given organisational situation.

The final principle addresses the issue of emancipation, again raised in the previous section. TSI requires that all relevant parties should be involved throughout the process. There is scope for debate and consideration about how to make such participation meaningful under certain circumstances – particularly where coercion exists.

17.3 THREE PHASES OF TSI

TSI consists of three phases of work: *creativity*, *choice* and *implementation*.

The first phase, 'creativity' asks questions in two modes: which metaphor best describes the current situation (the 'is' mode) and which best describes the desired situation (the 'ought' mode). A third approach to the enquiry is to consider which metaphors help to explain the difficulties and areas of concern. Metaphors suggested by Flood and Jackson indicate the organisation as a 'machine', 'organism', 'brain', 'culture', 'team', 'coalition' and 'prison'. This list is by no means exhaustive and any other metaphor may be used by the participants; what is essential, however, is that the description can be linked to one of the systems approaches.

Encouraging participants to go beyond the metaphors suggested by

Flood and Jackson may encourage more creative thinking about the situation. In one case, a large Hong Kong based corporation, the metaphor used was 'elephant' – slow-moving, lacking in colour (no flair), deliberate but instinctive rather than reflective. This perhaps suggests a mechanistic view with organismic overtones – a rather more complex description which captured the essence of the situation for the participants. The result of this phase is a choice of a dominant metaphor which is used to guide the selection of methodology(ies) in the next phase. It is legitimate to use 'dependent' or subordinate metaphors to capture areas of secondary concern.

The choice phase utilises Jackson and Keys (1984) 'system of systems methodologies' (SOSM) (figure 17.2) to provide a framework for choosing between approaches. The SOSM offers 'guidelines' to assist the participants in making their choices. The SOSM typology sorts methodologies according to two dimensions, the relative complexity of the system studied and the relative plurality of views of the participants.

A 'simple' system will have few elements, a low level of interaction, a high degree of determinacy and will be highly organised and highly regulated. It will be relatively static and closed to environmental influence. A 'complex' system will have a large number of elements in highly dynamic interaction,

	Unitary	Pluralist	Coercive
Simple	OR SA SE SD	SSD SAST	CSH
Complex	VSD GST ST Cont. Theory	IP SSM	?

KEY:

OR = Operations Research	Cont. Theory = Contingency Theory
SA = Systems Analysis	SSD = Social Systems Design
SE = Systems Engineering	SAST = Strategic Assumption Surfacing
SD = Systems Dynamics	and Testing
VSD = Viable Systems Diagnosis	IP = Interactive Planning
GST = General Systems Theory	SSM = Soft Systems Methodology
ST = Socio Technical Systems Thinking	CST = Critical Systems Heuristics
	? = No methodology available

Figure 17.2 **The system of systems methodologies**
Source: **Adapted from Flood and Jackson, 1991**

it will exhibit probabilistic behaviour, a lower level of apparent organisation and will be evolutionary.

Unitary, pluralist and coercive refer to the relationships between the participants in the system. A unitary view suggests common interests, values and beliefs between the participants with general agreement about ends and means and actions matching objectives. In a pluralist situation, the participants have a basic common interest but divergent values and beliefs. They can compromise on ends and means and will also act in line with agreed objectives. In a coercive situation there is no common interest; values and beliefs are in conflict, compromise is not possible and some parties may be coerced by others.

TSI interventionists must select a methodology (ies) (albeit it may be one of their own choosing or design not included in the SOSM) in order to move to the next phase, implementation. The framework of the SOSM should enable the users to select a methodology which reflects the characteristics of the situation studied.

Implementation rests in the coherent application of the chosen methodology(ies) to the situation in accordance with its own theoretical assumptions but constrained by the recognition of those secondary characteristics highlighted during the choice phase. Thus the approach to the methodology must be modified or 'tempered' to ensure that the use is suitable. Flood and Jackson (1991: 15–22) provide an example of the use of TSI in the quality context.

17.4 CRITICAL REVIEW OF TSI

TSI, while appearing complex, serves to simplify and perhaps demystify choice amongst systems methodologies, while also enabling coherent understanding and debate in a common language about the characteristics of a situation. It provides a framework for the exploration of issues of concern to an organisation and for the 'dominant' issues to be highlighted.

While the SOSM framework may appear to be almost reductionist in its approach, this is too literal a view. Flood and Jackson acknowledge this in their own critique and refer to the framework as offering 'ideal type' proposals. In any given situation, the practitioner must exercise professional judgement in choice of methodology and in recognising that most situations have a significant degree of 'grey' in their make up, compared to the 'black and white' so often sought by clients and apparently suggested by the SOSM. This area is one which demands sophisticated knowledge and understanding by the user (and may account for some of the inadequate uses of the TSI process).

In terms of use, TSI adds much of value to its users, provided that they are prepared to deal with the uncertainty and complexity which rigorous application of the technique may provide. For those who perceive all of an organisation's problems as simple and trivial the method is of little value since they have decided, before the start of the exploration, what the problem is and how it may be solved.

While the theoretical foundations of TSI appear fairly sound, there are two principal limitations. The approach is so complex in use that for managers without the appropriate background it may be difficult. For maximum benefit it requires expert facilitation. The first of these limitations may lead managers to avoid the approach, preferring something simpler and more straightforward. The second opens the whole model to the potential for abuse of power for which other models have already been criticised. In this context, the facilitators are the powerful and may divert the model to their own ends.

17.5 CRITICAL SYSTEMS THINKING AND QUALITY

Critical systems thinking has great relevance to the quality movement (and to the content of this book which reflects that thinking). Simply, critical systems thinking rejects the idea of 'one best way' of solving any problem (whether or not a problem of quality) proposing instead that each method has potential utility in organisational contexts which reflect the theoretical assumptions which underpin the approach and that human freedom and well-being is respected.

In the quality context this suggests that, far from any one Quality Guru being absolutely right and the others absolutely wrong – they are all right *and* all wrong. Similarly, the various strands of thinking being introduced in this part of the book are equally right and wrong, depending upon the circumstances in which their use is attempted.

Thus, in a certain situation the statistically based approach espoused by Deming may be most appropriate, while in another the participative approach preferred by Ishikawa may have greater utility. Equally, at a higher level of organisation, both of those approaches may be rejected in favour of a systems based approach which embraces the whole system of interest in the pursuit of quality.

A word of caution is appropriate at this juncture at the risk of offending some readers. It is not only quality methodologies and ways of thinking about the world that have different value in different contexts. These differences also apply to the words which we choose to use and the concepts which we attempt to apply. Thus such concepts as freedom of choice, participation and emancipation have different meanings and value in different contexts. These ideas are essentially products of Western thinking, reflecting primarily what philosophers consider important in societies which are relatively complex in both the economic and the social senses. They are aimed at furthering the interests of those parts of societies already supposed capable of exercising substantial political and economic choices and accustomed, even if for relatively short periods of history, to making those choices. Such parts of societies may be thought of as enjoying significant psychological maturity.

Other societies operate under different sets of opportunities, demands and constraints; they may be considered less psychologically mature. Thus while in a mature society the idea of participation in process design and improvement may be wholly applicable, in some contexts the members of the society may not be wholly familiar with the concept of a job. Consequently they may require a totally different (although not dictatorial) management approach, perhaps placing greater emphasis on the parental role of the manager. This difference in approach does not apply solely to emerging or developing economies but also to those parts of Western economies which have suffered high levels of unemployment over many years, for example, the steel, coal-mining and ship-building regions of most Western economies. In these regions there are significant numbers of people to whom the concept of a job is wholly unfamiliar since work has been unavailable to them, in some cases for two or more generations. This might be thought of, in part, as a product of the failure of employers and employees to embrace changes in management thinking and practice which might have enabled organisational survival. Critical systems thinking enables the thoughtful manager to recognise and reflect upon these aspects of the circumstances in which he works and to choose quality implementation methods accordingly.

17.6   TQM THROUGH TSI

In 1993 Flood undertook the task of exploring Total Quality Management through the ideas of critical systems thinking seeking to establish a sound platform for the theory and practice of TQM. His findings are encapsulated in the book *Beyond TQM* (1993).

He defines quality as: 'Quality means meeting customers' (agreed) requirements, formal and informal, at lowest cost, first time every time.' Flood sees ten principles (figure 17.3) emerging from this definition. These are to some extent a distillation and synthesis of the work of the gurus already explored in part two of this book.

The first principle, the call for agreed requirements, implies a need for a high degree of communication both within the organisation and with the customers in its environment. The demand for agreement implies that the communication must be focused on discussion rather than discourse – it must be a two way process of finding out and informing rather than a matter of giving orders. To be effective there must be understanding and voluntary consensus.

The second principle of 'first time, every time' reflects Crosby's call for zero defects. The clear implication is that there is no benefit to be gained from failing to meet customer requirements and that achieving quality is a matter of consistency. Third is the belief that quality improvement will reduce waste and total costs. The important issue here is the positive nature of the statement. Note that Flood uses the word, 'will', not may, could, perhaps or should. This is of great importance as a belief since many quality improvement programmes, initially at least, produce solutions which seem to have the opposite effect, increasing costs and waste in the short term while new techniques or processes are learned and embedded.

ROBERT FLOOD

Principle 1   There must be agreed requirements, for both internal and external customers.

Principle 2   Customers' requirements must be met first time and every time.

Principle 3   Quality improvement will reduce waste and total costs.

Principle 4   There must be a focus on the prevention of problems, rather than an acceptance to cope in a fire-fighting manner.

Principle 5   Quality improvement can only result from planned management action.

Principle 6   Every job must add value.

Principle 7   Everybody must be involved, from all levels and across all functions.

Principle 8   There must be an emphasis on measurement to help to assess and to meet requirements and objectives;

Principle 9   A culture of continuous improvement must be established (continuous includes the desirability of dramatic leaps forward as well as steady improvement).

Principle 10 An emphasis should be placed on promoting creativity.

Figure 17.3 **Ten principles of TQM: Robert Flood**

Often managements not fully committed draw back from the changes in response to this negative short term effect and hence fail to achieve any of the expected benefits.

The fourth principle, 'focus on prevention', again reflects ideas of the mainstream gurus and is fundamental to achievement of quality. If the previous principle is to hold good then clearly the process of achieving quality has to start with error prevention, since as soon as an error occurs extra cost is incurred in either rectification, rework or after-sales support. As Crosby suggests, 'It is always cheaper to do it right first time.' This links neatly to the fifth principle, planned management action.

Planning is at the root of success in all manner of activities in life. Planning implies intent which in turn implies commitment to a particular course of events. All too often managements attempt to deal with some form of operational organisational crisis (usually a cost based crisis) by trying to achieve 'quick hits through an instant TQM programme. This is sure to fail since the focus is wrong. The banner headline may read 'Quality' but the sub-text reads 'save money' and, since the latter is much easier to understand and measure, that will become the focus of the exercise. Some money may be saved, what is almost certain is that greater quality will not be achieved. A commitment to quality improvement is a long term commitment and planning is the key to success.

ENSURING FAILURE IN QUALITY IMPLEMENTATION

In late 1996 and early 1997 a food manufacturer decided, within the context of its overall quality improvement programme, to investigate the poor performance of an established food factory. The plant had been built some ten years previously but had never achieved the levels of productivity and profitability expected.

The investigation was undertaken by a team despatched from the head office who proceeded to conduct a thorough review of all activities at the plant. Their findings were extensive showing poor utilisation of equipment and labour, inadequate maintenance, poor record keeping (of production, quality, waste and yield) and abuse of the shift system by some employees. Findings were presented to the local manager, together with a well worked out performance improvement plan.

The manager demanded 'instant' improvements – a focus on the simple operational matters requiring attention – in order to reduce current year budget deficits. The team from head office argued for a systematic fundamental overhaul of processes and procedures, designed to achieve sustainable improvement over time.

No agreement was reached and eventually the team from head office was banned from the premises by the manager. The dispute was referred to the lowest level manager with reporting lines to both parties. At the time of writing, the dispute is unresolved and the original performance problems have not been addressed.

There are several mistakes evident in this process:

- the problem solving team was imposed on the factory rather than invited in;
- a 'them and us' situation was guaranteed by the exclusion from the process of any members of the factory staff;
- no 'agreed requirements' were developed between the 'customer' (factory manager) and the 'supplier' (head office team);
- no educational process was undertaken, that is, no sharing of knowledge by either party;
- not everybody was involved;
- the protagonists allowed themselves to be distracted into a 'tribal war' rather than focusing on the particular problem faced.

The sixth principle, 'every job must add value' is perhaps a recognition of the extent to which organisational processes are characterised by jobs and tasks which do not add value, being either unnecessary or obstructive to the process. An interesting point to note is that this 'every' does not just apply to production focused jobs but to every job in the organisation – from the board downwards! This again links to the seventh principle – the involvement of 'everybody' – all levels and all functions. This takes the responsibility for quality away from the quality assurance or inspection department and places it firmly in the hands of those responsible for actually doing the job.

The eighth principle – emphasis on measurement – is not taken as a call for reliance on purely statistical methods but as a recognition that without some form of measurement there is no effective basis for evaluation of performance.

The ninth and tenth principles can be taken together: calls for continuous improvement and the promotion of creativity. The first of these relies on the second. Flood specifically recognises in the ninth principle that continuous improvement should include 'dramatic leaps as well as steady improvement'. In this case we can argue with word choice and suggest that 'continual' improvement implies a more dynamic frame of reference for these 'dramatic leaps' than 'continuous' with its implications of incremental behaviour. Figure 17.4 attempts to highlight the difference perceived between continual and continuous improvement.

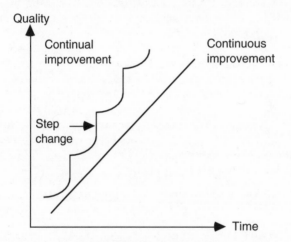

Figure 17.4 **Continual and continuous change**

Quality is then considered by Flood as a function of effective communication between the organisation and its customers. This communication clarifies expectations and is supported by consistent effort from all those within the organisation to meet those expectations. This necessitates meaningful measurement and a creative approach to continual improvement.

17.7 ASSUMPTIONS

Flood's assumptions about the world in the quality context will now be explored.

First it can be seen that Flood assumes a willingness on the part of organisations to communicate and negotiate with their customers. This suggests recognition of equality of power between the supplier and customer. In practice, such equality of power is rare, with one party or the other normally assuming a dominant role in the relationship. When power is unequal, that is, one party is reliant on the other for its continued existence or financial well-being, it is unlikely that equality will be maintained in negotiations about quality. For example, it is often the case in the motor industry that component or sub-assembly manufacturers rely on orders from a single manufacturer for the majority of their business. This means that the buyer can dictate quality standards, and prices. Similar behaviour is seen in the food industry where the major supermarket groups exercise enormous power over their suppliers. The banking industry has recently demonstrated similar characteristics in relation to its customers.

Second, Flood's approach assumes a willingness within an organisation to distribute power amongst the members – since this is the clear implica-tion of involving 'everybody, at all levels and across all functions'. Again, the relatively low power held by many employees and their vulnerability to loss of employment in many contexts, makes it more likely that managers will behave autocratically, dictating how things will be. This will not lead to full commitment and co-operation – which Flood requires – but does more accurately reflect the power relations in many contemporary organ-isations. This assumption is also implicit in the ninth principle – the culture of continuous improvement. It suggests again effective sharing of power within the organisation.

Flood's third assumption is that it is possible to be 'right first time, every time'. While in the manufacturing context this is not at all an unreasonable expectation, in the service and public sectors it is arguably extremely difficult. The technical aspects of any transaction are of course no more difficult to get right than the technical aspects of a physical product. Where the service and public sectors will always have difficulty is at the customer–organisation interface. While the technical aspects of any particular transaction are constant, each transaction is unique since it depends upon the mood and expectations of the particular customer and of the member of staff at the particular point in time. There are then three variables within any given transaction which are largely beyond the scope of the organisation to control. It is inevitable that there will be an occasional mismatch between expectations and delivery.

The final assumption in Flood's work which distinguishes it from that of others is the wholehearted embrace of the systemic approach. This comes through in his recognition of both external and internal customers and in the use of the word 'every' in relation to meeting expectations, to jobs adding value and to the involvement of all levels and all functions. He does not preclude the involvement of customers in this – although he does not specifically require it.

Overall, Flood's principles rely on a systemic world in which people behave as if they are in partnership. Power is distributed, with those having the information making the decisions, and collaboration rather than competition as the keynote of success. This is a rather different world to the one which many people experience each day.

Other aspects of Flood's approach will be examined in later chapters, especially the practice of TQM through TSI, which will be considered in chapter 26. This section has simply outlined his proposed overall process.

17.8   SUCCESSES AND FAILURES

It is probably too early to make properly informed judgements about the success or failure of this approach as, unlike the approaches reviewed in part two, it has not had the benefit of extended development and empirical study. It is reasonable though to attempt some preliminary evaluation of this work. The probable strengths are:

- it attempts to be truly holistic;
- it is systematic, methodical and iterative;
- it embraces much of value from the established approaches, overcoming some weaknesses previously recognised;
- it is rooted in a substantial appreciation of management and organisation theory.

Perceived weaknesses include the following:

- the theory and practice of TSI is not yet accepted as part of mainstream management theory;
- TSI is regarded by many practitioners as too complex in itself;
- there is a lack of widely reported case studies in the literature;
- substantial empirical development has been principally undertaken by Flood himself;
- as with the other approaches already considered the approach is of limited value in a truly coercive context.

Looking at the strengths, the truly holistic view stems from the meta-methodological, complementarist, framework of TSI which underpins the approach and tries to avoid the isolationist, pragmatic or imperialist criticisms made of other methods. The systematic, methodical and iterative process provides a heuristic aspect which reflects the Deming or Shewhart cycle of learning. The embrace of established approaches recognises that there are strengths in them and supports them with a broader conceptual framework, increasing their potential utility. Finally, the appreciation of management and organisation theory recognises that quality is only one aspect of organisational effectiveness and opens the pursuit of quality to the importation of ideas from other frames of reference within the total knowledge set.

With regard to the weaknesses, the lack of acceptance of TSI amongst mainstream theorists, is not necessarily a fault of the approach itself but a function of the different paradigms within which people are educated and work and the complexity of the world itself. Unfortunately contemporary problems cannot always be addressed through simple techniques. It could in fact be argued that many of the failures of problem solving approaches rest on their simplicity which is perhaps inadequate for the problems which they attempt to address.

The lack of available case studies and empirical development are functions of the time which has been available for such development. While the work of many others has been under development since the 1950s or more Flood's has only been in the public domain since the early 1990s.

The final weakness – limited value in truly coercive contexts – is common to all the quality methodologies reviewed (and indeed to other problem solving approaches). This weakness is one which no adequate methodology exists to address. For many practical purposes this may be regarded as relatively unimportant. Power relations in most organisations are distorted to some degree, but in most contexts there are practical limits. If the organisation becomes too oppressive the people will leave, thus the power of those in charge is finite. Employees in many contexts do have choices.

There are situations in fully developed as well as developing countries where a considerable degree of practical oppression does exist, where the employees do not have effective choices. This might occur in communities which have experienced high unemployment or where there is a single dominant employer. In these situations it must be hoped that the effective pursuit of organisational survival and quality will ultimately force those in power to adopt a less dominant position and engage the willing co-operation of the workforce by recognising that quality cannot be achieved without it.

17.9 CRITICAL REVIEW

Overall, Flood's adherence to the concept of a complementarist approach to organisation, and to problem solving, opens a new holistic avenue for the pursuit of the quality ideal. He precludes no ideas which are theoretically substantiated, requiring only that they be used in full understanding of the principles and world-views which underpin them.

The principal tenets of various strands of quality management are subsumed into his approach, thus ensuring the use of participation, the value of appropriate measurement, the informed use of a wide range of tools and the coherence generated by a deeper level of understanding. The approach overall then offers a considerably enhanced perception of the 'quality problem'.

The generality of the approach would appear to render it directly relevant to both manufacturing and service industries, although it will suffer many of the same shortcomings as the dominant approaches when dealing with the very soft aspects of organisational behaviour. For example, it may be possible to specify what words should be used in any given transaction – and this is often done. What cannot be specified is the sincerity with which the words are spoken and most certainly not the response of the particular customer to each utterance. The sincerity conveyed is probably more important to the customer than the exact form of words. Sincerity can only be attained when the staff member truly believes in what he or she is saying. No methodology exists which can guarantee such belief, although as will be seen, approaches do exist (chapters 28 and 29) which make it possible.

Pending further reported and substantial empirical work using Flood's approach by a broader range of practitioners the conclusion must be that it appears to have potential to enhance the implementation of quality programmes. This has yet to be proven.

SUMMARY

This chapter has introduced critical systems thinking and the use of the Total Systems Intervention methodology in a quality context. Readers wishing to extend their knowledge should consider the various works by Jackson (1991), Flood and Jackson (1991) and Flood (1993) to develop and enhance their understanding.

---

key learning points

CRITICAL SYSTEMS THINKING

Critical Systems Thinking has three goals
complementarism, sociological awareness, emancipation

Key belief
management problem solving has become divided amongst:

pragmatists, isolationists, imperialists

Total systems intervention (the meta-methodology of CST) has seven principles

- complexity demands sophisticated approaches;
- metaphors add value by aiding thinking;
- metaphors link to problem solving approaches;
- each method has strengths and weaknesses;
- differing approaches can be used in a complementary manner;
- problem solving must be systemic and iterative;
- participation and engagement of actors is essential.

CST and quality

- rejects the idea of 'one best way';
- all approaches and gurus are both right and wrong;
- beware of imposing an alternative value set;
- encourages reflection and choice.

QUESTION

What difficulties might be encountered in attempting to adopt a 'TSI' based approach to quality management?

chapter eighteen

BUSINESS PROCESS RE-ENGINEERING

ideas are good for a limited time – not forever.
Robert Townsend, *Further up the Organisation*, 1985

INTRODUCTION

Business Process Re-engineering (BPR) emerged as a formal business practice in America during the 1980s and early 1990s. An essentially pragmatic approach it resulted from observation and evaluation of the efforts of several companies to re-invent themselves. It can perhaps be most usefully thought of as a form of business strategy focused on gaining competitive advantage rather than as a theoretically rooted approach to management problem solving. Michael Hammer and James Champy (1993) formalised and crystallised the approach which is characterised as systemic and capitalises on many established problem solving methodologies and techniques.

18.1 WHAT IS BPR?

BPR challenges many of the assumptions which underpin the way organisations have been run for the last two centuries. First, it rejects the idea of reductionism – the fragmentation and breaking down of organisations into the simplest tasks – preferring the systemic recognition of flows of inter-connected activities with a common purpose. Second, it encourages organisations to capitalise on substantial developments made in technology, particularly those of the last decade. The role of information technology (IT) as an enabler of the radical redesign of organisations is emphasised – although it is stressed that using IT is not the point of BPR. Third, BPR enables organisations to take advantage of the more highly developed education and capabilities of the staff they employ. People are treated within BPR as McGregor's (1960) capable 'theory Y' individuals rather than as lazy, incompetent 'theory X' machine parts.

BPR embraces many of the developments in management thinking arising in the recent past, particularly those concerned with the manage-ment of human resources. Ideas such as empowerment are fundamental to the BPR oriented company.

18.2   DISCONTINUITY, CHAOS AND COMPLEXITY

Central to the BPR process is one key idea – that of 'discontinuous thinking', a notion raised by Hammer and Champy, but earlier given prominence by Handy (1990) in *The Age of Unreason*. Discontinuous thinking and the idea of 'discontinuity' demand some explanation.

The Western world relies on continuous thinking, largely derived from scientific thinking. It is an approach to development which is best thought of as incremental, that is, an apparently seamless, flowing approach. This has served extremely well and retains immense value in certain areas. It is reflected in the continuous improvement (*kaizen*) approach to quality adopted successfully by many companies throughout the world. However, it is now being suggested that this approach is inadequate to solve the problems besetting organisations. Readers will recall Handy's view cited in chapter 3.

The call for discontinuous change may be seen as 'special pleading' by management gurus and consultants seeking a 'new' product to sell – perhaps just another form of organisational snake-oil, a solution in search of a problem, after all it does represent the opportunity for major projects and large fees! This though would be an extremely cynical view and would ignore the substantial theoretical support which can now be drawn upon in this area from the 'hard' sciences, particularly biology and quantum physics. That Hammer, Champy and other writers in this area have not drawn on these sources does not negate the value of their work, it merely reflects different backgrounds and knowledge bases. It is fair to say though that their work would be substantially enhanced by the explicit recognition and use of these ideas. As suggested by Flood and Jackson, if there is no underpinning science to the work of management gurus they have nothing to rely on but experience and nothing to pass on to subsequent generations but stories.

The mathematically substantiated science of organisational cybernetics (which in its application to organisations has already been discussed in chapter 15) is concerned with the control of dynamical systems – those which are changing or evolving. This science has, in its contemporary interpretation, been evolving since the 1940s. It demands of organisations that they become discontinuous in the way they operate, embracing a whole new philosophy of management and decision making and distributing power in ways previously almost unheard of. Early development of this work involved mathematicians, biologists, physicists and engineers. As has already been shown this work has reached its most developed and useful form through the writings of Stafford Beer.

More recently, other developments of this work in the hands of physicists, biologists and others have proven (according to scientific methods) that discontinuities may be considered as natural phenomena. Catastrophe theory (a branch of mathematics) is cited as the original identifier of the 'butterfly effect' in which a butterfly beating its wings in one part of the world may generate a thunderstorm in another – the potentially massive consequences of a relatively minor disturbance or perturbation in a dynamic system.

Complexity theory (Waldrop, 1992), has shown how in dynamical systems equilibrium emerges from apparently random or chaotic behaviour and how indescribably complex systems can be studied and their behaviour understood. These systems again can be disturbed from their stable states by minor perturbations, and then, changing discontinuously for a period, settle into a new point of stability. The studies of complexity identify that patterns of behaviour emerge in what at first sight appear to be randomly oscillating systems.

Chaos theory (Gleick, 1987) – which some might argue is not significantly different to complexity theory – has shown how systems evolve, apparently chaotically while on closer examination order can be discerned in movements about a representative point in phase space. Often, system behaviour is almost repeated in a kind of spiral dynamics forming orbits around a fixed point. The orbit may never be the same twice but the fulcrum (or turning point) of the orbit remains the same. Again, minor disturbances can cause major effects.

These developments reflect much of the earlier thinking in the systems and cybernetics paradigms and are given great credence by the contemporary facility to model such systems on computers which allow us to observe the consequences graphically for the first time. Early studies, which did not have this advantage, relied upon the mathematical knowledge of the reader for their proof.

Grasping the concept that discontinuity is as natural (if not more so) than continuity, while discomfiting to many, must ultimately be seen as reassuring – since many discontinuities are met in life. The task of management is to drive and control the discontinuity, ensuring that it leads to survival of the organisation. The ultimate alternative is the discontinuity that is called death, or in the case of organisations, liquidation and bankruptcy. Discontinuity is sure to arise within organisational systems, but its consequences are a matter for management choice.

18.3 WHAT DRIVES BPR?

Hammer and Champy (1993: 1) suggest that the alternative to BPR is for 'corporate America to close its doors and go out of business'. The comment is related to the behaviour of organisations for many years, which when faced with increasing costs at home and competition from abroad have chosen, in effect, to export jobs rather than products, an argument already adequately explored in chapter 1 of this book. The same imperatives which drive the quality movement should drive BPR.

Thus a key impetus for BPR is the imperative of economic survival for mature nations. Whilst the focus of Hammer and Champy's work is the USA, the arguments apply equally well to the UK, Europe and to certain Asian economies. The message is to stop exporting jobs and start re-inventing the way we perform work in order to match the lower costs of manufacturing elsewhere.

It must be recognised at this stage that the imperative does not simply apply to the manufacturing sector but also to service industries and the public sector. The export of 'information processing' based tasks, supported by the explosive developments in the capabilities and use of information technology, is already exporting jobs.

Resistance to BPR and inhibition of its application in both the public and commercial sectors of the economy arises from the same sources. The focus of both tends to be short term, a product of government financial systems and commercial employment contracts. So long as there are profits (or an adequate budget) today, there is no need for action to be taken. Even where the need can be identified by those in power they often lack the will or commitment to take action since the consequences will not be felt during their own incumbency.

18.4 WHAT DOES BPR MEAN?

Hammer and Champy (1993) define BPR as:

> the fundamental rethinking and radical redesign of business processes to achieve dramatic improvements in critical, contemporary measures of performance, such as cost, quality, service and speed.

They comment that most established organisations have grown up with, and still adhere to, outmoded, traditional methods of work which are now relatively inefficient and often ineffective. These methods have often led to convoluted, complex ways of dealing with activities with many steps, checks and balances. These are, in many cases, rendered redundant by the development of both production and information technology, by the universal spread of education and by our current understanding concerning the needs and capabilities of people. Added to this should be the exponential

---

HAMMER AND CHAMPY

Key word 1   Fundamental

Key word 2   Radical

Key word 3   Dramatic

Key word 4   Processes

Key word 5   Performance

Figure 18.1 **Business Process Re-engineering – key words: Hammer and Champy**

growth in our understanding of the systemic nature of the world and the sophisticated methodologies and tools which have been developed in order for us to manage our organisations more competently. The key words (figure 18.1) in the definition will now be examined.

Key word 1, fundamental, is a clear call for the organisation to examine itself at the most basic level. Hammer and Champy suggest the question 'Why do we do what we do?' Perhaps we should go further and ask the question 'What do we do?' This second question demands that the participants focus on the purpose that they perceive for the organisation – that is, a redefinition of the organisation's goal – without which any improvement, however radical, may actually become trivial or banal. However efficient an activity, if it is focused on the wrong objective it serves little purpose.

For Hammer and Champy, key word 2, radical, means 'not making superficial changes or fiddling with what is already in place, but throwing away the old'. Ackoff (1981) offered, within the rigorous process of Interactive Planning, the process stage of 'idealised redesign'. This asks the question, put quite simply by Ackoff, 'If you were designing the organisation today what would it look like?' This implies *not* working from established processes and procedures but designing the organisation from scratch on a clean sheet of paper. In impact it is much the same as zero-based budgeting since it forces a fundamental re-appraisal of every activity within the organisation.

Key word 3, dramatic, implies that BPR does not seek to achieve marginal or incremental improvement in performance, the normal 5 to 10 per cent. For companies with that scale of problem (if they are sure of it) the process of BPR may be too powerful. Rather, the focus is on companies which want, or need, to achieve much more substantial performance improvements. Personal experience shows that through effective BPR practice improvements of 35 to 50 per cent are achievable. Within certain processes up to 70 per cent is claimed. It is suggested that every company should undertake a study of its processes to determine what level of improvement might be available. Simply being at or near best in class, which seems to satisfy Hammer and Champy, is not enough. If you are the best, but another organisation finds a way of being better, then you will face the re-engineering challenge anyway. Far better to undertake this activity while ahead of the pack and profitable than while running behind trying to catch up.

Processes, key word 4, are best defined as the 'value-chain' or 'cost-chain' running through the organisation and linking its inputs to its outputs. A process is the series of revenue generating or cost incurring steps involved in any activity. Certain industries, for example chemical and oil producers, are inherently process focused at an operational level. Processes are the way the organisation functions. Many other organisations are broken down into functional departments with 'baronial' (Jay, 1987) responsibilities for parts or sub-set activities. Those involved often have limited awareness that they form part of the overall chain, and sometimes no idea what value or cost they generate for the organisation. They are narrowly focused on a particular task with no knowledge or interest of what this contributes to fulfilling the purpose of the organisation or the needs of its customers. Readers will realise the relevance to quality in this aspect when recalling Deming's contribution to the quality movement in his recognition of internal 'supplier–customer' relationships.

Key word 5, performance, while not highlighted by Hammer and Champy, is for this author a very significant word. Performance does not necessarily mean profit – although this is the common interpretation. Rather, it should be taken to mean the fulfilment of the purposes of the organisation and the effective utilisation of resources.

BPR then relies on several unconventional ideas. First, is an orientation of the organisation towards its processes rather than its fragmented activities. Second, it requires the drive and ambition to make far-reaching and 'dramatic' improvements. Third, is what Hammer and Champy call 'rule-breaking', a willingness to challenge the conventions of the organisation. Finally, is the creative use of information technology. This means using it to enable genuine improvements in performance rather than to set in electronic tablets of stone the established ways of working.

Added to these should be the concepts of bravery and determination so often absent from corporate life. For as Machiavelli wrote in 1513 (*The Prince*):

> It must be considered that there is nothing more difficult to carry out, nor more doubtful of success, nor more dangerous to handle, than to initiate a new order of things. For the reformer has enemies in all those who profit by the old order, and only lukewarm defenders in all those who would profit by the new order, this lukewarmness arising partly from their fear of their adversaries, who have the laws in their favour: and partly from the incredulity of mankind, who do not truly believe in anything new until they have had actual experience of it. Thus it arises that on every opportunity for attacking the reformer, his opponents do so

with the zeal of partisans, the others only defend him half-heartedly, so that between them he runs in great danger.

Prior to concluding this section it is worth noting what is *not* meant by BPR. For Hammer and Champy what it does not mean is, downsizing, right-sizing, restructuring, automating or any other management activity which may or may not be necessary or desirable. These things should happen anyway, and of course may result from re-engineering, but that is not the purpose of the BPR process.

If that is how the organisation interprets re-engineering then two things are certain. First, that the process will fail (as do over 50 per cent of so-called re-engineering projects), that is the management commitment and understanding needed to really make it work will be absent. Second, the organisation will grow back all of the parts reduced in size since no fundamental change in its basis of operation will have occurred. The problem will simply be deferred rather than solved, dissolved or resolved.

BUSINESS PROCESS TINKERING

In 1995, the author was invited to present a seminar to senior members of a very large public sector organisation in Asia. The topic was to be Business Process Re-engineering.

Established knowledge of the organisation was reinforced through lengthy discussions with two managers concerning re-engineering projects then ongoing within the organisation. The organisation was essentially information driven and the projects rightly had a high information technology content. Study of the projects suggested that the organisation had rather missed the point of BPR. They had not even identified their core business processes, let alone modelled or critically examined them. Nonetheless the projects were going ahead with full approval and all possible speed. The projects were, in the author's view, tackling problems of such mind-boggling triviality to the organisation that they were probably not worth the effort, hence the expression 'Business Process Tinkering'.

Needless to say, this information and view was allowed to colour the presentation given to the senior management, and the live projects were used as examples of what not to do. The projects were set in the context of a different perception of the problems which the organisation needed to address – overstaffing in some areas, ineffectiveness in others, lack of resources in the 'front line', too many senior managers in 'make-work' jobs. The audience seemed to thoroughly enjoy the somewhat challenging, combative and participative seminar which concluded with a very lively and forthright question and answer session.

The most senior of those present arose at the end to propose thanks, concluding his short speech with the words: 'A fascinating and provocative seminar, but it seems to me that we need not take any further action.'

18.5 THE BRP PROCESS

The process of undertaking BPR draws on a wide variety of tools, approaches and understanding. Many of these have been or will be elaborated within this text for example, statistical methods, communication issues, problem solving tools, process mapping tools and the use of information technology. In this brief section the focus of attention will be on the overall process, called the 'business system diamond'. This is presented in figure 18.2.

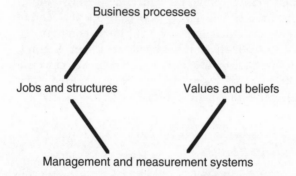

Figure 18.2 **The business system diamond**
Source: **Adapted from Hammer and Champy, 1993**

Adopting a process based approach to organisation first implies identifying what the key processes (value adding connected activities) of the organisation are. These in turn control the number, nature and content of jobs which leads us towards the definition of structure. Arising from the new expectations concerning desirable outputs (the results of processes) and the activities of employees, it is possible to define the management and measurements systems necessary for performance (and it should always be remembered that the tendency is for those characteristics measured to be delivered). Finally, with the other linkages in place, the values and beliefs of the members of the organisation will be modified.

It can easily be seen how each stage in the diamond drives the next. The diamond also suggests an iterative process – the re-engineering changes the culture towards one which is supportive of aspirations to further development. This may be interpreted as a call back towards continuous improvement.

18.6 BPR AND QUALITY

There is some ongoing debate as to whether BPR replaces or subsumes the pursuit of quality, or quality subsumes BPR. This debate is sterile. The pursuit of quality is about 'rightness' in all the actions and interactions of an organisation both internally and externally. The greater part of the quality methods and tools are incremental in their impact and lead the organisation towards the *kaizen* philosophy of continuous improvement. This implies linear, progressive change in the organisation. BPR is about embracing the hidden potential for change by recognising that incremental change only improves what is already done, while BPR may fundamentally change what is done. If a procedure or part of a process is redundant, in the sense that it adds no value to a product or service, improvement in its efficiency is a false gain. While efficiency improvement reduces the amount of waste, the procedure still remains as a cost in the system. The adoption of BPR techniques in process analysis can help to overcome this problem, eradicating procedures rather than improving them. BPR and quality are complementary, not competitive.

Perhaps somewhat perversely and as with the strategic process outlined in chapter 2, it is vital that the BPR process itself exhibits appropriate quality characteristics. If the BPR process is flawed, then the outcome will also be flawed.

SUMMARY

This chapter has introduced the concept of Business Process Re-engineering and placed it in the context of theoretical developments in recent years. The links to systemic approaches based on cybernetics, complexity science and chaos theory were explored. In the latter half of the chapter, BPR was defined and its key process explained. While this chapter draws heavily on the pioneers of BPR (Hammer and Champy, 1993), readers may wish to extend their knowledge by considering the work by Johansson *et al.* (1993), and by moving beyond this narrow focus to consider the work of systems thinkers in depth.

---

key learning points

BUSINESS PROCESS RE-ENGINEERING

BPR definition
radical reinvention of organisations on process lines

Key characteristics
pragmatic and empirical, not theoretically based, systemic, exploits developments in technology

Central themes
discontinuity, radical change, cybernetic understanding, complexity theory, chaos theory

Key drivers
economic, social, environmental

Method
The business systems diamond, process analysis, job and structure review, management and measurement systems, values and beliefs

BPR and Quality are complementary

QUESTION

What barriers would you expect to meet in designing and implementing a Business Process Re-engineering programme?

chapter nineteen

THE LEARNING ORGANISATION

Education makes a people easy to lead, but difficult to drive; easy to govern but impossible to enslave.

Lord Brougham, 1778–1868

INTRODUCTION

The chapters on 'Critical Systems Thinking' (17) and 'Business Process Re-Engineering' (18) have both espoused iterative, circular processes which should lead to the continuing evolution, and perhaps revolution, of the organisation. This chapter introduces the concept of 'the Learning Organisation'. Peter Senge (1990), author of the best known text in this area, identifies five principles for learning and seven learning disabilities which inhibit the development of truly successful organisations.

Learning, like the other two approaches, represents a circular process. Readers will recall Deming's 'Plan, Do, Check, Action' cycle and Crosby's exhortation to 'Do it all over again.'

19.1   WHAT IS A LEARNING ORGANISATION?

A 'learning organisation' is defined simply by Senge as one where:

> people continually expand their capacity to create the results they truly
> desire, where new and extensive patterns of thinking are nurtured, where

collective aspiration is set free, and where people are continually learning how to learn together.

The idea is supported in other parts of the literature. Beer (1979, 1981, 1985) writes about adaptive, ultra stable systems – organisations which are capable of reacting to situations and conditions not envisaged when they were designed. Ackoff's (1981) work and that of Checkland (1981) both call for participation, exploration and critical reflection – essential activities for learning. The critical systems work of Flood, Jackson and others can also be called upon to support this view with its calls for complementarism (requiring understanding of different theories and methodologies), sociological awareness (different cultures) and emancipation (the growth and development of human freedom). The most recent work in this area comes from Flood and Romm (1996) in which they elaborate an approach to 'triple-loop learning'. Senge also draws widely on the literature in organisation theory and business practice to support his work.

Looking at Senge's definition, there are a number of key words and phrases (see Figure 19.1). First, learning organisations are clearly focused on people. However, this is not in the sense of the mainstream human resource literature which aims to satisfy human needs and wants, but in an approach centred on developing human potential – which will in turn lead to those same satisfactions. Second, continually, implies a commitment to an ongoing process, a further move away from the static thinking which dominated earlier management science.

PETER SENGE

Key word 1　People

Key word 2　Continually

Key word 3　Create the results

Key word 4　New patterns of thinking

Key word 5　Collective aspiration/learning together

Figure 19.1 **The learning organisation – key words and phrases: Peter Senge**

LEARNING STIMULATES LEARNING

Berkshire Young Musicians Trust is a highly successful music education organisation. The public face of the trust is its highly successful bands which compete in music festivals at national level and regularly tour internationally, entertaining audiences in many countries. These competitive successes and international tours are seen by the head teacher as a bonus rather than being the real work of the trust. He sees the real work and achievement as the opportunity given to every child within the Berkshire community, regardless of ability, to take part in musical activities and succeed to their own best level.

The philosophy adopted is:

> every child can grow through music,
> every child should be given the chance.

The successes of the trust are attained through a number of factors such as enthusiastic staff, a large core of young musicians and exciting, stimulating music and projects. To enable this the trust operates on a highly devolved structure with day-to-day decision making delegated as far as possible. Understanding that the work of the trust stands or falls by its teachers, they aim to recruit the best and retain them. Performance is monitored through a system of curricular heads led by the Head of Education. Monitoring includes observation of lessons and assessment of problems as well as sharing of opportunities and experience.

The known strengths and weaknesses of the staff are seen as the basis for the development of training programmes designed to capitalise on the strengths and overcome the weaknesses. The opportunity is taken to use outside speakers when appropriate and bring fresh ideas and experiences into the organisation.

Staff are encouraged to find new and creative ways of stimulating the learning of their pupils, rather than simply regurgitating the lessons they themselves received as young musicians. Many members of staff write and arrange music specifically for their groups. They are passionate about music and aim to achieve the best possible results.

The only selection criterion applied to pupils wishing to study with the trust is their desire and expressed interest in the instrument. In discussion, the head revealed how recent research into the effects of learning music showed that this stimulated other learning by the child. Three groups of students were studied. The first group received music instruction, the second computer instruction, the third received no extra tuition. While the second and third groups demonstrated no change in their performance, the group receiving music instruction showed a 30 per cent improvement. The conclusion (however preliminary) is that learning music stimulates other learning.

Third, create the results, suggests that people's abilities enable them to control and create the future of organisations. This reflects the thinking of Ackoff and others. It must be acknowledged though that limits exist to the potential control exerted by organisations, these limits being enforced by the actions of others in a competitive world.

Fourth, new patterns of thinking, reinforces the points made earlier in the work. While not necessarily rejecting all the old thinking, the new should be capitalised on where appropriate. Finally, collective aspiration/learning together, here Senge appears to object to much of the development of Western society in recent years. This has seen a move away from collective, shared values and hopes, towards a rather more selfish world in which the individual considers him or her self, supreme. This is perhaps reflected in life in such areas as divorce rates, executive compensation packages, the increasing trend towards litigation over relatively minor matters and the drift away from religiously based societies towards a more secular approach.

The issue of learning is given real prominence when the leaders of large industrial organisations take it seriously. Senge quotes from Arie De Geus, then head of planning for Royal Dutch Shell 'The ability to learn faster than your competitors may be the only sustainable competitive advantage.' The American business guru, Tom Peters, makes the comment 'there is a surplus of everything', this is taken to mean that there is more capacity in the world to create goods and services than exists to consume them. This can only mean further competitive pressure, driving down prices and margins and consequently profits. It is not simply about learning to work 'smarter' to do better, but simply to survive.

19.2   THE LEARNING DISABILITIES

Senge suggests that even the 'excellent' companies may only be performing at a mediocre level (reflecting again some of the thinking behind BPR). He proposes that the ways we design and manage our organisations, the narrow, convergent ways we are taught to think and to interact create 'fundamental learning disabilities' (see Figure 19.2).

The phrase 'I am my position' argues that we become what we do for a job. The classic example of this is first meetings or parties when we introduce ourselves and are almost always asked 'What do you do?' Our response – 'I am a . . . ' define us as being our work.

The enemy is out there, reflects our human tendency to place blame or guilt elsewhere, rather than to acknowledge the faults in ourselves. This tendency has been recorded in the literature since at least biblical times.

LEARNING DISABILITIES

Disability 1   I am my position;

Disability 2   The enemy is out there;

Disability 3   The illusion of taking charge;

Disability 4   The fixation on events;

Disability 5   The parable of the boiling frog;

Disability 6   The delusion of learning from experience;

Disability 7   The myth of the management team.

Figure 19.2 **The learning disabilities**

Commenting on the illusion of taking charge, Senge suggests that when we think we are being 'pro-active', very often we are just being differently reactive. He proposes that 'true pro-activeness comes from seeing how we contribute to our own problems'.

Our reductionist views of the world, the tendency to scientifically analyse, leads us to a simple 'cause–effect' view of the world, hence the fixation on events rather than processes and interactions. This has already been challenged with the recognition of the systems based approach. Senge suggests in this area that our focus on events prevents us from seeing the patterns in gradual processes which tell us much about what is actually happening.

The parable of the boiling frog has been fully rehearsed in chapter 3. It is the recognition of the need for discontinuous change and, perhaps, learning to be uncomfortable with continuity in a non-linear world (chaos! complexity!).

Taken at the simple, individual level, if we reflect on our actions and their consequences then we learn. Unfortunately, we do not always learn from experience as, particularly in organisations, these consequences cannot be known in this way. They may well extend across organisational boundaries and have impacts for future time which we cannot be in a position to assess and learn from. Beer's Viable System Model starts to address this point with its emphasis on information management. The VSM calls for an internal model of the organisation within the development function and for abandonment of the traditional functional silos or stovepipes of management.

Suggesting that management teams are often little more than gentlemanly turf wars, Senge (following Beer and others) talks about the 'myth' of the management team. He recognises that appearances are often more important to people within organisations than reality. This means that often the management team is not a team at all, particularly when under pressure. Each member is fighting to defend his own credibility and position in adversity. Thus we end with what Argyris (cited by Senge, 1990) calls 'skilled incompetence' – 'teams full of people who are incredibly proficient at keeping themselves from learning'.

All readers will be familiar with these issues within their organisations. Senge requires that the familiarity is made within ourselves – a much more difficult task.

19.3 THE FIVE DISCIPLINES

Senge proposes that in order to overcome our difficulties with organisations and learning we must adopt five disciplines (see Figure 19.3), that is, become disciples of five beliefs. Readers will by now be familiar with the ideas of systems thinking. Senge's work draws heavily on the theories and practice of systems dynamics developed by Jay Forrester. Flood and Jackson (1991) offer a full critique of that approach. Here it is sufficient to say that the work studies the behaviour of non-linear dynamic systems.

```
FIVE DISCIPLINES

Discipline 1   Systems thinking;

Discipline 2   Personal mastery;

Discipline 3   Mental models;

Discipline 4   Shared vision;

Discipline 5   Team learning.
```

Figure 19.3 **The five disciplines**

Personal Mastery refers to the discipline of personal growth and personal learning. It demands of the individual an open-minded, inquiring approach leading to them creating their own future. Taking into account here the critical systems commitment to 'sociological awareness', it can be suggested that the extent to which Personal Mastery is achievable will be a product of the capabilities and the cultural and educational background of the individual.

Mental models are formed because it is clearly impossible to know in finite detail all there is to know – in our minds are carried only models of reality. These are necessarily abstractions from the full richness of the reality and as Beer (1985) suggests are 'neither true nor false but more or less useful'. Problems arise when the models are significantly flawed, which is often the case, or when it is forgotten that they are simply models, and become perceived as the reality. In these cases reliance on them is certain to be equally flawed. Senge suggests that learning to unfreeze and regenerate our mental models of the world is critical.

Shared vision is the call for all stakeholders in the organisation to have a common (or unitary) view of what the organisation is and what is to be achieved. Senge suggests that when there is shared vision the desire is for the same things for everyone. To achieve this the vision cannot be 'handed down from the mountain' like the Ten Commandments as is so often the case, but must be built from the ground. This calls for the sort of participative approaches espoused by Checkland (SSM: 1981), Ackoff (IP: 1981), Beer (Syntegration: 1994) and Ulrich (CSH: 1983).

Team learning does not easily occur but is driven by a number of key characteristics. Senge suggests that the team members must have first embraced the other four disciplines already described. The first key characteristic is alignment (the shared vision), the team can accomplish little unless there is a commitment to the same outcomes. Second, is the need to think and consider 'insightfully' [*sic*] about complex issues. Third is the need for co-ordinated action: here Senge refers to championship sports teams and jazz ensembles enjoined in 'operational trust'. Finally there is recognition of the need for the teams effectiveness to be spilled over into other connected (and usually) subordinate teams. This final point reflects the concept of recursion from the systems literature.

Holding all of these insights together is one, so far unstated, requirement. That is, the need for effective communication, both vertically and horizontally through the organisation. Effective communication requires a subtlety of approach often absent from daily dialogues. It means effective listening as well as effective speaking. It sometimes requires discussion and at other times dialogue. It does not mean the generation of conflict or the adopting, as is so often the case, of rooted, entrenched positions, nor reliance on dogma or ideology. These ways of 'communicating' lead more often to breakdown and obfuscation or unsatisfactory compromise, which conflict with the other disciplines.

19.4 WHAT IS ORGANISATIONAL LEARNING?

Organisations do not exist (except in the sense of a legal entity) other than through the interactions of their members. They are socially constructed devices assembled to achieve a common aim and cannot learn except through their members. The collective memory of an organisation is best described through its culture, that is, the ways of thinking and behaving which are common to its members. Organisational learning is not then about the addition of data to a corporate memory (although such memories

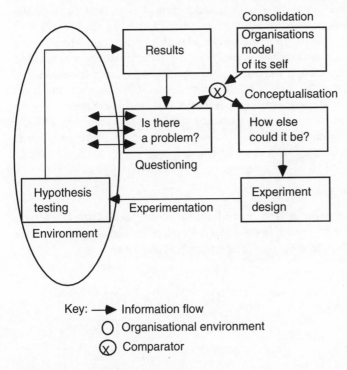

Key: ——► Information flow
     ◯ Organisational environment
     ⊗ Comparator

Figure 19.4 **A model of learning**

are capable of being created) but about change in the behaviour of the organisation through adaptation of the individual and collective behaviour of its members. Offered in figure 19.4 is the author's cybernetic interpretation of how such adaptation might take place.

This is explained as follows. Members of the company through their interactions with the environment come to question the way in which things are done (questioning), through comparison of their real world experience with the organisation's model of its 'self' (their model of the organisation and its environment). They conceive potential solutions to the defined problem (conceptualisation) and design an experiment to test their hypothesis (experimentation). The results of the experiment are fed back to them and the organisational model is modified according to their new experience (consolidation). They proceed to manage the organisation in accordance with the modified model. Learning fails to take place when the last of these steps, consolidation, does not occur.

Alert readers will have noticed the direct comparison which can be drawn here with other learning approaches such as the Deming Cycle (Plan, Do, Check, Action), Ishikawa's Quality Circles (which focus on problem solving) and Taguchi's prototyping methodology. Questioning, conceptualisation, experimentation and consolidation are drawn from Handy (1985).

19.5   QUALITY AND LEARNING

This brief section seems now almost redundant. The whole basis of the pursuit of quality rests in the idea of learning, that is, in finding ways of carrying out activities so that the outputs of an organisation more nearly match the requirements of its customers. If the same mistakes are repeated then clearly no learning is occurring, but equally, no quality improvement is being attained. The *kaizen* philosophy demands improvement in all processes all of the time. Learning is implicit in this. It can then be argued that any organisation successfully pursuing quality is also learning, and any organisation pursuing learning is also improving quality. The two words imply each other in the organisational context.

SUMMARY

This chapter has given a brief introduction to the idea of the 'Learning Organisation' and its founding principles. Readers should refer to the work of Senge to further develop their understanding and knowledge.

key learning points

THE LEARNING ORGANISATION

Key definition
a learning organisation is one engaged in an iterative, circular process of evolution

The seven disabilities

- I am my position;
- the enemy is out there;
- the illusion of taking charge;
- the fixation on events;
- the parable of the boiling frog;
- the delusion of learning from experience;
- the myth of the management team.

The five disciplines
systems thinking, personal mastery, mental models, shared vision, team learning

Organisational learning
Organisational learning means adaptation of individual and collective behaviour

learning implies quality implies learning

QUESTION

Compare and contrast the 'learning' models of the Quality Gurus with that outlined in this chapter.

part four

METHODS, TOOLS AND TECHNIQUES

USER GUIDE

In the first three parts of this book a substantial platform has been developed for thinking about quality. This platform is derived from management theory and the extended practice of the Quality Gurus.

Part four builds upon this theoretical platform by examining methods for implementing quality. The methods explored range from general techniques such as process analysis used in many management problem solving activities to those specifically focused on quality such as ISO 9000, statistical process control and quality circles. Equally both reductionist techniques and systemic methodologies are included, each having value in particular contexts. The part concludes with an afterword on the implementation of quality programmes.

This part of the book can be used in two ways. As with the others it can provide a simple critical introduction to a selection of tools for achieving quality which link to or are derived from the various theories already explained. For those with a practical focus, the section provides a comprehensive tool kit enabling the pursuit of a quality initiative in a way that is both practically informed and theoretically sound.

chapter twenty

PROCESS
ANALYSIS

Wherever there is an end, it is for this that the previous things are done, one after the other.

Aristotle, *Physics* II, 8

INTRODUCTION

This chapter introduces techniques associated with the identification and mapping of processes. Process mapping is a fundamental starting point for any quality initiative since it is vital to understand the whole of a process (or processes), if the use of other quantitative or qualitative tools is to become meaningful. Process definition and mapping helps to identify the processes and the location of particular quality problems. It is followed by process analysis and critical examination which are focused on generating improvements.

20.1 DEFINING PROCESSES

Defining processes in an established manufacturing environment is a straightforward activity – the process is largely defined by the flow of manufacturing. In a service environment it is often more difficult since processes are often not recognised as such, their elements being linked across separate functional areas. For example, in a bank, processing a customer's cheque may involve the signature of an official for authorisation of payment, a cashier, a computer input operator and a filing clerk. Each of these individuals may work in a different department (functional silo) within the bank, and the process may be subject to a number of variations and sub-routines, dependent upon circumstances. For this reason, fragmentation of processes has traditionally been the most used approach to process study and design. For an organisation serious about achieving quality, it is vital to move beyond this fragmented approach to something more coherent. Process definition is vital in this regard.

A process chart is valuable in providing an overall picture of a connected set of actions by recording, in sequence, each of the operations and activities. These operations and activities are recorded regardless of who does them or where they are performed. Functional boundaries within the organisation are ignored for mapping purposes.

Process charting can be carried out at a number of nested levels or recursions. At the first level, the 'Total Process', records the process outline from start to finish, with a minimum of detail and identifies where exceptions and sub-routines occur. The second level, 'Process Operation', details the specific actions taken at each stage, while a third level, 'Process Detail', studies the detail of the process potentially down to the level of individual hand movements (a work study level of analysis). For many purposes the Total and Operational levels are sufficient. Figure 20.1 shows how the three levels are linked.

The process charts are developed by identifying particular operations and linking them together along with any inspections, audits or delays. The process may be defined in either a vertical or horizontal flow – whichever is more convenient – and, for clarity and economy of effort, ASME symbols

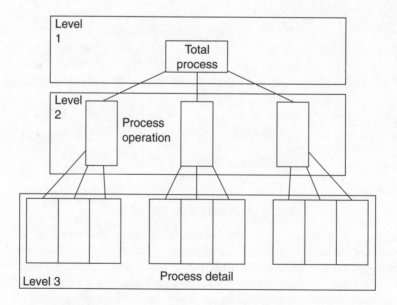

Figure 20.1 **Nested or 'recursive' process levels**

○   Operations

☐   Inspection/verification

◁   Movement

▽   File/end

D   Delay

◇   Outside scope of enquiry

✕   Destroyed/thrown away

▣   Inspection more important than operation

◉   Operation more important than inspection

Figure 20.2 **ASME symbols**

are used to indicate each stage. The ASME symbols, with some additions, are provided in figure 20.2.

For tracking and reference purposes it is common practice to number the sequence of actions. The process charts provide a record of the operation at various levels of detail and provide the basis for later process analysis and critical examination. They also provide a basis for deciding what should be measured and at which point. Such charts may usefully be overlaid on a scale plan or topographical diagram of the building layout, indicating paths of movement. This can prove helpful in eradicating delays and identifying why and where quality problems occur, for example storage of temperature sensitive materials in an unprotected area. An example of a completed 'Total Process' chart overlaid on a building plan is provided in figure 20.3.

This chart represents the receipt, preparation and despatch of a purchase order. The order is received by a storeperson who prepares a request form, creates a folder and passes the folder to the typist (that is three operations). The typist types the order and passes it to the checker who checks the typed order against the request form and (assuming all to be correct) passes the order to a progress clerk. The progress clerk passes the forms to the relevant buyer for signature, who, once they are signed, passes them back. The progress clerk then passes the order to the supplier, passes one copy of the order to the accounts department and holds the other in the buyer's file.

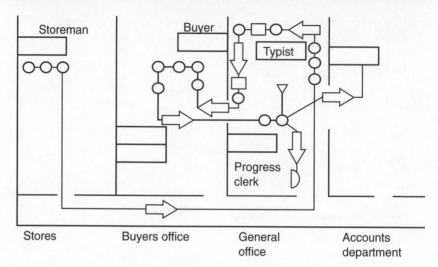

Figure 20.3 **A total process chart**

This process, which undoubtedly seems cumbersome to the reader, is a real example found in a UK factory in the early 1990s and is, in the author's experience, while obviously inefficient not unusually bad compared with other situations.

COOKING THE BOOKS

In 1992 a productivity and quality study was undertaken in a commercial bakery. This bakery, a subsidiary of a major public company, supplies cakes and other products to various supermarket chains. A map of the finishing process was created as the first step in the study, this was to act as a guide to understanding the process and as the basis for both quality and productivity measurement. The process was as shown in figure 20.4.

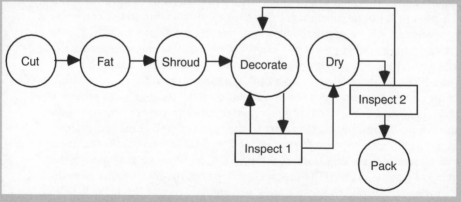

Figure 20.4 **The finishing process**

This map shows what will appear at first a simple, and efficient process, but it is important to remember that this map has been prepared at the 'Total Process' level. Other more detailed maps were prepared at lower levels, for example the operation 'Decorate' at the next level down sub-divided into between five and seven sub-processes depending on the particular product being made. Each of those sub-processes again contained sub-routines directly related to the product.

The company had never prepared such a map before. The map was used as a basis for evaluating the scale of the 'quality problem' which had been estimated by them as a 10 per cent reject rate. Discussion revealed that this rate was arrived at on the basis of the volume difference between the number of cakes entering the 'Cut' process and the number completing the process 'Pack'. There was no measure of intra-process rejects. The inspection process 'Inspect 1' was not even recognised by the management, or the supervisors undertaking it, as an inspection. Simple observation of the various process operations was enough to indicate major quality problems within the process. When numbers were recorded the actual reject rate, that is, the proportion of cakes recycling through various stages of the process, in particular 'Decorate', was found to be 35 per cent – a figure which did not vary substantially between products throughout a week of evaluation. Subsequent further studies confirmed the accuracy of the numbers.

This process map proved vital in three respects. First, it provided the management with a clear picture of how the production line actually operated, as opposed to how they believed it to operate – it helped them to modify their mental models. Second, it enabled the quantification of a problem which they had only vaguely suspected. Third, by examining the reject rate at different stages in the process it enabled sharp focus to be brought on the key problem area – the process 'Decorate'.

20.2 PROCESS ANALYSIS AND CRITICAL EXAMINATION

Once a process has been defined it can be analysed. Of particular concern in the quality management context is the recognition of where error or failure does or may occur in the process. This enables a focus to be maintained on those aspects of the process most in need of improvement or re-development. It also provides cues for key measurement points at which statistical process control techniques may be most usefully employed.

The purpose of analysing the process at the outset is to eliminate unnecessary or irrelevant activities and to identify the 'triggers' which start other processes and sub-routines. The critical examination should reveal the reasons for each activity and enable the compilation of a systematic and prioritised list of potential enhancements.

The benefit gained from critical examination is influenced by the attitude of mind of the analyst. The final result will depend upon the skill with which the process is recorded. Attention must be paid to the following points:

- Actions should be recorded as factually as possible.
- Pre-conceived notions and ideas should be abandoned.
- All aspects of the process should be challenged and verified.
- Hasty judgements must be avoided.
- Small details must be recorded at the appropriate level of analysis – these may be more important than the major items.
- Hunches and 'bright ideas' should be set aside until the recording is complete.
- New methods should not be considered until the undesirable or quality problem causing attributes of the existing method have been exposed.

In the context of work study it is common to classify each of the activities into one of three groups: 'Make Ready', 'Do', 'Put Away'. This refinement is probably inappropriate in the quality context since the primary issue of concern is not productivity (although processes with quality built in are normally more productive than those without).

Similarly, there is debate as to whether the productive or non-productive parts of the process should be examined first – the former tending to lead to more rapid productivity improvements. In the quality context the concern is with identifying where error and failure occur, and a systematic approach should be taken – following the process from the start. This is because errors made in early parts of the process may be driving failure at later stages, it is important therefore to eliminate these prior causes. Measurement of performance and error at key points of the process may be desirable as a means of identifying where failure occurs and in what proportions. The information so derived can be used to help in prioritising work.

The examination of the identified process can be carried out through a two stage sequence of questions which adopt the pattern shown in figure 20.5. In contemporary organisations it is useful to ask similar 'means' questions about the machines and technology used to support the process. That is: what machines are used, are they suitable for the task, are they reliable, do their outputs match or exceed the task requirements and so on.

Taken together, these questions enable the analyst to determine precisely what the existing process is, to question it and to identify its flaws. The movement towards quality is begun by proposing alternatives and highlighting failures. Properly supported by valid statistical techniques this 'is–ought' approach is useful.

20.3 METHOD DEVELOPMENT

Method development covers a range of techniques which can be used to identify alternatives to the established process and ways of overcoming quality problems. It relies on creative thinking about the situation which in turn requires an open and inquiring mind. A lateral approach is useful, which attempts to find fresh angles from which to view the process. Determination to succeed is important as is an acceptance that all ideas

CRITICAL EXAMINATION PROCEDURE

	Primary questions	Secondary questions
Purpose:	What is done?	What else might be done?
	Why is it done?	What should be done?
Place:	Where is it done?	Where else might it be done?
	Why is it done there?	Where should it be done?
Sequence:	When is it done?	When might it be done?
	Why is it done then?	When should it be done?
Person:	Who does it?	Who else might do it?
	Why do they do it?	Who should do it?
Means:	How is it done?	How else might it be done?
	Why is it done like that?	How should it be done?

Figure 20.5 **Critical examination procedure**

can, at the outset, be treated as equally valid, even though they may appear remote from the problem. Creative thinking is supported by a variety of techniques. Readers might wish to refer to the works of Edward De Bono for further inspiration.

Brainstorming is a method of enabling groups of individuals, normally between 4 and 12 in number (as for Quality Circles!), to generate ideas for problem solving. The process is relatively simple. The group leader outlines the problem and answers any questions submitted by the members. Thereafter the group generate ideas which are recorded without comment or judgement on flip charts, white boards, or sometimes on 'post-it' stickers. After about half an hour (or when the ideas dry up) the ideas are evaluated by the group. Those offering most apparent value being subjected to further evaluation and, where appropriate, experimentation and development.

It is vital that the leader of a brainstorming session is experienced in problem solving and is able to create and maintain enthusiasm amongst the group members.

Analogies are also useful. An analogy is an agreement or commonality in certain characteristics between things which are otherwise different. To use analogies is to apply alternative knowledge and experience to a problem. The problem solvers consider items which are different but possess similar attributes to the problem under consideration. This approach encourages cross-fertilisation of ideas from different professional backgrounds and disciplines. There are three types of analogy which are particularly useful.

- *Functional*:   What else does what this process does?
- *Simple*:   What does this process look like?
- *Natural*:   How is this done in nature?

This last is a particularly helpful approach since natural systems tend towards self-organisation (see chapter 14), effectiveness (if not always apparent short term efficiency) and evolution. A particular example of the use of a natural analogy is the invention of artificial fibre. The recognition by Robert Hooke in 1664 that the process of silk-spinning by silk worms could be emulated by man enabled Louis Schwabe, in 1842, to create a machine for making artificial filaments by forcing liquid through fine holes. This technique is used today in the manufacture of rayon.

Morphological analysis is a systematic method of creating possible lists of logical combinations of variables already known to solve a problem. It enables the range of possible solution spaces to be matched and a 'most reliable' method to be chosen. One example of this could be solving a delivery problem to a customers premises as follows:

- *Method*:   Post, courier, in-house delivery system.
- *Speed*:   JIT, same day, overnight, non-critical.
- *Packaging*:   Crushproof, airtight, palletised, unimportant.

The possible number of logical combinations of variables is $3 \times 4 \times 4$ – there are 48 possible solutions to the delivery problem (given that each combination of variables is possible, some, such as post and same day are 'illegal' solutions, that is to say, they will not work). Once the range of possible solutions has been defined, quality and other criteria can be applied to identify those which meet expectations and requirements.

Listing and combining attributes is another way of highlighting potential for improvement in a process. This technique requires the creation of a list of the attributes the process must possess in order to fulfil the requirements – such as Zero Defects. Changes to the process are then proposed which enable these attributes to be attained.

Heuristic analysis fits within the context of *kaizen* quality thinking. The heuristic method is to generate changes to the process, apply them and review the results. The results are then used as the platform for testing further changes, and so on in an iterative cycle. This is similar to the 'PDCA' cycle proposed by Deming and to the ideas of organisational learning outlined in chapter 19. Heuristic improvement should never stop, but to be effective must be used in a systematic rather than random manner. The principal disadvantage of the heuristic method lies in its incremental nature. A heuristic approach may never generate the sort of radical, discontinuous (or step) change in a process that may be provoked by the use of other methods.

Convergent and divergent thinking are also useful approaches. Convergent thinking occurs when the analyst (s) attempts to separate the essential items of the process from the incidental. In this way the aim is to focus on the most important issues, reminiscent of Juran's 'vital few and useful many'. Divergent thinking is the opposite and occurs when the analyst (s) expands the problem to take account of other information that is not central to the defined process.

The initial task of identifying the 'Total Process' suggested at the outset of this chapter may be seen as a representation of convergent thinking, while the second and third level analyses (Process Operation and Process Detail) represent divergent thinking. A further level of divergent thinking may be seen in expanding the 'Total Process' chart to encompass other interdependent processes.

SUMMARY

This chapter has introduced process mapping and critical examination as a fundamental technique for the pursuit of quality. This provides a platform for the other techniques which will be explored in subsequent chapters. Process analysis techniques can be further studied through books concerned with Organisation Methods, Operational Research and Business Process Re-engineering.

---

key learning points

PROCESS ANALYSIS

Key definition
the mapping, analysis, critical examination of processes

Key belief
it is vital to appreciate whole processes, not just functional parts

Examination techniques
process charting, process analysis, critical examination, method development

Development techniques
brainstorming, analogies, morphological analysis, attributes, convergent and divergent thinking

---

QUESTION

Use the techniques outlined in this chapter to map, critically examine and redesign a process in your University. (For example, the book management process in the library)

chapter twenty-one

QUALITY MANAGEMENT SYSTEMS: ISO 9000

to mistake the epiphenomena of the system . . . for the system itself.

(Stafford Beer, *Diagnosing the System for Organisations*, 1985)

INTRODUCTION

This chapter is concerned with effective quality management systems (QMS) of which the ISO 9000 series is the currently established, global standard. Without adherence to a QMS, it is impossible for the organisation to know and record how well (or badly) it is performing. The ISO 9000 series is featured in this text because it is the best known and most widely used of such systems. There are many quality management systems in existence which do not conform to this standard.

This chapter will not provide a full guide to the development and implementation of a QMS. That task is beyond the intended scope of this book and better left to a dedicated work of which there are several (for example Hoyle, 1998, Gilbert, 1994, Waller *et al.*, 1993, McGoldrick, 1994).

What this chapter does seek to achieve is a broad understanding of the nature and purpose of a QMS, its utility and limitations.

21.1   WHAT IS ISO 9000?

ISO 9000 is one of a series of quality management systems developed over a long period of time beginning with quality standards in the defence industry. For example NATO began developing quality standards in the late 1940s to enable a degree of harmonisation between co-operating military forces. These standards were consolidated and revised in DefStans (Defence Standards) 05–08, 05–21, 05–24 and 05–28 between 1951 and 1973. Dominant systems in the civil world include BS5750 (the British standard) and EN29000 (the European standard) as well as unique local systems which have been developed in several countries. However, ISO 9000 is currently accepted as the standard for quality practice in most countries.

A QMS constitutes a formal record of an organisation's method of managing the quality of its products or services. It enables the organisation to demonstrate to itself, its customers, and importantly to an independent accreditation body, that it has established an effective system for managing the quality of its products or services. Meeting the accreditation standards permits the organisation to claim quality certification for its products and services and to advertise the fact. This is seen as an important factor by many organisations and there is a trend in certain areas, notably the public sector and parts of the construction industry particularly in South East Asia, to only deal with quality accredited organisations. A QMS will also assist the organisation in attempting to formalise its operations and attain consistency of outputs.

The ISO 9000 series itself (figure 21.1) consists of two sets of documents. ISO 9000, 9001, 9002 and 9003 deal with quality assurance standards as the basis of assessment. These are particularly used in developing performance contracts. ISO 9004 deals with quality management itself.

As already stated, this chapter is not seen as the place for a full description of these standards. However, it is clear that they are comprehensive in their coverage, ranging from product or service development to after-sales service. There is within this series of documents a clear bias towards the manufacturing sector. This is after all where the process started and where greatest use continues to be made of the standards. There is a plan to harmonise all the standards and remove the bias by the end of the current century, although it is believed by some that the ISO 14000 series may largely replace ISO 9000 during the intervening period.

21.2   HOW IS A QMS CONSTRUCTED?

Construction of a QMS relies upon the use of the ISO 9000 series to provide guidelines and instructions adherence to which ensures that the

THE ISO 9000 SERIES

ISO 9000–0   Concepts and applications;

ISO 9000–1   Quality management and assurance standards: guide;

ISO 9000–2   ISO 9001/9002/9003 application guide;

ISO 9000–3   ISO 9001 applied to software development, supply and maintenance;

ISO 9000–4   Dependability Programme Management Guide;

ISO 9001   Quality systems: design, development, production, installation and service;

ISO 9002   Quality systems: quality assurance production and installation;

ISO 9003   Quality systems: quality assurance, final inspection and test;

ISO 9004–1   Quality management and quality systems elements: guide;

ISO 9004–2   Quality management and quality system elements: guide for services;

ISO 9004–3   Processed materials: guide;

ISO 9004–4   Quality improvement: guide;

ISO 9004–5   Quality plan: guide;

ISO 9004–6   Quality assurance for project management: guide;

ISO 9004–7   Configuration management: guide.

Figure 21.1 **The ISO 9000 series**

system will meet accreditation standards. As with every aspect of quality, the development of an effective QMS relies on a systematic approach.

Kanji and Asher (1996) propose a thirteen step programme (figure 21.2) of actions. Step 1, commitment to the quality management approach, has already been met on several occasions. This commitment is fundamental to any aspect of achieving quality. Unfortunately, managers find it far easier to commit themselves to a QMS than they do to commit themselves to quality. If you have the latter then that implies commitment to the QMS. If you only have commitment to the QMS then you have a system which will not only fail to assist the drive for quality, but will enable the manager to decide precisely who to blame (other than him or herself) for that failure. It will become an instrument of the penal system rather than a guide for the successful pursuit of quality. An effective QMS can only be created within the context of a fully supported quality programme.

KANJI AND ASHER

Step 1　Obtain management understanding of, and commitment to, the quality management approach.

Step 2　Define the scope of the activities to be included in the QMS.

Step 3　Define the organisational structure and responsibilities of those within the scope of the QMS.

Step 4　Audit the existing systems and procedures against the requirements of the standard.

Step 5　Develop a plan to write the necessary procedures.

Step 6　Train sufficient personnel to write their own procedures.

Step 7　Draft and edit the procedures and gain agreement to them.

Step 8　Compile a draft quality manual.

Step 9　Implement the system on a trial basis.

Step 10　Train internal auditors to carry out audits of the system and its operation.

Step 11　Revise the operation of the system in light of the results of audits and other information.

Step 12　Apply for registration (sometimes called third party approval) from an accredited body.

Step 13　Maintain the system by internal audit, using it as an opportunity to improve.

Figure 21.2 **Thirteen steps to a quality management system: Kanji and Asher**

Step 2, defining the scope of activities to be included, seems to be a little short-sighted. If an organisation is to be effective in its quality drive then every part of it must fall within the QMS. There will certainly be a need to assess priorities for inclusion in the QMS – production before personnel and the canteen perhaps – but the ultimate aim should be an all-inclusive system. This system may even extend to link with those of suppliers where appropriate.

Step 3, defining the organisational structure and responsibilities, while necessary, carries the danger of inhibiting necessary organisational change. While it is vital that the appropriate organisational structure is in use and that responsibilities are clearly defined, it is essential to realise that the correct organisational form is, or may be, a rapidly changing element. The dynamism and fluidity of the organisational environment demand this. It must be the case therefore that the organisational structure and responsibilities define the organisation of the QMS – not the other way around.

The fourth, fifth, sixth and seventh steps, audit of current systems and procedures and development of new procedures, are fundamental to the achievement of the QMS. It may be preferable, however, to place the sixth element in fourth place and extend the training element such that operational staff are trained to audit and review their own processes as well as develop the appropriate documentation. No one else knows a job better than the people who do it. Step 8, the draft quality procedures manual is a product of the four steps which precede it.

Step 9 reflects Taguchi's 'up and limping prototype'. The proposed system must be tested in action and validated or modified against empirical data. This links naturally to step 10. Training of internal auditors is vital and again should draw on the experience and knowledge of those who actually carry out the operations of the organisation. Use of the staff in this way, and proper training of them in the correct meaning of effective audit outputs – helpfulness, guidance and assistance to improvement – rather than oppressive policing, is likely to generate highly productive outcomes. This generates the modifications demanded by the eleventh step as an output of the audit process.

The twelfth step, accreditation of the QMS, should happen almost naturally. Within the context of the overall quality programme, accreditation should be a by-product. The application and registration should be easy to come by, if the organisation genuinely has quality and has taken the development of the QMS seriously.

The final step reflects the demand for continuous improvement, not only in the core activities of the organisation but in everything that it does.

It must always be remembered that the purpose of the QMS is not accreditation to a particular standard, but improvement to the quality of output of the products and services of the organisation. It has been observed that many more organisations have accredited QMS systems than generate quality products and services. It is perfectly possible to develop and implement a QMS with absolutely no improvement in quality whatsoever.

Conventionally, a QMS will require three core sets of information. The first will be a statement of the quality policy of the organisation. This may form the first part of the quality manual. The second set is the procedures which will be adopted to fulfil that policy. The third set is the task instructions which set out how each activity should be performed. With the increasing trend towards process oriented structures, it is useful to give serious consideration to documenting the procedures along process lines, rather than on the traditional functional basis.

To support these three sets of information, the organisation will also require a record system to provide the evidence that the quality procedures are being adhered to. This record system should be as simple and straightforward as possible but should also, as far as possible, be proof against corruption and fraudulent completion. If the data is not accurate then it is less than helpful. Accuracy will decline with complexity, volume of data and difficulty of collection. Wherever possible data should be recorded automatically.

BEAT THE SYSTEM

It is common today for service based organisations, particularly those which operate buildings open to the public, to install quality management systems for the public facing areas, particularly restrooms. They aim to ensure that these facilities are checked, serviced and cleaned on a regular basis, usually hourly. To facilitate monitoring that this servicing has been carried out, timed ticksheets are placed in each restroom for the cleaner to initial on each visit.

Imagine, a cleaner, or even a small team of cleaners in a twenty storey building, expected to check and service the restrooms on each floor every hour. Not only is this level of service probably unnecessary, but in many cases, with low levels of staffing it is impossible. Nonetheless, the ticksheets are initialled every hour. The QMS is working – or is it?

As one who regularly works in such buildings I take an interest in these things. It is far from uncommon (particularly at a weekend when the management are not about) to find that by 9 p.m. on a Friday the ticksheet for the weekend has been completed through to 7 a.m. on Monday. By Saturday afternoon the soap has run out, by Sunday morning (at the latest) there are no paper towels. The rest can be left to the imagination. The QMS is not working – although the records show that it is.

Such deceptions are commonplace throughout the world – this is by no means an exclusively British, European, Asian or American problem. It occurs everywhere in nice buildings and bad ones, in 'quality' organisations and in 'non-quality' organisations. They may have an accredited QMS – what they don't have is quality – somebody, somewhere, just does not care.

21.3   ISO 14000

The ISO 14000 series of standards for Environmental Management Systems was launched in 1996 in response to rising awareness of damage to the environment and the need for a common set of standards which could be adopted by any organisation. The standards provide guidelines on the elements that an environmental management system should have and on the supporting technologies. The standards prescribe what should be done by an organisation, but not how.

ISO 14001 and ISO 14004 provide the specifications and general guidelines for the series and allow it to fulfil business needs, for any organisation, from general guidance to self-assessment and registration. Achievement of the standards is claimed to lead to genuine business benefit with companies claiming process performance improvement, cost reductions, reduced pollution, legislative compliance and enhanced public image.

ISO 14000 has much in common with ISO 9000 and can capitalise on systems and procedures already established. It extends from the ISO 9000 criteria of meeting customer requirements to capture regulatory and mandatory environmental requirements. While ISO 14000 is established on a voluntary basis, there are indications that some countries may enshrine the standards in environmental legislation.

21.4   CRITICAL REVIEW

The ISO 9000 series is well accepted as the standard for quality management systems around the globe. It is comprehensive and has enjoyed substantial development over many years. However, as has been recognised in the inception of the ISO 14000 series, the scope of ISO 9000 is restricted to quality standards which are essential but not sufficient for contemporary organisations.

An effective QMS is a vital part of any quality programme; without it there is no basis for properly measuring and monitoring quality performance. It must not, though, be allowed to become an end in itself (as is so often the case). The QMS will inform the organisation how well or badly it is doing against the standards which it has set itself, nothing more. Unless action is continually taken to improve standards and performance, the measurement activity is sterile.

Documentation and procedures for the QMS should ideally be developed by the staff who actually carry out the tasks. Monitoring systems should be accurate, robust and generate accurate meaningful data.

Overall, a well designed QMS, within the context of a coherent quality programme should generate significant benefits to the organisation. Failure to heed the cautions outlined in this chapter will render the activity useless.

SUMMARY

This chapter has presented a brief overview of the core elements of a quality management system and the ISO 9000 series. The ISO 14000 series was also introduced. A QMS has been shown to be a relatively simple aspect of the overall quality initiative which may explain its popularity. Limitations to a QMS have been highlighted. Readers should refer to specific texts on ISO 9000 and ISO 14000 to further develop their knowledge.

key learning points

QUALITY MANAGEMENT SYSTEMS

Key definitions

the ISO 9000 series is the internationally accepted standard for quality management systems

the ISO 14000 series is the internationally accepted standard for environmental management systems

Quality management system

a formal record of an organisation's method of managing the quality of its product's or services

needs a systematic, ordered approach, leading to third party certification of the system, not the quality

Purpose

provides a basis for measuring and monitoring quality performance

QUESTION

Identify the strengths and weaknesses of an ISO 9000 standard quality management system. Consider how this system may be used to improve quality performance.

chapter twenty-two

STATISTICAL METHODS

'What is truth?' asked Pontius Pilate.
'It ain't statistics,' said a voice in the crowd.
Darrell Huff, *How to Lie with Statistics*, 1973

INTRODUCTION

This chapter introduces a selection of the primary statistical methods used in the pursuit of quality. It starts with Statistical Process Control (SPC) before looking at Control Charts and Statistical Quality Control (SQC). Key techniques such as Pareto analysis and the use of fishbone diagrams are featured; the use of certain techniques by the Quality Gurus is highlighted.

22.1 STATISTICAL PROCESS CONTROL

Statistical Process Control was briefly introduced in part two especially in chapter 6 (W. Edwards Deming). Its use relies on three key points:

- a pre-defined process;
- an established measurement system;
- operational (practical) definitions of the quality characteristics of the product or service must have been agreed and understood by all parties.

The method for process charting was outlined in chapter 20.

A measurement system is required to monitor the performance of the defined process with particular emphasis on quality achievement, that is, the proportion of defective parts or other outputs (such as services) in relation to the total produced. The measure of defective parts relies in turn on the operation definition of quality characteristics. Construction of a measurement system consists in deciding what should be measured and where, developing a recording and reporting system and, to be effective, taking action on the results. Decisions about the measurement system should be relatively straightforward once the process chart is constructed and enables the construction of control charts which are much favoured by Deming, Juran, Taguchi and others.

The platform for measurement is regular calculation and recording of standards achieved to establish a pattern of system behaviour over time. Measurements must be taken at time intervals appropriate to the process such as hourly, daily or weekly and should capture a suitable sample, for example, an individual operator, a group, shift or department. The plotted results provide the basis for corrective action and performance improvement.

Plotting of the performance measurements enables the calculation of control limits based on the actual performance of the process. While variations fall within the limits, the process is deemed to be under control, that is in a stable state. Variations outside the limits require immediate corrective action to restore stability.

Over time, the objective is to eradicate causes of variation outside the limits, what Deming calls 'special causes'. These may be removed through a variety of approaches, for example improved equipment, training or improvement in quality of inputs to the process.

Once special causes have been eradicated, the random variations within the control limits are considered to have 'common causes'; that is, the sources of variation lie in the process itself although it is considered to be under control. The reduction or eradication of these causes requires action on the process itself. This is seen as the responsibility of management since only they have the authority to make this level of change. Consistent and continuous effort is required to maintain the system in a stable state and to continuously reduce variation.

It should be noted that the control limits relate to the degree of stability of the process itself and are driven by process performance. They are not determined by the product or service specifications. Operational definitions are specifications for a product or service which include the acceptable limits of variation and the criteria against which they can be measured. These must be expressed in terms which can be understood by the supplier and the customer and must be useful in practice.

Specifications are important, since regardless of whether the process is 'in control' or 'out of control' they provide the targets towards which the process should be oriented. To have a process which is apparently in statistical control – that is, the process is in a stable state – yet producing parts which do not meet the specifications is useless. It is important therefore that the process is not only statistically in control but also capable of creating products or services which meet the specifications. The specification limits will often be narrower, at least at the outset, than the control limits of the process.

22.2   CONSTRUCTING CONTROL CHARTS

A control chart is used to record each occurrence of a particular event. This may be either measurement of a continuous variable, for example, temperature, humidity, thickness, weight or an attribute, that is, conformance to a requirement – specified as conforming/non-conforming, or acceptable/not-acceptable. Statistical analysis is used to determine upper and lower control limits for the process in its current state. The vertical axis of the control chart records the number of occurrences of a particular event such as a product failure or defective parts produced. The horizontal axis is normally based on time periods. An appropriate time period must be used for the particular process, that is, it must relate to the production time cycle. It is unhelpful to record defective parts produced in a week if the number of units produced is measured in minutes!

Figure 22.1 provides a sample control chart. A chart may also be constructed where the number of defective parts is measured against individuals or teams of workers. This may help to identify where problems are occurring within a set of common processes, say, where ten teams are working on identical processes, and can highlight where investment in training or other problem resolution techniques will bring benefit.

The upper and lower control limits for a 'variables' control chart are calculated using the properties of normal distributions. For a normal distribution, approximately 99.8 per cent of values fall within a band of 6 standard deviations, that is, plus or minus 3 standard deviations from

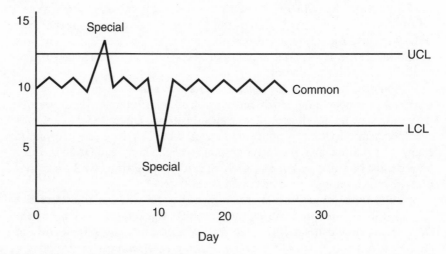

Figure 22.1 **Sample control chart**

the norm, and 68 per cent (approximately two-thirds) fall within one standard deviation. On this basis, the likelihood of an event falling outside the control limits is roughly 3 in every 1,000. It is considered therefore that any event falling outside is caused by a 'special' rather than 'common' cause.

The upper and lower control limits (± 3 standard deviations) are treated as triggers for action – any occurrence outside the limits must provoke an intervention in the process. Limits may also be set at ± 2 standard deviations from the mean to act as warning pointers to emergent deviation in the system.

In addition to using the basic information provided, the control charts may be used for trend analysis and forecasting purposes. These enable feed-forward control of processes which appear to be going out of control, and allow a degree of predictability to be generated.

Control limits for 'attribute' based charts are calculated differently. There are four versions of attribute chart (figure 22.2) chosen according to the sample size to be used and the quality characteristic to be measured. The upper and lower limits continue to be set at ± 3 standard deviations from the mean.

- *p* chart: varying batch size, varying sample size
- *np* chart: varying batch size, constant sample size
- *u* chart: component failure, varying sample size
- *c* chart: component failure, constant sample size

Figure 22.2 **Attribute control charts**

A *p* chart is used for defective items when it is not possible to take samples of a constant size, for example if the batch sizes or flow volumes vary. An *np* chart deals with the same problem but in situations where a constant sample is possible. The *u* chart is used for monitoring component failure where it is not possible to take constant sample sizes, the *c* chart when constant sample size is possible.

While this section has introduced control charts and provided the basis of their operation it is not intended to turn readers into experts in SPC. It is intended to provide only an introductory insight. All readers are recommended to employ the services of a qualified statistician if seeking to employ these techniques in any substantial manner. This is of particular importance in the choice of the appropriate tool (s) and in calculating such matters as sample sizes, validity of results and confidence limits. It is no use making changes to a process based on inaccurate or misleading data.

22.3 INTERPRETING CONTROL CHARTS

As well as informing the user whether or not a process is in statistical control, control charts can provide clues to help determine and eliminate special causes of variation.

A process which experiences only common causes of failure (that is those inherent in the process) will exhibit the following characteristics:

- all points will fall within the control limits;
- points will be distributed evenly either side of the mean;
- the pattern will appear random;
- most points will be near the mean, that is, less than one standard deviation.

In general, an 'in control' process will require modification or redesign in order for sustainable improvement to be achieved. For 'out of control' processes there are a number of cues for investigation/action.

A process which continuously or regularly produces results falling below the established lower control limit calls for two actions. First, is validation of the limit – have the calculations been performed correctly? The second action is to investigate the driver of the change and implement changes which reinforce the desirable improvement.

Second, any point falling outside the control limits should be investigated since it is likely to have a particular cause and the point of the system is to help identify and eradicate such causes.

Third, a continuing run of points to one side or the other of the mean, or a trend in one direction should be investigated. Again, a special cause may well be evident. Fourth, any apparently non-random, cyclical or repeated patterns should be investigated. These may relate to a particular operator or work group, a parts or materials supplier or may coincide with particular events (Monday mornings! Friday afternoons!). Again, desirable and undesirable patterns should be investigated to enable eradication or repeatability.

22.4 STATISTICAL QUALITY CONTROL

The concern of this chapter so far has been with measurements systems for recognising when a process is under control. It is considered that a reliable process will help drive the quality of the product or service. In this section other tools of statistical quality control (SQC) are considered. It is important to remember throughout this section that appropriate use of the tools relies not simply on following the correct methodology but also on the correct selection of tools in particular circumstances. The selection of tools to be considered is given in figure 22.3.

Vilfredo Pareto (1848–1922) was an economist. His research was concerned primarily with distribution of wealth. He found by analysing the distribution of total income amongst the population of a country, that a

- Pareto charts;

- Cause and effect diagrams (also called fishbone or Ishikawa diagrams);

- Stratification;

- Check sheets;

- Histograms;

- Scatter diagrams.

Figure 22.3 **Tools for statistical quality control**

small proportion of the population received a large part of the income. His early investigations in Italy revealed that about 20 per cent of the population received 80 per cent of the income and he devoted subsequent years to proving the universal applicability of this rule. The technique is now widely known as Pareto analysis.

Since Pareto's time, other economists and scientists have found that while the exact 80/20 proportion does not always occur the general shape of the curve remains. In the context of quality control, the application of Pareto analysis will indicate which areas, if improved, will give the greatest benefit for the least effort. It can also be used as a device for helping to separate what Juran calls 'the vital few from the useful many'.

The Ishikawa, or 'fishbone', diagram is also known as a 'cause and effect' diagram. It is used to reveal the factors which contribute to the achievement of a particular goal or objective, providing prompts for further investigation. It enables the creation of a complete overview of the situation being examined.

Essentially, an 'effect' is placed in a box on the right and a long process line is drawn pointing to the box. Major categories of causes are recorded on either side of the main line within other boxes connected to the main line. This enables each major cause to be considered independently. 'Sub'-causes are clustered around each of these lines. Figure 22.4 provides an example.

Major causes may include, machines, materials, workforce or money. They may also be technically or technologically oriented, for example, failure of components or processes. If a particular major cause group comes to dominate the diagram it may be worth isolation and separate investigation through another diagram.

The Ishikawa diagram is useful for exploring issues about which little is currently known and has power as a device for encouraging participation amongst those affected by the process being investigated. It can also be used in reverse as a 'solution-effect' diagram. This enables the exploration of the consequences of a proposed course of action. Figure 22.5 provides an example.

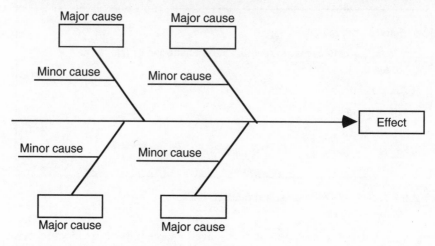

Figure 22.4 **Ishikawa or 'fishbone' diagram**

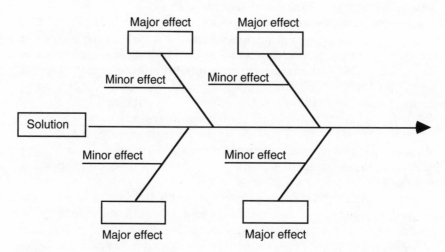

Figure 22.5 **Solution-effect diagram**

Stratification is a technique leading to what are known as 'strata charts', 'layer charts' or 'band curve' graphs. Each band of information is placed above the previous one. Totals are cumulative, so that each element of the whole is plotted one above the other. These again provide a useful visual representation of which elements in a process are incurring the greatest cost, or greatest number of faults, enabling decisions to be made about where attention should be focused. Figure 22.6 provides a self-explanatory example.

Such charts provide immediate evidence of the relative importance of the various constituent parts of a process or problem and are both easier to construct and easier to understand than Pareto charts. This makes them

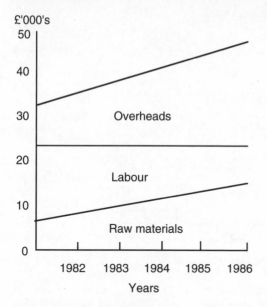

Figure 22.6 **Stratification chart**

more suitable for use in large scale presentations or where the educational level of the affected staff is relatively low.

Check sheets or checklists can be used in a variety of ways. In the context of quality, a common use is to investigate the customer–supplier relationship (the technique may be applied to either internal or external customers). It can help to investigate customer requirements and priorities, in the improvement of process definition and in creating an unbiased assessment of process performance and customer satisfaction. Any particular application may use more detailed or specific questions and may be supported by the selected application of statistical measures.

Histograms (or bar charts) are again ways of visually displaying sets of data and enabling comparisons between two or more characteristics. They are most often used to display frequency distributions and are helpful in summarising data, and appreciating measures of central tendency and dispersion.

Construction of a histogram is along two axes. The baseline (x axis) is divided according to the key divisions of data, the vertical (y axis) displaying frequency. A bar (or column) is drawn for each division. It is conventional for the group lengths (x axis) to be equal, meaning that the variation in the bars is in height only. However, in circumstances where group length is unequal the width of the bar may also be altered, that is, it may be proportional to the corresponding frequency. The height is defined as proportional to the ratio: group frequency/group length.

Uneven group lengths are only used where circumstances dictate this, for example, in small sample sizes. The histogram shape is likely to appear erratic. A sample histogram is provided in figure 22.7. A scatter diagram (or

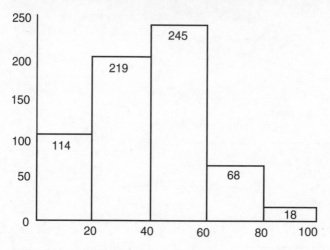

Figure 22.7 **Example of a histogram**

scattergraph) is used to determine whether a relationship exists between two variables. The scattergraph does not provide formal measures of these relationships, nor does it provide any means of establishing whether any apparent relationships are actually due to chance or not. It is normal to use other statistical devices in conjunction with a scatter diagram for testing of significance of the relationship. These methods may include linear regression analysis, correlation co-efficient and multiple regression.

Normally, a scatter diagram is drawn such that the independent variable is along the horizontal axis and the dependent variable on the vertical axis. The basic purpose is to discern whether there is any pattern among the points. If there is, a 'line of best fit' can be drawn with the same number of points on each side. An example of a scatter diagram is given in figure 22.8.

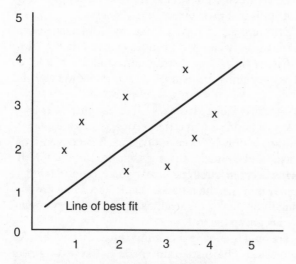

Figure 22.8 **Example of a scatter diagram**

22.5 CRITICAL REVIEW

Statistical methods offer the principal techniques for formally measuring and evaluating performance and performance improvement. However, they also offer the greatest scope for fooling both others and yourselves. They must be used properly, intelligently and with full understanding of their accuracy and implications.

Statistics are frequently used to support decision making – and support is their proper role. They should not become the only factor used to make a decision. There are a number of reasons for this. First, they may not be accurate. Even where machine counted, measures of volume, throughput and so on can often generate misleading numbers. When people are involved in the counting process a degree of error is almost inevitable – try counting sheep in a field or fish in a pond – the difficulty of counting is similar to counting finished products on a production line or service events in a retail outlet. Similarly, however accurate the actual numbers, if some critical process event has been overlooked (for example the 'within process' recycling in the bakery example in chapter 20), the measurements, and the statistics derived from them, will be wrong.

LOOKING BEHIND THE NUMBERS

A major retail organisation developed a staff productivity system for each of its various outlets. The system used output activity volumes to derive recommended staffing levels for each outlet. Procedures and processes within each outlet were standardised but the system was individually tuned to allow for physical peculiarities of different buildings, for example, working on multiple floors, and for the size of the particular outlet which sometimes required variations to procedures.

Despite the accommodation of these individual differences and the adjustment of staff numbers to reflect workload variations, it was found that certain outlets were under constant pressure with high levels of overtime. The managers of these outlets were placed under pressure by the senior management to bring their costs under control and match the productivity of the 'better' outlets. After some time it was found that there was no significant improvement in most of these cases, the complaints about pressure and the high levels of overtime continued.

Eventually short investigations were authorised in the problem outlets, focused on improving their productivity. Three drivers of the problems were identified:

- mismanagement of resources;
- inexperienced, untrained staff;
- high levels of business development activity.

The first driver was expected; after all, one purpose of the system was to assist managers in maximising the utilisation of resources. The second driver represented a major problem. The system assumed an 'average' level of competence and experience amongst the staff, whereas, in that fast growing organisation, the real 'average' was a lot lower due to high levels of staff turnover and continuing recruitment. Finally, the system only recorded 'successful' business development activity, that is, activity which led to a measured output. Any unsuccessful business development activity was excluded. The effect of this was that those outlets which tried hardest to develop new business were 'punished' by the inadequacies of the system.

Second, the statistics represent probabilities, not actualities – remember the number of 'averages' used in the calculation of standard deviation – particularly where batch or sample sizes vary. The answers given for these calculations are 'more or less' accurate – never precise. Third, since the calculations are to some degree 'wrong' pure reliance on them is bound to generate some degree of mismatch to reality, often leading to complaints and witch hunts.

Fourth, understanding how the numbers are driven is much more important than the numbers themselves. Pure reliance on the statistics leads to a focus on improving the statistics rather than improving the process which supports them. It is frequently observed that in a failing or struggling company the focus is put on reducing costs. Company wide cuts are imposed, for example 10 per cent of head count or 10 per cent of wage costs. While in the short term this might address the particular problem of immediate cash flow it usually does nothing for the medium to long term future of the company. Blanket reductions in staff not supported by changes in the volume of work simply lead to increased stress on those remaining (leading to higher levels of sickness), removal of key performers or simply to increased overtime for those remaining (which can actually increase costs). Problems with the organisation may anyway be related to pricing, competition, market behaviour, delivery problems or a whole host of other factors which the managers have failed to identify.

As it is with money so it is with quality. A short term hard-nosed push for quality is a recurring feature of organisations. However, unless changes are developed for the processes of production the common causes of failure are simply overridden. As soon as the pressure is released the system will revert to its previous behaviour. A further phenomenon is called squeezing the snake or 'corset' management. In this case a quality problem is identified at a particular stage of a process through the SQC mechanism. Managerial pressure is applied to that point and performance improvement is generated, the quality problem reduces. What is not realised until much later is that the problem has not disappeared it has simply been moved, either back up the process by constricting the inputs to the problem area or, further down the process by widening the exit point (usually by varying the criteria for quality).

Good, accurate statistics are vital for performance measurement, but they cannot replace competent, informed management. Good – that is, accurate, well founded and reliable – statistics can tell the manager much about what is happening within the processes of an organisation. That is the limit of their usefulness. The statistics say nothing about why the reported events occur – which is much more important. Statistics are nothing but a statement of the characteristics and events the managers have chosen to record. Demanding an improvement in the statistics – as managers often do – will ensure they get just that! The processes, products or services of the organisation will not change at all but the statistics will look better! Managers need to look below the reported numbers and consider the deeper aspects of the organisation. Aspects to consider might include the quality and amount of supervision, the reliability and accuracy or equipment, the feelings and attitudes of the staff, the expectations of the customers (many complaints are after all the result of a mismatch of the customers expectations – created through marketing – and the reality of the product or service – as produced by the organisation).

SUMMARY

This chapter has introduced the principal statistical tools of quality management. It is not intended that this chapter will create statistical experts, but, rather, provide an overview appreciation of the principals. Readers are reminded to develop their understanding further through the use of a good text on statistics.

---

key learning points

STATISTICAL METHODS

Statistical Process Control (SPC) requires
a pre-defined process, measurement system, operational definitions

enables monitoring of the outputs of a system, control charts are the output of SPC

these outputs are the basis for taking action

Statistical Quality Control (SQC) techniques
Pareto charts, fishbone diagrams, stratification, check sheets, histograms, scatter diagrams

Critique
principal methods for measuring performance, tell us *what* but not *why*,

need to be supported by competent, informed management

QUESTION

Using the process map developed at chapter 20, identify critical points where statistical data gathering would generate useful results. Select appropriate techniques for recording the values, justify your choices.

chapter twenty-three

BENCHMARKING

a disinterested endeavour to learn and propagate the best that is known and thought.

Matthew Arnold on criticism

INTRODUCTION

That an organisation is meeting the perceived requirements of its existing customers is insufficient to ensure long term success in today's highly competitive environment. If some other organisation is providing better (in the customer's terms) products or services then, over time, there is likely to be a drift of customers towards that higher quality supplier.

Equally, when commencing a quality programme, it is inadequate to define improvement relative only to existing internal performance and measurements. It is, of course, vital to define quality and improvement in terms of the customer's requirements and in terms of the 'best' competing products. The foundation for quality improvement then is knowing how good or bad one set of products and services are when compared to others in the same market-place. It is this foundation which benchmarking helps to establish. One particular benchmark now being used by many organisations is the ISO 9000 series which provides the standard for quality management systems and is thought by some to create competitive advantage.

Benchmarking is used by large and small organisations throughout the world to help them understand their own performance against the best that they can measure. This enables them to more profitably develop and grow their businesses.

23.1 WHAT IS BENCHMARKING?

Benchmarking essentially is a process of comparison between the performance characteristics of separate, often competing, organisations intended to enable each participant to improve its own performance in the market-place.

The objectives of benchmarking are first to obtain a clearer understanding of competitors and of customers' requirements. It is considered that this understanding, particularly of customers, will lead to reduced complaints and higher levels of customer satisfaction. Discovering process improvements will assist in reducing the costs associated with rework, rectification, waste and other quality problems. Benchmarking will also enable innovations (either of process or product) to spread more rapidly through an industry and across industries where appropriate – for example, in supply or distribution logistics where many problems are similar regardless of the industry.

Benchmarking involves a number of simple steps. The first establishes what, from the customer's perspective, makes the difference between one supplier of a product or service and another. For example, why one is considered adequate and another excellent. The second step is setting standards according to the best practice found. In other words, regarding best practice as the 'benchmark' for the organisation's performance. The third step is to determine by what means the benchmark organisation achieves those standards – which will always look challenging from the benchmarker's perspective. The final step is utilising the capabilities of the personnel to meet and, if possible, exceed the standards observed.

It is important to understand at this stage that what is important is not the industry but the core characteristics of the product, service or activity. While it may be ideal to benchmark one airline against another this may be difficult for reasons of competition, politics or law (for example where such behaviour may be regarded as anti-competitive or likely to lead to cartel pricing). On the other hand, it is perfectly reasonable to compare an airline's marketing or logistics function with those of a newspaper or a bread bakery since the products share a significant characteristic – nobody buys yesterday's bread or newspaper – no one can occupy an airline seat once the flight has left! Similarly, a useful comparison can be drawn between customer and enquiry handling in a bank with that at an airline counter or in a department store. The core process may be the same even though the particular questions may be very different.

Benchmarking provides a rigorous framework through which the benefits outlined above can be obtained. It enables a disciplined, demanding assessment of performance in areas which are crucial to the particular organisation. It also enables avoidance of the errors and mistakes already made by others, thus preventing further reinvention of the wheel.

Two major limitations on performance improvement can be usefully addressed through benchmarking. First, is the limitation to knowledge which so often affects organisational performance. The experience and knowledge which most people have of a process or product is gathered in a particular environment. Unless they have the opportunity of advanced training, perhaps through a business school, or some form of collaboration, they are largely closed off from developments which could improve their process. Thus they become content with the way things are – because they know of nothing different or better. The story of Fletcher Challenge Steel in China from chapter 9 perhaps reinforces this point.

Second, the syndrome known as NIH – Not Invented Here – can be overcome through benchmarking. NIH is a typical response by many organisations and employees to proposed changes to improve performance. It is often accompanied by remarks such as 'that may work alright in xxxx but it just wouldn't apply here', frequently supported by 'because we're unique', 'our circumstances are different' or 'our customers don't expect' or some similar excuse. The truth is that NIH is a defensive ploy intended to inhibit the disruption and effort that is often associated with a change programme. If the employees who will be affected by a change are involved in its design through the benchmarking programme, then they will be much less likely to resist the change and more likely to develop unique aspects which will 'make it work here'.

Overall, benchmarking first requires senior management commitment, particularly to supporting actions arising from the exploration. Second, it requires staff to be trained and guided in the process to ensure that maximum benefit is obtained. Finally, it requires allocation of part of the relevant employees time to enable it to be carried out.

23.2   HOW IS BENCHMARKING DONE?

There are only five steps (figure 23.1) to a benchmarking process regardless of the size of companies involved, although larger companies may indulge in greater amounts of data gathering than smaller ones and may have to be conscious of issues surrounding anti-competitive or monopolistic behaviour.

Step 1, appraising and identifying which characteristics to benchmark, can be achieved through Pareto Analysis. While it is possible to benchmark every characteristic of a process which can be measured, the return to the company from doing so will vary substantially. Remembering Juran's comment on 'the vital few, the useful many' it is worth trying to determine at the outset which activities the company needs to excel in to succeed in its particular business, bearing in mind that in the context of quality this should be expressed in terms of the customer's requirements. A substantial improvement in a process which delivers no benefit to customers will not necessarily and directly improve the competitive position, although it may generate improvement in profit performance which may be of great importance. Quality benchmarks might include aspects such as reliability, longevity, consistency, accuracy, levels of in-process rework or rectification, service intervals, after-sales response and so on. Factors which affect profitability – and which may enable more effective competition through

---

Step 1 Identifying what characteristics to benchmark;

Step 2 Identifying benchmarking partners;

Step 3 Designing the data gathering methodology;

Step 4 Selecting analytical tools;

Step 5 Implementing changes.

Figure 23.1 **Five steps in benchmarking**

reductions in prices – include reductions in rework, working stocks, inventory levels, and relationships between factors such as sales dollars (or other currency) per employee, enquiry to sale conversion rates, space utilisation and increasingly the effectiveness in use of management information systems.

The selection criteria for projects should be based on delivery of maximum benefit to the customer rather than on matters which might be considered as exciting or interesting to a particular professional group. Approaches based on the latter view often lead to major disappointment. For example many organisations since the mid-1980s have invested heavily in continually upgrading computer systems from the 286 chip technology of the late 1980s to the fast 266 MHz processors of the late 1990s. While the dramatic increase in processing speeds has undoubtedly been delivered (technically the machines work much faster than they used to), little genuine business benefit has been delivered to the users (most people type at the same speed they always did!). The processor speed is not of overriding importance so long as it is always equal to or faster than the operator. In terms of the customer, he or she generally has little interest in the speed of the machinery in use but a great deal in the accuracy of output of the process – an area where little evident progress has been made with many organisations still blaming 'the computer' for errors. It does not really need repeating that it is people that make mistakes, not machines!

Characteristics to be benchmarked should be, first, those which are of genuine concern to the customer and, second, those which are of material importance to the organisation. Other areas for benchmarking include those where the organisation knows that it is experiencing a problem either in relation to its customers or to its competitors. Issues might include staff training and development, recruitment and turnover, raw material and other input costs.

The second step is deciding which other organisations to benchmark with. In the case of a very large, perhaps divisionalised operation, it may be perfectly reasonable to start by internal benchmarking, for example, comparing the distribution logistics processes of two factories. If this is not possible then it is necessary to look outside the organisation for benchmarking partners. These may be domestic or overseas. A starting point is to again ask the customers who they regard as the best in your particular business; after all it is the customers whom you are trying to satisfy. This will also help to identify those characteristics of performance which the customers regard as important.

Other sources include the press, trade and industry associations, industry expert consultants or academics. Looking overseas, the various trade commissions, embassies, and state departments should be able to provide useful leads. For example, in Hong Kong the Productivity Council could help, while in the UK there are a number of organisations focused on benchmarking practice and co-operation.

There are four key issues to address in selecting benchmarking partners. First, do the companies have some knowledge of each other? For example, is there a customer–supplier relationship already? Second, is the experience of the proposed partner directly relevant to our needs? Third, are they as good as their reputation suggests? It is quite normal for a company's reputation to outlast the quality of its goods or services, equally some companies with established 'bad' reputations may have made substantial performance improvements. For example, in the 1970s the Fiat company developed a reputation for building cars which rusted very quickly and very badly. This has not been the case for many years yet the reputation still surrounds their products despite the evidence on the roads that the reputation is unfair. Finally, and as mentioned before, is the exchange of information with this partner permissible? Apart from any legislation concerning anti-competitive behaviour, organisations also need to be aware of limitations on the transfer of technology to and from certain countries and for certain purposes. These general cautions need to be supported by appropriate legal advice and of course the application of common sense.

Designing the data gathering methodology moves beyond the basics of ensuring that any statistical methods are rigorously applied and the results meaningful, to the real issue of how to physically obtain the information. The first and most readily available sources are in the public domain, for example, company annual reports, press articles, trade association journals and libraries, academic studies (where these have been undertaken and published), and from the various bodies and consultancies which specialise in enabling benchmarking. While normally direct competitors will only exchange data through a third party, such as a trade association, some may be amenable to a direct contact – particularly if the company approaching them is able to offer comparable assistance to them on another issue. For example, you may swap information on staff retention and development programmes for information on distribution logistics. As long as each party perceives there to be a fair exchange (in terms of problems solved) the volume of data will probably not be an obstruction. What is vital at this stage is that the data necessary to enable the benchmarking to be carried out is identified right at the outset – nothing is worse than having to return to the partner for more information, nothing is more unhelpful than designing improvements based on incomplete or inaccurate information. The services of a statistician and other suitably qualified professionals should be used to support the data gathering process, for example, consultants (either internal or external) with expertise in process mapping and analysis and so on.

The fourth step reflects the similar stage in process review already elaborated in chapter 20. The key difference is that rather than seeking general improvement, the search in the benchmarking exercise is for specific differences between processes which give one a significant performance margin over the other. This recognition of the performance gap is the basis for improvement, recognising always that what works for one company in one set of circumstances will not necessarily work for another in a different set.

The fifth and final step is implementing changes. Technically this is quite straightforward. New performance standards need to be set based on the improvement scope identified. The lowest level of management with an overview of the whole process affected, appropriately supported, needs to take direct responsibility for implementing the changes. Additional resources must be provided to support the changes if required. For example, overtime working may be necessary to to create a window enabling the absorption of disruption associated with a particular change. This might occur in a despatch unit where a redesign of the storage layout could demand that a significant amount of space be created in the short term. Finally, a performance monitoring programme must be implemented to make progress visible.

Benchmarking, like quality improvement, is never complete. It is a continuing process and although the incremental gains from the first exercise are likely to be the largest, the process should be continued to ensure that the organisation always reflects best practice in the particular area.

23.3   CRITICAL REVIEW

Benchmarking is essentially an exercise in organisational humility. It demands of the participants that rather than being complacent about how good they are, they respect the idea that there may be others in the industry who carry out a particular process more effectively than they do, that is, cheaper, quicker and more closely meeting customer expectations. They then have to set out to learn from those higher performers.

Technically, as has been shown, benchmarking is not a difficult process, each of the five steps is relatively straightforward, and overall it amounts first to emulating the best and, second, trying to improve on their performance. As any author will tell you, it is far harder to write an original book than to prepare a review or critique of another's.

The risk with benchmarking is that the organisation only aspires to be as good as the rest – and sets its sights according to that. This means it simply copies other's practices without adapting those practices to the particular and unique set of circumstances in which it operates. Relying on such a model (a model is simply a representation of reality), the organisation will never achieve the levels of performance of the organisation copied. This is because the model does not reveal everything about the organisation or its circumstances, only those characteristics which the modeller thought important.

The second problem with straight copying is of course that no competitive advantage is gained. The process simply levels the playing field further, reducing diversity in the market and thereby reducing effective consumer choice. If there is no measurable difference between products or services then purchasers will make their choices on other criteria such as convenience, accessibility or taste (fashion), the last of which is extremely fickle.

BENCHMARKING FOR SURVIVAL

Derwentside District Council

The Technical Services Department of Derwentside District Council proceeded to certification under BS5750 (subsequently ISO 9001) in June 1994. This successful conclusion was reached after a long and arduous process which started with a preliminary feasibility study and report submitted in September 1990. Commitment to the strategy ebbed and flowed over time dependent upon conflicting work priorities. However, the process was completed well in advance of the main target and achieved within budget.

The main motivation for applying quality management techniques was the prospect of competing in the future with private sector organisations under the rules of compulsory competitive tendering for professional services. The key element to the success of the initiative was to change the 'ethos' of the organisation through the drive and commitment of senior managers. The strategy was adopted on the perception that service quality aspects of the tender evaluation process would be most easily demonstrated through reference to a third party approved quality management system.

In addition to enabling competition with the private sector organisations, two other advantages were realised. First, the image of the department within the Council was improved. Second, the QMS provided a useful vehicle to support other necessary changes. Greatest benefit was derived where existing systems were inadequate or non-existent – particularly as it was in these areas that most resistance was encountered.

The system has been successfully in operation for three years and is now deemed 'mature' by the external assessors. The department believe that it has also given them an advantage in pursuing the 'Best Value' proposals made by the government.

Benchmarking their services against external standards has clearly served Derwentside District Council well.

Benchmarking is a potentially valuable technique for quickly lifting the performance of an organisation. However, establishing benchmarks must be used as the platform for significant improvement over the best, if it is genuinely to improve the competitive position of the organisation rather than simply keep it in the game.

SUMMARY

This chapter has briefly introduced the idea of benchmarking as a platform for performance improvement within the context of a quality programme. The major steps in a benchmarking process were considered and a critical review provided.

---

key learning points
BENCHMARKING

Key definition
the practice of formal comparison of processes and systems with other organisations as the basis for improvement

Key technique
identify key characteristics, identify partners, design data collection methodology, select tools, implement changes

Critique
demands humility, willingness to learn, risk – only match, not exceed competitor performance, hence danger of levelling not competing

---

QUESTION

What measures of performance would you use to select benchmarking partners?

chapter twenty-four

SUPPLIER DEVELOPMENT

Why beholdest thou the mote that is in thy brother's eye, but considerest not the beam that is in thine own.

(Matthew, 7: 3, New Testament)

INTRODUCTION

The issue of supplier development is not one which is well explored in the standard quality literature. However, suppliers, of both materials and services, are critical to the achievement of quality. The quality of material inputs to a manufacturing process are strong determinants of the quality of output. The quality of bought in services, such as perhaps distribution, accounting support, information technology support and building or machine maintenance affect either the production process or the interface with the customer, for example through deliveries or invoicing. Clearly, a part of being a quality organisation is ensuring that the external factors affecting the input and output ends of the internal processes meet the requisite quality standard.

24.1   WHAT IS SUPPLIER DEVELOPMENT?

Supplier development is best thought of as a business policy espoused by a company which is serious about achieving quality. It involves a commitment by that company to set and attain internal quality standards which meet the requirements of its customers, and to support its suppliers in enabling them to meet those same requirements.

Traditionally, companies wishing to exercise a degree of control of the upstream or downstream elements of the value chain have followed the route of vertical integration, either through development of their own services, or through acquisition. However, these traditional routes have proven less than fully successful. The company loses the focus of its core business, often operating the other parts of the business less successfully and at greater cost than the specialists, so that instead of excelling at one task it becomes mediocre at many. Equally, it is frequently the case that overall profitability is adversely affected. Supplier development moves away from this strategy, recognising its inherent difficulties and limitations, and respecting the expertise and knowledge specific to the fulfilment of a particular need.

Supplier development requires of the company that it change its posture in relation to its suppliers. Traditionally, the buyer–supplier relationship is adversarial, each party seeking to maximise its own benefit from the relationship. Supplier development requires that this relationship become co-operative or collaborative, such that buyer and supplier work together to maximise mutual interests. This also requires a change in the buying processes. The placing of orders based on lowest price and sealed tenders has to cease, with a change to open exchange of information and negotiations based on a willingness to achieve an equitable outcome for both parties. For example, the need of each party to generate an adequate return on its efforts must be respected.

A move towards using a single supplier is also advocated by some writers, (for example Deming, 1986: 35–40). This policy has both advantages and drawbacks. Positively, utilising a single source of supply should ensure greater reliability of inputs in terms of consistency, lack of variability (that is, closer adherence to standards), and the potential for continually improving standards and reduced paperwork. From the supplier's perspective, they are perhaps assured of a particular level of order, potentially higher order values, greater certainty in their business planning and longer production runs with bigger batch sizes (reducing down-time and set-up time which both in turn increase productivity), more reliable payment and availability of additional expertise (from their customer).

Looking at the negatives, the buying organisation may close itself off to other options, reducing the opportunity for speculative or spot purchases of materials (which meet requirements) and may reduce its leverage in price negotiations with the supplier, particularly when supplier power is high (Porter, 1980). The organisation becomes vulnerable to changes in strategy, tactics or performance by its supplier. This is particularly important when the product or service purchased is critical to the process. For example, if distribution is contracted out to a dedicated haulage firm which then, for reasons unrelated to the particular contract, experiences financial or other difficulties such as a strike or limitation on the availability of vehicles. From the supplier's perspective, becoming the sole source of supply to a particular organisation may involve the dedication of a significant proportion of its resources to fulfilling that order. In this case, it in turn may become vulnerable to any difficulties experienced by its customer or any change of product or strategy on their part. For example, if the buyer ceases to produce a particular product, or suffers from extensive competition leading to falling volumes, the fortunes of the supplier are similarly affected.

The foregoing comments are general considerations which must be addressed before any sole supplier relationship is agreed. It may be that both parties feel that the advantages outweigh the disadvantages and associated risks in the particular case and choose to proceed. On the other hand, one or the other may find that the relationship would make them especially vulnerable in which case they should instead seek alternative arrangements.

Clearly, there is a significant degree of risk to a supplier if the agreement with a buyer constitutes a significant proportion of the total business and limits, for whatever reason, the ability to undertake business with other parties.

That being said, there is also significant potential advantage to the buying organisation in successfully pursuing the strategy of supplier development particularly in the creation of a long term and stable relationship.

24.2 HOW IS SUPPLIER DEVELOPMENT UNDERTAKEN?

The decision to pursue a policy of supplier development can only reasonably be undertaken by an organisation already fully committed to quality and which recognises that improved input quality is necessary to support its implementation programme. To pursue this policy when the organisation is not already achieving high standards may well be seen by the supplier as an attempt to shift the blame for quality failure. Such an approach is unlikely to be well received.

Stage 1 Senior management commitment to supplier development;

Stage 2 Audit and evaluation of internal standards;

Stage 3 Define and quantify the desirable or necessary changes;

Stage 4 Develop agreement with identified suppliers;

Stage 5 Form joint teams and develop training programme (if necessary);

Stage 6 Teams define precise objectives, deliverables and timescale;

Stage 7 Implement changes and monitor impacts.

Figure 24.1 **Seven stages of supplier development**

Supplier development takes place in seven stages (figure 24.1). The first stage is, like the first stage in a quality programme, crucial. If the senior management are not committed to the process and its outcomes (including the need to provide short term financial support and to commit workforce resources to the strategy) it will fail.

The second stage is to audit and evaluate the processes in which the supplier's inputs are used to ensure that these meet the current internal expectations. Similarly, the inputs themselves must be formally evaluated. If a process is failing because of internal factors then no amount of supplier development will cure it. Similarly, if suppliers are to be approached to improve their performance it is vital that the buyer can precisely demonstrate the need by showing the impact on their own output.

CO-OPERATION OR COMPETITION?

As the public face of the food industry, the large supermarket chains adopt what might be regarded as supplier development strategies. They are committed to continuously enhancing the quality (by their measures) of the foodstuffs they sell and make use of this commitment in their advertising.

These organisations work closely with their suppliers through the buying process, evaluating not just the goods themselves, but the factories, farms and delivery systems. They agree exacting standards with the suppliers for all aspects of the product and reserve the right to refuse deliveries which do not meet those standards. Pricing is a difficult issue in this area with strong competition between the supermarket chains and consequent pressure on suppliers to reduce costs.

They do not always, however, adhere to the supplier development strategy outlined in this chapter. While the first three phases are usually completed, thereafter the process often breaks down. The agreement is often rather one-sided. The buying power of the supermarket chains coupled to the fragmentation of the food production industry with its many competing small suppliers tends to make those suppliers vulnerable to pressure. Similarly, stages five, six and seven are usually foregone with the supermarket expecting the supplier to conform to the new standards and to bear the cost of so doing. While in the short term this appears beneficial to end consumers, there is a danger in the longer term that the number of suppliers will be significantly reduced. In this circumstance, choice and variety will fall and prices will rise, reflecting the greater strength of those suppliers in their relationships with the supermarkets.

The idea of 'partnership' between buyers and suppliers, which supplier development strategies imply, would probably be most beneficial to all parties in the long run. Variety would be maintained, prices would be relatively stable as a result of continuing competition, and food quality would continually improve. This can only be achieved under co-operative rather than combative conditions.

Stage 3 is for the buying organisation to determine what standards it expects its suppliers to achieve and, consequently, what changes are necessary and which desirable. It is important to discriminate between those aspects which are essential to acceptable performance (that is, meeting requirements) and those which would be beneficial in the longer term but are not currently essential. This stage taken together with stage 2, defines the gap between the current performance of the supplier and the necessary performance. This defines the initial scope for the supplier development strategy and provides a basis for measuring subsequent performance improvement.

The first three stages simply prepare the ground for approaching suppliers. The buying organisation is now equipped with the information necessary to engage in meaningful discussions. Stage 4 is the development of agreement with the identified suppliers. Clearly, if the suppliers are not willing to join in with the programme then nothing is lost, since the organisation is fully prepared to approach alternative sources with a clear idea of its expectations. The supplying organisation must be prepared to make the same commitment to improving performance as the buying organisation. The basis of moving forward should be a written agreement setting out the aims and objectives of the programme and the benefits to be delivered.

Stage 5 is the formation of joint problem solving teams tasked with pursuing the various benefits. These should take the form of quality circles and may require training or development input in order to function effectively. Ideally, these teams should include representatives of all relevant functions in the two organisations. For example, a team made up exclusively of product buyers and sales staff would not be effective since they are likely to have only limited knowledge of the problems in use of the particular product or service. Operational staff must be regarded as fundamental to such a team which should have the authority to draw on other resources when appropriate, for example, accounting staff (for costings), statisticians (for the development of process control measurement) and so on.

Stage 6 is the implementation phase when the designated teams should initially define precise objectives, tasks and timescales in the light of the current performance gap. Implementation itself should more or less follow the pattern of quality circle operation using the same quality tools and techniques.

Finally, stage 7 is concerned with implementing any changes arising and monitoring the impacts against the expected benefits. It may be that for very large organisations a supervisory or steering board is required to oversee the implementation programme (particularly if a part of the strategy is to transfer the learning which takes place to other parts of the respective operations). For smaller organisations this should not be necessary.

Like most other aspects of a quality programme, supplier development can never be considered as complete. It is an ongoing, iterative process which aims to continually improve performance for the benefit of both parties.

24.3   CRITICAL REVIEW

There is clearly significant benefit to be gained by organisations working together to improve performance. They can streamline processes, reduce costs, enhance productivity and more adequately satisfy their customer's expectations. The drawbacks to this strategy principally surround the issue of vulnerability of either the supplier or buyer through dependence on a single source. This vulnerability relates to financial leverage and to the risks of failure to supply.

To be successful, a supplier development strategy relies upon absolute commitment by both parties to making the arrangement work and a willingness and intent to act in the utmost good faith at all times.

SUMMARY

This chapter has briefly introduced the concept of supplier development as part of the overall quality strategy. The issue has been paid little attention in the quality literature and the ideas expressed here provide a basic outline only.

---

key learning points

SUPPLIER DEVELOPMENT

Key definition
buyers working co-operatively with suppliers to improve quality throughout the value chain

Key technique
commitment, audit and evaluation, define changes, develop agreement, form teams, define precise objectives, implementation

Critique
benefits through streamlining, cost reductions, enhanced productivity, drawbacks from vulnerability of suppliers, unbalanced power within the value chain, potential to reduce choice and variety

---

QUESTION

Consider the food industry example just provided. Suggest ways in which a more equitable balance of power could be achieved.

chapter twenty-five

QUALITATIVE METHODS

Success nourished them; they seemed to be able, and so they were able.

Virgil, *Aeneid*, II, V. 231

INTRODUCTION

The aim of this chapter is to review a selection of the non-quantitative methods for achieving quality, showing how they may be used. Readers will recall the overall methodologies of the gurus from part two. In this chapter specific tools are considered.

25.1   QUALITY CIRCLES

Quality circles are usually considered to be the brainchild of Dr Kaoru Ishikawa but have been adopted in a variety of forms by many companies throughout the world. The circles exist (figure 25.1) to identify and solve quality problems associated with a particular activity or interest group within the organisation.

The aims of using quality circles are to improve and develop the organisation, show respect for people and enhance their satisfaction in the job and to stretch them to their potential. Each circle is made up of between 4 and 12 workers led by a supervisor or manager. The focus of attention is on problems within their own area although problems imported from a

---

- Improve and develop the enterprise.

- Respect human relations and build job satisfaction.

- Stretch human potential and capabilities.

Figure 25.1 **Aims of quality circles**

prior process should also be recognised. These become the responsibility of the supervisor or manager to address.

The effectiveness of quality circles depends upon a number of key factors. Prime amongst these is support from senior and operational management. If these levels obstruct, or inhibit the effort, even passively, then the initiative will fail. Similarly, participation by the workers must be voluntary, and both they and the leaders must be trained in appropriate techniques.

It is usually suggested that circle members have a common work background. This may be seen as perhaps inhibiting the development of solutions to problems that cross process boundaries. It is certainly the case that a problem within a particular area may be solved by a circle drawing its membership from within that area. This approach, though, will not necessarily help with problems which cross internal boundaries and denies the use of inter-disciplinary teams. Inter-disciplinary working has been found to be extremely helpful in the discipline of operational research and is now gaining popularity in many other fields. The principal benefit of a 'common background' circle is that the membership will not feel that a solution has been imposed by an outside, disinterested body. A sense of 'ownership' in solutions is generally recognised as a powerful means of overcoming resistance to change.

The orientation of the quality circle is towards solutions. It is very easy for quality circles to become enmeshed in complaints about the organisation. This may be made manifest in moaning about other parts of the process, or fruitless comparisons of working conditions, pay rates and other issues which are not central to the purpose of the circle.

Organisation of the circle should be a matter of normal good practice for meetings: that is, a specific (but limited) time set aside, circulation of an agenda and invitations to attend to all members, together with managers/supervisors at least as a matter of courtesy. It is recommended that the chair of the circle be rotated on a regular basis and that hierarchy in the circle be avoided. Apart from its benefit to active participation in the circle, this provides the opportunity for every member to try the role of manager, even if in a very limited sense. It may also be regarded as good training practice and an opportunity for a manager to see how individual workers might cope with more responsible and supervisory positions.

It is generally considered important that the efforts of the participants should be recognised, although debate continues about this aspect. One school of thought suggests that a participant in a quality circle is only fulfilling his or her responsibility to an employer by showing how improvement can be achieved. If satisfaction and increased job security are achieved through this then the effort brings its own reward. The other school believes that an employee is paid to carry out a particular task and that extra responsibility should carry extra reward.

This recognition and reward aspect needs to be related to the culture of the organisation and its geographical location. Decisions need to be made on the basis of the socio-cultural context of the particular organisation. This means that what may be appropriate in Hong Kong or Singapore may be wholly inappropriate in Tokyo or London.

Quality circles do not stand on their own as an approach to TQM, they must be supported by other initiatives. One important weakness in this respect is the lack of a quality circle hierarchy for working across organisational boundaries and at higher levels in the organisation. This means that interactions cannot be recognised and appropriately addressed within this conventional approach.

25.2 JOB DESIGN

Job design covers a range of issues associated with obtaining improvement in quality through enhanced job performance. It involves recognising that, to a large extent, jobs have historically not been designed, more often they have been described at the outset and subsequently allowed to evolve. Redesign may have been undertaken in the pursuit of greater efficiency and error reduction, including the application of work study and organisation and methods techniques, but this will have often served to fragment tasks into smaller parts. Decisions about particular tasks have often been made without understanding of the whole process or the purpose to be served.

This section proposes a variety of approaches which help to address the problems so caused, including dissatisfaction, fragmentation and ineffectiveness.

Often, organisations are not systematically organised and work is allocated on the basis of current workload and/or past experience. In this way work appears to move randomly around the organisation. Consequently, no sense of ownership or responsibility for particular aspects of the work is engendered amongst the workforce. On that basis of allocation the work has little or no meaning or value to them.

Creating natural work units (figure 25.2) means adopting a different approach whereby logical (or natural) groupings of work are created and allocated to individuals or teams, each accepting total responsibility for the work allocated. If the employees can identify with the work, there is a greater opportunity for them to take ownership and pride in accomplishment. A sense of ownership of the task and pride in its completion will often lead to improved quality through the sense of responsibility of the individual.

Natural or logical groupings of tasks may be developed along a number

NATURAL WORK UNITS

- *Geographical*: each worker is assigned work arising from a particular location, for example a Country/County/District.

- *Organisational*: each worker may be allocated work according to its divisional or departmental source.

- *Alphabetical*: customer processing work may be divided according to alphabetical groupings, for example A–D, E–K, L–R, S–Z;

- *Numerical*: work in a supply depot may be allocated to clerks according to bin locations or part numbers.

- *Customer (size or type)*: work may be allocated according to customer size or type. For example some banks have divided customers in to four principal sectors - large corporate, small business, high net worth individuals, mass market - and these divisions are reflected in their allocation of work;

- *Business type/industrial sector*: each employee specialises in servicing customers, or making products in particular market segments; for example engineering, property, education, medical and so on.

Figure 25.2 **Natural work units**

of dimensions, dependent on what is to be achieved. It is of course necessary to maintain an equal workloading in the creation of these work units. This may mean either allocating more staff to a particularly heavy workload area, or creating vertical or horizontal sub-divisions of the work. This can be achieved by cross-matching categories, for example, matching a geographical area with an industrial sector or by delimiting authority for taking action. An example of this is the use of lending authorities in banks which are often split both horizontally and vertically, for example, a lending officer may be able to authorise loans up to £250,000 in a particular market segment while another lending officer can authorise loans from £250,001 to £1,000,000 in the same sector.

Jobs have often been broken down into tasks (and even sub-tasks) so that in order to create a complete product or service a team of five or six people is needed. In the service industries, in particular, these people may be in separate areas or departments.

This is apparently highly efficient (in the sense of Adam Smith) since the individuals become highly adept at the particular task. However, simple, repetitive tasks often provide little or no challenge and hence provoke little interest from the employee. This lack of interest leads to dissatisfaction, falling productivity, increased error rates and absenteeism and often increased labour turnover – the last item leading to increased recruitment and training costs. This approach rests heavily on the work of Frederick

Taylor (1911), and may be considered at least partly responsible for some of the problems of industrial relations seen in Western countries throughout this century.

Re-combining tasks into complete jobs can help to counter this source of dissatisfaction, allowing the employee a sense of pride and achievement in what he or she has created. Using task combination, the employee is given the chance to manage his or her work, rather than being simply required to repeat the same simple task again and again.

To implement this approach it is necessary to have a comprehensive understanding of the work process. This can be obtained through the use of the process charting techniques discussed in chapter 20. Analysis will need to be undertaken at the process operation or process detail level. An alternative is to involve the affected staff in the redesign. They already know the process and, from experience, they normally have a good understanding of how changes and improvements can be achieved.

Perhaps the most famous, and certainly extreme, example of this is Volvo in Sweden. Volvo redesigned a whole car factory, abandoned the production line approach, and created a factory where teams built complete cars. Within this set up each team member employed a range of expertise to complete the task. This may be contrasted with a conventional, production line approach where each worker carries out only a single task on each vehicle.

Another example is the operation of postrooms in large organisations. A common sequence of work might be as follows:

1   Clerk 1 accepts and seals outbound parcel.
2   Clerk 2 weighs the parcel.
3   Clerk 3 affixes stamps.
4   Clerk 4 records the parcel in the postage's book.
5   Clerk 5 sorts and stacks the parcel for despatch.

It is clear that this fragmented process could be reorganised into a single task completed by one individual, rather than a team of five. Equally, it may be considered that other problems are inherent in the current fragmentation, for example can each clerk perform the tasks currently carried out by the others? It might easily be the case that the postroom ceases to function when one clerk is missing, not because of workload, but because only that one clerk has the necessary knowledge for the completion of a portion of the task.

THE KNITWEAR FACTORY

While it may sound farcical to suggest that a process may cease because of the absence of one person, a directly similar situation was experienced in a knitwear factory. This factory, in the Birmingham area of England, contracted out embroidery work to a range of specialists. Batches of pullovers were despatched on a daily basis to these specialists for completion of embroidery – they were in mid-process at the subject factory – needing to be returned for labelling and packing.

The despatch process was not unlike the postroom example with one exception, clerk 4 also selected an embroiderer from the approved range and recorded, in a notebook, the despatch address. It emerged that this was the organisation's only record of the allocation of embroidery work. The notebook was supplied by the clerk concerned and was kept by her 'so that I ensure a fair allocation of work'. During her absences on sick leave and annual holiday no embroidery work was despatched since the other clerks did not know where to send it! This of course brought the finishing process to a halt, not just for the factory concerned but also for the sub-contractors. The factory management were totally unaware of this situation.

There are a whole range of possible issues to emerge from the knitwear case, not least those of control and power in the organisation. For the current purpose, it is enough to recognise that the fragmentation of the despatch process created a major weakness in the organisation and, regardless of whether or not the control issue was resolved, the process depended upon the presence of every member of the despatch team, surely an undesirable state of affairs.

In most organisations, the worker works, while the supervisor or manager carries out the tasks of planning, organising, controlling and co-ordinating. Conventionally, tasks, performance standards, timeframes and objectives are set by the management for their subordinates with little or no consultation. This can mean that the worker feels no obligation to achieve those targets which they consider as belonging to the management rather than themselves.

Vertical loading consists of allowing responsibility to descend through the organisation so that workers are allowed a degree of freedom in setting their own standards, thereby accepting some responsibility for their achievements. Equally, degrees of latitude in decision making can be increased, empowering the employee to solve problems and take appropriate action.

Using the vertical loading approach can enable the reduction or removal of some control and checking activity, the assignment of more demanding tasks and increased levels of authority amongst the workforce. This, if properly handled, should lead to a virtuous circle of improvement at the lower levels and should enable managers to concentrate more effectively on the issues which really matter about their own work. Successful use of vertical loading depends upon three key characteristics (see figure 25.3) amongst the workforce. They must be willing to accept the additional responsibility, they must have the appropriate ability and the level of training and competence must be commensurate with the need of the task.

It is, of course, the responsibility of management to ensure that these conditions are met and to provide appropriate training where necessary. Management must also ensure that scope is provided for the empowered

- A willingness to accept responsibility;

- Ability which matches the increased requirements;

- A level of training commensurate with the new responsibilities.

Figure 25.3 **Key requirements for vertical loading**

staff to become accustomed to their freedoms and to learn to use them wisely. It is almost inevitable that at the outset mistakes and errors will occur whilst staff learn to apply skills of decision and judgement which were previously the exclusive preserve of the management. Mistakes must be accepted at the initial stage as part of the learning process and management must avoid the temptation to withdraw the freedoms and retake direct control.

Decision making is based on information. Very often employees exist in what might also be considered an information vacuum. They are unaware of performance standards (or even if they exist), receive a performance appraisal once a year (or once every two years in many public sector organisations), and gain no specific current information on how well, or badly, they are performing their particular task.

In these circumstances, the employees will set their own standards, either explicitly in conjunction with each other, or more commonly on an individual basis – doing what they think is best for them. Nature abhors a vacuum, and in the absence of information from management, the workforce will create their own. This may or may not be in line with management expectations. To correct this, task feedback information must be provided and to be effective must be driven by the process itself, must be as near 'real-time' as possible, must be continuously provided and must be meaningful to the recipient (see figure 25.4). Failure to meet any of these conditions will render the information useless.

The word feedback is one of the most commonly abused in the English language. In this book it means information drawn from the output side of a process which is compared with a target, the comparison being used as the basis for adjusting the input to the process.

- Driven by the process itself;
- Real time (or as near as possible);
- Continuous;
- Meaningful (that is it must be expressed in language which the recipient understands)

Figure 25.4 **Task feedback information**

Using the power of contemporary information technology none of these requirements is difficult to achieve. However, the most frequent difficulties arise with the last condition. What constitutes meaningful information for a manager may be very different to that for the worker affected. For instance, a manager may wish to work with reports expressed in terms of profit and loss, that is, with monetary measurements of performance. For the worker in the service department of a car dealership, monetary measures may be meaningless, he (or she) may measure performance in terms of the number of vehicles serviced, or the level of utilisation of servicing bays. It is useless then to provide information to these individuals on profit or loss, since that data cannot be used by them for control and self-management purposes. It is more useful and more effective to use information technology to provide information to each recipient which is meaningful in their own terms.

The idea of the self-managed work team is essentially an extension of vertical loading. While an overall task is set, the team are free to organise themselves towards its achievement, having either no supervisor, or appointing their own from within the team, often on a rotational basis. In extreme cases, the self-managed work team will take responsibility for organising holiday schedules and other activities which have traditionally been regarded as the exclusive province of management. The team will have the freedom and responsibility to devise improvements and changes within a process, and will often have ways of communicating successes and failures to other teams. This idea has been adopted in both the manufacturing and service sectors and by companies as diverse as General Motors and Texas Instruments.

Semco, a Brazilian company, has taken the concept of self-management to real extremes. Workers set their own hours, managers set their own salaries, the majority of the workforce are allowed to vote on corporate level decisions. Such an approach would appear to many as a recipe for disaster, yet Semco was one of Brazil's fastest growing companies and had a profit margin in 1988 of 10 per cent. Products include marine pumps, digital scanners, commercial dishwashers, truck filters and all kinds of mixing equipment; a range of products with considerable complexity. Semco is regularly named as the best company in Brazil to work for and receives 300 applications for every job – none of which are advertised! Interested readers may wish to study this case further in *Maverick!* (Semler, 1993) and *Organisational Fitness* (Espejo and Schwaninger, 1993).

25.3   ORGANISATION STRUCTURE

The issue of organisation structure will be further explored in chapter 27. In this section only the role and position of the quality function will be briefly examined.

A normal position for the Quality Control or Assurance Manager in many organisations is as a direct reportee of the Production Manager. This often serves to institutionalise the potential conflict between them and allow the Production Manager the final decision.

Such an approach enables the Production Manager to override quality decisions in the pursuit of some other interest, for example shipping a full order, regardless of quality, to satisfy the customer in the short term. It also enables the manipulation of other data such as productivity, labour utilisation and even reject/rework levels.

It is considered important that the Quality Assurance function enjoy a significant degree of independence from the Production function in order that effective inspection and audit become possible. In a company which has fully adopted the quality ethic, this becomes a much less significant issue, since quality ideas will be embedded in the workforce and quality standards will be clearly defined and recognised. In these circumstances the quality decisions, to a large extent, may make themselves. There will be limited scope for arbitrary decisions.

A key factor in creating an organisation for quality is the recognition of processes, and the consequent realisation that each part of a process has customers, either internal or external. A company which uses these processes as the cornerstone of the way in which it is organised, and sets its quality criteria in recognition of the needs of customers, will become an organisation for quality.

SUMMARY

The aim of this chapter was to move away from quantitative methods and consider a selection of the qualitative, human centred approaches which help in the development of a quality organisation. The use of quality circles, job design tools and organisation design approaches was considered. Each of these must be used intelligently and thoughtfully and within the context of an overall, systemically based quality programme. In isolation, none will achieve very much.

---

key learning points

QUALITATIVE METHODS

Key idea
while quantitative approaches are vital, these only measure what is apparently happening; qualitative approaches are focused on changing what happens

Key approaches
quality circles; job design – natural work units, task combination, vertical loading, task feedback, self-managed work teams, organisation structure

---

QUESTION

Consider the way in which tasks are undertaken in a fast food restaurant near you. How could the tasks be redesigned to increase job satisfaction? What do you think would be the effect on the organisation?

chapter twenty-six

TOTAL QUALITY MANAGEMENT THROUGH TSI

TQM is common sense.

Robert Flood, *Beyond TQM*, 1993

INTRODUCTION

Each of the methods introduced so far offers only a reductionist approach to quality, isolating and dealing with particular aspects of problems which are organisation wide. They do not deal with whole organisations but with parts and sub-parts, with processes and operations.

This chapter starts to introduce systems methods in the context of quality – approaches that attempt to deal with quality holistically, particularly with the concept of Total Quality Management. First, Total Quality Management (TQM) through Total Systems Intervention (TSI) will be considered.

26.1 TQM THROUGH TSI IN THEORY

Readers will recall that Total Systems Intervention is designed as a meta-methodological process intended to enable participants in an organisational situation to highlight the continually changing issues that are of concern to them in the organisation. This is achieved through the creative use of metaphors which enable them to capture particular characteristics of that situation and highlight dominant issues.

TQM through TSI becomes relevant when the dominant issue of concern in the organisation is with the pursuit of quality. This concern emerges from the *creativity* phase of TSI. Flood (1993) proposes that a TQM programme can be derived through the same basic framework used by the TSI process. This is illustrated graphically in figure 26.1. This shows that when 'quality' is dominant in the TSI process, the same three phases of creativity, choice and implementation can be used to select and implement tools for achieving quality.

This diagram reveals how the logical framework of TSI supports the application of TQM in the holistic context of all of the problems of the organisation. This will lead to better informed use of the range of tools and methodologies available for implementing quality, and in turn leads back to the further use of TSI to address other issues within the organisation. The process is iterative both through TSI and through TQM, reflecting the idea of continuation which is vital to TQM.

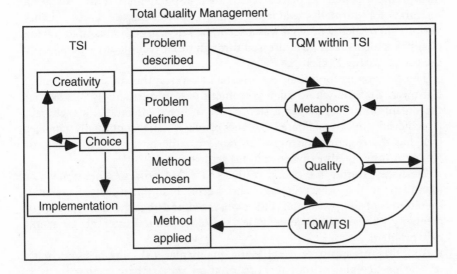

Key: ——▶ Information flows

Figure 26.1 **TQM within TSI within TQM**

26.2 TQM THROUGH TSI IN PRACTICE

It is important to appreciate that TQM through TSI is only appropriate when, within the TSI process, quality emerges as the dominant issue of concern. TQM is not proposed as 'the one best way'. If within TSI the dominant concern is with quality then it is suggested that the TSI approach to TQM should be pursued. In this context the tools of quality may be used in a complementary manner to the systems approaches. How might this occur?

An issue, or series of issues are identified by the management group of an organisation as giving cause for concern. The decision is made to address these issues using the process of Total Systems Intervention. The problem context is defined and debated and its characteristics elaborated. Driven by both internal factors (perhaps rework and rectification costs) and external factors (maybe falling sales and customer complaints) the primary issue of concern to the organisation emerges as 'quality'.

The group recognise (having already used the TSI process) that any one approach to quality will highlight and address particular aspects of the quality problem but not all of them. They therefore seek to adopt a complementarist approach. They re-enter the TSI process in the context of TQM seeking to identify, within the whole quality problem, those characteristics which are dominant, which in turn leads them to a choice of primary quality implementation methodology. That is not to say that the organisation simply adopts an approach based on the work of a particular guru, but that one approach, say statistical process control, is recognised as desirable as a first step, perhaps because there is no quality or performance measurement system in place. SPC is then implemented. This provides a platform for formally evaluating quality performance. Once quality performance is known, what was a secondary concern, for example solving quality problems, can be addressed through other techniques – perhaps by the use of quality circles.

The process is continual, the satisfactory resolution of one issue does not mean that the whole quality problem is solved, it simply means that the organisation has moved a step closer to being effective. As each gain is achieved and consolidated, so the primary issue continually changes bringing the organisation one step closer to the goal of zero defects or whatever other quality objective it has set itself.

Inevitably, during the course of the TSI/TQM process other issues not identified at the outset emerge and become dominant. It is essential therefore that the process of TSI is observed and that the three phases of creativity, choice and implementation are kept open to fresh innovation and new problems.

Adopting this approach to achieving quality places the emphasis of choice on the participants within the organisation rather than leaving it, as is so often the case, to choices imposed by those outside, such as consultants. This means that any solutions suggested should be closely aligned to the preferences of those within the organisation, since they are developing them. This approach dramatically increases the chances of success since the solutions are owned by those working with them.

In essence, the way of managing for quality through TSI has no end because it is an iterative process. In a dynamic, changing world there will always be newly emergent problems to solve or new messes to manage and the validity of the process remains constant although the particular methodology in use may be ever changing.

26.3 FLOOD'S TQM METHODOLOGY

Flood (1993) proposes an overall TQM implementation programme within which he proposes the use of TQM through TSI already outlined. This implementation programme is essentially straightforward and includes eleven steps (figure 26.2).

ROBERT FLOOD

Step 1   Develop an understanding of organisational design and organisational behaviour.

Step 2   Set up a steering committee.

Step 3   Set organisational mission.

Step 4   Set up next layers of Quality Councils.

Step 5   Design or choose educational modules.

Step 6   Set local missions.

Step 7   Undertake customer analysis.

Step 8   Choose projects for implementation.

Step 9   Choose tools for implementation.

Step 10   Implement educational modules and communicate details of the project(s).

Step 11   Implement projects.

Figure 26.2 **Eleven steps to TQM: Robert Flood**

The first step in this process addresses the requirement for quality to be taken not in isolation but within the context of a coherent understanding of management theory and practice. This reflects the concern that quality should not be taken as an end in itself but as part of the overall management of an organisation and that the vast body of established management knowledge should be drawn on to support and enhance the quality process.

Step 2, the establishment of a steering committee or 'Executive Council', is a recognition of the need for quality to belong not to an individual but to the whole organisation. The composition of the committee should adequately represent the functions and responsibilities through the organisation so that 'everybody is involved'. The responsibilities of the committee are to establish the quality mission, to guide and monitor the implementation process, to select and enable quality education programmes in the organisation and to establish lower level councils with specific responsibilities (either functional or organisational).

ROBERT FLOOD

- What do we think we do?

- Are we doing what we think we do?

- Why are we doing it?

- Are we doing the right thing?

- What else could we do?

- What would be the benefit of doing something else?

Figure 26.3 **Defining organisational mission: Robert Flood**

Steps 3, 4 and 5 are the primary responsibilities of the steering committee already outlined. For step 3, organisational mission, Flood (1993: 148) suggests six questions (figure 26.3) which need to be addressed to focus the attention of the organisation on its purposes.

Flood suggests that these questions focus the attention of the participants on what they want to achieve leading to the formulation of a crisp statement of purpose for the organisation. These questions, while useful, are essentially internally focused. To be systemic in defining the organisation's purposes, it is essential that outwardly focused questions are asked, especially questions concerned with the expectations of customers and other stakeholders in the enterprise. The literature on corporate strategy provides more rigorous and fully developed tools for dealing with this issue.

The selection of councils at the next and subsequent levels (step 4) will reflect the way in which the organisation is oriented. Selection should be based on the most appropriate format. For example, an organisation based in a single location may orient itself around products, processes, functions, or according to the tenets of some specific organisational paradigm such as cybernetics. A multi-outlet or geographically diverse organisation may first choose to use its geographical locations at the next level below steering committee and then to orient itself around some other criteria at lower levels. The essential rule is to ask what will serve the needs of the organisation best.

Step 5 reflects the need to enhance understanding of quality throughout the organisation. If consistency of approach to quality is to be achieved then a consistent approach to training will be needed to support it. The particular approach chosen will reflect the paradigm of those on the steering committee but must recognise the differing needs of other participants.

The sixth step is for each local council to establish a local mission. Again using the list of questions, they can orient the local approach within the framework of corporate thinking. It is essential that unity of approach is maintained. The local mission must always fit within this unity and complement the corporate view. If this does not occur then the initiative will fail, it is therefore essential that a protocol exists which will enable meaningful debate between the levels.

Customer analysis is step 7. This should be a relatively simple phase consisting of identifying who the customers are, determining (and agreeing) their requirements, evaluating performance against those requirements, identifying where improvements can be made and defining improvement projects.

The more difficult task is that of refining broad proposals so that they are converted into meaningful, appropriately prioritised and achievable tasks – identification of necessary resources, supporting measurement of the critical success factors and making clear allocation of responsibility for their completion. A mechanism must also exist (step 8) to enable comparative analysis of competing projects (even between local councils) where resources available to support the programme are limited. Ideas from Juran and others can be drawn upon at this stage.

Flood suggests that step 9, choosing tools, should be guided by the complementarist framework of Total Systems Intervention which is considered to provide an informed guide to methodology choice. Step 10 is implementation itself. Full and detailed planning of this phase is essential to ensure maximum effectiveness and efficiency – that is, no duplicated efforts, no gaps and appropriate scheduling since timing is of great importance to gathering meaningful information.

SALES PERFORMANCE REVIEW

A company decided to review the performance and standards of its sales force prior to recruiting additional staff to support a major business development thrust. The review had two purposes:

- Establish a best practice model;
- Develop an idealised staff profile to guide recruitment.

The recruitment drive was to commence in September, the decision to undertake the review was taken in late June. The basis of the study was for external consultants to interview and observe the behaviour of the established sales staff, to compare their observations with the results achieved by those staff and identify which characteristics were of greatest importance.

Unfortunately, the study was undertaken in late July and August. It was difficult to obtain appointments with the staff since many were taking annual leave during that period. At the same time the staff were finding it difficult to make their own appointments, since many of their targets were also taking leave and hence it was difficult to observe the staff working. Adding to the problems, initial discussions highlighted concerns over the way in which performance was measured and the accuracy of the results. When these concerns were discussed with the senior management it transpired that they shared the same concerns.

The review proceeded, many useful discoveries were made and a best practice model developed, notwithstanding the uncertainty surrounding the accuracy of performance measurement. At the final review meeting with the client it transpired that they had already recruited nearly half of the additional staff while the review was still in progress. A number of these recruits did not match the newly established profile.

This was a case of poor implementation of a good idea.

The responsibility of the steering committee at this stage is to oversee and co-ordinate the whole implementation programme, monitoring progress, ensuring that information is appropriately shared and reporting successes and failures. The steering committee may be viewed as the mechanism of organisational learning.

26.4   CRITICAL REVIEW

A critical review of TSI has already been provided and the same comments apply here. It is therefore only necessary to reflect on the additional aspects, particularly those derived from Flood's methodology.

The theoretical platform supporting TSI can, and no doubt will, be debated extensively. There are essentially two camps of protagonists. The first consider that TSI is a major step towards reunifying systems approaches which have become fragmented and non-systemic. The other suggests that the TSI process is itself reductionist, further fragmenting the systems discipline and reinforcing the barriers between differing schools of systemic thought, particularly through the 'System of Systems Methodologies'.

Regardless of this debate, there is value in the idea of TQM through TSI as a dynamic, iterative process. The continual engagement of all three phases of TSI brings home the understanding that the pursuit of TQM (through whatever means) is not a function of a single decision or a single act, but an ongoing search for ever higher standards. The conventional approaches do cover this point with their calls for reiteration at the completion of the particular methodology chosen, but the TSI approach emphasises that this can and should happen throughout and within the process, not simply when it is completed. All too often detailed decisions are made by senior management in an organisation with authority for action delegated to lower level staff. The decision makers, believing themselves to have discharged their responsibility in the matter, move on to the next issue. The TSI process demands that senior management are continually aware of and involved in the change process and refocus it when the situation so demands. Whether or not the organisation chooses to use the TSI process, it should embrace the idea of continual awareness and review of the situation and the methods being applied.

The implementation methodology proposed by Flood is in many ways simply a refinement and consolidation of the approaches espoused by others, and could be applied to almost any change process. However, in the context of TQM it adds value in two areas.

First, it demands that those responsible for the organisation develop a full appreciation of the theory and practice of organisational design and behaviour. While admitting (as a management scientist) to a bias in this regard, it is certainly the case that while many managers have undergone extensive training and education in their particular discipline their understanding of how organisations behave is often limited. Since quality is to be regarded as an emergent property of the behaviour of the organisation in its totality, the behaviour of that organisation must be fully understood. The failure of many quality programmes may perhaps be attributed to management inadequacies in this area.

The second significant contribution is the requirement for the establishment of formal Quality Councils at lower levels in the organisation. This approach helps to ensure the devolution of decision making power in respect of quality, while at the same time making responsibilities and accountabilities clear to all the participants. The idea of such devolution has already been met but not in this formalised, structured manner.

SUMMARY

This chapter has focused on the use of Total Systems Intervention as a guiding process for the pursuit of Total Quality Management both in theory and practice. Flood's programme for implementing TQM was reviewed and its particular strengths highlighted. Readers may wish to refer to the original works of Flood (1993) and Flood and Jackson (1991) to further enhance their knowledge and understanding.

---

key learning points

Key idea
if TQM is to be genuinely total then it must use a methodology which embraces all potential methods

Key approaches
TQM within TSI within TQM, Flood's implementation programme

Critique
is TSI systemic or reductionist?, added value through ideas of dynamic, iterative process, formally structured quality councils

---

QUESTION

What problems might you encounter in establishing a hierarchy of Quality Councils? How would you structure them to ensure that interactions between units were adequately catered for?

chapter twenty-seven

EFFECTIVE ORGANISATION

*because the instability feeds upon itself; and the catastrophic
collapse . . . is an inevitable output of the system.*
Stafford Beer, *Designing Freedom*, 1974

INTRODUCTION

The essence of effectiveness is viability – the capacity of an organisation
to survive in a changing environment. The keys to this are learning and
adaptation. The theory of the cybernetic approach which underpins viability
was explored in chapter 15. In this chapter Stafford Beer's 'Viable System
Model' will be examined as a practical, contemporary tool for the design
of effective organisation. Effectiveness – the achievement of a purpose –
drives the perception of quality. An organisation which is not effective in the
long term will not generate quality products or services. Organisational
effectiveness subsumes the concept of quality, rendering it redundant.

27.1 THE VIABLE SYSTEM MODEL IN THEORY

The Viable System Model (VSM) was developed by Stafford Beer from the
principles of organisational cybernetics which is concerned with steering
organisations into their future. Organisational cybernetics is the science of
effective organisation.

An organisation is considered to be viable when it is capable of survival in a given environment and capable of learning and adaptation to changes in that environment. To achieve this state, the process of it's management must have five functions: implementation, co-ordination, control, planning and policy, which taken together constitute the viable system.

The model enables multiple interpretations of any organisational situation to be developed, all according to the same principles, but focused on the different purposes imputed to the organisation by its various observers. Through this modelling process, dialogue and debate is generated, from which an agreed organisational purpose can be derived and a most useful modelling approach developed.

The approach to cybernetics espoused by Beer rests on five principles. First, Beer pays great attention to the role of the observer in defining a system, its purpose (s) and its design. Managers must recognise that they, and any experts they employ, choose the definitions which define the organisation. This guarantees them freedom in those definitions but means that they must accept responsibility for the outcomes.

Second, is the recognition of the systems principle, that any system has emergent properties that are possessed by none of its parts, and that each part has properties not possessed by the whole. Managers must therefore seek to deal with the whole system of interest, not just the parts. Practically, in the quality context, the definition of the organisation may be extended beyond its legal boundaries to incorporate suppliers, and in certain circumstances distributors of the product or service. This approach enables supplier development strategies to be coherent with the quality strategy of the organisation itself.

Third, is the 'black box' principle. This assumes that no complex system can be known completely but that managers can learn to control the system by manipulating inputs and monitoring the effect on outputs. This can be done without entering the 'black box'. This assumption should be contrasted with the traditional approaches to management which call for

---

FOUR POSSIBLE STATES OF A WORKING TRAFFIC LIGHT

- Red: Stop;

- Red and amber: Prepare to go;

- Green: Go;

- Amber: Stop, unless stopping would cause an accident.

To control this device, the traffic light regulator must be able to recognise and generate any of those four states. If it cannot do so it will be ineffective.

Figure 27.1 **Measuring variety**

detailed analysis and description of the organisation at every level from a pseudo-omniscient manager at the peak of an organisational hierarchy.

Fourth, is the principle of self-regulation. This recognises that a complex system may be expected to exhibit a degree of self-regulation arising through feedback loops within itself and between it and its environment. This tendency of complex systems to self-organise is of great benefit to managers, provided it is recognised and actively encouraged.

The final principle is known as the 'Law of Requisite Variety'. Elucidated by Ross Ashby, this states that to be effective, the variety of the controller (the management function) must be equal to that which is controlled (the organisation). Variety, in cybernetics, is a measure of the number of possible states of a system. An example of this is provided in figure 27.1. Readers should bear these principles in mind when studying the next section of this chapter.

27.2 VSM: CONCEPTION AND CONSTRUCTION

The VSM is an observer dependent, general model of any organisation. It is concerned with the mechanisms of adaptation, communication and control. It consists of a set of five sub-systems each of equal importance to the viability of the organisation. These sub-systems are richly inter-connected by a network of information loops in continuous operation. The whole system is capable of learning, that is, of adaptation. The five sub-systems are: implementation, co-ordination, control, planning and policy.

Implementation is, literally, what the organisation does, the products or services which it creates. The co-ordination and control mechanisms ensure cohesion of the organisation, yet at the same time, the model allows for the grant of maximum autonomy to the implementation parts. This tends to maximise the use of the self-regulating tendencies and enables the resolution of problems as near to source as possible. This is considered to generate two outcomes each of which has clear relevance to the pursuit of a quality approach: first, greater motivation at more junior levels in the organisation – a vital aspect of achieving quality; second, it frees higher management to concentrate on the issues which are of greatest relevance to them.

The planning function enables the organisation to interact with its environment, both influencing and being influenced. This function helps, for example, to ensure that customer requirements are known to the organisation – a vital part of the quality process. The policy function is responsible for the whole organisation, creating and sustaining its identity and arbitrating between demands for change and stability. It is the policy function which determines whether or not the venture will be organised for quality.

As a starting point it is useful to consider the organisation as embedded in an environment. The organisation consists of two parts – operations

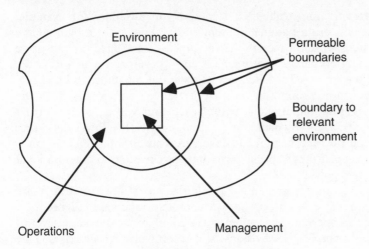

Figure 27.2 **The organisation in its environment**

and management (see figure 27.2). The boundaries between these three elements should be thought of as permeable membranes, open to flows of information. These membranes permit the continuous communication which is necessary between the elements. The diagrammatic conventions demand that these normally be shown as discrete information channels and this will be the case in subsequent diagrams.

This particular representation is of limited practical use, it provides a general conception rather than a detailed understanding. Figure 27.3 demonstrates the next step in building the VSM by separating the three elements and showing the communication channels.

Each of the communication channels is used to either amplify or attenuate variety. That is, the variety of the environment is absorbed by the organisation and its management, and the operational and managerial variety are amplified into the environment. The standard strategies by which this is achieved were reviewed in chapter 15.

Figure 27.3 provides an overview of an entire organisation interacting with its environment. Most organisations will consist of a set of operational

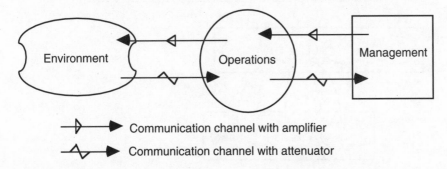

Figure 27.3 **The environment, operations and management separated**

and management units embedded in a total organisation, for example, the divisions of a multi-national company, the branches of a bank or the production lines within a factory. These units, taken together, constitute the implementation part of the organisation – those parts which fulfil the purposes of the organisation. Each must have the capability to be viable, within the constraints imposed on it by virtue of its membership of the containing organisation. Equally, within each unit will be found further lower level units, each of which must again be viable. The lowest level unit for practical purposes is the individual worker. This 'nesting' effect is called recursion and constitutes a special form of hierarchy built on organisational logic rather than power.

A chain of recursively embedded viable systems is presented in figure 27.4. Each oblong box encapsulates a complete recursion. Figure 27.5 shows all of the operational elements of a company at the same level of recursion, for example, the divisions of the company. As stated, this set constitutes the implementation function of the organisation, the parts which carry out the purpose(s) of the organisation. The communication channels are simplified in this presentation.

The diagram shows that for each division there is some degree of overlap between the environments. This could represent shared customers, physical

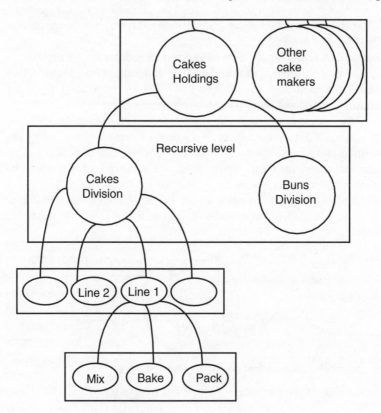

Figure 27.4 **A chain of recursively embedded viable systems**

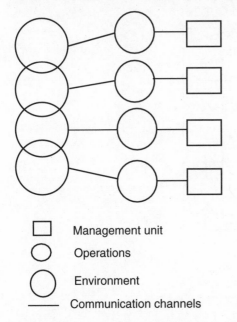

☐ Management unit
◯ Operations
◯ Environment
── Communication channels

Figure 27.5 **A set of implementation elements**

overlap between geographical marketing areas or competition for customers whose requirements could be satisfied by either of two or more product ranges from the same company. For example, for a computer manufacturer the overlap might represent customers whose requirements could be satisfied by either a large PC network or a mid-range system.

Conflict arising between the divisions could cause problems and inefficiency both within the organisation and in its dealings with the customers. It is necessary therefore to create a co-ordinating mechanism to deal with sources of oscillation or conflict. It would be possible to achieve this through a higher level edict – a set of rules or policies handed down by senior management. Such an approach, however, has two principal effects. First, every exception to the policy would need to be sanctioned at the highest level. This would increase the volume of communication and potentially overload the senior management with relatively trivial decision making. Second, the degree of freedom which the individual elements enjoy would be severely constrained. This would reduce flexibility at the operating level, inhibit the development of *kaizen*, and fail to fully utilise the self-regulating properties of the organisation. A final effect is that the organisation would come to be seen as oppressive, since individuals would perceive themselves to have limited freedom of choice and action.

The co-ordinating mechanism then needs to exist as a service to the operating elements and to be perceived by them as an aid rather than an obstruction. Prime examples of this are progress chasers/production controllers in factories, the creation of a timetable in an educational institution, the allocation of service bays in a car dealership or telling windows in a

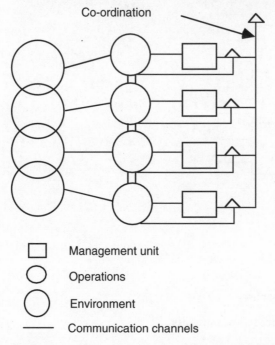

Co-ordination

	Management unit
	Operations
	Environment
———	Communication channels

Figure 27.6 **Operational elements with co-ordination and interaction**

bank. Each of these devices serves the implementation function, preserving the perception and practice of freedom and reducing the need for routine decision making at the higher levels. Figure 27.6 presents the organisation with the co-ordinating mechanism in place.

A second feature included in this diagram is the links between the operational elements. These represent the informal communication which always occurs between stages in a process, or divisions of an organisation. In the quality context they may perhaps be regarded as representing the internal supplier–customer relationships.

The next stage in the process of management is control. This is the regulation of the ongoing activities of the organisation. Control is concerned with the allocation of resources to the operational elements, with accountability for those resources and with adherence to corporate and statutory regulations.

It achieves this through two principal processes, resource bargaining and auditing. Resource bargaining is the process of budgeting for resources which is carried out in all organisations. The VSM requires this to be carried out on a negotiated basis. The control functions and the operational elements should engage in meaningful discussions about what resources are required and what objectives are to be achieved with them. The resource bargaining process should encompass all of the resources utilised and objectives set – money, staff, equipment, profitability, quality standards and so on.

The control function is made up of the various departments involved in regulatory activity. This would include units such as administration, personnel, production management, perhaps the general or divisional manager's office, quality assurance.

Audit is a sporadic intervention by each of the control departments in the operational elements. This serves to increase their knowledge and understanding of how those functions are performing. It is essential that these audits be sporadic, if they are not then they will lose their effect.

INEFFECTIVE AUDIT

Stories of ineffective audit are commonplace, examples are reported regularly on television and newspapers. Readers may be aware of action taken against some major accountancy firms because their annual audits have failed to reveal major errors or flaws in accounting systems.

Other, less public examples are equally frequent. In the UK, the Ministry of Transport (MOT) road worthiness test is applied to vehicles on a twelve monthly basis and, while the certificate states only that the vehicle was road worthy on the day tested, a further test is not required for twelve months. The vehicle user has a legal obligation to maintain the vehicle in road worthy condition at all times and the police and Vehicle Inspection Agency inspectors have the legal right to inspect a vehicle at any time. However, in relation to the number of vehicles on the road, such inspections are relatively rare, particularly for private cars. Motorists therefore ensure that on the annual test day their vehicle reaches the appropriate standard, but since the likelihood of inspection between tests is so small, many budget conscious motorists pay no attention to that aspect until the vehicle is again due for testing. This probably means that there are a significant number of vehicles in daily use which are not road worthy.

The benefit of the audit function to road safety is lost in its regularity. The system is designed to be ineffective.

The control function being in place, the organisation may now be considered to be self-regulating. It will be able to function effectively, carrying out its allotted tasks. Parallels may be drawn between this and devices such as heating/air conditioning systems which are self-regulating against a target temperature in the same way. Figure 27.7 presents the model at this stage.

An organisation which is simply self-regulating will not be viable in the longer term, since it cannot respond to environmental changes. Neither will it be capable of generating continuous improvement since it has no facility for development. This brings us to the next stage in the management process – planning.

Planning covers all of the research and development activity of the organisation. It may be concerned with market research and marketing activity, product development, financial planning, staff training and development, and most certainly is the root of quality planning. The planning functions

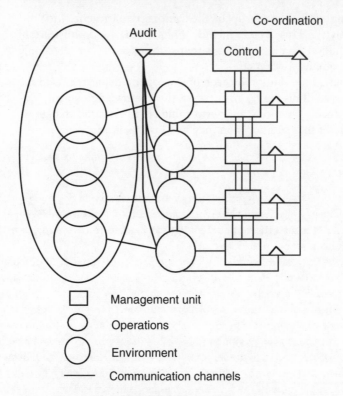

Management unit

Operations

Environment

Communication channels

Figure 27.7 **The self-regulating organisation**

interact with the emergent environment of the organisation considering possible courses of action either for adapting the organisation to the environment, or where appropriate, influencing the environment towards the organisation. The planning and control functions also interact with each other, continuously re-negotiating the resource allocations and objectives of the organisation.

This process of negotiation will almost inevitably lead at times to conflict and dispute, the control functions wishing to maintain the status quo, while the development functions wish to promote change. The conversation between them will be monitored by the last management function, policy, which will arbitrate between them according to the ethos of the organisation.

The ethos is the set of values and beliefs that underpin the philosophy of the venture. Without this policy function, the planning control debate can enter unmanageable oscillations, neither having the power to override the other. In this respect policy may be considered to be fulfilling an equivalent function to that of co-ordination at the implementation level. There is however one significant difference. The policy function, through its activities, represents the entire organisation to the outside world, and, is the formal link to the next higher level of organisation. The complete Viable System Model is represented in figure 27.8.

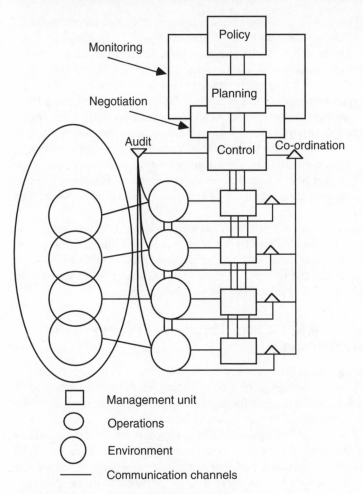

Figure 27.8 **The Viable System Model**

The responsibility of the policy function for representing the identity of the organisation to the outside world has been stated. At this stage, the model can be linked back to the prior writings on quality with the consistent demands from all writers for top management commitment. It is clear that without this commitment the quality initiative will fail and such commitment demands changes in both the words and actions of the senior management. If our organisations are as closely linked as is suggested by the Viable System Model (and from experience they seem to be so) then the actions and behaviour of the policy making group will soon come to affect the behaviour of those in the rest of the organisation. If they are serious about quality then this message will filter through very rapidly; if they are not, the message will move just as fast. Through the cybernetic model, the justification for senior management commitment to quality is realised because they transmit vital messages throughout the organisation and to the environment – the customers and suppliers of the organisation.

The model of an effective organisation is complete, and an organisation constructed in accordance with this framework will be viable, but there remain three major points to be made at this stage. First, the communication channels must be in continuous operation, and, second, they must be capable of carrying more information in a given time than the transmitting system is capable of generating. This ensures that information is not lost or distorted in the system. Similarly, it is important to remember that every time information crosses a boundary it must be converted into the 'language' of the receiving system. For example, a message concerning volumes or types of individual transistors or capacitors may have no meaning for a receiving department whose 'currency' is expressed in financial terms, or in units representing aggregations of components such as computers or keyboards.

Finally, it is normal to work with an organisation at three levels: the viable system of interest, called the 'system in focus', its containing system (one recursion up), and its contained systems (one recursion down). This is because the higher recursion exercises managerial control over the system in focus which, in turn, is managing the contained systems.

27.3   VSM IN PRACTICE: VIABLE SYSTEM DIAGNOSIS

The VSM can be used in three modes, descriptive, diagnostic and prescriptive. The following methodology shows how to model the organisation as it currently is (description). This forms the basis for comparison with the ideal model (diagnosis) which is in turn the basis for the rectification of organisational faults (prescription). The proposed methodology which modifies that crystallised by Flood and Jackson (1991) is from Beckford (1993, 1995) and assumes active participation by the members of the organisation. The process has three stages: identification of purpose, definition of the system and diagnosis.

The first stage is to agree the purpose to be pursued by the organisation (system). This is achieved through a process of discussion and debate centring on four questions (figure 27.9) and involving all relevant stakeholders in the system. It is essential that the purpose or purposes are identified at the outset in order that all parties are clear about what the organisation is trying to achieve. If this has not been done then any other activity will be fruitless.

Once the purpose to be fulfilled has been defined, it is necessary to identify the relevant organisational entity for achieving the purpose. This is called the 'system-in-focus'. It is important to remember that the purpose of a system is what the stakeholders consider it should do, and that this is achieved by the implementation function – so it is implementation that produces the system-in-focus.

The next step is to specify the viable parts of the implementation activities of the system-in-focus – those activities which contribute to the fulfilment of its purpose. It is then necessary to identify the apparently

- What constitutes the system?
- What are the system outputs?
- Do the outputs meet expectations?
- What other, or different, outputs are sought?

Figure 27.9 **Four questions for defining purpose**

enabling activities carried out within the system-in-focus – those things which it must do to support implementation. This might include the personnel and accounting activities, for example.

The next stage is to specify the viable system of which the system-in-focus is part, that is, the wider systems and environmental influences. This should be that system which is considered the most useful for the purpose of the enquiry and will normally exercise a management or controlling influence over the system studied. In a conglomerate or other large organisation this might be the parent company, alternatively it might be a purely conceptual organisation such as 'the motor industry'. This does not exist as a formal organisation but nonetheless there is a set of behaviours associated with membership of it; in this sense it exercises a controlling influence.

The purpose and identity of the organisation having been established, study moves on to the diagnostic stage. The general pattern (figure 27.10) from this point is to ask the participants to draw upon the cybernetic principles outlined previously in studying each part of the organisation. At each stage of the process the responses must be critically reviewed with the participants to help them explore and develop their understanding. The results should be amended as necessary.

The findings of the diagnosis usually lead directly to the generation of change proposals. Frequently occurring faults are highlighted in figure 27.11.

The methodology given has been that used in the general context of organisational problem solving. It is perfectly legitimate to use the methodology to specifically examine only a single aspect of the organisation. For example, at every stage the methodology tasks could be biased towards the quality issue, that is, to determine whether the quality management system is effective.

It is possible, and often useful, to model purely the quality management function. Such an approach ensures that the effectiveness of the quality programme is understood at all levels in the organisation. It may be found that while the senior management have implemented a quality programme, this has been done solely at the operations level and no changes have been made in other parts of the organisation to support it. For example, control may be focusing purely on volume as an output measure and ignoring the quality issue. Development may be focused on the demand for new products and ignoring calls for better quality (in the customer's definition) of existing products.

SIX STEPS TO VIABLE SYSTEM DIAGNOSIS

Step 1 Study the implementation functions of the system-in-focus and

- for each implementation element detail its environment, operations and localised management;
- study what constraints are imposed upon each implementation element by higher management;
- ask how accountability is exercised for each part, and what indicators of performance are taken;
- determine whether implementation managers have adequate authority and capability to enable the fulfilment of purpose;
- model implementation according to the VSM diagram.

Step 2 Study the co-ordination functions of the system-in-focus and:

- list possible sources of oscillation or conflict between the implementation elements and their environments and identify the co-ordinating mechanisms that have a harmonising or damping effect;
- determine whether 'soft issues' such as ethics, morals and culture are addressed through this function;
- ask how co-ordinating activity is perceived in the organisation (as threatening or facilitating);

Step 3 Study the control functions of the system-in-focus:

- list the controlling activities of the system-in-focus;
- ask how control is exercised;
- ask how resource bargaining with the implementation elements is carried out;
- determine who is responsible for the performance of the implementation elements;
- establish whether control and development activities are adequately discriminated from each other;
- how are the parts of control made accountable, at this level of recursion, for the resources which they consume;
- how is their performance in enabling the fulfilment of purpose measured;
- are all control activities necessary to the maintenance of the system;
- clarify what 'audit' enquiries are made by control elements into aspects of implementation;
- are audit activities sporadic or routine;
- understand the relationship between control and implementation

elements (is it perceived to be autocratic or democratic?) and find out how much autonomy implementation elements possess;

Step 4 Study the development function of the system-in-focus:

- list all the development activities of the system-in-focus;
- ask how far ahead these activities consider;
- question whether these activities guarantee adaptation to the future;
- determine if the development activities include monitoring what is happening to the environment and assessing trends;
- assess in what ways, if any, the development function is open to novelty;
- find out whether the development activities have a management centre/operations room, bringing together external and internal information and providing an 'environment for decision';
- question if development has facilities for alerting the policy function to urgent developments;
- how are the development activities made accountable, at this level of recursion, for the resources which they consume;
- how is their performance in enabling the development of the system measured;
- how is the relevance of development activity determined;
- how does the development function learn from the experience of the whole system.

Step 5 Study the policy function of the system-in-focus:

- ask who is in command (for example, on the 'Board') and how they act;
- determine what constraints are imposed on policy making by the next higher level of recursion;
- how do these constraints limit freedom to adapt;
- assess whether the policy function provides a suitable identity for the organisation (system-in-focus);
- ask how the ethos set by the policy function affects the perception of development;
- determine how the policy ethos affects the debate between control and development (which is taken more seriously?);
- investigate whether the policy function shares an identity with implementation or claims to be something different.

Step 6 Check that all information channels, transducers and control loops are properly designed.

Figure 27.10 **Six steps to Viable System Diagnosis**

FREQUENT ORGANISATIONAL FAULTS

- Organisational levels (recursions) have not been properly articulated.

- Certain implementation elements lack appropriate management.

- Central, enabling functions behave as if they were viable.

- Co-ordination is weak and its role poorly understood.

- Planning is not evident or is ignored.

- Senior management are engaged in control rather than planning or policy activities.

- Managers from the control function are engaged in day to day activities.

- There are no shared ethics (values and beliefs).

- Communication channels do not conform to those believed necessary in a viable system.

- Performance measurement is inadequate.

Figure 27.11 **Frequent organisational faults**

27.4   CRITICAL REVIEW

The VSM can be, and has been, applied to organisations of all sizes and types from one-man businesses to entire nation states. It has a general applicability and utility which exceeds that of other organisational models. The model fully embraces the interaction between the organisation and the environment in which it is embedded and caters for the definition of the organisation and its purposes by its stakeholders.

The model is criticised for being difficult to use in practice and although the methodology appears lengthy and complex, it can be very rapid in use. The standard modelling format generates great economy. On one occasion the author undertook a brief diagnosis of an insurance company subsidiary. Rather than the standard diagrams, individual milk, marmalade and butter portion containers were used to construct the model. The process took only 30 minutes and revealed to the management group a major flaw in the design of their organisation.

The model is also criticised for focusing on static rather than dynamic goals, although this criticism rather misses the point of the model. Similarly, it is argued that the model can lead to and support autocratic management behaviour. While this argument is easier to sustain, it must be noted that the principles of the model call for appropriate levels of autonomy and if this is not granted the organisation will not be viable. The major barrier to its use is the necessity of devolving power within the organisation and this requirement frequently generates resistance from those already in power.

SUMMARY

This chapter has introduced the Viable System Model, shown its relevance to quality management and how the model may be used. Readers should refer to the work of Stafford Beer (1979, 1981, 1985) and Beckford (1993) to further develop their understanding.

---

key learning points

EFFECTIVE ORGANISATION

Key definition
a system is viable when it is capable of survival in a given environment and capable of learning and adaptation to changes in that environment

Principles
observer defined systems, systems thinking, black boxes, self-regulation, requisite variety

Three modes
descriptive, diagnostic, prescriptive

Three phases
purpose, identification, diagnosis

Critique
general applicability, environmental interaction, observer definition, difficult to use, threatens established power bases, static not dynamic goals

---

QUESTION

Use the VSM to study your University or College? Diagnose its faults according to the cybernetic principles and recommend improvements.

chapter twenty-eight

EMPLOYEE PARTICIPATION

The process is the product.

Anon.

INTRODUCTION

Recognition of the desirability of employee participation in decision making goes back, at least, to the beginnings of the HR school of management thinking and has been a constant theme in subsequent work by many authors. This need is also made evident in the work of the established Quality Gurus. Crosby's entire approach is built around participation, while Ishikawa's quality circles emphasise his view of the need to interlink statistical and participative methods to achieve quality. From the work undertaken so far it is undeniable that active participation in the quality process by all the actors within the organisation will help to procure success in the pursuit of quality. The perennial difficulty is how to make that participation truly meaningful in organisations which are so frequently characterised by internal power struggles and dominated by small power groups.

This chapter introduces two systems methodologies each of which is designed to enable meaningful participation. They are Checkland's Soft Systems Methodology (SSM) and Ackoff's Interactive Planning (IP). Both are operational methodologies based on soft systems thinking which was outlined in chapter 16.

28.1 SOFT SYSTEMS METHODOLOGY: PRINCIPLES AND CONCEPTION

Soft Systems Methodology (SSM) (Checkland: 1981) rests on the assumption that the resolution of complex problems (of which achieving quality may be considered one) relies on the innate subjective views of the participants in the situation. SSM has been developed for use in ill-structured situations where there is an absence of clarity in the definition of the problem and no agreement as to what action is required to solve it. SSM enables a variety of viewpoints to be elaborated and evaluated by a group of problem solvers allowing them to make informed choices about the future. It is considered that by exploring the various viewpoints in an open forum and evaluating their strengths and limitations, an approach can be generated to which all participants will commit themselves. Solutions generated through the seven stage process of enquiry which is the methodology of SSM will normally lead to changes in three dimensions – attitudes, structure and procedures. It is considered that as many people as possible should be involved in the SSM process, and it does not have to be driven by 'experts', it can be used by managers as part of everyday working practice.

28.2 SSM: METHODOLOGY

As already stated, SSM consists of a seven stage process and should be used in an iterative manner (see Figure 28.1). Although the description in this chapter starts at stage 1, any other starting point would generate an equally valid result. The methodology is pursued by the members of the organisation although it may be facilitated by a 'problem solver' – often a consultant.

The first two stages take place in what is called the 'real world', that is, they are based on the experience and knowledge of the participants of how things are – to them. Stage 1 consists of exploring the problem situation and

---

PETER CHECKLAND

Stage 1 Finding out;

Stage 2 Rich picture;

Stage 3 Root definitions;

Stage 4 Redesign;

Stage 5 Real world comparison;

Stage 6 Debate and decision;

Stage 7 Taking action.

Figure 28.1 **Seven stages of soft systems methodology: Peter Checkland**

gathering information about it through observation, evaluating formal data (such as company records) and interviews.

Stage 2 is often an entertaining stage, and usually expressed in the form of a cartoon (called a 'rich picture'), this consists of creating a representation of the problem situation as it is experienced by the participants. Stages 1 and 2 taken together lead the participants to define a number of themes, or systems which they need to examine. These can usefully be thought of as processes within the overall organisation studied.

Stages 3 and 4 are abstract processes designed to explore how things could (and arguably should) be as opposed to how they are, as perceived by the actors. They are concerned with what Ackoff (1981) calls 'idealised design'. Stage 3 develops concise statements about the purpose of the various systems or processes, called 'root definitions'. The 'root definition' presents an ideal view of what the relevant system 'ought' to achieve and is refined through the use of six principal elements (figure 28.2) and six key questions (figure 28.3).

SIX ELEMENTS OF A SOFT SYSTEM

Element 1 – *Customers*:   those who gain by or suffer from the activity;

Element 2 – *Actors*:   those who perform the activity;

Element 3 – *Transformation*:   the action itself;

Element 4 – *Weltanschauung*:   the world-view of the situation which validates the action;

Element 5 – *Owners*:   those who can stop the activity (often the management);

Element 6 – *Environment*:   external constraints upon the system behaviour.

Figure 28.2 **Six principal elements of a system**

Stage 4 uses the validated root definitions to redesign the activities (the transformation process) aiming to overcome the limitations of current transformations. The 'conceptual model' developed identifies the minimum set of activities necessary to ensure that the transformation achieves its purpose. The set of activities is ordered into a process based on how the activities would occur in the 'real world' – this ensures that carts are not put before horses! It may be necessary to define sub-sets of activities which naturally group together, perhaps under the headings of operations, control, co-ordination and so on (rather like the VSM model seen in the previous chapter).

The aim of stage 5 is to compare the models constructed with the real world understanding of the group members. This enables them to highlight

'ROOT DEFINITIONS'

Question 1   What is required?

Question 2   Why is it required?

Question 3   Who will do it?

Question 4   Who will benefit?

Question 5   Who will be hurt or damaged?

Question 6   What external factors constrain the activity?

Figure 28.3 **Six questions for refining 'root definitions'**

possible changes in the actual situation to bring it closer to the systemic ideal now developed. Devices for this might include highlighting areas of difference, generating and ranking (for evaluation) options, and generating projections of possible futures (in the style of the scenario planning technique used by Royal Dutch Shell).

At stage 6 the comparisons drawn in the previous stage provide the basis for discussion and debate amongst the participants. This should lead to the selection of culturally feasible changes in the actual situation – that is, changes which are systemically desirable and are considered achievable within the culture of the particular organisation.

EXPLOITING INTERNAL MODELS

The Chief Executive of a large organisation was pleased with the progress which it had made under his leadership but had an uneasy feeling about the future. He invited a consultant to 'Come and have a look, tell me if you think anything is wrong.'

The consultant, with limited knowledge of the organisation and equally limited knowledge of the country and its culture was faced on the first day of the project with a room full of senior managers from the organisation. None of the participants, including the consultant, really knew why they were there. The Chief Executive had been very economical in giving out information. Introducing the consultant and saying 'I don't really know why he's here, or whether he will do us any good' the Chief Executive announced his departure on a business trip – extending for the duration of the consultant's visit.

The consultant chose to make a partial use of SSM at this point. This choice had several purposes:

- it would enable the development of a relationship between himself and the senior managers;

- it would facilitate the development of his understanding of the organisation;
- it would engage the senior managers in a participative dialogue – involving them immediately in the problem solving process. The immediate problem being that of defining the problem to be solved!

Introducing himself and explaining his background provided the mechanism by which the participants could be drawn into the discussion. Questions and their answers were used to draw comparisons between the consultants 'real-world' experience of organisations (his mental model) and the 'real-world' of the participants (their various mental models).

Within 30 minutes of the start of the process open and frank exchanges of views were occurring between the managers. The consultant was reduced to the role of referee. The problem of identifying the problem had begun.

There are few, if any, absolute rights or wrongs at this stage. The point of the exercise is more the process itself (for generating mutual understanding and appreciation) than for the outcomes – although unless these lead to practical and beneficial changes in the organisation it may be seen as somewhat sterile. The final outcome should be a set of changes to which all parties are willing to commit themselves.

The final stage of the process, stage 7, is taking action, that is, implementing within the real-world situation the changes that have been proposed. These may affect any part of the totality of the organisation studied, that is, its structure (organisation design, job design), attitudes (the culture and values) and procedures (the actual operations of the organisation). The total process is shown diagramatically in figure 28.4.

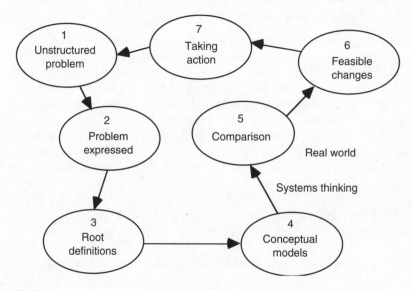

Figure 28.4 **Soft systems methodology**

28.3   CRITICAL REVIEW

While SSM does not preclude the inclusion of large numbers of people in the process, the approach is often recognised as working best with relatively small numbers. The methodology offers no specific help in using SSM in a situation where there are large numbers and where some degree of 'order' needs to be brought into the enquiry process, say in a factory employing 2,000 workers, or in a total organisation which might employ hundreds of thousands of staff in a distributed network of offices and factories. A more apparently useful approach for such organisations is Ackoff's Interactive Planning (IP) (Ackoff, 1981) which will be discussed in the next section. This approach adheres to the participative and subjective views recognised in SSM but provides a structured method for involving all of the people in the organisation in the process of creating its future.

SSM has great strength in its capacity to bring together groups with diverse opinions and offer them a structured process through which those opinions can be debated. However, it does not offer any form of desired, or ideal-type, outcome. It does not suggest any principles to which an ideal solution should adhere other than the forming of a consensus view. The solutions proposed therefore will ameliorate the concerns of those participating in the process but not necessarily others who either willingly or not are excluded from the process. Neither will it necessarily adhere to any specific organisational, cultural or procedural principles which might be thought desirable. Unless these things are already present within the *weltanschauung* of the participants or introduced at the problem definition stage, there is no scope for them to be considered.

28.4   INTERACTIVE PLANNING: PRINCIPLES AND CONCEPTION

Ackoff holds to the view that a planning methodology is required which enables people to plan for themselves, rather than be planned for by others. He sees this as enabling the participants to make their own values and ideals paramount in the planning process. This lets participants express their own view of 'reality' rather than having the reality of others forced upon them and it necessitates wide participation in the creation of the future of organisations. Reflecting ideas already met in other approaches, IP recognises three sets of interests in the organisation. Those of the organisation itself as a purposeful, viable entity, the interests of the wider community (environment) in which it exists and the interests of the individuals who work within it.

Interactivist planners take into account the past, present and predictions about the future as inputs to a planning process aimed at creating their future and the mechanisms by which it can be achieved. They work with their conception of the ideal future for the organisation.

Interactive Planning rests on the three principles of participation, continuity and holism. The participative principle is that all stakeholders should participate in the stages of the planning process. Ackoff, like Checkland, suggests that the process of planning is more important than the plan which is produced, since it is the process which enables individual contributions to be made and it enhances understanding of the whole organisation by those involved with it.

The principle of continuity recognises that values and ideals of the stakeholders change over time and that further problems and new possibilities emerge during the implementation of any plans. For Ackoff this means that the plans must be adapted to meet these changes such that they continually reflect the current circumstances; perhaps they should be considered as forever in final draft form! This idea reflects the notion of 'learning' examined in chapter 19.

The last principle is that of holism, that is, systemic thinking. This suggests that planning should be simultaneously and interdependently carried out for the entire organisation (or at least as many parts and levels as is possible). The notion of holistic or systemic thinking has already been explored in chapter 14.

To enable the participative principle of Interactive Planning to be practised, Ackoff proposes a particular form of planning organisation. This form is seen as embedding the planning process as an integral part of the

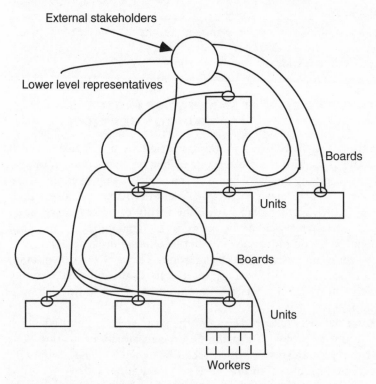

Figure 28.5 **Organisational design for interactive planning**
Source: **Adapted from Ackoff, 1981**

organisation. In this design the organisation is divided into planning boards. The heads of units within the organisation are members of boards at three levels, their own, the one above and the ones below. In this respect they act similarly to and may be characterised as like Likert's 'linking pins', or perhaps as the 'Policy' function in the Viable System Model which links recursive levels. At the highest level, external stakeholders are represented on the board, while at the lowest level all the workers are members of their unit board. This organisation could usefully be used as a design for linking the activities of quality circles within an organisation.

While apparently time consuming, with some managers belonging to as many as ten boards, the organisation is considered to derive major benefit through improved communication, co-ordination and integration of ideas. Morale is also improved. The organisation of Interactive Planning is represented diagramatically in figure 28.5.

It can clearly be seen that this structure does not replace the existing hierarchy, but interleaves with it. It is a hierarchy of planning rather than control. This generates possibilities of communication and debate which the power hierarchy itself tends to inhibit. It is particularly noteworthy that the approach explicitly incorporates the views of external stakeholders who might for example, include local government representatives, community leaders, suppliers and perhaps customers or consumers of the product or service. This has evident implications for organisations pursuing quality programmes. For example, where a supplier development strategy is being pursued, suppliers can be linked into the planning process of the organisation. Similarly, customer feedback becomes truly meaningful when the customers form a part of the organisation.

28.5   IP: METHODOLOGY

The methodology for IP includes five steps (Figure 28.6). Holding to the systemic requirements of the approach, the process may be run in any order and the whole should be regarded as an iterative process with plans as already suggested being always in the latest 'draft' form.

RUSSELL ACKOFF

Step 1   Formulating the mess;

Step 2   Ends planning;

Step 3   Means planning;

Step 4   Resource planning;

Step 5   Design of implementation and control.

Figure 28.6 **Five steps to interactive planning: Russell Ackoff**

Formulating the mess (step 1) consists of a SWOT type analysis intended to highlight the strengths, weaknesses, opportunities and threats faced by the organisation. Ackoff proposes that a useful device is to work out the 'future the organisation is currently in'. This is a scenario for the future of the organisation if nothing is done about its internal situation and the environment continues to develop along the lines anticipated. Ackoff suggests that this requires three types of study (figure 28.7). A synthesis of the three sets of results is considered as a reference scenario of the current 'mess'.

THREE TYPES OF STUDY

- *Systems analysis* – which will detail the organisation, how it works and its environment;

- *Obstruction analysis* – which will unearth the obstacles to corporate development;

- *Reference projections* – which predict future performance by extrapolating current performance in the given environment.

Figure 28.7 **Three methods for formulating the mess**

Ends planning (step 2) seeks to specify the future the organisation wants. It begins with idealised redesign – a vision of the sort of organisation the stakeholders would create if they were free to do so. This involves selecting a mission, specifying the attributes of the design, and designing the organisation. Normally, two versions of this are created – one constrained by the existing wider system, one unconstrained. The difference between these two idealised organisations indicates to what extent the organisation must address its efforts towards modifying its environment during the planning process.

Idealised redesign is a creative process and as such permits only two constraints. First, the design must be technologically feasible, that is it must not rely on a potential future invention or breakthrough. Second, it must be operationally viable, that is it must be capable of functioning if created.

Flood and Jackson (1991, 151) suggest that the design should answer to the criteria of the best 'ideal seeking system' that the stockholders can imagine. From this point it is clear that the organisation designed must be capable of learning and adaptation. Ackoff's outline design for such a system requires it to be capable of:

- *observation*: to recognise opportunities and threats;
- *decision making*: enabling a response to those opportunities and threats;
- *implementation*: actually doing something;
- *control*: performance monitoring and self-correction;
- *communication*: the acquisition, generation and dissemination of information.

The alert reader will by now have identified similarities in ideas between IP and other approaches already discussed such as the VSM with its requirement for implementation, co-ordination, control, development and policy – the five functions of management. It must be stated though that there are some fundamental differences in the theories underpinning the approaches.

Means planning (step 3) is the term used for the process of generating the 'hows' which support the 'whats' of the first two steps. It is concerned with making operational the changes considered necessary by those involved. Alternative 'hows' should be generated, perhaps using some of the techniques outlined in earlier chapters of this book and comparisons made to find the most effective.

Resource planning (step 4) looks at the requirements for materials, supplies, energy and services – all of the inputs to the organisation – as well as at facilities and equipment, personnel and money. For every aspect it is necessary to determine what changes need to be made in order to support the idealised redesign. This stage is very similar to the 'Internal Business Audit' in a strategic review process as it attempts to assess the capabilities of the organisation and its personnel.

Implementation and control (step 5) is concerned with ensuring that the decisions made are carried out. This involves the allocation of tasks and the monitoring of their completion. The outcomes of implementation should be fed back into the planning process such that necessary modifications and further changes can be made.

28.6 CRITICAL REVIEW

IP shares with SSM the criticism that it's outcomes are bounded by the knowledge and expectations of the participants in the process. For quality to be addressed as an issue it must be highlighted at the outset as part of the formulation of the mess. Similarly, at the implementation phase, the need for knowledge of quality theory and practice must be recognised.

While IP and quality circles appear to have much in common, they are differentiated in two ways. First, quality circles operate only at a single level within the organisation whereas IP links all levels. Second, quality circles are focused on purely localised operational problems whereas IP, used properly, has the scope to capture strategic perspectives from the lowest levels of the organisation. Quality circles may be thought of as a problem solving technique, IP may be thought of as a way of managing the organisation.

Like SSM, IP is oriented towards defining the problem. It is focused on providing a methodology for generating solutions. It does not offer any guidance as to what those solutions should be, demanding only that they are derived in an emancipatory manner.

SUMMARY

This chapter has reviewed two methodologies for participation in the creation of a quality organisation. Readers should refer to the work of Checkland (1981) and Ackoff (1981) to further develop their understanding.

---

key learning points

SOFT SYSTEMS METHODOLOGY

Key definition
solving complex problems relies on the innate subjective views of the participants in a situation

Principle
engage participants in the organisation in changing its operation, improve commitment to outcomes, purposes must be defined before means can be decided

Method
seven stage process of enquiry – finding out, rich picture, root definitions, redesign, real-world comparison, debate and decision, taking action

Critique
best with small numbers, brings 'order' to a debate, caters for diverse opinions, no desired or ideal-type outcome other than consensus

INTERACTIVE PLANNING

Key definition
participants values and ideals must be paramount in the planning process

Principle
plan or be planned for, ends must be agreed before means can be decided

Method
five stage process – formulating the mess, ends planning, means planning, resource planning, design of implementation and control

Critique
outcomes bounded by expectations and knowledge of participants, multi-level participation, structure enables mass participation, potential for strategic perspective, means oriented, no 'ideal' solutions

---

QUESTION

Compare the two methodologies outlined in this chapter. Under what circumstances would you use each?

chapter twenty-nine

STAKEHOLDER
PARTICIPATION

*hierarchy is endemic to the human experience of social system.
And yet it seems never to suffice as an organising principle.*
(Stafford Beer, *Beyond Dispute*, 1994)

INTRODUCTION

The methods, tools and techniques so far reviewed in this book have one prime, common theme; they are all designed to improve the quality performance of the organisations in which they are used. Similarly, they all rely on an assumption that what is good for the organisation is good for society and for the individual workers. Nowhere in this set of tools is this assumption either exposed or investigated. The focus is on practical issues of what to do and how best to do it; the question of whether or not it should be done is simply not asked.

Flood (1993) suggests that when 'freedom by debate' (enabled through SSM or IP) fails, 'people become emprisoned.' They become trapped in a way of thinking or a set of assumptions about the world which represent other people's interests rather than their own. They may be subject to practical constraints which, either by accident or design, lead them to conform to the expectations of a more powerful individual or group. People are trapped either by the limits of their own knowledge and understanding or by the structure of the society and organisations in which they exist. It is suggested that a means is necessary through which those affected by a change or process can work with the powerful group to review the assumptions and consequences of the change. The process for addressing these problems is called Critical Systems Heuristics. It will be the subject of this chapter.

While the idea of stakeholders is one which has much currency in political science and sociology it has only recently become used in the language of management. In this context a stakeholder is defined as anyone (or group) with a legitimate interest in the behaviour of a system. This would include those who are involved in it, those affected by it (whether involved in it or not) and those affecting it.

29.1   CRITICAL SYSTEMS HEURISTICS: PRINCIPLES AND CONCEPTION

The work of Werner Ulrich, *Critical Heuristics of Social Planning* (1983), broke new ground in systems thinking by setting out an emancipatory systems approach. This approach enables critical reflection upon the means and goals attained through hard systems thinking and the nature of consensus achieved through soft systems thinking.

The approach is intended to reveal the normative aspects of a proposal – the underlying value assumptions, consequences and side-effects for those affected by planning. Ulrich suggests that whereas the dominant tools of systems thinking consider the means or ends in problem solving there is a need to consider 'whether' – that is to ask what 'ought to be done'? This is seen as enabling freedom of choice to create better social systems and leads to the development of procedures whereby those who are subject to the consequences of designs can challenge the rationality of the planners.

Ulrich's approach is considered to offer a method for proceeding in coercive situations, those where the powerful in society can impose their views on others. It is suggested that CSH enables the true interests and motivations underlying proposals to be revealed and that plans must be supported by all stakeholders if they are to be considered rational.

By 'Critical Systems Heuristics' Ulrich is considered to mean:

- *Critical*: an approach which explores the assumptions underpinning a particular approach (in much the way this book has explored the work of the Quality Gurus);
- *Systems*: the network of elements and interactions to be studied;
- *Heuristics*: the iterative search process for developing a solution free from the bias of the planners.

The last part of this definition is suggestive of an 'ideal' seeking process which maintains the assumptions and presuppositions at the forefront of the process of enquiry. They must be constantly open to question and debate.

Ulrich establishes a basic distinction between those 'involved' in a planning decision and those 'affected' but not involved and creates a framework of twelve critically heuristic categories around this, together with three (Flood and Jackson, 1991: 201–202) 'quasi-transcendental ideas', systems, morality and guarantors. CSH rests on four principles (figure 29.1) which incorporate these three ideas together with a concept of purposefulness.

WERNER ULRICH

Principle 1 Purposefulness;

Principle 2 Systems;

Principle 3 Morality;

Principle 4 Guarantor.

Figure 29.1 **Four principles of Critical Systems Heuristics: Werner Ulrich**

Purposefulness requires that the ability to determine purpose should be spread throughout the system. The system should generate and disseminate knowledge relevant to purposes thus enabling debate. All plans should be critically examined in respect of their normative content.

The systems principle provides a critical standard against which understanding of the world (assumptions) can be measured. The moral principle requires system designers to continually seek to improve the total human condition through their designs.

The guarantor principle recognises that there can be no absolute guarantees of improvement. This principle requires that system designers seek opinions from a wide range of experts and from various stakeholder groups in creating proposals and that these proposals should be agreed by both the involved and the affected.

Essentially, Ulrich's approach may be considered as an endeavour, in a relatively practical way, to ensure the meaningful participation in social systems design by all those who are members of, or interact with, that system.

29.2   CSH: METHODOLOGY

The methodology of CSH consists in essence of two parts. In the first part twelve questions are employed in two modes – 'is' and 'ought'. The first use, in the 'is' mode, is intended to reveal how the interests of four groups relevant to the system are served. These groups are: the client, the decision taker, the designer (s) (those involved) and the witness (es) (those affected but not involved). The questions explore the value (normative) basis of the design by considering the basis of power and the basis of the design's legitimacy. The second use is in the 'ought' mode, examining whose

TWELVE QUESTIONS FOR CSH IN THE 'IS' AND '(OUGHT)' MODES

Question 1   Who is (*ought to be*) the actual client of the design of the system?

Question 2   What is (*ought to be*) the actual purpose of the system's design?

Question 3   What is (*ought to be*) the in-built measure of success?

Question 4   Who is (*ought to be*) actually the decision taker?

Question 5   What resources and constraints are really (*ought to be*) controlled by the decision taker?

Question 6   What resources and constraints are not (*ought not to be*) controlled by the decision taker?

Question 7   Who is (*ought to be*) actually involved as planner?

Question 8   Who is (*ought to be*) involved as expert?

Question 9   Where do the involved see the guarantee that their planning will be successful? (*Who ought to be the guarantor of success?*)

Question 10   Who among the involved witnesses represents the concerns of the affected? (*Who ought to get involved*).

Question 11   Are the affected given an opportunity to emancipate themselves from the experts? (*To what extent ought the affected be able to escape the influence of the experts?*)

Question 12   What world view is (*ought to be*) underlying the design of the system?

Figure 29.2 **Twelve questions for Critical Systems Heuristics**

interests perhaps should be served by the system. The questions are shown in figure 29.2.

Question 1 is concerned with defining who belongs to the group whose purposes (interests and values) are served, as distinct from those who do not benefit but may have to bear the costs or other disadvantages of a particular system design. Question 2 seeks to evaluate what is achieved as opposed to what the planners claim will be achieved. Question 3 considers the measurement of success in terms of what is actually achieved.

Question 4 seeks to establish who can actually change the measure of success by asking in whose terms success is measured. Question 5 tries to determine the resources necessary and constraints to be overcome to enable successful planning and implementation of the system.

Question 6 is concerned with defining the boundaries of the system, by attempting to determine which aspects fall within the system to be managed and which fall outside. Question 7 is concerned with identifying those who are undertaking the planning while question 8, tries to differentiate between the expertise being offered and that which is desirable to develop a solution – questioning the legitimacy of their involvement. Question 9 is seeking to establish how the promises made can be fulfilled while question 10 seeks to establish who will be affected by the operation of the system but is not involved in it – and therefore has no direct influence on its operation.

Question 11 follows this by requiring the inclusion of representations from the 'affected but not involved' so that their views may be taken into account. Question 12 brings reflection upon the assumptions about the world which underpin the proposals being made. For example, in the quality context, question 12 might cause the participants to consider whether quality improvement was necessarily a good thing or whether it was simply a function of a particular set of assumptions and expectations about the world.

The gap between the two sets of answers is the basis for the second part of the methodology, the 'polemical employment of boundary judgements'. More commonly, the adoption by those engaged in the process of the standpoint of 'devil's advocate'. The objective of this dialectical debate is to force the system designers (the 'problem solvers') through the process of debate, to demonstrate the validity of the boundaries to the system (the parameters under which it would operate and the expectations from it) which they have selected. Thus, rather than those 'affected but not involved' having to prove that their alternative views are correct, the planners must prove the superiority of the original boundaries.

The affected are able to demonstrate through this process that:

- the planners have employed boundary judgements in creating their proposals and calculating effects;
- that the experts are not able through their expertise to prove, or justify, their own position, or alternatively to falsify those of their critics;
- that experts (planners) who are unable to justify their proposals on the basis of their 'knowledge' are employing dogmatically or cynically held positions and hence disqualify themselves from the debate.

The employment of this polemical process is considered to generate an equality of position between the parties, enabling 'reasonable dialogue'.

THE WRONG QUESTION

The UK, in common with many other nations, employs a system of public enquiries to explore issues of national or regional importance. The objective of such enquiries is to enable open and fair debate on a particular proposal reflecting some of the ideas of

Critical Systems Heuristics. Recent examples include the enquiry into the Newbury Bypass (now being built) and the fifth terminal at Heathrow Airport (enquiry expected to last until the middle of 1998).

The rules of public enquiries in the UK guarantee that every interested party will have the opportunity to express their views to the enquiry officials and these views must be catered for in the final outcome.

The public enquiry process has two major flaws. First, the enquiry officials are selected by the government of the day. Whilst independent of that government, and bound by a duty of equity and impartiality, there is potential for political interference in the process. Second, and of much greater concern, the public enquiry is established to address a particular question, and no other. That question is *not* defined in a way which reflects the CSH process. The enquiry therefore may derive a fair and equitable answer to what many of the affected regard as the wrong question.

The same flaw may exist in any process of debate such as that outlined in this chapter.

Through the process of exploration and debate outlined, it is considered that system design can be explored and modified to better meet the needs of those both involved and affected.

29.3 CRITICAL REVIEW

The process of CSH is, of course, only useful where all parties are willing to contribute to the process and to make adaptations based upon the findings. Where overt coercion exists, (in other words the circumstances in which this approach is most fully justified), it may be considered unlikely that the powerful would willingly engage in debate with the weak. They are more likely to simply use their power to overrule.

The approach is most useful in the pursuit of quality at the outset of a TQM programme. Considered use of CSH at this stage may enable the revelation of barriers to the quality movement by enabling both the involved and the affected to highlight hopes and fears which usually remain unexpressed. It is these hopes and fears, the 'hidden agendas' of the participants, that often prove fatal to the quality initiative.

Examples of this might be a management who recognise the need for improved quality in order for their organisation to continue to compete and survive, but recognise that this may generate threats to their own positions as well as that of the workforce – they are involved and affected. The workforce itself may also consider threats to be present – to job security, to accepted and accustomed working practices, indeed to a whole way of organisational life.

The CSH approach should enable all of these fears and hopes to be expressed through the questioning and debating process, enabling them to be accounted for in the system design, and granting the experts insights which they would not otherwise have. Equally the affected, though not initially involved, will be better able to understand the motivation and rationale of the management.

One of the most beneficial effects may be the need which the process generates for 'self-reflection' by the powerful. The debating device will force them to express their understandings and, in so doing, to justify them to themselves. If they cannot do this then they may well change their approach.

As with other 'soft systems' based methodologies, the use of CSH does not lead to any specific problem solution. It will not generate a new organisation chart or a different way of working. What it will do is enable the rationale behind any particular solution derived from another methodology to be justified in terms of the people affected.

SUMMARY

This chapter has introduced the need for an emancipatory approach to be taken to quality – creating freedom of thought and action for all. The second part of the chapter introduced the theory and practice of Critical Systems Heuristics. Readers should refer to the work of Ulrich (1983, 1987) to further develop their understanding of this complex and demanding approach.

---

key learning points

STAKEHOLDER PARTICIPATION

Key definition
an emancipatory systems approach for developing true consensus

Principles
purposefulness, systems, morality, guarantors

Method
CSH methodology of stakeholder participation, dialectical debate

Critique
useful only where the powerful permit debate, overt coercion stops the process, may enable barriers to quality to be identified, develops understanding, no ideal-type solutions

---

QUESTION

What difficulties might you encounter in using Critical Systems Heuristics in a corporate situation?

chapter thirty

IMPLEMENTING QUALITY PROGRAMMES

Suit the action to the word, the word to the action.
Shakespeare, *Hamlet*, (III, ii)

INTRODUCTION

It is necessary, but not sufficient, that those pursuing quality management should be competent in the use of the wide variety of tools and methods available. It is also essential that those tools should be used in the context of a well organised and overarching project. A fragmented or partial approach will only generate partial quality management! It should be acknowledged that although implementing quality is a continuous activity and must become an embedded part of the management process of the organisation, initiating a quality programme depends upon a successful first project.

The basic approaches of the Quality Gurus were outlined in part two of this book, from Crosby's 'fourteen steps for quality improvement', through Deming's 'seven point action plan', to Feigenbaum's 'four steps to Total Quality Control' and Ishikawa's 'Company-Wide Quality Control'. Each of these suffers from the limitation that it is designed to achieve those things which the particular guru finds important and neglects other aspects of the process. Flood's (1993) holistic process attempts to overcome this difficulty by commencing the TQM initiative with an educational programme and encouraging eclectic use of all of the ideas of quality – in context and fully justified. Flood's process was outlined in chapter 26. A thoughtful manager can work from the sets of principles for achieving quality outlined in this book, select appropriate tools and develop a quality programme which will work in his or her organisation. To provide a further general TQM methodology would be redundant, so this chapter will examine some general issues of project management, implementation and control.

30.1 PROJECT MANAGEMENT

This section assumes that the quality process has been commenced using some of the tools already outlined and that what is required is to implement the projects. Project implementation consists of three sets of activities (figure 30.1). It is a dynamic, iterative process which continually steers a project towards its goal – a goal which may itself change during the life of the project. In a large scale project it is quite likely that the 'target' will move during its lifetime. For example, the benchmark against which original objectives were set may change, a new technology may move from the research laboratories into the mainstream, or the customer base of the organisation may change substantially, all leading to a revision of plans.

QUALITY IMPLEMENTATION OUTLINE

- Planning;

- Implementation;

- Control.

Figure 30.1 **Three activities of project implementation**

Before commencing any project it is vital that the project managers consider the major tasks to be completed, the order in which they should be undertaken, the resources required and the availability of 'float' or 'slippage' time within the project. They also need to take account of any constraints upon the project such as the availability of working capital, the effect of seasonal weather changes and the delivery commitments given to the client (s).

A small project with a limited number of variables and activities can be undertaken with a minimum use of the formal tools of project management. Larger projects, including TQM initiatives, should draw on these tools to support the process and ensure the best results are obtained.

There are a number of approaches available for project planning. One of the oldest, and probably best known, is the Gantt chart. This device breaks the project down into its constituent parts and these are scheduled against the timeframe of the project. Progress is indicated by use of shading. While useful – the Gantt chart is very simple – it does not take account of interdependency between separate elements and ignores 'slippage' or 'float' time. During the life of the project it can be difficult to maintain awareness of activities which are behind schedule and whether the project can be completed on time. An example Gantt chart is provided in figure 30.2.

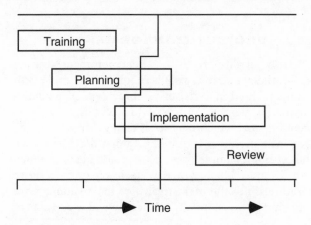

Figure 30.2 **A Gantt chart**

The technique of network analysis (or critical path analysis) provides a more comprehensive system for planning and controlling large projects. Unlike Gantt charts, it recognises interdependency and highlights those parts of the project which are critical. Critical aspects are those which if not achieved on time will delay or prevent completion of the project. It is useful in the programming of resources and in the minimisation of project costs. The network process consists of two stages: preparing the network (figure 30.3) and analysing the network.

In the quality context, shortening of the project time may be desirable in order to meet the requirements of a key customer, or to establish a quality margin against a competitor whose activities constitute a threat. Major benefits are derived simply from the construction of the network since this forces the planners to consider every aspect in detail well in advance of implementation. This process should lead to improvement in the plan provided a 'critical' stance is taken.

Each activity is represented within the network diagram by an arrow with a circle at each end. A letter is used to denote the activity, and numbers are used within the circles to denote events. Some activities within a project will be dependent on the completion of a prior activity, whilst others will be able to occur simultaneously. Where activities are carried out simultaneously, dummy events are introduced simply to resolve the logical difficulty of

CRITICAL PATH ANALYSIS

Preparing a network:

- Define the scope and purpose of the whole project.
- Identify the various activities.
- Determine the logical relationships between activities and events (the start or end of individual activities) and construct the network diagram.
- Determine for each activity, the probable duration, resources required and any restrictions, for example a starting date, daytime working only and so on.

Analyse the network:

- Analyse the network to discover which jobs are critical in determining completion time.
- Determine whether or not it is economically feasible (or desirable for other reasons) to shorten the completion time.

Figure 30.3 **Critical path analysis**

having separate activities defined by the same pair of events. Figure 30.4 provides a simple example.

In this case, activity P can be carried out simultaneously with Q and R, but Q must be completed before R can commence. Activity S can be carried out simultaneously with Q and again must be completed before R begins. A dummy event T is introduced to enable the separation of the Q and S lines. Line lengths are of no significance, duration is given by the number below the line.

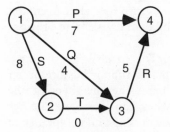

Figure 30.4 **Example of a network**

The 'critical path' is the route through the network which occupies the minimum time passing through all the critical points. In the case given, the route would be 1, 2, 3, 4, giving a duration of 13 minutes, since S must be completed before R is started. Activities R and S in this example are the critical activities since delays affect the entire project, whereas P and Q are non-critical. They could be delayed by 6 minutes and 4 minutes respectively without affecting the overall time. This permissible delay time is called the total float.

The network provides a 'time budget' for the project (and may even be used to develop the financial budget if cost and time are directly related). As with any budget, it should be updated during the course of the project to incorporate 'actual' values achieved and the balance of the project should be modified and replanned accordingly. Software packages are now available which will conduct and support network analysis.

30.2 IMPLEMENTATION STRATEGIES

Implementation (through whichever set of methods and tools) can be achieved in two primary ways: expert-owned – a consultant or quality specialist driven programme, and self-owned – a programme owned and driven by the staff but supported by consultants or specialists.

Expert-owned programmes are most common and commence with the appointment of a project manager and implementation team. Normally, such a team will take full responsibility for the project, identifying and making appropriate changes and handing over the new system or approach to the subject staff on a 'turnkey' basis. This team will deal with training, debugging new systems and procedures and ironing out any difficulties before handing over the project.

Such an approach has significant advantages in certain circumstances, such as in 'greenfield' situations where there are no established methods or preconceived ideas. It can be very rapid (and consequently cost-effective) in the short term. The approach can take advantage of functional specialisms that would perhaps otherwise be unobtainable or very expensive. Its primary disadvantage, and particularly so in an established situation, is that it places ownership of the new methods in the hands of the project team rather than the affected staff. This has the effect that success or failure is allocated by both management and staff to the project team, and it is usually the case that barriers or objections to change are not eradicated but by-passed – those affected are overruled. This in turn may slow or inhibit the process of change and generates the possibility of reversion to previous approaches, in effect negating the work done.

The self-owned approach is more effective. This involves appointing a project manager from within the affected group and supporting him or her with functional specialists as necessary, while using members of the working staff as the implementation team. They can then generate the changes for their area themselves, promoting ownership and acceptance of the changes and avoiding the difficulty of imposed change.

The role of the functional specialists then becomes to support the initiatives of the staff, rather than to take those initiatives themselves. This approach combines the high expertise of the functional specialists with the grassroots knowledge of the staff in the organisation to produce solutions acceptable to all sides. The principal disadvantage of this approach is that it can take longer to achieve the desired changes. This extra time (which perhaps bears an additional cost) must be balanced against the greater likelihood of creating permanent, accepted change.

A further advantage is that the staff involved will learn from the functional specialists and thus enhance their own knowledge and understanding. While difficult to measure, this is a substantial benefit as it establishes a 'change orientation' amongst the staff and they come to recognise what is and is not possible from a new perspective. Experience of working in both implementation styles leads the writer to suggest that the second of these methods is to be preferred.

30.3 CONTROL

Control rests in a constant monitoring of project progress with information 'fedback' from the project used as the basis for comparison with expectations usually derived from the Gantt chart or Network. The results of the comparison are used as the basis for altering the inputs to the project or perhaps changing the objectives with consequent replanning of resource allocation. Readers will recognise this as a cybernetic process.

Altering the inputs to a project might include increasing or decreasing the level of resources used, enhancing the level of expertise employed when a particularly difficult problem has emerged, or bringing in new resources or expertise to deal with unexpected events or obstructions. Deming's PDCA cycle at the 'check' stage, for example, would be expected to highlight difficulties or unexpected results from experiments which would lead to redetermination of other changes, which were themselves consequent upon the experimental change. Such unexpected results should not be regarded as failures, as is so often the case, but as part of the process of learning associated with an evolutionary activity. Experiments which do not produce the expected results are as valuable as those which do. Knowing how *not* to do something, is at least as important as knowing how to do it. Used intelligently this information enables further failures or continuation of a failing method to be avoided.

Equally, the unexpected success is a further opportunity for learning. It may be a conceptual or practical breakthrough which makes some future step in the process of change redundant, or a new opportunity arising as a result of the change. It is important that the control system can recognise these aspects and take advantage of them.

It is quite common in managing change programmes to persist for long periods with a particular experiment or trial and meet nothing but resistance from the workforce. This can, quite suddenly, be overcome and it is important that the breakthrough moment is recognised and the advantage gained capitalised upon. Such a breakthrough in one area commonly creates the opportunity for breakthroughs in others.

MANAGEMENT AND KEYBOARDS

A large institution employed staff who strongly resisted the introduction of PCs and an electronic mail system. They were accustomed to armies of PA's and typists producing all work requiring keyboard skills.

A key part of a service quality initiative for the organisation involved shortening the timescale for responses to written enquiries (both internal and external) and it was recognised that this could be achieved by removing steps from the production chain, that is, encouraging staff to produce their own mail. It had also been demonstrated that this could be more cost-efficient up to quite senior management levels, could lead to a reduction in numbers employed and save significant quantities of paper.

Resistance was organisation wide. The staff would not accept the idea, and the IT experts could not confirm the cost–benefit case using their own costing model. The breakthrough arose when the directors were persuaded to allow a pilot study to be undertaken in one location where the general manager was open to the innovation.

In what could be seen as a coercive move, a wide area network was installed and staff were told that they were to receive these machines – not that they had to use them. In addition to 'e-mail' facilities the machines were equipped with spreadsheet and database packages which supported the 'non-correspondence' activities of the staff. They were trained in these facilities, having accepted already that they would improve performance and being able to measure the advantage to themselves of such a system. They soon 'discovered' the 'e-mail' facility and started using it because they found that it enabled them to perform various tasks much more quickly. Within a month, the staff were typing the bulk of their own correspondence, the previous objections having been forgotten. They recognised, for themselves, the benefits of the system through acceptance of what had been originally a subsidiary use.

Once these staff acknowledged the benefits, resistance throughout the organisation crumbled, and there was a sustained clamour of demand from many other locations for the same facilities. The IT department were able to prove the cost–benefit case (since they were able to amend their model to reflect a new reality), and indeed claimed credit for the whole operation, creating a model system for themselves within their own department!

This breakthrough in acceptance of one change created the possibility of other changes, previously equally strongly resisted, being accepted right across the organisation. These changes affected job descriptions, management roles, staff numbers employed and a whole range of systems and procedures, all of which could be redesigned to support the quality initiative.

Changing of project objectives becomes possible when the progress made indicates that the original objectives cannot be achieved (for whatever reason), or more demanding objectives have become accessible due to unexpected breakthroughs or progress. Frequently, those involved in the project will be criticised for setting objectives incorrectly, or for making 'mistakes'. It is a sign of good management that the need to change objectives has been realised and that action is proposed. This is a fundamental part of most quality approaches – a constant seeking of higher goals and higher achievements.

30.4   CRITICAL REVIEW

It is not possible to give other than a brief overview of the implementation of a quality programme in a text such as this. There are myriad techniques for project management available and in use, most of which will contribute value.

The overall pattern of planning, implementation and control applies just as much to the writing of this book, or to undertaking a journey as it does to completing a quality programme. Nonetheless, the techniques identified are considered of great value in helping to understand the total implementation process and can be used at every level within the organisation. For example, a Gantt chart could be prepared for the whole quality initiative and used as the driver for all of the lower level (recursive) quality initiatives. Hence, if Flood's programme were being used, each Quality Council would employ its own Gantt chart and these would be derived from and linked with each other. If the plans are not integrated in this way then inevitably some aspect of the programme will fall through the gap. The important point is to use these tools thoughtfully, exploring how much they can help the organisation rather than deriding them for how little they achieve on their own.

SUMMARY

This chapter has briefly introduced the overall process of quality implementation and shown how the three phases of planning, implementation and control can be managed.

---

key learning points

IMPLEMENTING QUALITY PROGRAMMES

Key idea
quality projects *must* be holistic

Methods
variety of techniques, Gantt charts, critical path analysis, Project Management from within the group (s) affected, ongoing control and adaptation of programmes

Critique
tools must be used thoughtfully, use tools systemically, recognise links between projects, managers must behave as they expect others to behave

QUESTION

Study the quality programme of one of the gurus featured in this text. Decide which activities you think fit into the three phases of Planning, Implementation and Control. What additional steps would you add to these programmes to enhance them?

Afterword

'Whatsoever is rightly done, however humble, is noble.'

(Henry Royce)

The single most critical issue in the pursuit of quality is that of management commitment to it, without this the programme will fail – as so many do.

Each of the writers on quality mentioned in this book mentions this commitment – normally listing it as the first step in the programme. None however are very specific about how it can be obtained. The reasons given for pursuing quality are most often negative – to avoid failure, to reduce costs, to avoid defeat by overseas competition. While these are all conveniently measurable they are also all inherently short term. They cause management to focus on the return from pursuing quality – and often quality consultants will package their programmes in terms of the direct cost–benefit case, reinforcing the approach. In terms of Maslow's hierarchy of needs (1970), quality programmes focused on avoidance are addressing basic organisational needs of physiology and safety.

These objectives are all in themselves worthwhile. It is important to achieve all of them. However, once they are achieved (in terms of the initial cost–benefit case) the focus of the organisation may well – and often does – move on to some other short-term objective such as increasing market share or improving margins. The pressure for quality will subside in the face of increased emphasis on some other objective. Quality, in the absolute sense, can never be achieved. There will always be scope for further improvement, but once the pressure for improvement is released the organisation may tend to slide backwards towards a lower level of achievement.

In the context of an effective organisation (one which is to be viable in the long term) quality is not an objective, it is a given. The essence of effectiveness and survival for the organisation rests in 'rightness' – being perceived as providing a quality product or service. This 'rightness' arises from an attitude of mind which obtains satisfaction from doing the job, whatever it may be, correctly for no other reason than that is the way the job should be done. This attitude most frequently comes out as a sense of caring, the sense that it matters to the individual whether or not the job is done correctly, not for the measurement system nor the purposes of statistical process control, but just because it is right. This parallels Maslow's idea of self-actualisation – to be all that one can be.

This attitude is most often met in those who work in what we call the 'caring' professions: doctors and nurses, vicars, priests and rabbis. Similar behaviour can be observed in craftspeople whose only 'benchmark' or measure of quality performance may be against themselves – are they pleased with what they have done? Is it the best that they could do?

It is met, though more rarely, in those pursuing other occupations. This attitude is met in unexpected places, it is remarked upon. It does delight the customer and may exceed their expectations.

Throughout this text the concentration has been upon quality as an exercise in technical correctness – that reflects the literature on which it is based. However, 'caring' reflects the other aspect of quality – its aesthetic. Management must focus on pursuing quality not just for its short term extrinsic benefit but for the intrinsic worth in attaining quality of product or service. They must truly believe in and pursue quality for its own sake.

Glossary of terms and abbreviations

AGIL Adaptation, Goal, Integration, Latency

Aphorism a short clever saying expressing a general truth

Benchmarking formal comparison of one organisation against another with the aim of performance improvement

Black box a technique for studying the behaviour of complex systems

Business Process Re-engineering (BPR) a process oriented organisational performance discipline

Business systems diamond a meta-methodology for BPR

BS 5750 British Standard quality management system (now subsumed in ISO 9000)

Call-centre a centralised telephone enquiry service

Comfort zone an accustomed way of behaving and working

Complementarism an approach to problem solving in which choice and use of methodology is guided by the characteristics of the situation and understanding of the theory underpinning the method

Cowpaths naturally developed processes in organisations

CSH Critical Systems Heuristics

CST Critical Systems Thinking

Culture the set of values and beliefs which guide behaviour in an organisation or nation

Deterministic/determinism entirely predictable system behaviour

Direct costs of quality the visible costs of quality failure

Emergent properties behaviour which is exhibited by a whole system but by none of its parts

Empirical derived from practice or observation not theory

EN 29000 European Standard quality management system (now subsumed in ISO 9000)

Feedback communication enabling self-regulation

GDP per capita the amount of income generated by a nation divided by its population

Guru originally a Hindu spiritual teacher now used to refer to leaders in a discipline

HACCP Hazard Analysis Critical Control Points - a food production management system

Heuristic a process of trial and error

Holism/holistic the attempt to deal with whole organisations rather than parts

HR Human Resources

Invisible costs of quality consequential and hidden costs of quality failure

IP Interactive Planning

ISO 9000 International Standards Organisation guidelines for a Quality Management System

ISO 14000 International Standards Organisation guidelines for an environmental management system

Just-in-time (JIT) a system of supply which delivers parts to a production process when they are required, obviating the need to hold stocks

Kanban the operating system to support JIT

Kaizen a Japanese belief system oriented towards continuous improvement in *all* aspects of life

Mechanistic a view of organisations which suggests that they and their staff can be organised to behave like machines

Meta of a higher logical order

Methodology a systematic set of methods for studying issues and problems

NIH Not Invented Here – a barrier to change

Normative concerned with defining ethics and social standards

Organisational cybernetics the science of effective organisation

Organismic/organic a view of organisations as being like organisms

Paradigm a personal framework of thought or system of beliefs

PDCA Cycle Plan, Do, Check, Action – a systematic continuous improvement cycle

Poka-Yoke defect = 0

Probabilism/probabilistic behaviour which is partly random or unpredictable

Process all the operations required to complete a task

QA Quality Assurance

Quality Circle/(QC/QCC) a problem solving team for quality issues

QC Quality Control

QFD Quality Function Deployment

QMS Quality Management System

Recursion structural invariance at different levels of an organisation

Reductionist/Reductionism a way of studying organisations through fragmentation and analysis

Replacement cycle the time period between repeated purchases of a good or service

Rework fixing or repairing finished goods before despatch

Self-regulation the ability of a system to manage itself

Slipping clutch syndrome an effect on productivity and quality when a production system is placed under pressure

SMED single minute exchange of die – a fast change process for machine tools

Soft systems the study of human activity systems

SOSM system of systems methodologies

SSM Soft Systems Methodology

Stakeholder any person or organisation affected by or involved with an organisation

Statistical Process Control (SPC) a quantitative system for monitoring process performance

Statistical Quality Control (SQC) a quantitative system for monitoring quality performance

Supplier development a business strategy of co-operation between buyer and supplier to jointly improve quality

Systemic an approach which deals with whole systems and the interactions of their elements and the environment

Total cost the lifetime cost of purchasing and maintaining a product

Total quality control Feigenbaum's approach to quality and management

TQM Total Quality Management

TSI Total Systems Intervention

Variety engineering techniques for managing probabilism

VSD Viable System Diagnosis

VSM Viable System Model

Zero defects a quality target focusing on error free production

Further reading

Throughout this book reference has been made to a wide selection of sources which have been found informative and interesting in the attempt to understand the role of quality in the wider context of management thinking, organisation theory and emergent social issues. Following is a list of texts which will help the reader to explore further the themes and issues raised in this book.

Beer, S. (1974) *Designing Freedom*, Wiley, Chichester: Beer discusses the impact of conventional management thinking on the development of society and suggests ways in which the apparent threats to freedom can be overcome. This book is Beer's most lucid attempt to elaborate his philosophy.

Crosby, P. (1979) *Quality is Free*, Mentor, New York: Crosby introduces his quality approach in a highly readable, accessible text.

Deming, W. E. (1986) *Out of the Crisis*, The Press Syndicate, Cambridge: Deming elaborates his fears for the future of American industry and proposes solutions based on his quality thinking and practice.

Feigenbaum, A. V. (1986) *Total Quality Control*, McGraw-Hill, New York: This text provides a full explanation of Feigenbaum's approach to managing for quality.

Flood, R. L. (1993) *Beyond TQM*, Wiley, Chichester: Flood develops his holistic approach to Total Quality Management drawing on his background in systems science. The book is readily accessible to non-specialists in systems and quality.

Galbraith, J. (1974) *The New Industrial State*, Penguin, London: Galbraith develops an argument about the power of big corporations in the future economy of the world.

Hannagan, T. J. (1986) *Mastering Statistics*, 2nd edition, Macmillan Education Ltd, Basingstoke: Hannagan provides an introduction to the development and use of a wide variety of statistical techniques.

Hoff, B. (1994) *The Tao of Pooh and the Te of Piglet*, Methuen, London: Hoff provides an insight to Western systems thinking through a re-interpretation of elements of Chinese philosophy.

Hoyle, D. (1998) *ISO 9000 Quality Systems Handbook*, 3rd edition, Butterworth-Heinemann Ltd, Oxford: Hoyle provides an easy to follow guide to developing and installing a quality management system.

Huczynski, A. and Buchanan, D. (1991) *Organisational Behaviour*, 2nd edition, Prentice-Hall International (UK) Ltd, Hemel Hempstead: This text provides a substantial and reader friendly guide to the principal strands of management thinking which dominate contemporary organisations.

Huff, D. (1973) *How to Lie with Statistics*, Pelican, London: Huff explores in an entertaining but ruthlessly critical manner the ways in which poor understanding of statistics are used to manipulate decision making.

Ishikawa, K. (1986) *Guide to Quality Control*, 2nd edition, Asian Productivity Organisation: This book, based upon Ishikawa's practical work was originally developed as a guide for the work of Quality Circle members.

Juran, J. M., (1988) *Juran on Planning for Quality*, Free Press, New York: This substantial and detailed text provides the most useful guide to Juran's thinking and his approach to achieving quality.

Kanji, G. P. and Asher, M. (1996) *100 Methods for Total Quality Management*, Sage, London: The authors provide an easy to follow, simple 'how to' guide covering the major activities in a TQM programme.

Logothetis, N. (1992) *Managing for Total Quality*, Prentice Hall International, London: Logothetis provides a guide to the statistically based methods for achieving quality.

Lovelock, J. (1979) *Gaia: A New Look at Life on Earth*: Lovelock explains the development of his theory of the environment. Appreciation of this perspective helps in understanding the environmental imperative for the pursuit of quality.

Oakland, J. S. (1993) *Total Quality Management*, 2nd edition, Butterworth-Heinemann Ltd, Oxford: Readable and well structured, Oakland elaborates in detail his programme for attaining quality.

Ormerod, P. (1994) *The Death of Economics*, Faber and Faber, London: Ormerod explores the assumptions which underpin much of currently dominant economic theory, highlighting the weaknesses and flaws which he perceives.

Pirsig, R. M. (1974) *Zen and the Art of Motorcycle Maintenance (An Inquiry into Values)*, Black Swan edition, Arrow Books, London: Presented as an account of a man's journey with his son, the book reflects a process of enquiry into two strands of quality thinking, the technical and aesthetic.

Shingo, S. (1987) *The Sayings of Shigeo Shingo*, (trans. A. P. Dillon, Productivity Press, USA 1987): Shingo's message is expressed through his many mottoes for achieving quality.

Taguchi, G. (1987) *Systems of Experimental Design*, Vols 1 and 2, Unipub/Kraus, International Publications, New York: Taguchi's own guide to his process for developing quality within the product and the production process.

Waldrop, S. (1992) *Complexity*, Simon and Schuster, New York: Waldrop reports the development of complexity theory giving insight to thinking about organisations as non-linear dynamical systems.

References

Ackoff, R.L. (1981) *Creating the Corporate Future*, Wiley, New York

Allen, R. E. (1995) *Winnie the Pooh on Management*, Methuen, London

Ashby, W. R. (1956) *An Introduction to Cybernetics*, Chapman and Hall, London

Bank, J. (1992) *The Essence of Total Quality Management*, Prentice-Hall International, London

Beckford, J. (1993) 'The Viable System Model, A More Adequate Tool for Practising Management?', Ph.D. thesis, University of Hull

Beckford, J., (1995), Towards a Participative Methodology for the Viable Systems Model, in, *Systemist*, UK Systems Society, 17(3): 112–128

Beer, S. (1959) *Cybernetics and Management*, Wiley, New York

Beer, S. (1974) *Designing Freedom*, Wiley, Chichester

Beer, S. (1979) *The Heart of Enterprise*, Wiley, Chichester

Beer, S. (1981) *Brain of the Firm*, 2nd edition, Wiley, Chichester

Beer, S. (1985) *Diagnosing the System for Organisations*, Wiley, Chichester

Beer, S. (1994) *Beyond Dispute: The Invention of Team Syntegrity*, Wiley, Chichester

Bendell, T. (1989) *The Quality Gurus: What Can They Do for Your Company?*, Department of Trade and Industry, London, and Services Ltd, Nottingham

Burns, T and Stalker G. M. (1961) *The Management of Innovation*, Tavistock, London

Burrell, G. and Morgan, G. (1979) *Sociological Paradigms and Organisational Analysis*, Heinemann, London

Carroll, L. (1866) *Alice's Adventures in Wonderland*, Macmillan and Co., London

Checkland, P. B. (1978) The Origins and Nature of 'Hard' Systems Thinking, *Journal of Applied Systems Analysis*, 5 (2): 99

Checkland, P. B. (1981) *Systems Thinking, Systems Practice*, Wiley, Chichester

Checkland, P. and Scholes, J. (1990) *Soft Systems Methodology in Action*, Wiley, Chichester

Clemson, B. (1984) *Cybernetics: A New Management Tool*, Abacus, Tunbridge Wells

Clutterbuck, D. and Crainer, S. (1990) *Makers of Management*, Macmillan, London

Crosby, P. (1979) *Quality is Free*, Mentor, New York

De Bono, E. (1970) *Lateral Thinking: A Text-book of Creativity*, Spain Press, London

Deming, W. E. (1982) *Quality, Productivity and Competitive Position*, Massachusetts Institute of Technology, MA

Deming, W. E. (1986) *Out of the Crisis*, the Press Syndicate, Cambridge

Espejo, R. and Schwaninger, M. (1993) *Organisational Fitness, Corporate Effectiveness through Management Cybernetics*, Campus Verlag, Frankfurt and New York

Fayol, H. (1916) *General and Industrial Management*, SRL Dunod, Paris (trans. Constance Storrs, 1949, Pitman, London)

Feigenbaum, A. V. (1986) *Total Quality Control*, McGraw-Hill, New York

Fiedler F. E. (1967) *A Theory of Leadership Effectiveness*, McGraw-Hill, New York

Flood, R. L. (1993) *Beyond TQM*, Wiley, Chichester

Flood, R. L. and Carson, E. R. (1988) *Dealing with Complexity*, Plenum, New York

Flood, R. L. and Jackson, M. C. (1991) *Creative Problem Solving*, Wiley, Chichester

Flood, R. L. and Romm, N. R. A. (1996) *Diversity Management: Triple Loop Learning*, Wiley, Chichester

Galbraith, J. (1974) *The New Industrial State*, Penguin, London

Gilbert, J. (1992) *How to Eat an Elephant: A Slice-by Slice Guide to Total Quality Management*, Tudor, London

Gilbert, M. (1994) *Understanding Quality Management Standards*, Institute of Management, London

Gleick, J. (1987) *Chaos*, Heinemann, London

Hammer, M. and Champy, J. (1993) *Business Process Re-engineering*, Nicholas Brealey, London

Handy, C. (1985) *Understanding Organisations*, 3rd edition, Penguin, London

Handy, C. (1990a) *The Age of Unreason*, Arrow, London

Handy, C. (1990b) *Inside Organisations*, BBC Books, London

Heller, R. (1989) *The Making of Managers*, Penguin, London

Herzberg, F., Mauser, B. and Synderman, B. B. (1959) *The Motivation to Work*, 2nd edition, Wiley, New York

Hofstede, G. (1980) Motivation, Leadership and Organization: Do American Theories Apply Abroad? *Organizational Dynamics*, Summer: 42–63

Hoyle, D. (1998) *ISO 9000 Quality Systems Handbook*, 3rd edition, Butterworth-Heinemann Ltd, Oxford

Huczynski, A. and Buchanan, D. (1991) *Organizational Behaviour*, 2nd edition, Prentice Hall International (UK) Ltd, Hemel Hempstead

Ishikawa, K. (1985) *What is Total Quality Control? The Japanese Way*, Prentice-Hall, London

Ishikawa, K. (1986) *Guide to Quality Control*, 2nd edition, Asian Productivity Organisation

Jackson, M. C. (1990) *Organisation Design and Behaviour, An MBA Manual*, University of Hull, Hull

Jackson, M. C. (1991) *Systems Methodology for the Management Sciences*, Wiley, Chichester

Jackson, M. C. and Keys, P. (1984) Towards a System of Systems Methodologies, *Journal of the Operational Research Society*, 35: 473–486

Jay, A. (1987) *Management and Machiavelli*, revd edn, Hutchinson Business, London

Johansson, H. J., McHugh, P., Pendlebury, A. J. and Wheeler, W. A. (1993) *Business Process Re-engineering*, Wiley, Chichester

Johnson, G. and Scholes, K. (1993) *Exploring Corporate Strategy*, 3rd edition, Prentice-Hall, Hemel Hempstead

Juran, J. (1988) *Juran on Planning for Quality*, Free Press, New York

Kanji, G. K. and Asher, M. (1996) *100 Methods for Total Quality Management*, Sage, London

Logothetis, N. (1992) *Managing for Total Quality*, Prentice Hall International, London

Lovelock, J. (1979) *Gaia: A New Look at Life on Earth*, Oxford University Press, Oxford

Lovelock, J. (1988) *The Ages of Gaia*, Oxford University Press, Oxford

Lovelock, J. (1991) *Gaia: The Practical Science of Planetary Medicine*, Gaia Books Ltd, London

Lynn, J. and Jay, A. (1982) *Yes Minister*, BBC, London

Machiavelli, N. (1513) *The Prince*, (trans. G. Bull, 1961) Penguin, London

Maslow, A. (1970) *Motivation and Personality*, 2nd edition, Harper & Row, New York

Mason, R. O. and Mitroff, I. I. (1981) *Challenging Strategic Planning Assumptions*, Wiley, New York

Mayo, E. (1949) *The Social Problems of an Industrial Civilisation*, Routledge & Kegan Paul Ltd, London

McGoldrick, G. (1994) *The Complete Quality Manual*, Longman, London

McGregor, D. (1960) *The Human Side of Enterprise*, McGraw-Hill, New York

Morgan, G. (1986) *Images of Organisation*, Sage, London

Oakland, J., (1993), *Total Quality Management* 2nd edition, Butterworth-Heinemann Ltd, Oxford

Oliga, J. (1988) Methodological Foundations of Systems Methodologies, *Critical Systems Thinking, Directed Readings*, (Flood, R. L. and Jackson, M. C., 1991, eds) Wiley, Chichester

Parsons, T. and Smelser, N. J. (1956) *Economy and Society*, Routledge & Kegan Paul, London

Peters, T. J. and Waterman, R. H. (1982) *In Search of Excellence*, Harper Collins, New York

Porter, M., (1980) *Competitive Strategy: Techniques for Analysing Industries and Competitors*, The Free Press, Macmillan, New York

Porter, M., (1996), What Is Strategy?, *Harvard Business Review*, November–December: 61–78

Pugh, D. S. (1990) *Organisation Theory*, 3rd edition, Penguin, London

Pugh, D. S. and Hickson, D. J. (1976) *Organisation Structure in its Context: The Aston Programme 1*, Saxon House, Aldershot

Pugh, D. S. and Hickson, D. J. (1989) *Writers on Organizations*, 4th edn, Penguin, London

Pugh, D. and Hinings, C. R. (eds) (1976) *Organizational Structure – Extensions and Replications: The Aston Programme II*, Gower, Aldershot

Schoderbek, P. P., Schoderbek, C. G. and Kefalas, A. G. (1990) *Management Systems: Conceptual Considerations*, 4th edition, Business Publications, Dallas

Semler, R. (1993) *Maverick!*, Arrow, London

Senge, P. M. (1990) *The Fifth Discipline*, Century Business, London

Shingo, S. (1987) *The Sayings of Shigeo Shingo*, (trans. A. P. Dillon, Productivity Press, 1987)

Singleton, W. T. (1974) *Man-Machine Systems*, Penguin, London

Taguchi, G. (1987) *Systems of Experimental Design*, Vols 1 and 2, Unipub/Kraus International Publications, New York

Taylor, F. (1911) *The Principles of Scientific Management*, The Plimpton Press, Norwood

Townsend, R. (1985) *Further Up the Organisation*, Michael Joseph, Sevenoaks.

Trist, E. A. and Bamforth, K. W. (1951) Some Social and Psychological Consequences of the Longwall Method of Coal-getting [*sic*], in *Organisation Theory, Selected Readings*, (D. S. Pugh, ed.) 3rd edition, 1990, Penguin, London

Ulrich, W. (1983) *Critical Heuristics of Social Planning*, Haupt, Berne

Ulrich, W. (1987) Critical Heuristics of Social Systems Design, *European Journal of Operational Research*, 31: 276–283

Waldrop, S. (1992) *Complexity*, Simon & Schuster, New York

Waller J., Allen, D. and Burns, A. (1993) *The Quality Management Manual*, Kogan Page, London

Weber, M. (1924) Legitimate Authority and Bureaucracy, in, *Organisation Theory, Selected Readings*, (D. S. Pugh, ed.) 3rd edition, 1990, Penguin, London

Wiener, N. (1948) *Cybernetics or Control and Communication in the Animal and the Machine*, The Massachusetts Institute of Technology, Cambridge, MA

Woodward, J. (1965) *Industrial Organization: Theory and Practice*, Oxford University Press, London

Index